Gerry Marshall

Gerry Marshall

HIS AUTHORISED BIOGRAPHY

JEREMY WALTON

GREGOR MARSHALL

Haynes Publishing

A catalogue record for this book is available from the British Library

ISBN 978 1 84425 648 8
Library of Congress control no. 2009936974

Published by Haynes Publishing, Sparkford, Yeovil, Somerset BA22 7JJ, UK
Tel: 01963 442030 Fax: 01963 440001
Int. tel: +44 1963 442030 Int. fax: +44 1963 440001
E-mail: sales@haynes.co.uk
Website: www.haynes.co.uk

Haynes North America Inc.
861 Lawrence Drive, Newbury Park,
California 91320, USA

Designed by James Robertson

Printed in USA

CONTENTS

INTRODUCTION

This is the story of a big, big man who died a motor racing legend on 21 April 2005 at Silverstone, the self-styled 'home of British motorsport'. Naturally tall and muscular, at more than six foot in his youth, Gerald Dallas Royston 'Gerry' Marshall was a man of strong character and extreme behaviour, with a high IQ and a tongue that tipped between wit and whiplash. Yet he could also be extraordinarily generous and deeply supportive of friends and family, even unknown racing drivers got cash earmarked for his household bills!

Many readers will be attracted to this book simply by his motor racing exploits. However, thanks to the recollections of his three ex-wives and others who shared his 63 lusty years on Earth, it is also possible to reflect on other aspects of his life, which reveal him to have been a man of as many facets as a fly's eye.

Gerry became a larger-than-life character when he discovered alcohol, eating out and the enjoyment of living the high life. His closest associates and family agree that Gerry 'never did know where the kitchen was in a house', and none can remember ever eating a meal that the big man had cooked.

Gerry's story already appealed to readers over 30 years ago, when my 1978 book *Only Here For The Beer* was published, but one key criticism of that original book can now be addressed. When Gerry was alive, he hardly ever started telling one story before another bubbled to the surface, and his biographer therefore had to stay alert – battling both uncontrolled laughter and alcohol overdoses – to desperately try and capture the point he was making. These difficulties led to some critics pointing out that Gerry's original biography might be hilariously action-packed, but it was frequently difficult to follow. Its chronological continuity suffered not only because the author was inexperienced (he pleads in mitigation that it was his first book), but also because the pre-computer technology of cut-and-paste made alterations cumbersome.

Now, however, the author has 21st-century Apple technology, and no Gerry to blame, although he may try and shift responsibility to Gerry's son Gregor. A product of 1977, Gregor is introduced here – completely out of chronological order – because it is he who has enabled this fresh assessment of his father to be made. Gregor has logged over 1,400 of Gerry's racing, championship and trophy statistics, as well as guiding the author through Marshall family lore. Marshall junior also did his best to restrain the author's crass interview intrusions into the inevitable personal and professional sensitivities left in the wake of his Dad's tumultuous life.

Armed with Gregor's astonishing crosschecked record of his father's motorsport achievements, the author was also allowed access to Gerry's family, wives, fans and friends – all impossible in 1978 when Gerry was alive and his first biography was published.

So, let's start at the beginning and see how long it is before I lose the thread this time.

Jeremy Walton
Wiltshire
Spring 2010

OPPOSITE *Just one picture introduces our hero: racer, business and family man. Gerry, seated, with his helmet on the roof of 666 DTV road [and occasionally track] droop-snoot Firenza. First wife Carol, mother of their three children, sits on the 1974 Honda motorcycle. Behind, the collection includes the blue Firenza SL Sport company car, Jensen 541, stunning red first-edition Lotus Elite, and rare hardtop for the Daimler V8 registered 25 NMG. At the back is just one of the many tractors (this one a Farmall) that were Gerry's favourites from his toddler years. In the lane behind you can see another Firenza coupé in gold, probably the machine that brought the Luton factory photographer to this mid-seventies assignment.* [Vauxhall Motors/Marshall Family Archive]

CHAPTER 1

Dramas from day one

S adly, it is no longer possible to talk to Albert, Gerry's father, as he died in 1993, but we can improve dramatically on previous accounts of Gerry's early life. This is because Gerry's mother, Ruby, was alive and well in 2010, still living in the Harrow house that she and Albert bought as the first owners over 20 years ago. Ruby's memories, approaching her 93rd birthday, allow us a much deeper insight into Albert and Gerry's father and son relationship than when they were both alive, as do the memories of Gerry's two brothers.

Gerry was the first of three boys born to Ruby and Albert Moses. Gerry arrived in 1941; John during 1947; and Martyn in 1954. Both his brothers had adult connections with the motor trade (John) and motor sports (Martyn), but neither had quite the same ultimately fanatical interest that was evident in Gerry from a disconcertingly early age.

Ruby started our benefit of hindsight with a proper beginning. 'Gerald was born on November the 16th, 1941, a Scorpio. He was quite a big baby at eight pounds eight ounces, but very good-looking, with such curly blond hair – I entered him in a local beautiful baby contest once – and he won!' remembered Ruby fondly. 'He was born in Southoe, Hunts, as we lived there for part of the war; and Gerald's ashes are now buried in Southoe too,' she added.

RIGHT *Life on two wheels is fun! Gerry was an avid motorcycle rider for more than 45 years, from first moped to superbikes.* [Jenny Cook]

ABOVE *Ruby and Albert Marshall in November 1990. Albert died in 1993, but Ruby was an invaluable 2009 source of witty and observant memories to add a special dimension to the characters of father Albert and son, Gerry.* [Marshall Family Archive]

Their first son was christened Gerald Dallas Moses, but was usually simply known as Gerry. Ruby said: 'We chose "Gerald" simply because we liked it, for it was not an inherited family name. The "Dallas" part came purely out of the blue, and I think I got it from visits to the cinema.'

There would be more name modifications, as Ruby explained: 'The family surname was changed from Moses to Marshall, with two Ls, after the war, when Albert returned from five and a half years' service with the RAF, most as a Flight Sergeant.' Born in 1913, Albert was the third generation of a family business that had started with Jewish immigrants from Poland arriving in the UK in 1862. During Gerry's post-war upbringing the business was a builders' merchant, but other branches of the family also had related property and building companies.

'We got married in 1937,' Ruby continued, 'and the war changed my husband: it increased his confidence. Although he was not a big man, he had a big voice and could command attention, especially when he had to instruct recruits to shoot properly.' Gregor added subsequently that 'from Granddad, down through my Dad and myself,

the shooting ability has stayed constant. Like Jackie Stewart, we are all good shots. It must have something to do with the hand-eye co-ordination that's vital for motor sports.'

As we have already seen, by the mid-'50s the family had grown to five with the arrival of Gerry's younger brothers John and Martyn, of whom Martyn was the first to start with the Marshall surname from the outset. Their firstborn, meanwhile, had become Gerald Dallas Marshall.

This was not the end of Gerry's name game. He adopted the initials 'G.D.*R*.M.' from 1964, when writing reports of events he contested for weekly sports papers like *Motoring News* and *Autosport*. 'We don't know exactly why he added that name,' comments Gregor, 'but we do know that the R stood for Royston. We can only assume that he took on the "Royston" part in honour of the Hertfordshire town, which was near Bill Blydenstein's later Shepreth premises for DTV [Dealer Team Vauxhall].' Gerry could not have known he was going to be a DTV driver, but we know he did have early contact with DTV founder and resident genius Bill Blydenstein before he stepped into his first competition Vauxhall, Bill competing against Gerry's Dad, Albert. So we can only assume that the name was added to increase his sporting profile.

Ruby said: 'Gerald was a slim boy right up until he married. I think all that good-living was what changed the way he looked so much.' Walton hazily remembers starting interview days with Gerry in 1978 with a fried breakfast, but I asked his first wife Carol in 2009 if that was truly his normal routine. 'Yes, he always started the day that way, that's what he wanted.'

Ruby pulled us back on chronological track. 'We came back to London before the war ended and Gerald did most of his schooling at Harrow High, which was a very good school. He had a good upbringing, with annual holidays, and he was always particular about personal cleanliness, how he spoke and table manners.' Gerry's children Tina, Justine and Gregor confirm that their father was strict, but could be less than formal about shutting the bathroom door!

Sport that didn't involve a motor was not the strongest pull on Gerry's time – although he obviously much preferred it to the classroom. His parents tried to encourage an interest in team games like football and cricket, but to little effect, though Gregor still possesses a cricket bat handed down by his Dad.

Ruby recalled that Gerry did some ice-skating (he knew sports car racing driver/owner Michael Wheatley as a rink rival long before his racing days), 'but his best results came from his running. He was a sprint champion several times, and I've still got some of his cups.' Family lore has it that Gerry's school sprint records were unbeaten until brother John came along, and as an adult he won hundreds of pounds in wagers when unwary racing rivals took him on. His sprinting abilities clearly presaged his fantastic getaway starts in motor racing.

Ruby felt that 'Gerald did not take school seriously, but he was actually very bright. His father bought a weekly motoring magazine and, before he could read, Gerald would go through it with his Dad and memorise all the different car types. He could tell you which car was which. Later on he would never forget things like the registration number and all about that type of car.'

Motorised mischief was never far from this Marshall's mind. 'Gerald never could leave anything with an engine alone. He disappeared one day and so did a friend's tractor. He was stuck in it!' Ruby confirmed contemporary accounts from classmates that 'Gerald was always in trouble at school. He got in the headmaster's car once and started it up.'

His friend Roger Bunting's recollections allow us a contemporary's view of what was hidden from his parents' eyes. 'I first met Gerald in the junior school of Harrow High School in Peterborough Road, Harrow. It must have been the early 1950s.

ABOVE *Albert Marshall was a regular racer through the 1950s, and enjoyed the social side of car club membership. He is seen here in a borrowed Healey, rather than his legendary MG Magnette.* [John Marshall]

LEFT *Albert's pride and joy: Wife Ruby, John and Martyn [two of his three sons, Gerry is absent] and a plum 2.4-litre Jaguar.* [John Marshall]

ABOVE AND RIGHT
*MG Magnette LDL 156
in its usual pristine
state before and after
its 1959 rollover
accident at Snetterton,
from which it was
driven home! Sadly,
we could not trace
this historic ex-Monte
Carlo MG's history after
Albert's ownership,
although we do know
it was repaired.*
[John Marshall]

We had a very attractive form teacher called Miss Williams. Very top-endy, which, even as 11-year-olds, we were very aware of.'

Another Bunting memory confirms a growing reputation for mayhem. 'I remember the school had arranged a trip to see a Cinerama film in London. On the day before the event it was announced in assembly that there was a spare ticket and "would anyone like to go apart from Marshall?" Poor GM had quite a reputation even at that early age for causing mayhem!'

Bunting recalled an unlicensed 15-year-old Gerry's brief career as a driving instructor. 'It was probably about 1956. I was given my very first driving lesson by GM on Albert's Austin A40 Somerset, which GM used to proudly valet on Saturdays [a lifelong clean car habit – JW] at the rear of Dad's builders' merchants in Queensbury, North London. I was treated to a demonstration of GM's teenage expertise.

'Unfortunately GM had forgotten to shut the bootlid before his manoeuvres commenced. Guess what? The poor drop-down boot lid suffered severe contact with the garage. Not sure how this was resolved with Albert. But I know it curtailed my driving lesson…' quipped Roger in 2009.

Bunting concluded: 'We were at that school together until we both failed to achieve any significant academic qualifications and left at about 16 years' old. By which time we were both hooked

ABOVE AND LEFT
Gerry liked speedy boats as a lithe youngster, also taking a holiday as a teenager with life-long friend, Roger Bunting. [Both Marshall Family Archive]

on anything motorised or attractive and female on two legs.'

Ruby believed that Gerry's overwhelming motor sporting ambitions came from her husband, but we'll find in later chapters that his contemporaries were just as much to blame. Ruby, however, asserted that 'Albert was to blame.' She chuckled. 'Albert was a keen amateur driver and a member of MG Car Club, North London Enthusiasts' Club and Harrow Car Club. At one time he had both an MG Magnette and a Dellow, and the MG was a very interesting car that had been used in rallies. It had a small sink in the back and was an unusual green and raspberry two-tone colouring.'

Family lore says that the MG (registration number LDL 156) was a serious ex-Abingdon factory car prepared for the 1954 Tulip Rally, then a major event. That does not mean it was the fastest thing on wheels, but it literally had everything, including the kitchen sink. Martyn also recalled the duotone paint scheme that Ruby remembers, and the boot-mounted sink, and added that the plumbing supplied hot and cold water! 'It was an amazing car: it also had a Remington Razor, an electric kettle,

plus those period stick-on screen heaters, a Hellfors spotlight in the centre of the screen, Halda rally timing gear and high-back leather seats.'

Then over 40 years of age, Albert Marshall used the MG mainly for sprints, but he also raced the car a lot more than previously recalled, and competed against Gerry's future racing manager, William Benjamin ('W. B.') Blydenstein. John Marshall explained in 2009 that 'Dad used to drive the car to meetings with the family aboard, but he usually had a set of Michelin Xs for competition, then got some proper racing Dunlops.'

'Albert did not take his motorsport too seriously,' recalled Ruby. 'He joined those motor clubs as much for the social side as anything, the "Noggin and Natter" sessions as they used to call them. But his attitude to the sport for his family did change when he rolled the MG over!' This defining moment was during a 1958 meeting at Snetterton, also recalled by Martyn, then a toddler, so it was a traumatic occasion. Both John and Martyn agreed that it was the only time they ever saw their Dad cry. 'He just loved that car.'

Ruby said: 'I remember I went along to all his events with the three boys and on this occasion

BELOW *Look at the middle row. Late in his school days, Gerry [fourth from the left] and Roger Bunting [second from left] in a rare uniformed moment of official order.* [Marshall Family Archive]

Gerald was a teenager. He sprinted to get to his Dad's crash, jumped on somebody's car, which didn't make him or her very happy. Then he was on to the track and was about the first to reach the scene.' There were pictures of Gerry posed alongside the crumpled MG, now lost.

John remembered that the family had all watched the race from the flat roof of the main start/finish straight buildings. 'You looked back to the Esses, and we saw Dad's car go over. Then there were ploughed fields, and it must have got caught up in there and flipped over. Mum was not very happy and the car was a right mess, with the driver's door folded back and the roof down. But we'd 100 miles or more to do to get home, so there was no alternative but to lash it up with string and rope, the boys holding it in place! Fortunately it steered straight and we got back OK.' Ruby likewise recalled that 'we drove back with the doors all tied up with rope'.

John recalled that the MG was officially a write-off but that 'a bloke in the back streets of Kilburn did a beautiful job rebuilding it. In fact we went on holiday in it the following year, 1959. Sadly it was sold on to one of Dad's employees, and he did all sorts with it – after that we lost track of it.' Gregor and I did ask MG enthusiasts to try to track it down in 2009, but without luck.

Ruby added cheerfully that 'the boys were all in the back as we drove this poor car home from the accident.' She grew more thoughtful. 'After that Albert saw the dangers of the sport, and I think that was one of the reasons he was quite anti when Gerry wanted to take it up. So far as I know, Albert only ever went to watch one of Gerald's races, in 1991, but he did watch him on BBC *Grandstand*. Deep down, he was terribly proud of his son's achievements, but could never say so to Gerald: he would always tell all his Rotary and car-club friends about Gerald. It was a shame – they could both have got more out of life together with that common interest.'

In 2009, Martyn – who now runs his own hardware store in Bedfordshire – confirmed that 'Dad was very anti-motorsport for all of us boys. It was just that Gerry had the drive to do it. Whatever Dad said, Gerry would say the opposite to wind Dad up. I was the quieter type, tended to stand back a bit. It was always a job to get a word in anyway with those two about!

'However, I did have a go at the sport with Gerry's help.' Martyn certainly did, but that's a 1970s' story…

Roger Bunting recalled how much Albert cared what his son was up to when he had access to an internal combustion engine. 'Gerry's first motorised transport was a BSA Bantam, 125cc. First thing Gerry did was have 30-thou shaved off the cylinder head, when I think it went slower. Anyway,

ABOVE *Superb period picture of one of a chain of Marshall Bros Builders' Merchants that were located in and to the west of London. The gent on the right with overalls buttoned is Albert Marshall, Gerry's Dad. This picture was taken in the early sixties, prior to a massive redevelopment that saw the shop demolished after 75 years continuous trading.* [Martyn Marshall]

this machine was purchased much against his parents' wishes.

'As soon as Gerald was mobile, he just took off. His Mum and Dad were permanently worried – with just cause – knowing the wildness of their prodigal son. Albert turned up one evening at my parents' house in his 100E Ford van, looking for his missing son. I guess this was about 1957 [Gerry would have been around 15 – JW].

'Albert asked if I'd go with him to some of our haunts to try to find his missing son. Gerry's new machine could well be terrorising the roads of Harrow. I jumped in with Albert, and we set off.

'We were just ascending Harrow and Wealdstone railway bridge when a memorable sight greeted us. Exiting the 60° bend from the top of the bridge at an amazing rate of knots appeared the poor punished Bantam, lent right over on the footrests, sparking on the road – with GM on board, of course. He was wearing his blue gabardine school rain mac, billowing out like a balloon, and wearing Albert's white corker crash helmet. It was a stunning sight: I was much impressed.

'But I thought Albert was going to have a heart attack, seeing young GM putting on a performance that even Valentino Rossi would have been proud of,' reported Bunting.

Bunting reckoned Gerry's interest in motorcycles was straightforward. 'I don't think Gerry had a great passion for bikes any more than I. It was just that you could get motorised cheaper and a year earlier on a bike. And all our crowd had a bike, so GM had to have one too.' There was a link, too, in the fact that his pal Peter Kitchen's father, Bill, was a famous speedway racer. But again, Roger felt that the truth was more prosaic than Gerry's eyes being filled with Speedway stardust. 'I don't think we knew much about Bill Kitchen in those days to influence any of us, although Bill was captain of Wembley Lions speedway team and runner-up in the World Championships one year,' Roger recalled.

A brace of even more painful two-wheeler tales associated with Gerry's early motorcycle career also come from the Bunting store. The first concerned the successor to Gerry's abused Bantam. 'In 1957 or '58 I had acquired a Panther 250 twin two-stroke bike. Meanwhile, Gerry had his first experience with that poor tortured BSA Bantam. Somehow he came across an offer of this new single 197cc Villiers-engined Panther in Gamages store. As soon as he got it, Gerry had to race straight to my house in Harrow Weald to show me his new acquisition. But before he even arrived, his enthusiastic riding had managed to break the chain! Anyway, with this duly sorted and the bike not yet run in, we were off to Brands on the Sunday.

'I can remember following GM at full chat down the hill on the A20 to the roundabout just before Death Hill and Scratchers Lane. Suddenly this black line started appearing from beneath the back wheel. Yes, he'd seized the brand new engine! After cooling down it did restart, and we were able to continue.

'Before the poor thing was returned to its makers with a catalogue of GM-induced problems, repeated rear footbrake-induced 180° spins – achieved by applying the considerable weight of the GM physique – had managed to snap the brake rod!'

Roger added that 'when the family were living in The Fairway, North Wembley, there was some sort of falling out between GM and his parents re his motorcycle dramas. I think the bike had been rendered undrivable for the umpteenth time and they refused to fund it any more. The result was that Gerry had punched a hole through the plaster wall of his bedroom and announced he was leaving. He arrived here at the garage with his packed suitcase hoping to stay with me.

'Fortunately it got resolved and I didn't end up having a boarder,' chuckled Roger.

As our January 2009 chat concluded, Ruby observed: 'Nobody would have guessed it, but deep down Gerald was a shy man.' Gregor explains that 'you would never have thought it, but Dad was not only shy, but got extremely nervous before each race. He had to put on a front and I don't think any of us knew how hard he found it making himself ready for a race or other public occasions. He'd be going to the toilet all the time, winding himself up with the wisecracks.'

By contrast, recalled Ruby, 'Albert had a strong personality and he was nobody's fool. His business was housed in a spacious old Kilburn church for a long time.' Gregor remembers that the crypt was 'creepy and quite smelly!' Gerry quipped in 1978 that his Dad 'actually bought a church, not bad for a good Jewish lad!' Gerry also remembered Albert 'moving into the old St Cuthbert's vicarage, which he bought off the vicar'.

'There were other North London enterprises,' Ruby told us, 'including a shop at Kenton, along with three shops stretching out to Ruislip in West London. All were sold up by the early 1990s. Gerald worked for his father for two to three years … I was surprised they lasted that long, working together – especially as Gerald turned the warehouse into a car factory!' she laughingly recalled.

Then, at 76 years old, Albert decided to retire.

This unexpected decision impacted on Martyn's working life most: he had worked for his father for 17 years on 'nothing wages. I mean *really* low.' The first he heard about it was a phone call 'just to let me know he'd sold the business'. No doubt about it, Albert could be tough on his sons; but, Martyn tellingly revealed, 'at teatimes, any meal times, it was Gerry who was a stickler for correct table manners – he really was fastidious. And it was usually him who checked me, before my parents could.'

Subsequently an unexpectedly tender side of this wild character was revealed to Martyn. 'Gerry loved me to pieces. When I was about three and he was a teenage 15 or 16, with girlfriends, he'd take me on the bus to see them, or take me along to swim. There's not many teenagers who would have wanted their three-year-old kid brother around with the current girlfriend!'

But mischief and wheels are never far from the Marshall legend. While Martyn was still a toddler, Gerry 'decided it would be good fun to pack the boot of my trike with a bundle of firework bangers. He told me to peddle like hell and off I went down the pavement … They went off all right, blew the lid off my little three-wheeler's trunk! Mind you, the neighbours did give him a right telling off.'

You can be sure that this wasn't the last time they had to remonstrate with Gerald!

LEFT *Martyn Marshall, wearing a moustache that had been shaved before this book appeared, was close to Gerry (back to camera) personally and through a later motor racing alliance. Seen supping quietly in the background, head inclined, is later-life friend, John Llewellyn.* [Marshall Family Archive]

CHAPTER 2

Marriage and the man

B y 1964, Gerry's 23rd year of rumbustious existence, there were signs of increasing adulthood, with proper jobs and the girl he would marry already part of his life. However, racing also had a hold on Gerry following his April 1964 debut in a proper motor race, as did extreme sociability when near a glass, so our story unfolds with the streak of wild unpredictability that entertains us but caused some of his nearest and dearest to sigh in sorrow and (often justified) anger.

A good example of the exasperation Gerry could cause comes from his youngest brother, Martyn, who tells a revealing story concerning their Dad's 50th birthday and Gerry's saucy reaction. 'This would be in 1963, when Dad was 50. He decided to give himself a treat and went out to buy a Jaguar. He always told us, "You're nobody unless you've got a Jaguar and a Mini," and at this time both my

LEFT *Wedding day laughter all round and some significant influences in Mr Marshall's life abound, aside from bride Carol (centre). To the right of Carol is Martin Lilley, who owned both TVR and Barnet Motor Company. Also at the wedding was Gerry's life-long friend Martin Mulchrone. Carol also remembered the presence of Neil and Bruce Duncan, Chris and Pam O'Donahue (Chris became Gregor's Godfather), John and Anne Broomer, Anna Graham and Sarah Keighley, Carole and Alan Keefe, Frank Meaden and significant TVR figure John Woollen.* [Marshall Family Archive]

older brothers did have Minis. Anyway, Dad wanted a 3.8 Jag, the top model, but when he went to insure it the company told him they would only insure him on a 2.4. When Albert demanded why this was, the insurance company told him it was because Gerald was nominated on Dad's insurance, and had made so many claims!'

Martyn continued: 'Dad got his 2.4 in opalescent maroon, and then Gerald said he wanted to borrow the money for a Jag too. Dad told my brother that it took him 50 years to get a Jag, so he was not going to lend him the money.

'Next thing we know, Gerry draws up outside with a fantastic 3.8 Jag in full John Coombs specification, a proper car!' reported Martyn. Guildford-based Coombs was famous in the 1950s–'60s for fast road and track Jaguars. 'Now we all knew that this couldn't be right – where had Gerald got the money? Dad didn't want to know anything about Gerry's Jag, but when Dad went back into Kilburn his bank manager said he "wanted a word".

'Manager: "About this new loan you've acted as guarantor for, Albert."

'Albert: "What loan?"

'Manager: "The one your eldest son took out to buy a car – you know, the Jaguar he got to be part of your business, the business he is going to inherit very soon, when you retire…".'

Martyn chortled, but the consequences for Gerry were immediate. 'Dad went mental. Told the manager he was not going to guarantee or pay for any such loan. Finally, I think Gerald sold it on pretty pronto to one of Carol's family!'

The person that would stabilise Gerry through a marriage that lasted from 1965–81, and mother of his three children, was a young lady called Carol Maynard. Relaxed in early 2009, despite a recent hospital stay, Carol looked back over 40 years. Chatting from a comfortable sofa in the living room of the house she shares with her second husband, Miles Hutton, Carol rewound those years with frequent bursts of laughter and exasperation, back to the tempestuous time when life with Gerry was 'never boring, but certainly challenging'.

How did Gerry and Carol meet?

'I was a Harrow Hill girl,' Carol explained. 'On Sundays, I often went to the notorious John Lyon pub that so many of the local motor racing boys hung around. My sister's boyfriend, Sydney [now deceased – JW], introduced me to Gerry and I found out they both knew each other through a common interest in Riley 1.5s. Gerry had one at the time.

'So I hold Sydney entirely responsible for everything that happened,' Carol said, with the kind of light laughter in the face of adversity that made so many men think she was an attractive saint rather than a mortal. That impression was reinforced when she commented 'I was convent-educated and 17 years old, so some of my life going out with Gerry – like the weekly porn film shows at the famous Charles Crichton Stuart–Frank Williams flat [in Pinner Road, Harrow – JW] were a big shock!'

Carol recalled that 'back then I didn't drink, so I did a lot of the driving when we went out. We'd go to places like the Steering Wheel Club, where Gerry met a lot of motorsport people.' These included two significant influences on his motoring life, Gregor Grant and John Wingfield. Grant was the founder and editor of *Autosport*, the weekly bible of the British – and later international English-speaking – motorsport community, and Gerry would cultivate excellent contacts with not just the senior editorial figures, but also talented juniors. John Wingfield and Nancy, his mother, would become Gerry's trading partners in the successful Marshall Wingfield car sales establishment at Temple Fortune in Finchley Road, North London.

Now let's get back to life with Gerry in the mid-1960s.

Gerry always quipped of his 1964 engagement to Carol that she wore 'a Mini Cooper on her third finger, left hand,' because he sold his first racing Mini to buy the ring. Commenting on that trade, Carol said cheerfully: 'Yes, it was true, but he wasn't without a racing car for long.'

Carol was and is an enthusiastic driver. Her Mini Cooper has delighted her since 2002, when Gregor worked for BMW and arranged a discount purchase. Carol sometimes shared cars with Gerry in '60s club sprints. There's a picture of a very ratty-looking Ford Anglia that they shared, which had its engine built in their front room and the narrowest steel wheels outside a handcart.

Carol recalled that she and Gerry shared a love of fast cars. 'My favourite, then and now? Oh, a Jaguar E-type would definitely do it for me,' laughed Carol, with a meaningful look at second husband Miles.

Still chuckling, Carol remembered being stopped for speeding on a number of occasions, including one when speeding was not on police minds. 'I was in a stripped-out racing Mini Cooper. It was terribly noisy, and I don't expect it had a speedometer. When I saw the police car following me, I just left it in second gear and crept along at what I guessed was 30mph. The patrol car overtook me and pulled me in. So far as I remember it the conversation went like this:

'Policeman: "Everything OK, madam?"

'Me: "Yes, what's the problem?"

'Policeman: "You were going so slowly we thought you must have had a problem – a car like this is built to go faster. Go on, show us what it can do!"'

The lady did as she was told and 'left them standing!'

Gerry and Carol were married 2 October 1965, Carol's 19th birthday. Carol recalled all too vividly their character-building wedding day. 'My Mother

ABOVE AND BELOW *Not quite what they seem. Gerry always loved loose-surface competition, but the shiny Riley (above) is being conducted without the hindrance of competition numbers or a crash hat, and the road-car Mini Cooper in dusty action (below) carries fashionable spot-lamp accessories and no numbers either.* [Both John Marshall]

ABOVE *Gerry's Riley 1.5 was a shiny wonder that led to a grubby (but effective) Mini racer.*
[John Marshall]

BELOW *Everyone gets roped in when a man goes racing, and Carol's numerals were a lot tidier than Gerry's…* [John Marshall]

said on the day: 'You can still change your mind. You know a leopard never changes it's spots.' A pause for the cliché to sink in, then Carol quipped 'Unfortunately she was absolutely right!'

To illustrate the point, Carol added of her special day that 'First of all he had to be best man to somebody else that day. Then we spent time – a very long time – in The John Lyon pub before we went to The King's Head Hotel, Harrow on the Hill, a really nice place I knew from family dos. In fact I dug out the receipt for our wedding night the other day, and it came to £17, almost a week's wages in those days.

'Gerry was very ill through the night, which was slightly embarrassing. In fact we never went back there. Gerry was racing the next day and he turned up at the track still wearing his wedding suit! He then threw up in the scrutineering bay, but he very probably won his race…'

Gregor has the programme from the event and confirms that on 3 October 1965 Gerry contested a Brands Hatch event around the Grand Prix track in a Barnet Motor Co TVR, winning a round of the Redex Championship for Special GT cars. The 1965 year and race season was significant in Gerry's life, as he also started working for Barnet Motor Company, which took him beyond the mad Mini brigade and into some serious TVR and Lotus exploits.

Despite the volatile nature of life with Gerry, he and Carol enjoyed a strong home life, with increasingly comfortable houses in Hertfordshire, to the north of London: all were handy for the M1 commute back down to town. Carol commented: 'Incidentally, that house you came to, to start each interview day in 1978, was the third we'd had in that area. We chose this location because it was handy when Gerry had a job at Barnet Motor Company [1965–7]. I always remember it because the garage was centrally heated and carpeted, so I always said it was more comfortable than the house!'

As their family grew, so did their houses. Tina was born 24 September 1966 and Justine arrived on 14 November 1969, her birthday just two days earlier than that of her father. Gregor (named after *Autosport* founder-editor Gregor Grant) was a later, 1977, addition, also born in November but this time on the 7th.

Incidentally, Gerry's brother John married Carol's cousin Anne. John recounted that 'Anne and I had met as kids, as the families knew each other, but it was Gerry and Carol who reintroduced us when I was a teenager. Carol and Gerry were going along to a barn dance and we went along with them. Subsequently Anne was a bridesmaid at

Carol and Gerry's wedding, but Gerry and I were distanced a bit when he and Carol got divorced.'

John added in 2009: 'As you'll hear, I was involved with Gerry's early adventures and racing outings, but he didn't always want me around. I wasn't a great drinker and I didn't have the cash that he and his friends apparently had. Gerry went his own way with his own circle of racing friends as time went on.'

However, Gregor recalls that John and Gerry enjoyed brotherly banter in later years when they went to visit their mother Ruby.

Carol still has 'a heavy right foot' today and has been known to feature in speed camera photography, but she is pretty unmoved by such incidents when she rewinds to the wild motoring exploits of her ex-husband, and some of the car-collection missions she tackled 40 years ago.

'I can remember one post-Steering Wheel Club late-night session. Gerry had an E-type and Willie Green had brought an Aston Martin along. I just *knew* the two of them would race back! I think it took them just 17 minutes to get from that Mayfair club to our house in St Albans.' Yes, the roads were emptier then, especially in the early hours, but that run must have made any TV car chase of the period look tame…

Carol's worst moment came at much more mundane speeds, but was potentially deadlier. 'I used to collect cars for Gerry all over the place. The first time I took a car on a trailer was scary. I stalled on a level crossing and got pretty stuck.' Fortunately she did get the tow-car restarted, but many have suffered fatal consequences in such circumstances, and unmanned railway crossings can still be deadly places today.

Both Gerry and Carol were especially proud when Carol was invited by Eba Grant to join the British Racing Driver's Club (BRDC) Doghouse charity in 1968, when all other members were the wives of single-seater drivers. Carol maintained a long association with the Doghouse Ball and other charitable Doghouse activities, including a spell as chairwoman.

Carol recalled the day that a loose BRDC connection lead to her meeting A-list film star and racer Paul Newman. 'Gerry and I met Paul Newman through a 5 November 1975 BRDC ball and a Vauxhall connection that [double World Champion] Graham Hill arranged. Newman was to accompany Hill to a test at Brands and then test-drive a standard Firenza. This was in the mid-1970s. Gerry got to hear about it and offered to lend the star his own, much modified, Firenza … I think it was just after the "Droop Snoot" model had come out,

and Gerry always had every tuned go-faster bit on his cars.'

Carol smiled as she cast back over 30 years to a truly memorable meeting. 'Gerry told me I'd be taking his Firenza down to Brands Hatch for Paul Newman to drive. I thought it was a wind-up, so the next morning I didn't put on any make-up or anything to make me presentable to just about the biggest film star of the time. I just didn't believe Gerry, and I still didn't right up until I drove Gerry's Firenza into Brands.

'There were no General Motors personnel about. I asked at the gate if Graham Hill was still there and he had come and gone. I was a bit late – say 12, for an 11 o'clock appointment. And I still thought it was a wind-up, as there was just nobody about. I drove right through to the old Paddock café-bar area, the thing they had before the Kentagon. One of their top men at the track, Geoff Clark, said , Hi, Carol, Paul Newman's waiting for you! You're late and we've all been waiting for you.'

'I met Newman then. He was a smaller, slighter figure than I had thought from films, but oh, those eyes! So, so blue – just magnificent. He made no fuss about being kept waiting, just got on with it,

BELOW *Gerry ready for Mini battle, twiddling a wood-rim wheel in a period peaked helmet. We guess he put the door stickers on himself, they are so badly crumpled!* [John Marshall]

did a few laps, said it was fantastic compared to the production cars he'd driven.'

Her eyes still alight with the unexpected excitement of it all, Carol remembered: 'I drove back home in a daze. Paul Newman had driven *this* car. I was sitting on the seat where *he* sat, and turned *this* steering wheel. Ooh!

'The only shame of it was he never asked me for a date!' closed Carol, with an unexpected giggle.

Gerry did not simply just join Barnet Motor Company and set the tracks and sales ledgers alight. There were preliminary steps. He revealed that 'In February 1965 I joined Brew Brothers in Kensington on the commercial vehicle sales side. About three weeks after I joined, the manager of the department left for Australia, bequeathing me his Hillman Imp [registration CYP 986C] and his job. I think it was the car – which we called the Hillman Limp – that drove him to this,' Gerry quipped.

Was Gerald now on the fast track to managerial and racetrack glory?

Life was never that simple. He became involved in a substantial drinking session after the *Daily Express* meeting at Silverstone on 20 March was waterlogged. His planned race in a Newtune Mini was abandoned after 'we had all been strapped into our accidents' (as friend James Boothby put it). The post-meeting intake of alcohol and consequent pranks around the twilit circuit included testing the long-suffering loyalty of dealing and racing friend, ex-pat Canadian Robbie Gordon, who would play an important part in Gerry's early racing life (being owner of some of the machinery he raced). The post-meeting sessions with the Imp involved Robbie 'holding the gear lever in when it kept dropping out of third'. This was significant to Gerry's erratic progress homeward, as the sudden mid-corner loss of a ratio led to the abused Hillman falling over outside Towcester – this despite Gerry 'doing all the clever things one does. You know, waggling the wheel, and pushing up and down on the pedals, and generally acting the goat.'

As could only happen to Gerry, the kind gentlemen in a Cortina who helped Mr Marshall put the Imp back on its wheels were members of the constabulary. 'It was such a horrible car I don't think it made much difference to it,' was Gerry's verdict, but the consequences were not so funny for GM. The policemen were kind, but they had to report what they had seen. Gerry's fast-track career at Brew Bros was unsurprisingly abbreviated, as his fictional accounts of the incident, trying to remain employed with the Imp buried, were uncovered.

In those days – and into the 1970s – some notable racers managed to preserve their

OPPOSITE *Married, and Mrs Marshall's education in the world of alcohol begins with a ceremonial sip. Her new husband had a heavier night, but still raced the TVR V8 forcefully the next day.*
[Carol Hutton]

ABOVE *A life about to change, forever. Carol Maynard before she became Mrs Marshall.*
[Carol Hutton]

BELOW *Posing with Carol, the red road car that became a heroic two-tone racer. MMT 7C was a fine perk for Gerry courtesy of a Sales Manager's job at Barnet Motor Company.*
[Carol Hutton]

competition licences, despite being disqualified from driving on public highways, so Gerry's motorsport ambitions remained undimmed. He enjoyed a very promising season in club racing and the British Saloon Car Championship driving a Mini running a 970 S motor, as the detailed racing chapters will relate.

Now we trace the encounters that led to Gerry's Barnet Motor Co employment. Loyal Marshall friend Robbie Gordon supplied some of the background during an interview at his home in the West Country in 2009. Retired RAF squadron leader, racer and motor trader James Boothby

was involved in the buying and selling of TVRs when he was not busy being a constant drinking companion to Gerry at a Kensington establishment rather bucolically named The Hereford. Gordon also remembers that pub as being the venue of one of his first encounters with Gerry, along with a road adventure involving a twin-engined Mini and Robbie's Cobra, recounted in the next chapter.

Gordon did some trading with Boothby, as did Gerry from premises at 11 Reece Mews. Also drinking and working in this posh London postal zone were John Wingfield, later to become Gerry's motor trade business partner, and future TVR and Barnet Motor Company owner Martin Lilley, who caught the motor racing bug badly.

According to Gerry, Lilley invested in TVR shares just weeks before the company went bankrupt. Carol Hutton recalled the vendor as David Northey, her second husband's cousin and a friend of Gerry's. Martin Lilley bought a Griffith V8 from Boothby and crashed it thoroughly after it performed the period TVR trick of losing a wheel – a trait Gerry experienced twice at one race meeting, and six times in his later motoring column accounts!

Martin Lilley and his father, Arthur, showed true commitment to TVR, buying TVR Cars in 1965 and forming TVR Engineering. They inherited some serious debts but stuck with the company through some tough times and saw its reputation and sales improve.

In 2009 Robbie Gordon recalled: 'I got to know Martin Lilley quite well at Barnet Motor Company.

RIGHT *The first marital home for Gerry and Carol was this Hertfordshire semi-rural cottage, which cost under £10,000 in the sixties.* [Carol Hutton]

He was younger than Gerry and I, very affable, slightly shy and immature with occasionally a short temper. I sold him the famous lightweight E-type CUT 7 [a Jaguar registration we shall hear more about later – JW] around this time and knew him as a wealthy young man. As I remember it, Gerry called most of the shots in the daily business at Barnet – quite a responsible job for somebody in their early 20s.'

Robbie 'drifted away from the James Boothby life' and went on to work at Barnet Motor Co himself. He underlined that successful businessman Arthur Lilley dealt with 'all the financial aspects at Barnet, including lining up to get our pay'.

For Gerry the Lilleys were life-changers. Martin installed him as sales manager at Barnet Motor Co, a decision Robbie laughed at, quipping 'I think both the job and Gerry's drives in Martin's cars show just how difficult it was to say no to Gerry when he was at his most persuasive!'

Gerry was able to provide both the Lotus and TVR brands with some excellent motorsport results and to support his growing family with a worthwhile job while still feeding the Marshall passion for fast cars.

Another link between TVR and the Marshall family exists today. In September 1966 Carol and Gerry had their first child, Tina. From November 1965 to the Turin, London and Paris Shows of 1966–7, TVR had built a pair of little sports prototypes with the lightweight Hillman Imp power trains. These show cars were initially displayed as an unnamed convertible, but subsequently appeared in Turin and Paris in 1966–7 as the Tina Convertible and Coupé, named in honour of Gerry's daughter. Both models had styling by Trevor Fiore that echoed the contemporary Trident (also by Fiore). Classic rumour has it that Gerry made up the 'Tina' badge by cutting up a Ford Cortina logo.

The original plan was to sell Tina soft-tops for less than £1,000 each, but sadly approaches to manufacturers like Rootes Group (Imp manufacturers), Aston Martin and Jensen produced no cooperative deals. It's estimated that Martin Lilley spent over £15,000 at 1960s values before the project had to be abandoned.

Today Gerry's daughter Tina lives in a converted Lincolnshire pub and – slowly, as is the nature of these things – is restoring her own Tina coupé, a vehicle that Gerry had acquired and stored for over 20 years.

Gerry was not present for Tina's 1966 birth, being otherwise engaged on the Isle of Man contesting the Tholt-y-Will hillclimb. Family lore has it that his memory for his two November-born offspring's birthdays (Justine's in 1969 and

Gregor's in 1977) was patchy, even though it was also his own birthday month. Gregor views the missed birthday cards philosophically, Justine less so, especially as her arrival was within two days of her father's birthday!

Carol commented: 'From the day we got married to the day we divorced [in 1981], Gerry never changed. He could be a rotten husband and father, but a great driver. That does *not* mean he didn't adore his kids – he did, but on his terms. If he wanted to see them when he got home at midnight, he'd want to get them up to see Daddy!'

In 2009 daughter Tina added to Carol's verdict of Gerry as a Dad: 'He was not a conventional father in any form, but he was incredibly loving, and also very generous when he was about.' Tina added that Gerry would become the most attentive of grandfathers, and stressed that 'he would do *anything* for any of his friends. I would like that to be shown, most importantly, because he was the best friend any of them could ever have had. They all lived off his fame, off his humour, his spontaneity, and some took advantage of him. He had such loyalty to his friends, especially John Llewellyn and Colin Pearcy.'

Gerry's complicated love life included an on/off relationship that began in 1971 and led to a briefer (1983–8) second marriage. Jennifer Cook

LEFT *Carol with Justine and Tina in 1975. The trophy shelves are already groaning.* [Marshall Family Archive]

ABOVE *TVR's Tina coupé on Motor Show duty. Gerry's daughter, Tina, had this sharply styled fastback undergoing restoration in 2010.* [LAT]

was 20 when she appreciated Gerry's company whilst her father, Eric, raced a Mini, and she joined Gerry's drinking crowd along with her father. This resulted in Albert Marshall accidentally inviting her back to his home on one post-pub occasion. Carol was naturally furious when she subsequently heard about Jenny's apparent acceptance at her husband's parental house, but Albert was not to know that Jenny was anything more than another of his eldest son's increasingly numerous casual acquaintances.

Martyn Marshall recalled that his grandfather Albert, like Gerry, often enlivened mealtimes by making controversial statements. Albert would assert 'You're nobody until you've got a Jaguar and a Mini,' or, more provocatively, 'You're nobody until you've got a mistress!' Martyn laughed in 2009 when he looked back on the Jennifer home invitation. 'When Dad found out that Jennifer was having an affair with his son, Gerry had the perfect answer: "I don't know what you're making a fuss about – you told us we'd be nobodies unless we took a mistress!"'

Jenny recalled in February 2009 that 'I just kept as low a profile as I could. When we were together in 1971, Gerry was married with kids. From 1971 to the night before his death in 2005 we were in

pretty constant contact, and I travelled with him to many races and some rallies.'

Over three decades Jennifer experienced aspects to Gerry that contradicted his 'life and soul of the bar' public persona. Former teacher Jenny explained: 'I knew Gerry through motor racing, but that was not the real attraction. That was his personality. Yes, there was the larger than life character everyone talks about, but what made him the centre of attention was equally fascinating in more private times. He just had such a quick mind, and that was a big part of the rapport we developed. At home, he would read and read, had a real thirst for knowledge, and it was not all motor racing stuff. I have seen a listing of all his books, and it says a lot about the man.'

Jennifer added: 'He had a tremendous vocabulary. I could try almost any word from a dictionary, he would know what it meant, and that came out in both conversation and the columns he wrote for various magazines. I liked all the silly names he made up for real people, and I know that the ads he used to do for his business at the back of *Autosport* were often the first things readers went on to look at after they'd read his columns.'

Gerry's hand could be detected in the trade ads back to Barnet Motor Co days. *The* established

Marshall motor business became Marshall Wingfield when he joined forces with John Wingfield in 1972. The company survived beyond John's death thanks to the support of John's mother and employees, business cohorts Brian 'Slim' Atthews and 'Lord' David Atkinson.

Jennifer also remembered Gerry's love of music. 'He enjoyed pretty well all sorts, but when he had those big old cartridge players ['an eight-track – Dad always loved his gadgets,' says Gregor] we always used to tease him about it.'

His favourite artists?

Unhesitatingly Jennifer nominated Dean Martin. 'He was always on in the car back then.' Subsequently she added: 'Gerry also loved Chas and Dave. Gerry became good friends with them and we went to their live concert in Watford. It was his type of music. We had complimentary tickets to a live Pink Floyd concert and took Tina and Justine, but he managed to fall asleep through the best bits!'

Gregor on Dad's musical tastes: 'Yes, he was a Dean Martin fan but equally loved Frank Sinatra (*Singing in the Rain* being the all time favourite), and also Country and Western. On long journeys home from various circuits I'd eventually have to fall asleep to drown it out!'

Jenny recalled: 'Gerry always suffered from claustrophobia and would sometimes get too hot in a public place, like a restaurant, and would have to go outside. Even at home he would have air conditioning fitted and working whenever possible.' There was also a superstitious side to his nature: 'He hated going racing on the 13th. I'm sure one of the times the Firenza lost a wheel was the 13th.'

Gerry married and divorced three times, had early girlfriends, and spent the latter part of his life – when he bravely endured many medical treatments and hospital stays – with final companion Gwen Howard. He gave and received love on a generous scale and avoided facing life alone.

His brother Martyn summed up Gerry's attitude succinctly: 'I think he loved them all – all the women in his life. He was a big enough man to love every one of them. He was not a conventional man, and that was perfectly reflected in the funeral service, with all three wives and Gwen attending.'

That is a generous view of an incredibly complex character and emotional life. The other side of the coin, however, is that Gerry's divorce from Carol left the first Mrs Marshall living in a top-floor Council flat with three young children (Gregor was four) – which was a much tougher existence than

his other wives or lovers experienced, although third wife Penny was left significantly poorer by their marriage.

Carol did not talk about her bleak 1980s existence, but family members revealed that she and the children had nowhere else to go when the divorce went through in 1982. It was only the existence of the Right to Buy scheme, second husband Miles Hutton's support and some borrowed money that finally saw that flat disposed of in 2000.

Carol and the kids did not live in penury, but the early post-divorce years were tough on her. That she managed to laugh through so much of our 2009 interview tells you why daughter Tina still believes 'that if push came to shove, Dad would have called Mum and vice versa, despite everything – and I'm not a romantic fool'.

Such shifting scenery in Gerry's relationships often made life difficult for those bumping into him at public events with the 'wrong' female companion or a later wife. This led to several fractured friendships.

Carol summed it up best when she recalled the 2008 funeral of Bill Blydenstein. Carol explained: 'I still occasionally get unwelcome reminders of my marriage to Gerry, and Bill's funeral was one of them.' Warwick Banks ('Barwick Wanks' to readers of Gerry's columns) – renowned racer, especially in Minis – approached Carol at the funeral and commented: 'You know it was damn difficult sometimes with you at one end of a paddock and Jenny at the other.'

Not half as difficult as it was for Carol. But let's get on with unravelling our racing story against that backdrop of supercharged emotions.

BELOW *Tina holding her baby Imogen in April 2009, with husband Brendan alongside holding Nathan. To the right of Tina are boys, Daniel and Harry.* [Tina Lynch]

CHAPTER 3

Boy racer to maximum Mini-man

How can you do justice to a man who gave so much entertainment to so many, for so long? Participating from 1961 to 2005 in the sport he loved most in life, Gerry tackled more than 1,400 races, rallies, sprints and assorted motorsport adventures. These outings brought an unrivalled 625 wins and a massive array of trophies and trinkets, faithfully catalogued by son Gregor to form the backbone of the astonishing story we now unravel.

Although Gerry always was fanatically keen on motor cars and associated competition, his path into racing a car himself was as protracted and convoluted as any Marshall pub tale. Gregor's records show September 1961 as his father's first outing in his very special Austin A35. Gerry was just nineteen years and two months old. The shorter Brands Hatch club circuit was the venue, but despite a best-in-class qualifying performance he did not complete the formal Sprint, for the meeting was over-subscribed and he had only a reserve entry. So his first motorsport result had to wait until October that year, when he took the same radically modified A35 to second in class at Eelmore Plain. Just how long it took to get the big

RIGHT *By 1965, Gerry had made headline impact on saloon car racing with this June performance at Crystal Palace. Steering Newtune's 970 S-type in traditional tyre-smoking style, he headed the striped Cooper Car Company works entries, here in hot pursuit. Gerry eventually finished second in the 1-litre class, fifth overall.* [Evan Selwyn-Smith]

ABOVE AND RIGHT
The (in) famous Marshall Austin A35 was heavily modified mechanically, often using contemporary Speedwell parts from a company then associated with double World Champion Graham Hill. The A35 frequently sported modified panels because of the owner's exuberant apprentice racing driver moves!
[Both John Marshall]

man into racing his own cars can be judged from the fact that his motor-race debut – at Snetterton circuit – was not until April 1964.

What held him up through those years, aside from the usual youthful financial cramps?

In an uncanny prediction of his own later role entering other drivers in competition cars he owned, Gerry's racing ambitions were initially controlled by watching his circle of friends in motorsport action and discovering 'all about women – or something about women anyway!' Gerry remembered of those formative motorsport years: 'I hadn't got any spare cash, time, energy or even the enthusiasm to go racing. Funnily enough I was always frightened to race myself. I was always the team manager or procurer of parts, rather than the driver.'

Of this period, Gerry recalled that 'I used to knock about with Roger Bunting and John E. Edmond Miles, the two of them apprenticed at Middlesex Motors. John had a Sprite which we modified and Roger had an A35 van with a really demon engine. I was as envious as hell.' Gerry attended Silverstone 8 Clubs and MG Car Club race meetings during the late 1950s and early '60s, but never as a driver. Wistfully he remembered Roger 'went very well' in the A35 van, such commercials being not a rarity in low-cost motor sports back then: Tony Lanfranchi, later one of Gerry's closest racing mates, earned considerable respect in a Ford commercial.

Another of young Gerry's acquaintances, Philip Morris, had an MG Y-type with transplanted TF1500 motor, dubbed MG YB. He and Gerry would share many adventures, which according to Morris 'cannot be printed, even at this late stage!'

Gerry eventually found a way of following the A35 performance route to his motorsport ambitions, swapping his long-suffering Ford Pop road transport for 10 CRO. That was the registration of the long-desired Austin of Barry Hall, a friend of Bunting's and a member of the Marshall motorsport circle. It came with a 1960s personal pedigree that included minor rallying royalty in the form of previous owner Mike Butler. It had been tuned by then hot-shoe heaven providers Speedwell. This North London company was originally co-owned by double British World Champion Graham Hill and later relocated to High Wycombe, Buckinghamshire.

According to Gerry, the A35 dramas and a frenzy of speed uprates started almost immediately. 'I had it two hours and broke the crankshaft. Tim Conroy, who then worked at Speedwell, rebuilt the engine. I never looked back from that moment on with the car … It was a never-ending drain of money!'

ABOVE AND LEFT *A 1963 Snetterton bar deal turned Gerry's immaculate Riley 1.5 (WYR 191) into a scruffy racing Mini, YCD 436, seen outside the family home in its DIY coat of white paint.*
[John Marshall]

Gerry concluded: 'I finished up with what must have been the fastest A35 on the road, at any time. I bought all the remains of Doc Shepherd's A40 racer from Brian Claydon at Newtune, Cambridge.' Claydon transferred some authentic race-proved items from the famous Shepherd A40 (registered UCE 13) and quite a lot of hardware that was not on that proven winner – stuff like a Weslake cylinder head and the legendary BMC 649 camshaft, an essential modification for just about every competition Mini Cooper S of the later 1960s. 'I had things on that road car that even people who were racing didn't have. I had a ZF limited slip diff – nobody used them, they couldn't afford them, and they used locked diffs. It also had the dubious distinction of being the first A35 with a 45 DCO Weber [carburettor] on it, and I eventually also had one of four high-ratio steering boxes on as well.'

The A35 took Gerry to his first personal participation at the wheel of a competition car, but there were other adventures on the way to that September 1961 debut. He had found a lady around five years older than him who was willing to share life's pleasures. Gerry almost forgot about motorsport until 'my parents went to Spain on holiday. I thought this was a good move on their behalf and decided to enter a sprint in my A35. I was up all the previous night, and I polished the car nicely. I also borrowed the safety belts out of my father's [famous ex-works] MG Magnette. Bearing in mind belts were something of a novelty in those days, I find it a bit surprising how convinced I was that they were a Good Thing. It wasn't easy

ABOVE *Gerry's mechanical prowess did not match his driving skills, but he got down and dirty with the best of them. Our man changes the Mini's miniscule brake pads.* [John Marshall]

RIGHT *Philip Morris (wearing crash hat, talking to Gerry through the window of YCD 436) was a very influential racing companion in the earliest Marshall forays. Philip's Riley Elf Mini variant, sits behind Gerry's Mini in the Snetterton pit lane.* [John Marshall]

screwing the full harness belts from the MG, I can tell you. Anyway, I managed to get them in and set off down to Brands Hatch and practised.'

Although he was fastest in the class, Gerry's status as a reserve entry meant that practice runs were all he got. But that was not the end of the adventure. 'I was very unhappy about all this, having been there all day, and I drove off for home. I was unbelievably tired, having been up all night polishing the car, and all the tension and worry of what my father was going to say when got back, if he found out. I got past Hyde Park Corner and was driving down the Bayswater Road and I literally dropped off to sleep – smack! – into the back of a parked car.'

It sounded amusing the way Gerry told the tale, but his sleeping lady companion got a facial cut in the accident. A relative subsequently instigated court proceedings, which were not amusing and stirred up yet more trouble for our debutant.

Gerry's youngest brother, Martyn, told us a trio of excellent A35-period tales from the early 1960s that have passed into family folklore, and middle brother John added some more colour to the years before Gerry was racing regularly.

Martyn began: 'Us three brothers were out in that super-tuned A35 with Gerry one day, following an Austin Healey 3000. It turned into a good little road race, great fun. Eventually we drew up at some lights. The guy in the Healey had the hood down and was curious as to how this little Austin could keep up with the big Healey. "I say, what have you got under the bonnet?"

'Gerry kept a straight face and assured him it was "strictly standard, old boy," – then squealed off the lights!'

During the notoriously snowy winter of 1961–2, Gerry 'parked the A35 up on the drive in a hurry and shot into the house one night. He seemed breathless and puzzled us when he told us he'd left some coal in the garden. I suppose we had about ten minutes to try and figure this out, before a coal lorry drew up outside. They must have spotted the Austin in the drive, because there's no way they could have caught Gerry in that. Anyway, they asked my bemused Dad for their coal back. He was so embarrassed ... Gerry had seen it fall off the lorry, sprinted over and scooped it up to bring home in a big hurry.'

Similarly, Martyn reported that on another occasion 'again the A35 squealed into our drive. This time Gerry bolted upstairs, undressed and reappeared in a dressing gown, plus Dad's pipe! Again, we had a while to figure it out. This time it was the police, and Gerry went to the door for their "Is-this-your-car?" routine.'

Gerry swore he had been asleep, thus the dressing gown. Furthermore, the Austin had 'not been out all evening'.

'The police must have known Gerald was telling porkies,' Martyn commented. 'For a start the engine was pinking, the brakes were probably smouldering and the tyres stank of hot rubber – but he got away with it!'

John Marshall remembered the infamous A35 well. 'It really did have every trick part on it, especially when Gerry had the connection with Graham Hill's mechanic – Tim Conroy – at Speedwell. Graham must have had one of the fastest A35s in the world at the time, and Gerry was not slow to inherit any tuning parts.' Mind you, such leading-edge technology had its snags, as John recalled: 'At one stage it had a Formula Junior engine and four Amal motorcycle carburettors on it and was always catching fire!'

John recalled that the A35 spent much more time creating havoc on public roads than in motorsports. The incident that particularly stuck in

ABOVE *Brian Claydon of Newtune works on the Philip Morris racing Elf, with Gerry's race Mini, bonnet up in the background, awaiting attention.*
[John Marshall]

BELOW *Bottoms up!
Despite the lack of
racing overalls, Gerry
is the figure in the crash
hat getting ready to
race his Cooper Mini.
Brian Claydon (front)
tends the clockwork.*
[John Marshall]

OPPOSITE

*Our second study of
Gerry (sunglasses) and
Brian together was
necessary because all
our other pictures show
Brian buried in engine
bays!* [John Marshall]

his mind was 'when, with a new girlfriend on board,
Gerry overturned the Austin into somebody's
garden in heavy snow.' Gerry described this in my
earlier book, *Only Here For The Beer*, but only
admitted to inverting the car 'right opposite my
old school. I had to drag my father out to come
and tow us in!' John added that there were several
repercussions to this, including Gerry dragging
in best friend Philip Morris as an independent
witness, all negated when 'our Dad rushed up to
Phillip and greeted him as an old friend! – this
when Phillip was meant to be a stranger describing
how a dog ran across the road and caused Gerald
to swerve…'

Gregor's records show Gerry entering
the notorious A35 just twice in full-blooded
motorsports. Both appearances were in 1961
sprints – the first has already been recounted, while
the second, on 1 October, is recorded as a second
in class at Eelmore Plain, with a silver ashtray as
the reward.

Gerry competed twice more in 1961, in the
Philip Morris MG YB with transplanted motor
during November. He shared the car with its owner
at the MG Car Club Brands Hatch sprint, and it was
sold the following Monday after having scored a
first (Philip) and second in class over the weekend.

As well as his second sprint drive, Eelmore Plain
near Aldershot was the unlikely venue for several
other early Marshall forays. Sometimes hapless
rental car companies found themselves the source
of essential motorsport hardware. From the safety
of 1978, Gerry recalled that some 1961 outings
were courtesy of a Wembley-based business called
Hire-a-Car. 'We used to go down there and hire
Minis. These poor bloody Minis, we used to give
them some stick – I used to get seconds and thirds
in the up to 1,000cc class in rented Minis.'

The Marshall men did not restrict themselves to
just Minis, though – a respectable Wolseley 1500
and a Barnet Motor Co Jaguar E-type faced the
Eelmore ordeal in 1964. As Gerry later explained,
'We had some fun – Philip Morris and myself and
Martin Mulchrone. Martin had his Zephyr Zodiac
Mk2 and he used to pound round too.'

After Gerry's initial flurry of 1961 appearances,
the 1962 season is a blank, as Gerry became Mr
Fixit for his racing friends. He became the racing
cohort of Martin Davidson, who raced a very special
Mini under the alias Harry Martin because of total
parental opposition. Gerry explained a decade later
that 'Hairy Harry, as we used to call him, bought
WER 113, an ex-Doc Shepherd car. His father
thought he was buying an ordinary road Mini! When
he got home, of course, all hell was let loose. His
father soon put the car up for sale in *Autocar*, but
we bought it on HP before a buyer could step in.'

Martin Davidson won his first race at Brands
Hatch with Gerry in the pits, but a subsequent
Brands outing was more sobering. After battling
with long-time Marshall friend and fellow
motorsport man Barry Hall, Davidson severely
damaged his Mini at Paddock Hill bend and
required a hospital stay. Gerry commented: 'It was
a terrible business and shook us all.' However,
the Mini was repaired and raced in Cooper
specification for 'a couple of good seasons, which
were great fun'.

The fun encountered some rough passages,
though, including quarrels over various romantic
liaisons, but what changed Gerry's motorsport life
was an episode in 1963. He painfully recalled the
embarrassing details of a Snetterton bar-room deal:
'Martin had been racing [his] Mini in the wet, and
he'd been beaten by somebody I reckoned should

never have beaten him. I started drinking and laying down the law to him in the bar afterwards, generally being rude to him. Telling him I would have done better than that.

'There was a chap listening called Tim Farr – a nice chap. He had been racing Minis in his first season. His car was an old one with two halves stuck together, a new 997cc Cooper engine and sub-frames fitted by Frank Hamlin, who worked at Newtune Garage in Cambridge. Farr's father had offered him a new Marcos if he passed his law examination and gave up motor racing,' explained Marshall. 'The upshot was that I went home in a battered old Mini racing car and he went home in my beautiful Riley! No money changed hands, but I couldn't believe it when I woke up and saw what I'd "bought" – nor could my father!'

That deal changed Gerry's motorsport life, and was to lead in time to his talent for self-promotion and his writing ability being revealed. The Mini, then registered YCD 436, acquired a coat of DIY white paint and became his weapon of choice in tackling more sprints and for his long-postponed racing debut.

Sometimes using first wife Carol's Maynard maiden surname, Gerry began to write accounts of his adventures – and those of the rest of the field – which appeared in the weekly motorsport journals *Autosport* and *Motoring News*. This was the period during which his 'G.D.R.M.' signature, with the addition of 'R' amongst his initials, first surfaced. By the 1970s, Gerry's wit underwrote successive columns for contemporary motoring magazines *Cars & Car Conversions*, *Motor* and, inevitably, *Autosport*, the weekly bible of the English-speaking motorsport fraternity and the only title to survive into 2010.

Gerry was a lifelong *Autosport* reader, developing consistent dialogues with the junior – but extremely influential – editorial staff from his earliest appearances. Most of those he met or wrote for in the 1960s became established seniors at the magazine or parent company Haymarket Publishing. These included names such as Mike Kettlewell, who departed to run his own publishing and motoring book sales company; *What Car?* founder editor Richard Feast; and subsequent (*Autosport* editor) and, at the time of writing, Haymarket non-executive Director Simon Taylor.

John Marshall shared many of his elder brother's early racing forays and seemed to spend much of his life wondering how many more seconds he had left on earth as they plummeted towards the next motorised incident. Over 40 years later, John recalled that 'Gerry wasn't a spanners man. He'd change a tyre, we'd do a set of plugs at home, but

otherwise he'd have somebody else do the work.

'As a schoolboy teenager I went along on the many trips to and from our home up to Cambridge, where an ex-Don Moore employee called Brian Claydon had a back-street garage and did a lot of cylinder head work. Gerry did have a small company called Cranleigh Conversions at one time, and we often used to take customer heads up there for polishing and the like.'

John also recalled how Gerry coincidentally met Robbie Gordon, who, as we have already seen, would become a great racing friend and financial supporter in later business ventures. 'At the time, Gerry was driving a twin-engine Mini that the owner wanted to convert to Cooper power units. We were on our way up to Newtune, just outside Biggleswade, when a then pretty new AC Cobra came up behind us. Gerry said "We'll show this bloke how to go!"

'I thought Gerry was mad [not for the first time, I suspect – JW], but the Mini was fine on the

The Terrible Trio

Throughout his 40-year professional racing and trading life, Gerry's name was associated with those of Tony Lanfranchi (*aka* 'Big Tone') and Barrie 'Squeaker/Whizzo' Williams, and they were frequently described as 'The Terrible Trio'. Like Lanfranchi and Marshall, Williams was often underrated because of his apparent party lifestyle, but he was not a heavy drinker like Gerry and Tony, even though he was often at the bar with them.

Significantly, Williams was the only survivor of the trio by the summer of 2009. Tony died of cancer in October 2004, less than a year before Gerry passed on.

April 2008 saw the publication of a book featuring Whizzo's life and times as told to Paul Lawrence (*'Whizzo': The Motor Sporting Life of Barrie Williams*). There are some pearls within, and my respect for Williams as a supremely versatile driver remains. Some passing references to Gerry are as mean as Gerry and Tony could be to Barrie in the bar. Barrie's disjointed intro might

make you think Gerry was still alive and pouring pints into Williams' innocent little frame!

When Gerry Marshall first met Lanfranchi is not recorded, but a bar was undoubtedly in the background. Tony was also resident at Brands Hatch as chief racing school instructor for more than 21 years and the pair often drank there, as did many others of the era; but Thruxton was a personal driving favourite for Gerry, and Snetterton was really his home track. He racked up many, many test and race miles in Norfolk, including 24-hour races and record-breaking runs.

Gerry worked for Lanfranchi occasionally in the 1960s, and beyond that Tony often drove Marshall-owned machinery, most notably the Mayfair Opel Monza through the 1976 season, when the duo also shared a Vauxhall at the Spa 24-hours (see Chapter 7).

Peter Lanfranchi, writing a personal column in Barrie's biography, some years after brother Tony's death, said: 'My brother Tony, Gerry Marshall and a few other drivers were extremely lucky. They lived

corners of course, and it held its own, although it was hellishly noisy with one of the engines right by your ear. Gerry really belted down the road, then there was a bang and the Mini filled with smoke.'

They stopped quick enough to save the engine and John-the-obscure-parts-finder trekked off to find the sump plug that had fallen out. Meanwhile Cobra man had stopped and paid his respects, asking how he could help. John takes up the story, 'Well, that was Robbie Gordon, the son of a Canadian banker, and he turned out to be a very good friend to Gerry. I found the sump plug – just one of lots of jobs like this I got from Gerald over the years – and the two of them became great mates.

'Robbie and Gerry got me my first Mini,' John added, 'because they bought an 850 when they came out of a drinking club after the buses had stopped running and the taxis had all gone home. Saw the Mini by the kerbside "For Sale", knocked the owner up and bought it on the spot! They brought it back home, didn't want it any more, so it became my first Mini. That got all tuned up by Newtune too, even though I didn't want it tweaked up.'

John's connections with Gerry and motor cars were maintained in later life through his employment as an expert stores man with particularly strong Jaguar connections, as he explained in 2009: 'I worked for Henleys for 22 years between 1965–86 and then for Tony Hildebrand of Straight Six for another 11 years, until that shut down. Like Gerry, Tony was a great character and eccentric, so they got on really well, particularly with a common interest in classic Jaguars.'

Robbie takes up the '60s story: 'I remember the Mini breakdown encounter – one of many dices Gerry and I enjoyed – but also that my Cobra was a bit special. It was actually the car shown on the 1963 British Show stand. After a year it had to be exported to preserve its tax-free status, and it went to Canada, taking a year for the only dealer to sell it on over there.

'Anyway,' Robbie continued, 'Gerry and I developed quite a friendship and it was me who owned the ex-Trevor and Anita Taylor Mini 1275 S, the Mini Gerry shared so successfully with David Wansborough at Snetterton in 1965' (when Robbie himself was 'in Scotland with my bride to be'). In an intriguing aside, Robbie added in spring 2009 that 'I had that 1275 racer detuned and used it on the road for a while as 110 NNM. It then vanished, but I got a call in 2008 from a man living not ten miles from me in the West Country who was restoring it to our original specification.'

Robbie would also own (twice – these were wheeler-dealer times) a 1-litre Mini Cooper S that Gerry originally owned in partnership with Mike 'Weber' Walton. Gerry raced that 999cc S

through an era when motor racing paid them to live, not a flash life, but a glamorous life cheaply. Barrie was never a big boozer … Gerry and Tony were serious boozers, not alcoholics, but they drank more than their fair share. Barrie and I would go out and have a couple of pints and feel a bit giddy. You could start drinking with Gerry and Tony at ten o'clock in the morning, and they'd still be throwing them down at midnight, but Barrie wasn't into that and, as a result, both Tony and Gerry would tease him.'

They certainly did, and it could get cruel, but Barrie was certainly not the only one to be the butt of Marshall & Lanfranchi's cutting comments.

So what was a 'serious boozer' in the first division?

Tony Lanfranchi gave us this clue in his 1980 biography *Down the Hatch*: 'Now and again he [Williams] gets to believing he's a serious drinker. Unfortunately he moves straight from the lower half of the second division to international class, or at least the first division, when he comes in with Gerry Marshall and me. But he doesn't really stand the pace. Six or seven pints, and Barrie's down on his hands and knees, so to speak, having decided that he can't keep up.'

So what did Marshall and Lanfranchi regard as serious drinking? Walton cannot remember lasting more than six pints in the company of the premier league duo, who once hung him out of the window at the Steering Wheel Club for his parsimonious ways, which they saw as worryingly teetotal! However, a teenage drinking companion from Harrow remembered Gerry scoffing 17 pints at a sitting, and he felt that subsequent regular practice would have increased this total significantly.

No wonder we called the original book *Only Here For The Beer*.

Talking to me for *Classic & Sports Car* magazine in October 2000, Tony described his friendship with Gerry as 'an annual fallout about one thing or another'. Actually, Gerry and 'Tone' shared more than either would care to admit over four decades, and Tony remembered that their friendship was first kindled because 'not many people kept up with me on the track and in the bar, but Gerry was one.'

Gerry's longest racing and personal friendship portrayed here in two late-sixties portraits with Tony Lanfranchi (seated in single seater No 6). The lady standing alongside big Gerry is Tony's earlier partner, Tina, a lady who could lap chart a 24-hour race without a break. [Both Marshall Family Archive]

prominently in 1964, beating Warwick Banks in the factory-backed Cooper Car Co S-type, and John Fitzpatrick in the benchmark Broadspeed 970 S, at Snetterton's British Championship round.

A seriously impressive result in those factory-financed days!

Brian Claydon and his Newtune company became a vitally important racing and commercial contact for Gerry. Claydon's wife Daphne had the final say over many decisions, and Newtune was a significant factor in Gerry attracting attention in his formative Mini racing years against formidable opposition. Gerry competed in Minis of various sorts, including one borrowed through most of 1963–5 from later (1971–3) triple British Touring Car Champion Bill McGovern. Bill was a fellow John Lyon local pub denizen, and he and Gerry made their racing debuts on the same day and track.

Our emergent ace also shared Robbie Gordon's Newtune Garage-entered Mini Cooper 1293 S for the prestigious European Touring Car round at Snetterton, to finish an excellent ninth overall with class-winning success against first-class Mini maniac opposition, including Janspeed Mini ace Geoff Mabbs, the inevitable Lanfranchi and Vic Elford.

Gerry's co-pilot, the modest David Wansborough, said in 2009: 'I greatly enjoyed sharing the [Robbie Gordon] Mini with Gerry for the European Touring Car Championship race at Snetterton in 1965. It was a car I had been racing regularly, but Gerry's times were significantly better than mine (I have conveniently forgotten by how much), and he must certainly take the lion's share of the credit for our success. I'm sure his tyre wear was a good deal greater than mine!' It was an outstanding result, but sadly it was the only time he and Gerry raced together.

David paid this personal tribute: 'I shall always remember Gerry as one of the great characters in the world of club and national racing. His passion for life and racing showed unmistakably in his driving, and in his boisterous personality around the paddock and in the bar. Any sport needs characters like Gerry, and racing was fortunate to have Gerry for so many years, as the number of others of his ilk gradually dwindled'.

Amusingly, Wansborough said of his own driving CV: 'I had a short career in a D-type Jaguar and other big sports cars in the early '60s, during which I gained a reputation as a fast but sometimes erratic driver. In 1965 I was mainly driving the Mini and the low-drag E-type CUT 7. I only did a few events in the latter, having put it in a lake at Oulton in the Tourist Trophy in April, which rather undermined my own and my sponsors' confidence in me!'

David added this fascinating period insight to the legendary CUT 7 Jaguar's pedigree: 'The authentic CUT 7 was raced for several seasons by Dickie Protheroe before Robbie Gordon and John Fellowes bought it with the intention that I should be the principal driver. We had ambitions to do Le Mans and other major internationals, but the lake incident put paid to all that – possibly a blessing in disguise, as if my career had developed as I then hoped I probably wouldn't be here to tell the tale. Racing was a dangerous game in those days. That car is now owned by Lord Cowdray, and raced regularly in historic racing.'

We know today that Gerry almost certainly tested CUT 7 at Snetterton back in the 1960s, and also that Lord Cowdray had been in correspondence with him regarding the eligibility of key motor components in the '60s that could therefore be used authentically at FIA international racing level in the 21st century.

Gerry tackled 40 events as a Mini racer in 1963–65. In 2009, pioneering Vauxhall Viva rallying guru and former Mini specialist Chris Coburn provided this time-warp reminder: 'It's strange what time does to one's recollections. The majority of time I spent with Gerry was through DTV, but my memories of him are as strong from his Mini driving as in the Blydenstein DTV Vauxhalls. How such a big man, with the entire weight disadvantage he had, could be so competitive in such a small car will remain a mystery to me forever! The front-wheel-drive Minis lent themselves to an even more spectacular

driving style than most remember him for in the Vauxhalls. Perhaps that's where his exciting driving style came from? Bill McGovern's name can't be lost in all of this, as he also entertained, competing with GM.' (Bill was subsequently more famous for earning a BTCC triple title with George Bevan Sunbeam Imps.)

A scan of Gregor's records for his father's 1963 to August 1965 Mini forays shows 40 entries in all Mini-brick types from 850 to full blooded 1275 S. They reveal 16 class wins (mostly in sprints), including two outright race victories. The first of Gerry's 625 class and outright wins was scored on 30 August 1963 over the Brands Hatch Club layout. Marshall and Minis would be reunited as racers, but this was the end of Gerry's regular Mini motorsport participation. To succeed you had to beat a lot of mad Minimen, and Gerry had proved a worthy and skilfully aggressive member of the Mini club.

Time to step up to V8 power with TVR, and relish classy Lotus pace.

BELOW *Gerry with the third member of the terrible trio, Barrie Williams, both trying to look credible enough to bid for the show-stopping Porsche turbo in Martini stripes.* [LAT]

CHAPTER 4

Big power, classy sports car era

Gerry's first non-Mini drives were connected with Jaguar E-types. We have a result for a one-off outing in that Barnet Motor Company Jaguar E-type in 1964, but Gerry also tested the fabled low-drag E-type CUT 7 at Snetterton. However, Robbie Gordon – contemporary friend and short-term cohort at Barnet Motor Co – commented in May 2009 that Gerry never actually *competed* in CUT 7. 'I'm sure Gerry never drove this car competitively whilst I owned it. I sold it to Martin Lilley in December 1965, which would make it a year too late for Gerry to use at Eelmore .... Gerry had lots of contacts with probable access to E-types.'

Sitting in the kitchen of the Somerset cottage where he and his wife have lived more than 30 years, Robbie went on to tell a typical period E-type tale. 'We had one or two E-types at Barnet Motor Co for sale when I was there, but they were standard road cars. One we sold to two likely lads from the East End – for cash, of course. About a week later the cops turned up to interview me (the nominal owner, as I'd paid for it), because it had been used in a big bank heist in South London! None of us went to jail,' quipped Robbie cheerfully, with the insulation of 45 years' hindsight.

Today Gregor credits reportedly strong outings

LEFT *Young man in a Lotus hurry. Gerry wheels a Barnet-entered Elan with typical determination around Brands Hatch GP circuit in October 1965. Marshall was sixth overall and had originally been entered in a TVR.* [Marshall Family Archive]

Gerry Marshall
3, Morton Close
Pitstone Green
Nr. Leighton Buzzard
Beds. LU7 9BQ

The Viscount Cowdray
Cowdray Park
Midhurst
West Sussex
GU29 0AY

28th May 2003

Dear Michael,

I must apologise for the delay in replying to your letter. I can only say that it got lost in my lack of system!

I would confirm that when I drove CUT 7 in 1965, it had slide throttle injection. It was then the property of Robbie Gordon. He owned the car for some time then Martin Lilley, who I worked with at Barnet Motor Company, bought the car and between us we raced it (mostly Martin). When we bought the car it was with a load of spares; an alloy block, 4 speed gear box, wheels, tyres etc. everything Protheroe had for the car. Robbie stored these at Somersham Garage who went bust and when we went to collect our parts the gypsies had broken in and removed them including the alloy block– irreplaceable!

I then sold the car to Charles Bridges who sent Brian Redman down on the train from Manchester with a paper bag full of £5 notes. I demonstrated it on the Barnet Bypass and he then gaily drove it home on the road for a race the next day at Oulton Park. They only had the car for a little while as they needed to complete a Jaguar Team for a relay race. It was then sold to Mike Wright who hill climbed it.

If you need any further details or fuller anecdotes feel free to ask.

See you at Goodwood.

All the best,

Gerry Marshall

GOLD MEDAL

Tel. 01296 668252
Fax 01296 662556
Mobile 07836 515386

LIFE MEMBER

ABOVE *The 2003 correspondence between Gerry and Lord Cowdray confirming the 1965 history of CUT 7, most famous of British Jaguar racing E-types. Robbie Gordon and then Martin Lilley owned the legendary Jaguar in this period, before its sale to Charles Bridges for a certain Brian Redman to drive home from Barnet after a G. Marshall public-road demonstration!* [Marshall Family Archive]

in the legendary Jaguar E with making others look at his father's racing capabilities beyond Minis. An Eelmore sprint outing in an E-type preceded Gerry's employment by and regular appearances for the Barnet company in TVRs and Lotus Elans in 1965 – outings that severed the Marshall Mini habit. By the way, it should be noted that the BarMoCo premises were opposite the police station, so little walking was involved in accounting for numerous scrapes with motoring law…

The man who facilitated that 1964–7 Barnet employment, on and off the track, was Martin Lilley, who as we have seen became the owner of TVR itself in 1965, and remained in control of the Blackpool company until 1981, when he sold it on to Peter Wheeler, who died in June 2009. Sadly, TVR was sold to Russian owners in 2004 and the Blackpool factory was shut in October 2006; as I write this three years later production has still not resumed.

Of Gerry's working and racing relationship with Lilley junior, Robbie recalled that 'it was complicated. Marshall was so much the mover and shaker, the absolute dealer. Martin was relatively shy, so Gerry tended to be the frontman, but Arthur Lilley remained very much in charge of the finances at Barnet. Still, it was always difficult for anyone to say no to Gerry, and he often got away with murder!'

A good example recollected by Gordon involved a 1966 sprint. 'Gerry was there with the Griffith and I had Gerry's 1-litre Cooper S. We had a puncture in the Marshall Mini in the practice runs and there was a valve problem we couldn't fix. Gerry and the chief RAC scrutineer, plus myself, repaired to the bar. Gerry said casually to me, "Want to drive the Griffith this afternoon?"

'I tried not to look too eager as I agreed.

'Gerry turned to Big Cheese Steward and said, "That'll be alright, won't it?"

'"Don't see why not," said the RAC steward, loath to interrupt his whisky.

'I drove the afternoon runs and I had the bad manners to beat Gerry in those tests!'

Robbie remembered of his time at Barnet Motor Co that 'we were young men with fast cars to play with. We just had a ball.'

An excellent speedy experience he highlighted was an informal race with Gerry at Snetterton. 'He had the Griffith up there and I had the E-type. The Jag was quick and well proven, so we were evenly matched, as I never claimed to be as quick as Gerry. We must have done six to seven exciting laps when I spun at the hairpin and ended our unofficial dice. I was in over my head and he really had the legs of me,' concluded Robbie.

Talking in 1979 about the break Lilley had given him in TVRs, Gerry said: 'I will never forget the mid-'60s and the way we used those V8s for anything. I once did an autocross with one, finishing second to the factory driver in another TVR, and we would often sprint standard models. I even went to the Isle of Man a couple of times and thoroughly enjoyed doing Tholt-y-Will hillclimb. It was over three and a half miles long, and, I remember, in 1966 we finished in the top five overall with the V8 TVR.' Gerry won the class that time out, and in 24 outings in the Barnet Motor Company V8 TVR between September 1965 and March '67 he recorded four outright race wins and nine class or overall victories in races and sprints.

Gerry's driving style was a supreme magnet for apprentice journalists trying out their superlatives in *Autosport*. Over the Whit Holiday in June 1966, Richard Feast reported from Brands Hatch of Gerry's class-winning third overall on Sunday, 'BarMoCo's TVR dashingly driven by Gerry Marshall'.

On Whit Monday, Simon Taylor saw Gerry out in two TVRs at Snetterton – the second car was the class-winning 1800 S – and was most inspired by Gerry in the smaller TVR. He wrote: 'An equally exciting argument ensued over the 3-litre class between Gerry Marshall in the Barnet Motor Company 1800S and Lionel Mayman in the 1964 Liege-winning Healey 3000. Marshall was slipstreaming Mayman down the pit straight, with Mayman weaving furiously to shake him off. Marshall got past around the outside at Sear, then Mayman took Marshall again, then Marshall took Mayman and pulled away slightly.'

Reporting from Snetterton later in June, Taylor gave this account of Gerry's presence: 'The race for marque and GT cars settled into a loud exchange of exhausts, and a three-cornered race soon developed between Charles Bridges with the E-type, Bob Ellice's Elan and Gerry Marshall (TVR Griffith). Fortunes changed; Bob Ellice spun the Uptune Elan and dropped second place and Charles Bridges took over, but the Griffith thundered ahead, pulling out a fair lead by the flag.'

However, the most heroic Marshall performance in the TVR was reported in an early May 1967 *Autosport* by the established Francis Penn. Gerry attended the Tholt-y-Will hillclimb in the Isle of Man with the BarMoCo TVR. Over 3.6 miles, and ascending from 200ft above sea level to 1,215ft, just below The Bungalow on the legendary TT motorcycle road circuit, the course was challenging enough before the rains came down.

On Saturday Gerry was 'an astonishing second', beating at least three single-seaters with competent drivers aboard. On Sunday, Penn wrote: 'The first man

LEFT *Generation game: The early racing and road-car insights in this book owe much to John Marshall (left), appearing here alongside Gregor at the 2006 Vauxhall Bedford Opel Association [VBOA] annual event put together at Billing Aquadrome by ex-Vauxhall employee Ian Coomber. Dave Wheatley's brilliant recreation of Old Nail was displayed alongside many other increasingly appreciated performance Vauxhalls.* [Marshall Family Archive]

ABOVE AND BELOW *Gerry drove plenty of smaller capacity TVRs in his 1965–67 era at Barnet Motor Co. The head-on view is of Martin Lilley steering, the side shot is of Gerry driving subsequent business partner John Wingfield's 1800, registered XPG1. Gerry appeared in the 1965 Redex Championship with this 1800 at Brands Hatch and set the first sub-1-minute lap for the TVR around the club track, finishing third overall in a rare early-career non-Mini appearance.* [Both Evan Selwyn-Smith]

to crack the 200-second barrier was Gerry Marshall, who set a resounding 199.46 secs, a superb run which was BTD [Best Time of the Day].' That was until another single-seater flew up and sunshine set in. The drying tarmac meant the best formula cars could get beneath the 190-second mark, but Gerry had more to give than any other class winner. Penn added: 'Marshall got the TVR up in 192.49 – just great!'

That meant Marshall was just about five seconds slower than John Butterworth, the fastest hillclimb specialist in a supercharged Brabham BT14, and some three seconds behind the 4.5-litre Brabham BT 7 of multiple British hillclimb champion David Hepworth. Respect!

The April 1966 issue of *Sporting Motorist* carried a Brian Smith track test of MMT 7C, the silver and blue V8 Griffith in which both Gerry and Martin Lilley competed regularly. By then Gerry had sprinted the TVR twice with Best Time of the Day results, but the journalist had less luck as his Brands assessment was marred by heavy rain and standing water. However, there are some interesting period observations.

Sporting Motorist reported that 'Martin Lilley originally bought a standard TVR Griffith from the factory about a year ago. Martin ran it on the road and in a few races, until a wheel came off at the London Motor Club's Brands meeting in June [1965], and the car was virtually a write-off. TVR supplied Martin with a second-hand chassis and body, the body being presented as a lightweight one. It turned out that it had in fact been fitted with a sunroof and boot [but these had been filled in with glass fibre] and was not a lightweight unit anyway. In fact, when they had rebuilt the car it weighed 24 hundredweight [2,668lb/1,213kg], which is about 4 hundredweight [448lb/204kg] heavier than standard! At this point the only things fitted from the original car were the engine and bonnet.'

This description ties in with Gerry's *Only Here For The Beer* account and other published material. It also highlights that father and son Arthur and Martin Lilley bought the TVR company in Blackpool *after* the purchase of the race Tuscan and its three-wheeler accident. However, the Lilleys' reasons for buying TVR aside, some of the personal remarks Gerry made in 1978 about Martin's acquisition of the company and the road/racing Griffith understandably upset Mr Lilley considerably in 2009, and JW does not feel it fair to repeat them.

Given Gerry's winning record in MMT 7C, it was remarkably standard in the engine department. In 1966 Brian Smith reported that 'the 4.7-litre Ford V8 engine is left absolutely standard except for the fitment of a Carter carb in place of the Holley unit to cure cutting out on corners'. Given that the car was gradually developed, Gerry's description of the carburettor swap seems more likely: 'I did acquire the single multiple choke Holley carburettor from Mike Salmon's successful F. English Mustang.'

Smith added: 'A different silencer is fitted, but in fact the engine still gives the standard 271bhp and is fantastically flexible,' as the journo proved by managing one standing start in third gear and 'the engine didn't protest at all!' Gerry subsequently recalled: 'The beauty of the TVR Griffith was it had an enormous range of power: it would go from 3,500 to 7,200rpm … Going down the old Norwich Straight at Snetterton we used to reckon that was 150-plus mph. It was a fabulous thing, dead reliable too, but it wouldn't stop!'

Other reported modifications in the track test included a Mustang four-speed mated with a 'Cobra one plate diaphragm clutch' and a Jaguar E-type Salisbury 3.77:1 final drive with limited slip differential. Top speed was reckoned at 155mph, but Gerry's quip to the reporter was one to treasure: 'Gerry Marshall has seen 5,800rpm on the tachometer

before braking for Paddock at Brands and he says this gives 122 mph and a feeling of insecurity!'

The dynamics had some useful uprates including Armstrong Firmaride damping, apparently working with showroom coil front springs, whilst the rears were attributed to 'Barnet Motor Company specifications'. The half-shafts were also uprated, whilst wheels, braking and tyres were replaced. As far as we can tell over 40 years later, it looks like the calipers were replaced from Mercedes 230 SL and Aston Martin DB5 sources. Wheels were spinner-nut Cobra 6 x 15in fronts, half an inch wider on the back with Dunlop R6 race rubber.

The eight cylinders also stayed cool at a reported 75°C, 10° hotter when left to idle with the aid of an electric fan. Fuel consumption was reported as 20–22mpg for public roads and 16–18mpg racing, which seem seductive figures by most competition V8 standards.

John Marshall reminded us just what a different world racing in the 1960s was. Remember that Gerry was driving a winning car at national level in the Barnet TVR Griffith? Well, the Barnet company

BELOW Both Gerry and Martin Lilley used the versatile V8 TVR MMT 7C for every kind of motorsport, as the rear-end shot reminds us. Here it monsters a Brands Hatch Sprint, the tail light showing that autocross was not beyond the V8's off-course experience! During February 1966, the hard-worked TVR appeared at least twice in Brands sprints, winning its class on each occasion [LAT]

ABOVE AND RIGHT

March 1966 Snetterton and we have two cracking pictorial records of Gerry's appearance in the BRSCC GT & Marque race. Gerry qualified fastest, but retired in the race. [Both LAT]

were also fielding an Elan, which John remembered as 'a beautiful car, well turned out, but the body was so paper-thin it would wear through in places. Still,' joked John, 'they probably needed that with Gerry's weight!' He confirmed an earlier Gerry report that the lightweight Elan was unregistered: 'They would run about on the road with the publicity registration BAR 1, which was not theirs!'

In John's words, 'the TVR Griffith was usually driven to and from events on the road. Any major repairs had to be done in Blackpool, so a driver would have a long trip to and from north of London.' Since the exhausts were of the straight-through artillery battery variety, some sort of primitive noise reduction was a requirement. John recalled that 'they used to run the silenced extensions to the race pipes back up over the rear screen to the roof.'

John also remembered a bit of informal road testing one Saturday, ready for a Sunday race. 'Gerry had the thing flying along the Barnet bypass, could have been doing 180mph from the noise it was making, when there was a bang. We found the

fan belt had flown off, and they couldn't get one in time to race the next day. Guess who was detailed to go and find it? Right, me and a friend hunted all along the bypass until we found the thing.'

Barnet Motor Co was about more than racing the high-profile TVR Griffith V8. For Gerry it marked a steady and increasingly high-profile role as sales manager, but he also raced Lotus products, especially the Elan. You could say he made an impact, particularly in a full demolition job at Brands Hatch, but the young Marshall also showed such speed that it led to later track offers.

The Elans arrived in Gerry's driving hands by accident, as he explained a decade later. 'Martin [Lilley] had also bought himself a competition Lotus 26R Elan that year, but that lightweight Elan wasn't ready until the end of 1965. That was my original Elan – I nearly always drove it.' That was the first of the BarMoCo Elans and was equipped with a 1,650cc oversize Lotus-Ford Twin Cam motor. 'That was a fabulous car,' Gerry remembered, 'and won

ABOVE *Two Ford-powered V8s at Coram Curve, Snetterton, in September 1966 for the* Autosport *final championship race, Bernard Unett's Sunbeam Tiger showing a lot less lean than Gerry's TVR. The Marshall-TVR combination won at this venue in September '66, but had to be content with fifth on this occasion.*
[Marshall Family Archive]

ABOVE *Mallory Park saw Gerry in social and circuit action over five decades. Here's the Barnet Elan 26R at Devil's Elbow, probably part of Marshall's double drives on October 17th 1965. Gerry was second in the Lotus and sixth overall in a second event with the Barnet TVR Griffith – he was still appearing in Tuscan V8s (albeit in the contemporary one-make series) at Mallory in 1991.* [Marshall Family Archive]

practically everything it did in its original form – FTDs, race wins and God knows what.

'I had no intention of driving it originally, it was really for Martin, but it was so easy to drive,' Gerry concluded, having proved the point in his first race with the Lotus. The 24 October 1965 event was over Lydden Hill's tortuous contours close to Dover in Kent. Gerry plus Elan played bumper cars with Chris Meek's Ginetta on the first corner, and he took the Elan on to a second place overall with a new lap record, earning a few drinks from others who had received similar treatment from Meek. That was a well-publicised meeting because Lydden had recently opened to motor racing and the promoters benefited from the support of radio pirates 'Wonderful' Radio London.

The BAR 1 registration first appeared in September 1965, with Gerry driving at Eelmore Plain to a second in class. That was the first of 17 BarMoCo-backed outings that Gerry completed, in at least three different Elans; his last Lotus outing for BarMoCo came in March 1967. They would score at least eight class wins, including one outright race victory. The latter fortunately took place in front of an impressed Bill Blydenstein, spectating with Carol Marshall at Lydden in July 1966, when they also saw Gerry win in the Griffith.

Unfortunately the 1966 season was not an Elan success, as Gerry explained: 'We thought our previous car had been so successful we could sell it, minus engine and gearbox, and buy a new one from Lotus and have the new engine. So the car

was duly sold and the new one painted the same colour as the one before' – which led many to assume it was the same BAR 1-registered Elan. Even though it had one of the first dry-sump twin cam motors and trick short-stroke dimensions, it proved very fragile and retirements became routine during 1966. Marshall finally put it out of its misery with a big off at Brands Hatch in an end of season sprint.

The second competition Elan was rebuilt, 'but I didn't want to race it again,' felt Gerry. Barnet found another driver for the car, but without breaking its poor results record. Legend has it that when the ill-starred Elan was sold in 1967 its new owner was killed in his first race in it.

As stated, Gerry used at least three Lotus Elans in competition, and a story told by first wife Carol in 2009 illustrates that even cars in Barnet Motor Company stock were not safe from Marshall-Lilley motorsport passions. Carol remembered an outing that tells us much about the Lilley-Marshall partnership in hindsight.

The shared drive that made Carol laugh was this: 'I was lined up at a '60s sprint in a very smart Lotus Elan, ready to rush off. I could see Gerry and Martin looking pretty agitated outside. Then they gave me my final instructions, almost on their knees to plead with me – "Doesn't matter how slow you are, *please, please* don't scratch it!"'

Carol thought for a moment in 2009 and said dryly, 'From that I gathered that the Lotus had been sold, or was a customer car in for service!'

According to a recently unearthed diary entry, Gerry left Barnet Motor Co on 11 September 1967. The diary's last recorded entry for Gerry in a BarMoCo car was for a TVR 1800S in the *Autosport* Championship final at Oulton Park on Whit Monday, 16 September, but we have found no corresponding race report. Gerry certainly raced Snetterton's European Championship event that weekend, in Rex Finnegan's Cooper S, retiring before five laps elapsed.

Likely confirmation of Gerry's September departure from Barnet comes from the Tholt-y-Will Manx hillclimb a weekend later. Martin Lilley wheeled the Barnet Motor Co's now Paxton-supercharged TVR to class front-running effect. We are confident that Gerry went back to Tholt-y-Will hillclimb in 1967 with a very second-hand E-type and won his class.

The Barnet departure came 'after the inevitable humungous rows', as one family member revealed, but not on this occasion with Martin Lilley. Martin remembered in early 2009: 'I was not actually there when Gerry went, I was up in Blackpool running the company. It was my Dad who actually dismissed him. I never did get to the bottom of why it happened, either from my father or Gerry.'

Research in the 21st century indicates that the real reason was Gerry's road-accident rate. We have heard of at least three write-off incidents, and Vauxhall rallying guru Chris Coburn recalled one TVR outing that ended when 'a road accident caused him to scatter TVR parts over a wide area while he had only a seat left attached to himself'.

As he left Barnet Motor Co in 1967, Gerry formed a company with Martin Maudling (son of contemporary Tory politician Reginald) and Bruce Duncan. Carol explained that 'it was to make glass fibre bits'. Gerry was more specific in 1978 and reported they were aiming primarily at MGB owners, 'but it never really got off the ground, so I started trading from home, though it was very difficult with such a lack of capital'.

However, help – limited at first, but subsequently becoming a chance to earn a racing living – was at hand.

'As it happened I was standing next to Carol Marshall, then shortly expecting their first child. I remember saying how I thought it worth coming a very long way to see him in action.' That is how the late Bill 'Billy B' Blydenstein recalled watching Gerry handle the Lotus Elan at Lydden Hill's short track in summer 1966.

Speaking in 2009, Carol felt that 'Gerry had a lot of respect for Bill. And Bill could handle Gerry most of the time, which a lot of people could not.'

Dutch-Norwegian Anglophile Bill was an ingenious engineer and a winner, even when (as you'll recall) he competed against Gerry's dad in the Borgward Isabella he famously engineered and drove. Blydenstein was also a front-runner with the Mini at international level, which commanded the wild young Gerry's attention. Gerry had tested Bill's Mini briefly at Snetterton in 1966, when it reached a demonic 8,600rpm, and would race it with success.

Gerry reported that 'it had no torque at all, it was a super screamer and I was really half frightened of it, because a front-drive car with a limited slip differential and no torque is a totally different kettle of goldfish to a TVR 4.7 with no brakes and no road-holding, all driven on the throttle'. That Blydenstein-Marshall Mini was sold to Gerry in 1967, and he racked up four class wins in it. Actually, it was a part-ownership, for Gerry shared title with Ken Ayres and was forced to sell the Mini as he exited Barnet Motor Co.

Bill Blydenstein became not just the father of the Dealer Team Vauxhall (DTV) racing saloon car team, but also the mentor Gerry Marshall needed to introduce a degree of discipline into his competition future.

ABOVE AND BELOW *The alliance of Bill Blydenstein and Gerry was formed before the Vauxhall era. Here Gerry waits his turn in Bill's flyweight Mini at Snetterton 1967, while our other period shot shows Bill in a later familiar role, handing over an award and a cheque to Gerry!* [Both Marshall Family Archive]

CHAPTER 5

1967–71: The Viva era

As Gerry and the V8 Griffith became an established outright winning combination in upper echelon British club races, the unlikely foundations for his next decade of motorsport were created – foundations that would lead to our hero being paid regularly, initially as much as £10 a race! His cashflow improved (as you will see in the next chapter) and he was invited to join the British Racing Drivers' Club (the BRDC), a membership that he maintained until his death at the club's Silverstone circuit some 34 years later.

Now, let's see how Blydenstein nurtured an exploratory 1.2-litre Viva to become a professional programme of outright winners, with consequent professional driver benefits to Gerry.

Unlike Ford, the larger General Motors (GM) corporation had complied with an earlier US 'gentleman's agreement' not to participate in motorsports, and they officially stayed out of the limelight. This meant that for subsidiaries like Vauxhall, any branch of motorsports was out of public bounds; but – as in the States – there were,

RIGHT *Gerry's lightning starts and total commitment were particularly rewarding around the tighter twists of Brands Hatch. He enjoyed many podium places at the Kentish circuit in 1969, but this picture – proving he could leave even a pedigree ex-British Touring Car Championship Ford Falcon V8 struggling to pass the Mini – would be a favourite memory. The Falcon owner-driver was 21st century Lola Cars owner, Martin Birrane.*
[Marshall Family Archive]

ABOVE AND RIGHT
These fine images show Bill Blydenstein – beside trailer and in action at a sprint – hard at work on development of the 1,256 Viva on original J.A. Pearce Magna wheels at Snetterton, before Gerry became his regular driver. There is also evidence of factory interest at this stage, thanks to Bill's persistent politicking.
The action picture is particularly interesting, as Bill shared with Gerry at the 29th October 1967 CUAC Sprint. This is Bill driving, because we had a picture of Gerry at the same corner in Only Here for the Beer! *[Both Marshall Family Archive]*

effectively, rebels in engineering and marketing who evaded the corporate handcuffs.

Vauxhall had been a prestige sporting marque in 1908 – the alternative Bentley of its era – before GM bought it in 1925 for $2.5 million. Transatlantic grey corporate sludge overcame the 'English Chevrolet's' proud competition heritage through the 1950s. Then, during the early 1960s, Vauxhall's sporting VX4/90 appeared for a brief foray in international rallying, and Mr W.B. Blydenstein worked his magic on cylinder heads for the team. After that, he returned to his extraordinarily effective engineering of lighter and faster Minis.

Bored by working on the same Mini boxes, Bill looked at Vauxhall again in 1966 and wrote a formal letter enquiring if some support would be available to back a then new Viva HB in motorsports. The Vauxhall newcomer was an attractive interpretation of GM's contemporary 'Coke Bottle' curvy styling and looked positively advanced on the suspension and chassis side, compared to the ageing rival Ford Anglia, sporting properly located wishbone front suspension and a coil-sprung rear axle.

Bill was not the only one to investigate the Viva; double Grand Prix World Champion Jack Brabham's Surrey-based tuning company sold a street-performance kit for the boxy first (HA) Viva, and in 1967 offered a conversion for the Viva

HB. Blydenstein and Coburn marketed their own speed kits from just £66. *Motor Sport* tested Bill's ex-Vauxhall Viva HB, registered KXE 658D, for its March 1969 edition. It shaved some four seconds from the production 0–60mph time, leaving it at a still underwhelming 15.3 seconds allied to an 88mph maximum speed. I tested this Viva again in May 1970, with 60,000 miles on the clock and a Lydden race to its credit. It now had a 1.6-litre motor delivering 0–60mph in 12.1 seconds and almost 100mph top speed. Gives you an idea of what a struggle it was to turn this family car into any kind of racer…

Inside Luton, a couple of important allies heard the Blydenstein message. First to bend corporate discipline and offer 'very limited help' was then Vauxhall product information manager Jeremy Lawrence. Other Vauxhall personnel in at the start were senior engineer Colin Wood (who had been involved with Billy B on the VX4/90 rally programme) and Roy Cook. 'Cookie' became the higher profile face of DTV's factory links, enthusiastically pushing engineering uprates to assist competitiveness.

All these characters, plus Gerry and Bill Blydenstein, knew exactly how to work with the media for maximum support, headline ink and, later, TV transmissions. They delivered the

ABOVE *In the earlier years, the big problem was to make the bulkier Viva faster than the Mini horde. At Snetterton, there was enough grunt to stave off the Mini pack, leaving a Cortina and even a SAAB in its wake. We have nine appearances logged for Gerry in the 1,256cc original S&K Viva from October 1967 to March 1968, when the 2-litre car took over.* [LAT]

ABOVE *More Mini action as Gerry scares off the attentions of another marauder, in 1968 at an autumnal Snetterton, with a touch of opposite lock in the 2-litre Viva.* [LAT]

leverage to make the most of any GM cash and components, rewarding Vauxhall dealers Shaw and Kilburn – backers of the first Blydenstein Viva and subsequently DTV – with maximum PR value for every pound spent.

Bill knew Gerry from earlier 1960s encounters, when Bill had a fine British and European racing record in machinery as varied as Borgward Isabellas and Minis. Gerry drove Bill's flyweight Minis, which always made Bill giggle uncharacteristically, but

Blydenstein knew he had found a talent that would develop alongside his engineering ambitions.

A young Dutchman called Han Akersloot, who was Bill's hands-on mechanic in the Mini era, also drove Billy B's machines. Akersloot returned to Holland after Bill discovered he could lap his Minis and the Viva significantly faster than his protégé! Although Bill was pleased to discover the potential of his creations, he had already experienced success as a driver and his ambitions now lay in engineering, preferably for a major player who had a larger chequebook than a club racing budget.

He started trawling for a driver who matched his pace, which would leave him free to concentrate on the oily bits. In one of many interviews at Shepreth between 1969–75, Bill told me: 'It was difficult enough just to keep your head above water financially in a rapidly expanding conversion business. I had seen far too many businesses go bust because *le patron* went motor racing. I decided I wanted to hire a dog rather than bark myself.'

The first four-cylinder competition Viva that Blydenstein built at his Therfield home was retrospectively and partially funded by selling his flyweight (1,064lb/484kg) 850 Mini – constructed outside Royston during 1967 – to Gerry Marshall, as mentioned in the previous chapter.

Working with Akersloot some five years before DTV was formed, the Viva was very much an exploratory creation, one that Bill drove at 1966 sprints and hillclimbs, including an event at Woburn's stately home and lion park.

RIGHT *'I was getting up to my ears in mud driving the Coburn Rallycross car at Lydden Hill.' Gerry usually enjoyed Lydden, taking the Viva's first outright victory at this venue, but rallycrossing (then a huge TV spectacle) a Viva to a class second place did not please the man at all. Especially as his mate Lanfranchi was picking up a podium at Brands Hatch in Gerry's usual race 2-litre Viva over the same December 1968 weekend.* [Marshall Family Archive]

A belated 31 March 1967 press release described the embryo competition Viva as having 80bhp from the standard 1,159cc. When media men like Rex Greenslade and future *Autosport* editor Simon Taylor saw it compete it at the end of February 1967, the Blydenstein Viva was already described as bored and stroked to 1,256cc. Fed by a downdraught Weber IDA twin-choke carburettor, it developed a maximum of 95bhp. All the interior trim was removed and kerb-weight was estimated at 1,792lb (814.5kg). Bill had it in much that specification for it's first race with him at the wheel on 13 April 1967, when it was ninth overall.

Other racing Viva technology included JA Pearce Magna alloys of 4.5in width coupled to 12in (front) and 13in diameters. The only major development that escaped them in 1967 was Bill's own set of close ratio gears – a very successful 1968 development that was also profitable for Bill, with over 50 such gear sets manufactured for customers.

Gerry quipped in 1979: 'I still say Bill took the limited slip for the original S&K Viva from a lawnmower. Still, the driver was demanding the astronomical fee of £10 a race, so there wasn't much left for luxuries!'

The Marshall-Blydenstein connection was natural, for Bill watched Gerry compete in the Barnet TVRs and Elans, having allowed him out in his own Mini. Gerry, TVR-mounted, had also won the Cambridge University (CUAC) sprint outright, where the media men saw the Viva a class winner in 1967. Later that season Bill arranged for Marshall to test the Viva at their favourite Snetterton. It was not instant magic

– the Viva felt 'totally and utterly gutless! I mean, it wouldn't stay with a 1300 Mini in a straight line, but it handled,' Gerry emphasised a decade later.

It took several laps before Gerry understood how Bill was extracting the best out of the useful chassis, limited power and comparatively high weight. After that three-lap intro he proved he could do the job, and was DTV's top dog for the next decade. Gerry was unmatched in his driving versatility, from V8 Firenza to rallying's rough stuff

ABOVE *Whoops, there goes a cone Mr Marshall! Development of the 2-litre Viva GT was fast-tracked, with multiple 1968 appearances at Woburn (Bedfordshire's stately home) hillclimbs, Gerry sharing, as here, with Bill. Best result was a third overall in July, and now they could afford proper Minilites!* [Bruce Stevens]

LEFT *Those pesky Minis! Gerry contested the Redex Championship in a busy 1969, the Viva 2-litre second in class for this January season-opener at Brands Hatch. The Marshall-Blydenstein Vauxhall combination secured second in the series.* [Colin Taylor Productions]

and an assortment of other rides undecorated by Vauxhall's Griffin.

Following the Cambridge Sprint and a reported preliminary race outing at Brands Hatch, 19 November 1967 saw Gerry *race* the Shaw & Kilburn Viva by Blydenstein – an event previewed in the sporting weeklies, which wanted a change from the usual Ford Anglia, Hillman Imp versus Mini contests. One eagerly anticipated: 'Marshall, aged 25 years, renowned for his tyre smoking, sideways, attitudes in Minis and TVRs: should be good value for money in this Viva!'

Gerry had little in the way of firepower on his side, but after a close battle with one of the inevitable Minis – so close that the Mini spun and light contact was made – Gerry took eighth overall in the Swiftsure Challenge ten-lapper. He was 'furious' about the scrape, thinking, 'My first race for Bill and the car's got damaged already!'

This is how Gerry described that November 1967 Viva outing to 1970s *Motor* column readers: 'The car was uncompetitive, being some 20bhp or so down on the equivalent Cooper S and a lot heavier. But the preparation, handling and friendly team spirit was enough inducement to make me stay.'

Gerry and Bill managed six S&K Viva outings that Gregor and I have traced – races and sprints – during the closing months of 1967, plus one appearance at the traditional March CUAC sprint to open their 1968 account. Here the 1.2-litre Marshall-Viva combo came second in class. An eyewitness account of a September 1968 Harewood climb by Marshall and Viva can be found in the sidebar headed 'Early fan goes the distance'.

The S&K-backed Viva with its smaller capacity four-cylinder whirring madly to propel a small, plump saloon body along was due for some serious 1968 refreshment: a 2-litre slant four-cylinder had arrived from the parent General Motors, nicknamed with quiet irony 'Generous Motors'.

1968

The second season of Viva by Blydenstein in Shaw & Kilburn colours, with Gerry Marshall energetically conducting, saw significant changes and the first outright victories. The larger 2-litre slant four from Vauxhall and the late-season adoption of fuel injection were vital for success, as was hiring Gerry Johnstone as chief technician. By 1973 the Shepreth premises would have 12 or so on the payroll, including Gerry's overworked and utterly loyal mechanics at most events, Dick Waldock and Geoff Hall, who both joined in 1970.

The first sprints on record for Gerry in the 2-litre Viva GT are dated May 1968, with fourth and fifth class placings. On 6 October the combo was third in class at Woburn, but by that time the GT and Gerry had won a race.

The 2-litre Viva's race debut at Brands Hatch on 9 June was ragged. Although this was the original S&K 1,256 Viva, it was not sorted for the racetrack – and it showed. Gerry had experience with the 2-litre in a couple of sprints and hillclimbs, but racing was trickier.

The 2.0 Viva was moody all of the first Brands race day, prone to heavy understeer – which did not please its conductor Gerry, who generously and undiplomatically shared his opinions with the media. The GT lapped 3.8 seconds per lap slower than the best Ford Escorts, and contemporary race reports reflected that lack of pace.

Bill Blydenstein wrote to the press more in sorrow than anger. They were sympathetic to his cause, as this piece from Paul Harrington – a freelance for both *Autosport* and *Motoring News* – illustrates: 'The Viva Special makes a welcome break from the tedium of Ford and BMC. Excellent turnout and Gerry Marshall's fiery, but skilful

OPPOSITE Brands Hatch Viva action with Gerry fighting the traditional Ford foes from very different eras. The wild-looking insect of a machine (top) started life as a Ford Popular before Mike Berman took hold of it and campaigned it with 1,650cc front-running success in 1968–69. The Portobello Anglia on full opposite lock (bottom), as Gerry sneaks by on the kerbs at Druids, is that of regular rival, Mike Chittenden. [Brian Kreisky/Dave Knowles]

Driving the last of the Marshall Viva GTs

Back in August 1971 Walton was allowed to drive, at Silverstone, one of the last DTV Viva GTs. As ever, the Vauxhall was beautifully presented and four people drove that day without incident.

This was the Viva that was involved in the famously large accident with its teammate in November 1971, as described in the main text; and it did indeed feature the numb and light steering action that Roger Bell reported.

Gerry Marshall set a benchmark 1m 6.8s; JW was 1.5 seconds slower. We all marvelled at the progress Billy B had made, for the original 1967 S&K Viva with 1,256cc was almost exactly ten seconds a lap *slower* than the 2.5-litre driven on that club-circuit day. Most laps were spent running in, which still allowed a calculated 95mph through the fastest corner.

Bill confided that the Viva GT racer cost around £3,500 new, £2,000 after a season. DTV had run through the following engine sizes and outputs, all based on Vauxhall's slant four and standard block casting. Tecalemit Jackson rated the 2.0 litres at 176bhp by 7,000rpm; 2.2 litres recorded 195bhp at 6,500 revs; 2.3 litres saw 200bhp. For 2.6 litres, 210 horses were indicated, although the predominant characteristic was accessible torque, as expected from an 87mm stroke versus the original 2-litre's 69.2mm.

Bill and team resorted to production parts to cut costs and this could damage race durability. The suspension was based on the Vauxhall coil-spring system, reportedly lowered by a local blacksmith's press, with Spax or Koni damping, and restrained by front and rear anti-roll bars. 10in wide Minilites wearing staggered Goodyear sizings massively enhanced grip.

The transmission remained a four-speed but with Blydenstein's own close ratios, and a Borg Warner limited slip differential lived inside the new but obsolete 1964 VX 4/90 rear axle.

driving must always be a hit with the crowds. A win cannot be far away.'

The following weekend Gerry got closer to an outright win around the old Brands smallest track layout, so short it was lapped by a Mini in less than 39 seconds! Harrington noted in *Autosport*: 'Gerry Marshall was out in the Shaw & Kilburn Viva GT, now far more sorted than on its previous appearance. He made a great start, but … a Group 2 Cooper S slipped by', only to subsequently retire. Gerry fought to hold off an angry Anglia for much of the race, but it too slipped by before the race ended, leaving the Marshall-Viva combo an encouraging second.

The first outright win for the team's 2-litre and Gerry came just two races later, at Lydden Hill on 20 July. Harrington reported that the main excitement at Lydden that day was the first use of a remotely controlled live action camera 'in car', now accepted as routine in BTCC. Unfortunately the camera was placed in an all-Mini race, so Gerry and the 2-litre GT's moment of history went without a BBC record of the event. Marshall and company became, in Harrington's words 'the first Viva, other than the Chevrolet-powered car, to win a race'.

The Viva would win a second time at Lydden the same year (22 September), this time by almost 14 seconds against mediocre Mini opposition.

More important to Bill and Gerry as competitors was that the Viva GT was credible as an outright competitor and had seen off the Brabham Viva opposition in a public confrontation. Perversely,

they were both subsequently members of the same Viva DC team for Britain's longest club race of the period, the 750MC's Holland Birkett 6-Hour relay.

Some 17 clubs entered, and the Blydenstein Viva looked a lot more effective than the comparatively standard-looking Brabham device. Even though Brian Muir drove with typical ace pace – returning to the pits on three wheels in the late stages! – the Brabham effort was not professionally presented.

We originally believed that the Viva team finished third overall, but there were unexpected post-race protests to muddy this usually sporting event. A 2009 crosscheck indicates that the team were actually outside the top ten, Gerry's GT demanding a time-consuming blown head gasket replacement.

The Viva GT was worked hard in '68, with at least 20 appearances in sprints, hillclimbs and club races, finishing in the top three overall, or in class, on at least 14 occasions. One race was entrusted to sparring partner and drinking companion Tony Lanfranchi. Why did Lanfranchi drive Bill and Gerry's pet project to a professionally unfussed third overall at that Brands meeting?

Gerry supplied the snappy answer: 'I was getting up to my ears in mud driving the Coburn Rallycross car at Lydden Hill.' This was a truly foggy, muddy and ghastly weekend, when the BBC TV cameras had a hard time recording the Saturday runs. Gerry did get a pot for his pains, second in class, but he did not rallycross again. And he had a pang of rallycross regret when he got back to Brands in time to see his mate Tony out in *his* racing Vauxhall.

Coburn Improvements – originally in North London, subsequently Banbury-based – were responsible for all Vauxhall off-road sport at this time, up until the operation was moved under Blydenstein's Shepreth wings in March 1975. Chris Coburn told us in 2009: 'The overall DTV budget was divided between racing and rallying activities, but not equally. Vying for funds was always "energetic"! When poo really started to spin off the fan, and personal relationships were put to the test, Gerry passed with flying colours. Enough was enough for me. Gerry and I went separate ways but a really good personal relationship always remained.'

Chris amplified on this life away from motorsport rivalries: 'It was probably away from driving that Gerry and I enjoyed the best times together. Being a large man, showing all the signs of good living, he could have looked shabby in over-casual wear. He had the sense to know that and dressed well. He never minded spending to achieve a stylish persona. This was a good balance to me, personally being well known as a skinflint!'

BELOW *A brave sortie to spread the GM-Vauxhall racing word in Europe saw Gerry in action at Zolder, Belgium. The Shaw & Kilburn Viva GT pursues the locally-driven, but British-prepared, Ford Escort TC. Our hero came home with an eighth and a fourth overall over the September 5–6th weekend.* [Marshall Family Archive]

ABOVE *A fortnight after Zolder, Gerry appeared in a three-day meeting at one of the tracks which he respected most, and where he had much success. This is the grid at Spa-Francorchamps for the two-part* Trophee des Ardennes. *Much publicity was generated for an heroic practice session to take second on the grid in the wet at the earlier Coupe des Spa in April 1970, where Gerry raced to fourth amongst the V8s. On this September '70 occasion, he qualified seventh (centre of third row) and retired in the race.* [Marshall Family Archive]

RIGHT *Winner's laurels and a pot to display – the Osram GEC Championship was a happy hunting ground for Gerry and the club racing Viva GT in 1970–71. Here is the happy 1970 class winner at Oulton Park.* [Marshall Family Archive]

He concluded: 'A really good trick of Gerry's was to have one of his car sales company's staff dress in chauffeur's uniform and drive us to events.'

Jenny Cook added these observations, which tie in with Chris Coburn's respect for Gerry's dress code: 'He always carried a small comb in his overalls and brought this out at the end of a race to comb the few strands of hair on the top of his head before he received the winning laurels. There would be a real panic if he lost that! He did like to look presentable in front of the cameras. He was part of the Old School and thought it very important to wear a shirt and tie and dress appropriately for the occasion.'

Gregor confirms that his father 'hated jeans and trainers'.

Tecalemit Jackson's injection system debuted on the Viva GT on Boxing Day, and was used on the single and twin overhead camshaft Vauxhall slant fours thereafter. Combining the injection with other 1968 moves on camshaft profile and exhaust woke up Vauxhall's slant four considerably. At the slant four's summer 1968 race debut it was reckoned to have 125 carburettor horsepower, about ten horses up on the showroom. By the close of '68, some 160bhp at 6,500rpm was claimed.

Gerry recalled: 'The whole thing of driving the Viva was now very different. Where before I had been getting maximum power at 5,800–6,000rpm, I was now having to use 7,000rpm with no torque. In fact the lap times weren't any quicker, but it seemed it.

'Now we had a racing saloon car as opposed to a racing saloon with a modified engine: this meant we could do the thing properly and it would go bang at higher revs.'

1969

Thanks to a disinterred 1969 diary, we have an intimate picture of Gerry's working life at the track as the Viva 2-litre developed. Chief opposition to the Viva in the Redex Championship materialised from garage proprietor George Whitehead's self-prepared Ford Anglia, backed by *Cars & Car Conversions* magazine (then the Walton's employer).

Inevitably, there were failures on the work-in-progress Vauxhall, but racing routines were often interrupted by numerous media links that Bill arranged and Gerry completed. They delivered useful press and TV coverage, a trait that continued into the 1970s. In one January 1969 week Gerry's diary shows that he worked with two magazines, one of them the influential *Car*, ably represented by Mike Twite.

Early in the Redex season, Gerry raced spectacularly at Brands Hatch, fighting a V8 Falcon piloted by 2009 Lola boss Martin Birrane. Gerry made one of his fabulous starts, able to 'challenge for the lead on the first lap,' said the press. Despite a spin on the grass as he jostled for position against such a heavyweight opponent, Gerry still gathered the plot up to the point where he was second in class, fourth overall – and thereby gathered some Redex Championship points.

In March, Bill's technical curiosity meant the Viva GT travelled to the Motor Industry Research Association's grounds in Leicestershire to measure its acceleration. The Blydenstein-engineered Vauxhall hit 0–60mph in 6.6 seconds, completed the standing quarter-mile in 15.2 seconds, and comfortably cleared the 20-second barrier for 0–100mph at 17.6 seconds.

Gerry's reward was a tenner for the driving and Bill's was the knowledge that his Viva had recorded sensational statistics. Blydenstein's budget-conscious conversion accelerated faster than a contemporary 6.3-litre Jensen 4x4 Interceptor tested at the same track!

Early Viva media reports

An independent assessment of Gerry's early association with Bill Blydenstein and Vauxhall came from former motoring journalist and British Touring Car front-runner Rex Greenslade. Rex has lived and worked in the USA since 1987. He currently heads up a PR and marketing agency (G Works Inc) that provides communications services to multinationals such as Mercedes-Benz, GM, and Jaguar.

Rex recalled: 'I first met Gerry at the CUAC sprint at Snetterton in October 1967. Gerry was there on one of the very first outings with the Blydenstein Viva 1,258cc and I was initially much more interested in the car than the driver. That was because I was a first-year engineering student at Cambridge, sponsored by Vauxhall, and here was someone *racing* a Vauxhall: what kind of nut does that?

'You couldn't help but be captivated by Marshall's wit, the self-confidence and larger-than-life presence, physically and as a personality. Yet anchoring all this, you suspected there was a suggestion of a roguish undertone: a rough, second-hand-car-dealer, and let's-shake-hands-but-count-your-fingers-afterwards undertone – all done with the best possible smile.

'On the track it was all business,' reported Rex, 'and I watched mesmerised as he methodically maximised traction off the line to get a good launch. That's what sprints were all about, and I imagine that these repeated runs helped develop one of Gerry's trademarks: his ability to do phenomenal starts.'

Yes, that's 1979 Triumph Dolomite Marshall teammate Greenslade. More from him later.

Gerry's 1969 diary entries regularly report 7,800 to 8,500rpm motor speeds, albeit the last one was accompanied by a laconic 'blew up after 8 laps' comment for a 7 June Oulton outing. Bill was undaunted; a new cam profile was fitted for a Snetterton test 12 days later and Gerry reported 8,600 revs in top gear.

A Silverstone press day in July was used to debut a close ratio gear set, but these weekly demon tweaks were not bringing immediate race rewards. Retirements that month included a knotted gear linkage, loss of steering, and a puncture. Progress continued to be erratic, with a broken crankshaft and connecting rod in separate September incidents, but there was also an outright win at Oulton Park – this despite the diary note, 'Without gear lever or belts, couldn't get second gear.' Hardly surprising, with Gerry stirring just the stump left by the snapped gear lever…

That '69 season saw Gerry record 28 outings in Vivas with capacities from 2.0 to 2.3 litres. He reckoned to have scored ten wins by 1 November, and some 16 outright and class wins in all vehicles during the entire busy season.

He certainly won the second Redex race of two at an initially wet Brands Hatch final in November. His diary records that they used the 2.3-litre motor and that he collected £150 from his Redex efforts – he finished second in that series – and £15 for the drive. Whitehead won the 1969 Redex title, but Gerry was too busy to mourn that loss. He was off to Thruxton the following weekend for the BBC televised meeting of 15 November. His note-form diary reminders of a day watched by millions state: 'Second in class, third overall: all led for a bit.' He took home £15 for the drive and a fiver for his 50 per cent of the prize money.

1970

Headline Marshall-Viva GT action in 1970 came in contesting two British championships – one the premier BTCC saloon car series – and a quintet of overseas outings, three to Zolder in Belgium and twice to the classic Spa-Francorchamps circuit, then in its original eight-mile lap road-circuit format.

Those Spa outings were not for the 24-hour hardy annual, but the early season Coupe de Spa equalled his best overall overseas result at that point. His fourth position could have been better still if wet conditions had persisted, judging by his grid time. Although it was Gerry's first visit to the Spa, practice conditions were familiar to a Brit: pouring rain. He underlined what an underestimated talent he was with second fastest time, ahead of Grand Prix and multiple Le Mans

ABOVE *Trouble ahead! Walton slipped in this picture gratuitously because he thought Gerry would have liked it. Mr Marshall seized the 1970 Osram Class title in the Viva, but what happened to the lady in Hot Pants is mercifully unrecorded…* [Marshall Family Archive]

winner Jackie Ickx, who had the benefit of a muscular Mustang V8 (on hire from Dennis Leech in the UK) for the fast swerves of the Ardennes. Chris Tuerlinckx won in a 6.5-litre Camaro followed by two locals in an Alfa GTAm and a BMW 2002.

Iconic *Motor Sport* GP reporter Denis Jenkinson commented: 'Among all the continentals with their BMWs and Alfa Romeos was a Vauxhall Viva giving as good as it was getting. It was driven by an English clubman, one Gerry Marshall, and he was really enjoying himself.' Praise indeed from the irascible DSJ.

Gerry also drove a Brabham BT8-Climax in the 1,000km World Championship sports car race at this meeting, qualifying 30th, but it failed to finish.

Tony Lanfranchi – instructor and assessor of a thousand and more apprentice driving talents up to Grand Prix potential – commented of Gerry's Spa prowess in 1980: 'I'd been to Spa three or four times and knew what it was about. And then when it came to Mr Marshall performing he was seven seconds a lap *quicker*. I couldn't believe it. But Gerry was incredibly quick round Spa. I have

Early fan goes the distance

Ian Senior – Atlas website 'The Nostalgia Forum' regular – wrote to us: 'The first time I saw Gerry was at Harewood hillclimb in September 1968. The exact date escapes me; it shouldn't really, as it was also the first motorsport event I ever attended. Gerry was a bit special to me. He was the first racing driver I ever saw live, as opposed to televised.

'Harewood was my first brush with motorsport on the hoof. On arrival, bale out of the car and head to see what's happening on the track. Blimey – a Vauxhall Viva. Surely not? I mean, a *Viva*, for God's sake?

'Anyway, the bloke driving it is giving it a right good go. He crosses the finishing line, which comes immediately after a sharp right-hander, with a lurid tail slide, beautifully controlled.

'Fantastic!

'Must get this bloke's autograph. Run straight to car when it returns to paddock, and out gets a big man with a huge grin on his face. Doesn't look like what I'd call a racing driver, but I guess they don't all look like Graham Hill or Jackie Stewart.

'"Can I have your autograph, please?" I ask.

'"Bloody hell," he says, "I'm famous!"

'I think this sticks in my mind more than anything else I ever saw in motorsport, as it was my first event, first driver (and a spectacular one), an unlikely car, a great character – it had it all, really.

'I've lost count of the number of times I saw Gerry drive after that – so many cars, so many circuits, so many years – in fact, sometimes it was hard to avoid him!

'But that first time was the best!'

a theory about it. You have to produce a theory pretty quickly when you get blown off quite so comprehensively.

'It amounts to this: Gerry is a wild man and around the short circuits in Britain he is forever sideways here and sideways there. Very spectacular, but not – in my opinion – very quick. Quick, yes. But not *that* quick. But let him get to a place like Spa with 140mph bends (200mph bends for that matter, if you had a fast enough car) he has to drive smoothly. And then he is quick. Really and truly quick.'

The 2-litre Viva also scored a fourth overall at zigzag Zolder's punishing layout, but back in Britain the first division BTCC gave the Blydenstein-Marshall-Vauxhall triumvirate few breaks. Technically the Vauxhall had to shed all its low-cost weight-saving glass fibre panels and had to use an engine of less than 2 litres, conforming to a much more expensive set of international Group 2 regulations.

The opposition was world class, two transplanted Australians in imported Trans-Am pony cars: a Mustang V8 (Frank Gardner) and Chevrolet's similarly big-power Camaro (Brian Muir). The supporting cast included Ford Escorts in every class and future triple BTCC championship-winning combo, Harrow mate and fellow first-race debutant Bill McGovern in an Imp by George Bevan that dominated its 1-litre class.

Gerry's BTCC year started off with an adventurous twentieth overall and tenth in one race at the Brands Hatch International meeting, but in the second heat he inverted the Viva. He reckoned that 'it clipped the kerb and, oh so slowly, it toppled over. That was OK, but the marshals then rolled the car up the right way, over the good side! I thought that was most unnecessary.' Even Bill saw the funny side, but for a different reason. 'He had a brand new set of belts in the car but just couldn't get them undone. Can you imagine it? Eighteen stone of Marshall trying to get loose.'

At the Snetterton second BTCC qualifying round, Gerry turned in a cracking early practice time, right up amongst the Escorts. Blydenstein acknowledged that Gerry came in complaining of low oil pressure and a vibration. There was no immediate answer, so Gerry was sent back out. The consequent destruction of the oily bits meant that, in Bill's words, 'when we got back to the workshops we discovered it was literally the sump that was holding it together!'

Race results were patchy. Getting inside the top ten overall on three occasions was tough enough, but the Marshall and Viva combo managed a best of seventh overall at Silverstone in April. More encouraging from a Vauxhall viewpoint was that Bill Dryden's SMT Viva holding tenth backed up Gerry's ninth overall at Silverstone in June.

Head gasket failures interrupted play at two BTCC rounds, but the Marshall Vauxhall's practice speed was underlined with a fifth overall at Croft before a collapsed gasket dragged it back to last. Another accident occurred at the July Brands supporter to the Grand Prix, when, racing John Bloomfield's Escort for tenth to the last corner, last lap, saw the differential 'locked up solid,' explained Gerry. 'I went into the bank backwards, which didn't enamour me to Bill at all.'

The smaller Fords were *the* BTCC targets for GM-Vauxhall, but as well as having the best drivers a Ford wallet could attract, the 1,301–2,000cc Escorts would get motor implants during the season. They graduated from effective class dominators with 170–180 horsepower Lotus 8-valve twin cams to screaming 16-valve Cosworth BD-series motors. These could challenge for outright wins, blending pedigree Formula 2 racing outputs with a larger capacity to durably realise over 200 horsepower. This must have been a significant factor in Billy B not returning to the BTCC in 1971.

There were 1970 compensations. The BARC-Osram GEC Championship allowed the Blydenstein

Vauxhall to be developed around the 2.3-litre production crankshaft at club racing's cheaper costs. Racing from March to October, with more than 200 horsepower at Gerry's disposal, was rewarded by a large silver trophy to mark an Osram class victory, five class or outright wins, and regular front-running results.

1971

Top event in Gerry's Vauxhall racing life this season was the official formation of DTV, from January planning to a June public announcement. The other debutant was a Firenza coupé that would be nicknamed 'Old Nail', the subject of our next chapter. DTV also tried a 2.6-litre variant of the Vauxhall's four-pot, the biggest raced.

Gregor has logged an astonishing 58 events for Gerry in 1971, mostly in Vauxhalls. GM senior returned home with 34 class and outright victories, one championship title, and another BARC-Osram class title. GM-DTV lap records came at Lydden Hill, Cadwell, and Llandow.

Quality opposition was provided by then Post Office engineer Mick Hill (Capri V8) and ex-Harrow sparring partner Dave Brodie. 'Brode' turned out in

a slick black and gold Escort Twin Cam of 2.1 litres, with the logo *Run Baby Run*.

There was no instant win for the Firenza's public debut in September. Gerry practised it before an epic Crystal Palace dice with Mike Crabtree's Willment Escort Twin Cam and the large V8 Camaro of Martin Thomas, the latter later working with Gerry 'DTV' Johnstone in a Bedfordshire racing restoration business. The Firenza was not to the Big Man's liking at this stage, and he raced the 2.5 Viva GT.

The race in the South London park was immortalised before BBC cameras, complete with Murray Walker pedigree commentary – one that hints that not only were Murray's trousers on fire, but so was the commentary box. The Camaro rumbled off to lead much of the race, harried by Crabtree and Marshall so successfully that it finally slid off. Crabtree finished first, but was demoted for a jumped start, so the legendary result was a celebrated Marshall Viva victory. Gregor commented in 2009 that 'Dad knew Crabtree had jumped the start and didn't hassle him, he just kept close enough to win without risking anything.'

Former *Motor* magazine editor and respected racer Roger Bell nominated that Crystal Palace

ABOVE *The 2-litre Viva GT was redeveloped for the more restrictive regulations of the premier RAC British Touring Car Championship in 1970, making it a lot heavier. Gerry tried as hard as ever – look at the tyre smoke! – but Ford flung finance, serious talent and numbers at the series. At this March 21–22 two-race Guards Trophy weekend to open the 1970 season, the best Brands results saw the Shaw & Kilburn pioneer sixteenth in qualifying and pressed to crack the top ten overall. [LAT]*

adventure amongst his favourite Marshall races. Writing in 2008, he told us: 'Gerry was such an extrovert driver – make that a spectacular driver. He defied the law that sideways is slowest. Gerry was very quick on the corners, witness that 1971 dice at Crystal Palace with a screaming RS and a thundering American V8 Camaro, both of them well-driven by top clubbies – and a lot quicker than Blydenstein's half-developed Vauxhall. Yet on every corner Marshall would close right up to their bumpers, showing magical car control while trying to squeeze by without knocking anyone off. It was wonderful stuff to watch.

'In my experience, Gerry was a very fair driver who steered clear of trouble,' concluded Bell. 'Forceful, yes, but fair.'

Just 15 days later Gerry and the team took the Firenza to bumpy Llandow in South Wales and took a brace of victories, one in the saloon car event and a second in the Allcomers event. That started a run of nine wins just in 1971 for the Firenza, but as Gerry commented, he had 'no choice' about using the Vauxhall Coupé rather than his beloved Vivas after a 20 November '71 BBC saga at Lydden Hill.

At that event, Gerry was ensconced in the fresh Firenza whilst his temporary teammates, Messrs Crabtree and Bell, appeared in the DTV Vivas. Gerry won after the most ferocious fight with Brodie's Ford.

Bell tells the remaining race story with 37 years' hindsight: 'Ah yes, Lydden Hill, where Bill Blydenstein bravely fielded three cars, GM in the quickest of the three. His runaway win hardly compensated for the first corner crash, caused by me spinning off and collecting the chasing Mike Crabtree in the third Vauxhall head-on, demolishing – almost before the race had started – two-thirds of Billy B's racing team. It was an awful embarrassment.

'At the time I couldn't explain it. To implicate the steering – which on "my" car was kind of vague and lacking in feel for a racer – sounded like a feeble excuse. Later on (I mean years later on), when tyre temps became a commentator's talking point (which they weren't at Lydden), I realised I must have committed the cardinal sin of plunging into a first-corner melee on cold and largely gripless rubber. It caught me off guard and oversteer – which, as a pupil of the Gerry Marshal school of driving, I should have countered – flicked me through 180°. Poor Mike Crabtree was an innocent victim of my accident.'

Gentleman Roger should be comforted that the lasting Lydden controversy was not over his accident – these things happen in racing, right up to Grand Prix teammates – but rather the fate of the brace of Vivas. As stated in Gerry's original biography both Vivas were written off the books of

BELOW *Some key movers and shakers in the formation and operation of Dealer Team Vauxhall and its forerunners are seen here. In the back row, we have top management and dealers, plus Vauxhall Motors marketing man Jeremy Lawrence (farthest right) who was the pioneer inside the company who listened to the calls to competition action. Front row, left to right; a smartly suited Gerry M, Roger Willis of Castrol Competitions Department, Jean Ames (DTV publicity queen), Billy B and Chris Coburn.* [Vauxhall Motors]

DTV, but they were privately reborn, and there is a reference to Gerry transporting his 'old Viva GT risen from the Lydden ruins' to a Belgian show in *Only Here For The Beer*. Gerry raced both again, but *not* for DTV.

Son Gregor described subsequent DTV Viva history to me in 2008: 'This has always been misreported, and subsequent debates are also misleading. In the Lydden accident, one spun and the other hit head on, a big impact and very badly damaged, so much so that DTV wrote them off. What happened next, though, was that Dad's friend and neighbour farmer John Pope bought one and straightened out the chassis with his tractor! John

RIGHT *Before the battle, Gerry chats beside Vauxhall No 74. It is June 1971 and Gerry elected to race the 2.5-litre Viva rather than the new Firenza coupé at this legendary encounter with fellow front-row occupants Martin Thomas (5.7-litre Camaro) and Mike Crabtree (2-litre Escort TC).* [Marshall Family Archive]

restored the car and raced it (Dad even raced it) and he then built it into a twin-turbocharged Aston V8-engined Magnum that he used in Special Saloons – and Dad raced that, too.

'The other Viva was bought by Gerry Johnstone and Stan Burge. The body/chassis was scrapped and all the running gear was built into a Firenza. Gerry J and Stan raced it, as did Dad: he even dented it, and I have pictures to prove that. It was always said the cars were written-off and I think people always took that to mean scrapped too, which wasn't the case.

'But it literally was true that neither car survived as it was before, and they were built into other racing Vauxhalls.'

In November 1971 Gerry made a diary note of his fees and prize money shares for the month from DTV. It delivers an excellent snapshot of his intense winter schedule, with eight outings logged. We do know that in the first half-season the Firenza racked up a succession of six winter wins through November and December, all bar one at Brands Hatch. There was also a one-off at Santa Pod, two test sessions at Snetterton netting £20 apiece, five race or sprint appearances in the DTV Firenza at £30 each and a half-share in £90 prize monies. Total Marshall rewards for a UK month that most racers would cheerfully avoid? £255.

Gerry's fame spread, for at least two of his epic races that year were televised, and he started his first column for a motoring magazine in October 1971. It offered a dodgy diatribe of jokes, tractor tales and a comparatively serious account of the Viva in its final format before the Thames TV Firenza, star of the next chapter.

The Norman Abbott Brands Hatch race controversy – when the crowd booed Gerry roundly after a Boxing Day win for alleged unfair contact with Abbott's flamboyant Ford – hogged the letters pages of the motor sporting weeklies into 1972.

TIMELINE TO DTV 1966–71

1966
Bill Blydenstein looks for something 'beyond shoehorning engines in and out of Minis'. Approaches Vauxhall via a formal letter for help competing HB Viva.

March–April 1967
Bill tests and announces (in 31 March press release) competition Vauxhall Viva HB at slightly uprated 80hp from the original 1,159cc. Debuts Viva in 1,300cc class of Cambridge University (CUAC) sprint, Snetterton. Wins class comfortably. FTD goes to Gerry Marshall (Griffith V8). 9 April: Blydenstein makes Viva race debut, Snetterton. Finishes ninth overall.

October 1967
Marshall sprints the Blydenstein Viva bored and stroked to 1,258cc, yielding possibly 95bhp, in an autumn CUAC sprint, Snetterton (see 'Early Viva media reports' sidebar). First test for Gerry Marshall in Blydenstein Viva follows.

November 1967
Marshall debuts Shaw & Kilburn-decalled Viva at Romford & DMC's Brands Hatch meeting: eighth overall.

June–July 1968
Marshall debuts 2-litre/125bhp sohc Viva GT at Brands Hatch; eighth overall in June. Wins first outright victory for Vauxhall Viva in S&K colours on 20 July.

October–December 1968
Gerry Johnstone joins Blydenstein. Development of 2-litre/160bhp Viva GT, targeting 200+bhp.

Early 1969
Blydenstein occupies old Shepreth Railway Station premises that in 1971 become home to DTV and the Marshall-Vauxhall racing legend.

May 1969
210bhp is claimed for oversize 2.3-litre club racing Viva.

August 1969
2.3 Viva takes first outright win.

March 1970
Gerry debuts Group 2 international version of Viva at 170bhp in Brands Hatch BTCC opening round. DNF.

May 1970
Viva GT-Marshall debut at Coupe de Spa, Belgium: qualifies second, races to fourth overall.

May 1971
Marshall's winning Thruxton debut for ultimate 2.6-litre stretch of Vauxhall four-cylinder.

June 1971
Dealer Team Vauxhall founded with support from more than 600 dealers. Silver and red livery adopted for DTV in place of Shaw & Kilburn's orange and white. DTV colours amalgamated with other sponsors including Thames TV and Castrol in later years, usually with prominent Vauxhall logos on leading edge of the bonnet.

November 1971
Infamous televised Lydden Hill crash of two DTV Vivas. Marshall wins in Firenza in controversial battle against Brodie's Ford. Vivas not used by DTV again.

ABOVE *Battle joined. In the earlier stages the Thomas Chevrolet rumbles away from hidden Crabtree Willment Ford, a sideways Gerry and fourth-placed John Bloomfield. Thomas spun away his lead under pressure from Crabtree and Marshall, but Gerry was retrospectively awarded the race as Crabtree was penalised for a jumped start.* [Chris Todd]

CHAPTER 6

TV star car and televised mayhem

'I have to think hard to remember it retiring from more than two races. A great credit to everyone at Shepreth, that car. I always point out that I never put a scratch on "Old Nail" – the boys did more damage dropping it off the trailer!'
– Gerry's verdict on a famous Firenza

The showroom Vauxhall that in many minds would define the image of Gerry at DTV – and beyond – was revealed in 1970, and is the star car in this chapter. This racing Firenza became so familiar as an outright or class winner in 66 events that it earned the affectionate nickname 'Old Nail' from its creators and chief conductor. Gerry's 50th win in the legendary DTV Firenza came on 27 June 1974 and marked the Blydenstein-DTV-Marshall partnership's transition from Viva apprentices to a dominant force in UK club racing.

Other Vauxhall outings for 1974–7, marking the end of Gerry's racing contract with DTV, are reported in the next chapter, but for now let's get back to the tale of a charismatic Coupé…

LEFT *'The most attractive car we ever did', was Gerry's verdict on the official 9th September 1971 debut of the Firenza coupé in Thames Television livery. This is a pre-release publicity picture at Shepreth; here DTV's former railway station premises is the backdrop to preparation skills that can also be seen in the two Vivas parked on the platform behind. It was not long before Vivas passed into history and Firenzas, and later Magnums, became central to Gerry's racing life.* [Vauxhall Motors]

THIS PAGE *Wherever the Thames TV Firenza appeared it attracted maximum attention, but as our other pictures show there was a lot of dirty work to be completed behind the pristine preparation standards of the Blydenstein boys in subsequent seasons.* [Vauxhall Motors/ Marshall Family Archive]

The Vauxhall Firenza two-door coupé promised a modest improvement to the Blydenstein Viva racing platform in showroom format, when it cost around £1,000 at introduction in 1970 and was rated at 127bhp with a possible 100mph max. The initial performance option was the Vauxhall slant four-cylinder at 2.0 litres, but that became a 2.3 (2,279cc) in later life, when the name Magnum was adopted for the Coupé and usually superseded the Viva and Firenza badges from 1973–7. The exciting Firenza coupé derivative became the November 1973 Motor Show premiered 'Droop Snoot' limited-production item. Just 204 were reportedly manufactured, sold at an introductory £2,271.31p price with a five-speed gearbox, aero bodywork and an uprated version of the 2.3-litre four-cylinder that allowed 132bhp on the road.

The nose-coned two-door was more than a match for Ford equivalent RS2000s, which had little over 100 horsepower and four-speed gearboxes, but such low production ensured Ford – and to a lesser extent British Leyland's ingenious 16-valve Dolomite Sprint – reaped any profits to be found in this affordable high performance sector.

These production Vauxhall Coupés affected Gerry's racing equipment. The Vivas disappeared from DTV front-line use after the Lydden debacle, and the backbone of special saloon assaults became the gradually redeveloped Firenza, which was born through 1971. It was always referred to as a Firenza until 'the Firenza name was dropped when the Droop Snoot was canned,' comments Gregor. 'It then became either the Magnum or Viva HC two-door Coupé.'

Gerry and Vauxhall-mounted challengers were encouraged to use Firenza or later Magnum coupés in production formulae. Production racing had grown in the UK from unofficial handicap races in 1971 to a brace of fully-formed production racing championships backed by

ABOVE *A winning day: 26th September 1971 saw Gerry debut the 2.5-litre Firenza at Llandow, South Wales, with victories in the Saloon and Modsports/ Allcomers separate races. He also finished fourth in his third race of the day, in the Escort Mexico that would secure the 1971 Ford Championship...Mr Versatility reigns, OK?* [Marshall Family Archive]

Britax and Castrol in 1972. The 1972–3 production
rules dictated categories based on price, not the
traditional cubic capacity classes, but cubic capacity
prevailed subsequently.

More on that later. Meanwhile let's take a look
at the 1971 club competition coupé that became a
legend in its racing lifetime.

Presented to entrants and vital publicity links
Thames TV (an ITV broadcaster) in grey and blue
livery in September 1971, Gerry voted it 'the most
attractive car we ever did' in his DTV era. As one
of the original prototype Firenzas, it was certainly
the coolest racer of 1971, sporting tinted glass!
More seriously, it weighed 112lb less than the
largely glass fibre-panelled Vivas at an estimated
1,736lb/789kg. The Firenza special saloon was
the first of the DTV racing Vauxhalls to be fully
wind-tunnel tested, but it would be improved

aerodynamically over its five-season life, particularly
when the flat front went in favour of a droop snoot
and a deeper front spoiler was counterbalanced by
a rear blade.

When Thames stepped out of the sponsorship
limelight for 1972 the Firenza became silver with
a black bonnet and orange side-stripes before
adopting Castrol livery in 1974, which meant silver
primary colouring shared with the oil company, as
Castrol backed DTV comprehensively in racing and
rallying. The car still retained this livery in 2010.

The Firenza started race testing much as
a coupé Viva. Redeveloped around its own
technical character, 'Old Nail' carried ever more
sophisticated firepower and aerodynamics to a
reported 63 victories between September 1971 and
May 1975.

Gerry's later 1971 season fortunes were tied to

the arrival of the Firenza. The demands of the huge (over 600) Vauxhall dealer network required as much standard content as possible. Major publicity was made of a 70–80 per cent production content at various stages, versus an estimated less than 25 per cent for rival Fords. This helped contain costs and strengthened the link between showroom and racetrack, but often conflicted with Gerry's needs.

Unfortunately, the Firenza's standard front engine location was well forward compared with many rivals, who shifted their motors back, low down in the frame, to improve their race cornering capabilities. DTV personnel (dubbed by Gerry 'Bill and Ben the engineering men') struggled to deliver competition handling and eliminate persistent understeer, a natural opposite to Gerry's requirements on all but the faster corners – which are rare in shorter British events.

Although much of the Viva GT racing hardware lay beneath the Firenza's two-door coupé lines, the handling was stubbornly different. Bill Blydenstein commented of the embryo racing Firenza, at the time of initial testing, that 'it jumped around like a kangaroo!' Gerry commented six years afterwards: 'This had us fooled for a bit, as all weights, suspension and settings were identical to those on the Viva GT.' This meant adapting production parts, such as by reinforcing front wishbones and redrilling mountings to deliver front-end negative camber. Solid (rose) joints were not adopted until 1972. The four-link rear axle was also modified from production sources, whilst the front disc brakes were transplanted from the six-cylinder Ventora. Reportedly a commercial limited slip differential replaced the in-

house locked diff, but Gregor notes it has a Coburn LSD today.

Gerry had two-wheeler testing moments before DTV found a combination of softer coil springs and slimmer anti-roll bars that worked with the stiffer Firenza body. Even at that famous BBC-televised race from Crystal Palace in September 1971 the Firenza practised a second a lap slower than the faithful Viva. That was the reason we saw Gerry plus Viva take on the Crabtree Escort RS and the Thomas Camaro V8.

The 1971 race Firenza specification carried over the single camshaft eight-valve. The 2.5-litre stretch of the Vauxhall slant four hauled just 1,736lb/789kg. This was now rated at 214bhp by DTV, but Gerry observed that although it was down on ultimate horsepower this capacity was 'very much up on torque and throttle response'. This was a supremely

1972

The most successful sorties were those with the Thames Firenza, which won the Forward Trust Special Saloon Car Championship outright and recorded 14 victories. The title was taken after Gerry had flown from a production race inversion at Snetterton to contest a race finally abandoned at Thruxton, one that sealed the Forward Trust series for him.

The Firenza took on the 2.3-litre single camshaft motor that DTV-Shepreth had developed as a saleable unit to customers. Gerry commented at the time: 'Although down on bhp it was very much up on torque and throttle response, giving the very agile Firenza a decided advantage out of the corners.'

The Firenza was working towards its 'Old Nail' status in 1972 with 20 assorted outings in races and sprints, but Gerry topped that with at least 25 appearances in three production racing Firenzas for DTV. This was the first season for an alleged showroom formula in which the classes were decided on price rather than cubic capacity.

In production racing, the Firenza grew from 2.0 to 2.3 litres and brought a surprising amount of class wins – especially as the season also featured the loss of a rear wheel (twice!), a disqualification for an over-bored motor, and a brace of accidents. Despite this, Gerry won his class in the year's Castrol series.

There were also winning appearances in the 2.5-litre John Pope Viva, rebuilt from Lydden Hill wreckage. A quick Opel Commodore served for

ABOVE *Maximum attack! Gerry tackles Cadwell Park, Lincolnshire's 'mini-Nürburgring', to win outright in April 1973.* [K. Lancaster]

BELOW *Pacey! April 1973 early Forward Trust Championship round sees Gerry win outright and a Vauxhall estate wheeled out to honour his success over the victory lap.* [Vauxhall Motors/Marshall Family Archive]

accessible power band, one that suited corner-infested British tracks, which were regular fare for such modified saloons. The PR material reported the race Firenza was geared for 140mph max and was expected to achieve 0–100mph in 13 seconds.

Blydenstein reckoned you could duplicate the Firenza's specification for £4,500: the 210 horsepower motor swallowed £1,200 of that total. The regular power plant from first race through most of the initial 12 months into 1972 was the 2.5-litre single cam.

Although it did not receive its race baptism until September, with a double-win score at Llandow, the Firenza quickly racked up seven overall wins in its first season.

There were a lot more to come…

Gerry's first Spa 24-hour race – it qualified 14th overall but blew in the first hour – and there was even a Mini reunion, at Brands, where he hauled off a second in class for old times' sake.

The BARC recognised his unique and sustained racing record by awarding him the President's Cup.

1973

Again the faithful Firenza-Marshall combo carted home 14 outright race or sprint wins during a strong year of race-car development over 21 outings, during which the very special Vauxhall went through its biggest technical makeover. By March the Lotus-developed 16-valve cylinder head arrived, and a tail spoiler. Both contributed to a reported 15mph jump in maximum speed.

To accommodate the lighter alloy motor and its long induction trumpets, a frightening peak also grew in the bonnet. Consistent lap times benefited from a 2in spread in rear Minilite wheel widths at 12in, the fronts running at the previous 10in widths. Rear disc brakes were scheduled for this Firenza, but were removed later.

A later beak nose coincided with the launch of the Droop Snoot Firenza, raced with a deeper front spoiler in place of the original flat front and smaller blade.

The Lotus-headed motor measured 2.0 litres but was given a longer stroke to race as a 2.2, subsequently also using a 2.3-litre 16-valve. After a June explosion in the motor department at Silverstone, that redeveloped unit saw DTV's first use of a dry sump lubrication system. This system supported production-based reciprocating component durability, including the cast iron crank and reworked, lighter connecting rods. Peak power was reckoned at 230bhp for one unit, 250 horses at best. Maximum torque dropped – by comparison with the Blydenstein bigger displacement single-cam units – to 170lb/ft.

Summarising the effect of Firenza developments from the driving seat, Gerry felt that the 16-valve motor was 'worth about a second a lap. It sounded different but now we had a problem with the reliability of other components. The gearboxes just couldn't take the power and we had to soften the clutch. We went back to our old Ventora clutch rather than the triple plate we had been using – you just couldn't change gear smoothly enough for the four-speed to survive, so we went back to the ordinary Ventora one we'd used for years.

ABOVE *Classic stuff! Gerry captured in September 1973 at the Thruxton chicane by the excellent local photographer, John Gaisford. Gerry qualified second, but this kind of driving in these conditions saw him win once more.* [John Gaisford]

LEFT *BMW day battles featured in Gerry's 1973 August. Here we see him take on the British BMW-ALPINA Batmobile, driven by affable expat Australian, Brian Muir. Gerry qualified quickest, but had to settle for second in the race. On the same day, he also qualified a BMW 2002 on pole in a celebrity thrash, racing to sixth.* [Chris Todd]

ABOVE *Through the Complex at Thruxton in October 1973, the crowds gasp as Gerry rides the kerb in his successful efforts to hold off the amazing DAF-V8 of Tony Hazelwood. Gerry qualified third for this well-attended closing round in the Forward Trust series and won outright, clinching the class championship for the '73 season. During this season, the Firenza grew a power bulge to accommodate the trumpets on the 16-valve engine and adopted a simple front spoiler.* [John Gaisford]

This allowed a certain amount of give, and I had to make sure I treated the box very gently. We had to nurse the whole car the whole time. When we got oil surge we developed the dry sump system and so on, developing the car the whole time. In fact I was not able to drive it really hard until the time we first used the five-speed 'box.'

The ZF quintet arrived publicly on 6 October, for a Firenza four-cylinder confrontation with a 6.4-litre Javelin V8 at Silverstone. Even the wet weather could not offset the American car's V8 power along the straights and Gerry finished second, a strong class winner. Later a key figure at Donington Park, Robert Fearnell wrote the *Autosport* report, in which he praised Gerry as follows: 'But the highlight of the race was put in by Gerry Marshall who gave a superb example of his superb car control, having a whale of a time as he hurled his Firenza through Woodcote with armfuls of opposite lock and vast wheelspin.'

Never mind, the DTV-Gerry-Firenza combo won the next day at the well-publicised *TV Times* Race of the Stars meeting, held around the Brands Hatch Club circuit. Bob Constanduros of *Autosport* saw the 15-lapper: 'Last race of the day was a fine exhibition of how the home team wins, Thames TV taking the honours thanks to the faultless and very quick driving of Gerry Marshall still in the Firenza. He lapped all but second and third, the former being Colin Hawker's DFV-engined Capri.' Hawker set the fastest lap, but this was hardly surprising

since Superspeed employee Colin had a Grand Prix Cosworth V8 packed under the smart Ford's hood!

This had been a typically entertaining and effective two days of racing from Gerry, underlining why he was such a crowd and media favourite – a status underlined at the final Forward Trust round at Thruxton later that month, where he secured the class championship, the overall title going – as was customary in those days – to a smaller-class car, in this case an 850 Mini. He took a fine win around the ferociously fast Hampshire track against friend Tony Hazelwood's V8 DAF, as Brian Cutting's unique Martin V8 Escort expired, 'Gerry performing his customary sideways power slide out of the chicane,' commented *Autosport*. It was a quick conclusion to 'Old Nail's' 1973, with Gerry averaging over 96mph. Hazelwood set a fastest lap at a sliver over 100mph, but sadly Brian Hough lost his life driving a TVR Tuscan during an otherwise stunningly sunny Autumn weekend.

1974

Fitting in a prolonged visit to General Motors' facilities in the USA and beginning a column for *Motor* magazine, 1974 proved a productive year for Gerry. It also marked Vauxhall's first overall championship title rather than a class title (though Gerry himself had famously earned his own first outright championship with an Escort Mexico in 1971, for which see Chapter 9).

Despite the availability of V8 power for Marshall in the troubled 'Big Bertha' Ventora (for which, and 'Baby Bertha', see below and Chapter 7), and ever more powerful opponents, 'Old Nail' seized ten outright or class wins in its 19-event season, whilst the new Ventora scored only three and was written off following a brake failure in August 1974.

So it was 'Old Nail' that earned the majority of the points that made Marshall 1974 Forward Trust Saloon Car Champion.

The opening round of the Simoniz Special Saloon at Brands Hatch saw the fastest Firenza lose its Thames TV livery. *Autosport* reported: 'Prospects for the large-engined Simoniz saloon

ABOVE *Ready for the off. Gerry's lightning starts could offset some of the gathering V8 Ford firepower, as 'Old Nail''s 4-cylinder motor reached the limits of its development. But such major Silverstone battles as this convinced Vauxhall and DTV that a V8 was the only way forward.* [Marshall Family Archive]

LEFT *The Irish Mondello racing weekends were hectic socially and on track. Here Gerry is the meat in a home Vauxhall team sandwich, Des Donnelly leading. This June 1974 weekend brought two retirements for Gerry after constant problems in practice left him on the second row for the first event and last in the other session.* [F.E. Hall]

car race looked great with the front row comprising Colin Hawker's Capri-DFV, Nick Whiting's Escort FVC and Gerry Marshall's 2.3 16-valve Firenza, featuring the new type Firenza nose section, and all three looked absolutely immaculate. Tyre-wise Marshall sported Goodyears to the other two Firestone runners and it was the Firenza that screamed into the lead, followed by Whiting and Hawker.'

Sadly for those – including Gerry – who liked nothing more than a real race, both Fords suffered mechanical problems. Whiting finished 17.2 seconds adrift of easy winner Gerry. A 7-litre Mustang was third, which tells you something about the pace these four-cylinder flyweight special saloons demonstrated.

The Firenza was repainted in Castrol colours after starting the season in the black, silver and orange livery described earlier. Goodyear, Vauxhall and DTV Sportsparts were the primary corporate logos.

The Firenza's winning streak continued through the gestation of 'Big Bertha' with three straight wins (Brands, Mallory, and Silverstone), before the

'big gun' in DTV's armoury arrived on the last day of March 1974. However, although 'Bertha' won on her debut she was not very well behaved after that, and DTV resorted to 'Old Nail' frequently. The most charismatic Droop Snoot of all returned to the Special Saloons in late April and early May with a class win and an outright at Mallory Park and Brands. The 19 May Simoniz round at Brands Hatch saw Marshall and 'Old Nail' both off-colour, so it was Fords to the fore, with Whiting's Escort-FVC beating Hawker's Capri DFV V8, leaving Gerry third.

The end of May – the 27th, to be precise – should have seen a great weekend for Gerry at Thruxton, for he was entered in three Vauxhalls. However, the only Droop Snoot to turn in a result was one from the first batches of road cars, in which Gerry scratched home in a rough race, second to Barrie Williams (more in the next chapter). Registered OTP 554M, this car lived on in Ireland in 2009.

June was luckier for Gerry and 'Old Nail'. Whilst 'Bertha' exhibited development tantrums, the Firenza sailed over the Irish Sea to contest the Simoniz Special Saloons event at Mondello on the

BELOW *Not pretty, but functional. DTV experimented with the aerodynamics on the front of the Firenza at Oulton Park in 1974. They subsequently adopted the much neater droop snoot front end with a simple blade spoiler. Note typically thorough Blydenstein team preparation in the electric elements for the front screen to combat misting. [Alan Cox/ Marshall Family Archive]*

Quids in: 1971–4

Driving the earlier Vivas was never going to earn a fortune in pre-DTV days, but Gerry recorded driver fees of £849 up to the end of December 1971, wryly noting, 'These figures include some expenses!' This refers to entertainment and overnights, as well as straightforward commuting to meetings and test days.

Besides fees for steering-wheel services on track, Gerry collected a retainer of £500 in February 1972, which represented a half-year post-DTV payment, for he collected £1,000 at the start of 1973 as a retainer. According to Gerry's records, retainer payments picked up to a further £1,000 at half-yearly intervals for the remainder of 1973 (he earned £3,000 in total that season), whilst just the first six months of 1974 is recorded as another £1,000.

In the year following DTV's 1971 formation, Gerry's income from driver fees jumped as sharply as the overall results. He logged it at £2,846 – but that was not a fortune in 1972, when the average industrial wage was around £3,000 a year and the early Firenza Coupé cost £1,016.

For 1973, driving netted £3,564, and ten months accounted for in 1974 saw £4,718 received, reflecting success bonuses and prize monies. These

are not the total benefits Gerry received because there were (inevitably) other deals. Sticking to DTV/Vauxhall income, it's worth noting that Gerry reckoned his free car and servicing were worth £750 a year in the 1972–4 period.

Those of you who passed basic maths exams (unlike Walton) will find that these 'accounts' do not crosscheck. That is partially because Castrol payments were incorporated in the retainers during this period; but we can report that Gerry reckoned the total value to him of DTV-Castrol payments was around £4,000 in 1973, and 1974 was valued at £5,750, including the fully expensed use of a Firenza.

Ever the gentleman, Bill Blydenstein added these words to the formality of the 27 July 1973 contract letter: 'I am extremely grateful for your services to Dealer Team Vauxhall over these last two years. The fact that you have driven for me and us for all of five seasons is perhaps the most telling fact of all. That you have managed to win so many races with, initially, a rather uncompetitive motor car, and without any major accidents, speaks volumes for your ability.'

The financial terms for 1975–7 are covered in the next chapter.

ABOVE *Into Paddock Hill Bend at Brands Hatch once more. As was regular mid-'70s race fare, it's G. Marshall in the DTV hardware taking on local Nick Whiting's beautifully presented and engineered Escort. Note that the Firenza now sports a droop snoot and integrated spoiler to support the limited production model.* [Jeff Bloxham]

Gerry outwitting Whiting to take second place in an outstanding special saloons field that also featured Hawker's Formula 1-motor Capri in fourth. Near neighbour and recreator of the Lydden Viva John Pope 'had some moments taking the left-hander with Marshall overtaking around the outside'!

The pace was relentless for 'Old Nail' that year: from July to December, Marshall and the Vauxhall coupé appeared another nine times, five of those outings being at Brands Hatch in the later winter months. Though this secured the over-1,300cc Simoniz Championship class, the overall title was won by a smaller capacity entrant – again.

The last Simoniz round was a two-race affair at a chaotic Brands Hatch on 13 October in which Gerry finished second to Whiting, handicapped by a broken first gear incurred in the first race getaway.

1975

Although V8 power from 'Baby Bertha' now became the DTV race-winning formula, Gerry's final season with 'Old Nail' still saw two outright wins in seven outings before the V8 took over front-line duties in May. The combination of these cars also contributed to Gerry's annexation of a Forward Trust and Tricentrol Special Saloons championship double.

'Old Nail's' first outing of the season was at Brands Hatch on 2 March, Gerry typically busy with a second appearance at this meeting with a Hamilton Motors-sponsored 2300 Magnum. Both returned as winners, the Magnum with a class result in the Radio 1 racing-by-price production saloons event, and 'Old Nail' with another outright victory in a non-championship special saloon thrash.

These were not straightforward outings, for 'Nail' blew an oil seal on a new shorter-stroke motor in practice and Gerry was uncharacteristically slow off the line. Nick Whiting took natural advantage and looked set for the win until, according to Chris Witty's *Autosport* account, 'Marshall quickly closed the deficit'. In the third lap 'an inviting gap left by Whiting tempted Marshall. It was a tiny choice, but with the door then closed, the two touched and Whiting returned to the pits. The damage was superficial but tempers were shortly high. They cooled fortunately as Marshall meanwhile slipped and slithered his way to yet another win, entertaining us greatly as he did so.'

The Magnum performance was even more spectacular, Gerry humiliating all the 3-litre Capris with the ex-Greenslade Vauxhall. Witty observed that 'his pace took him miles clear of the larger

---

ABOVE Championship alliance; Gerry Johnstone, DTV's top technician, and Gerry M within Champion No 1 'Old Nail', line up for another wintry Brands Hatch confrontation with Nick Whiting. 'Old Nail' scored four outright wins and a class victory just in November-to-December 1974 appearances at Brands. [Marshall Family Archive]

OPPOSITE Demon start! Marshall may have qualified on the third row for this Ingliston 1974 encounter in the droop-snoot-modified Firenza, but it didn't take him long to hit the front in the first-corner scramble: he finished second. [N.A. Kenyon]

16th. Always a favourite with Gerry – himself a firm crowd and party favourite – that outing saw the 50th win record for 'Old Nail'. Here is how Brian Foley saw it for *Autosport*: 'Nick Whiting led the over 1300cc Simoniz round for just one lap, and once in front there was just no catching the wheel-lifting and/or sideways Vauxhall Firenza of Gerry Marshall, who had 2.2 seconds to spare over Whiting after 15 laps.'

Later in June 'Big Bertha' redeemed herself with a win, but (as you will see in the next chapter) the first 'Bertha' passed on to that big racing car paddock in the sky during the same season.

'Old Nail' wheeled out for another classic confrontation with the Whiting Escort. Paul King commented in *Autosport*: 'Again the DTV Firenza and the All Car Equipe Escort-FVC put on a good show. Nick Whiting had pole, but Big Gerry got a superb start from the middle and led into Paddock. They circulated as close as this for 11 laps, but then the Escort developed a puncture and Marshall was left with an easy win.'

'Old Nail' tackled three consecutive later July meetings with a brace of seconds and an outright victory. Such rewards came at Scotland's tight but spectacular Ingliston track, Oulton Park, and an easy (seven seconds) win at Mallory. The Ingliston defeat was handed out by Mick Hill's 5-litre Capri V8,

capacity Capris, which are now in the same class and had been thought of as certain class winners. Not, it seems, with Gerry around.'

From that 2 March meeting to its last official appearance for DTV, 'Old Nail' and Marshall notched two outright wins (Brands and Snetterton), a brace of Oulton Park seconds at the same meeting, one third around Silverstone Club, and in their last official outing fourth.

That final DTV official appearance for 'Old Nail' was at Silverstone Club layout on 4 May, and was suitably dramatic. Starting at the back of the grid, the agile Vauxhall coupé, in its fifth racing season, finished fourth overall. Sounds simple, but it had both handling and alternator problems before the start, arriving so late for the start that Gerry and 'Nail' commenced their last DTV race from the back of the grid.

There was some heavy metal up the front, headed by an 8.1-litre V8 Corvair (safety campaigner Ralph Nader asserted that the rear-engined Chevrolet was unsafe, with a weedy flat six on the street!), in which Ian Richardson set the first 100mph lap for a saloon around the Northamptonshire club layout. Gerry lapped in the 98mph bracket, 'Marshall entertaining the crowd with a lot of sideways stuff,' as a contemporary

Short pants

John Llewellyn, who gave the personal tribute address at Gerry's 2005 funeral, recalled: 'Our friendship started in 1972 at the Cambridge University Car Club sprint at Snetterton. I had borrowed my mother's Mini and Gerry was there in the Firenza. I've still got the programme.

'They had a straw chicane down the back straight. Gerry went immediately before me and had straight-lined it. So, when I arrived there was straw everywhere and no obvious route: on returning to the pit I protested to him.

'I was allowed a rerun, but our friendship began – in the bar, of course.'

As with many of Gerry's friendships, roots extended back into childhood, as John explained: 'When I was racing my VW Scirocco in 1982 at Mallory Park, my parents came to watch. They lived not far away and, after the race, they came to congratulate me on my class win, and I introduced them to Gerry.

'I said, "Dad, this is Gerry Marshall." They shook hands and my Dad commented, "Pleased to meet you. I used to bring John to watch you when he was in short pants!" This was true, my brother and I used to make it to Mallory whenever there was a race meeting on, and that's when my admiration started with the Big Man. At big meetings they used to go for lunch at the shed by the lake on Stebbe straight and Gerry was always last to leave.

'Little did I know that my hero of those days was going to become my best friend.'

report states, 'although it was a serious handling problem this time, not playing to the crowds.'

'Old Nail's' most successful seasons had been in 1972 and '73, with 14 outright victories in each. In all Gregor has traced 47 outrights amongst 'Old Nail's' official total of 63 wins, which included class victories. But the four-cylinder Firenza could not remain an outright winner, even for Gerry, in the face of ever larger and more sophisticated V8 opposition on the faster circuits.

'Big Bertha' was not the answer, but between Gerry's last race in 'Old Nail' and the testing debut of a new V8 weapon housed in a Droop Snoot Firenza outline there was a gap of just 17 days. Enter 'Baby Bertha', and with it another chapter in Gerry Marshall's career – the thunderous 'Bertha' era.

'OLD NAIL' FIRENZA TIMELINE 1971–5

September 1971
Firenza coupé in Thames TV colours revealed 9 September. Gerry wins twice and sets new lap record at Llandow, South Wales, on 26 September.

November 1971
Infamous televised Lydden Hill crash of two DTV Vivas, but Marshall wins in Firenza again.

March 1972
DTV-Castrol contest UK-based Castrol and Britax production racing-by-price championships. Marshall drives 2-litre Firenza initially, 2.3-litre later homologated.

OPPOSITE *Our excellent study of 'Old Nail', in April 1975 action at Oulton Park, depicts the rarity of Special Saloon-battling Group 1 front runners. Gerry tackles Stuart Graham's Brut 'Splash it all over' Camaro on the way to second overall.* [LAT]

LEFT *Life after a racing career saw a lot of cleaning sessions and show appearances. By 2009, 'Old Nail' had clean dry quarters at the Donington Museum collection, one of the few racing saloons to appear amongst the blue blood single seaters.* [Chris Todd]

ABOVE *Another race day, another garland. 'Old Nail' and Gerry Marshall gathered garlands like no other racing Vauxhall. The 66 wins – 63 from Gerry, the rest from Scotland's Bill Dryden – contributed to four major championship titles, Gerry securing the 1972 BARC Forward Trust Championship and class titles in the 1973 Forward Trust and 1974 Simoniz Saloon Car Championship. In 1975, the charismatic Firenza contributed to Bill Dryden's class-winning points tally in the Scottish Saloon Car Championship.* [Marshall Family Archive]

October 1972

Excellent Marshall season with Thames TV Firenza at 2.5 litres. Wins Forward Trust Championship, nine wins in thirteen outings.

March 1973

Firenza adopts Lotus LV240 16-valve motor at 2.2 (later alternative: 2.3) litres. Gerry debuts at Mallory Park with a win and fastest lap. Class Champion, Forward Trust Services.

June 1974

Marshall and DTV's 50th win for Firenza, at Mondello Park. Class Champion, Simoniz series.

March 1975

DTV take on rallying responsibility from Coburn Improvements. Chevette hatchback debuts, a new weapon for DTV rallying armoury. Old Nail helps secure Scottish Championship.

May 1975

'Old Nail's' last official DTV outing with Gerry driving, at Silverstone. Finishes fourth. Later in '75 the underrated Bill Dryden achieved Scottish wins in three outings with 'Old Nail', with SMT support, to win the Scottish Saloon Championship.

Winter 1977

'Old Nail' presented to Gerry by Bill Blydenstein at the DTV Christmas party.

February 1978

Gerry runs 'Old Nail' and a Chevette HS2300 at Chiltern Circle & Harrow MC's Brands Hatch sprint. Set FTD with the untouched Firenza, which Gregor records as 'its 63rd victory in Dad's hands'. Gerry also seized a class with a Chevette, before selling it immediately afterwards.

In 2009, Gregor Marshall commented on 'Old Nail's' post-DTV life with his Dad: '"Old Nail" is still in the family (owned by my two sisters and I), as Dad never sold her – the only racer he kept! Everything is completely original from the day she was presented to Dad, nothing new in 30-ish years. Bill asked Gerry Johnstone to take the dust cover off, give her a clean-up, make sure everything was working, and then DTV presented her to Dad.

'After that Dad competed in a 1978 sprint at Brands Hatch and I think they did a demonstration run at his benefit meeting in 1979, but she has never run in anger since.

'The timeline since Dad's ownership is a bit patchy, as Dad always had it in hand (I wasn't expecting him to leave so suddenly!), but the Droop Snoot Group also borrowed the car for some shows.

'From 1979 to 1987 it sat in Dad's various workshops when illness, divorce and recession forced him to close his garage and race team. During 1987 to '89 the car resided in an old lady's garage in Garston, and was rarely seen by Dad other than to pay for the garage and put air in the tyres. From 1989 to 1990 the Firenza lived at Dad's house.'

Thanks to Gregor we can identify these primary moves in 'Old Nail's' post-DTV life…

1979–90

'Old Nail' remained remarkably untouched in private Marshall local storage.

1990–9

Retained in a private museum. Went for auction at Coys in 1990, but failed to reach its reserve price.

1999–2007

Moved to Vauxhall Heritage Museum.

2007–10

Still owned by Gerry Marshall's children, but now part of the Marshall collection at Donington Park Museum.

LEFT AND BELOW
Remember us this way…'Old Nail' in maximum spectator-entertainment mode at Thruxton, and a superb 1975 portrait of Gerry at the height of his DTV-Vauxhall career – caught after an Oulton Park appearance with 'Old Nail', knowing that 'Baby Bertha' promised to continue his winning ways. [John Gaisford/ Alan Cox]

CHAPTER 7

1973–7: 'Big' & 'Baby Bertha' times

I n May 1979 Gerry summarised his DTV decade of dalliance thus: 'I drove Vauxhalls officially for almost exactly ten years, November 1967–77. From the original 1,258cc Viva HB to the fabulous "Baby Bertha" Firenza V8, DTV slaved to give me the best and really made the Vauxhall name mean something to enthusiasts. Just what a pace they worked at you can judge from the fact that the original Viva was hard-pushed to get on terms with 1300 Minis: less than ten years later "Baby Bertha" was the most successful saloon in Britain, holding lap records all over the place and rushing along at fearful speeds.'

DTV-Marshall had a lot more stuff to strut in 1973–7, including two charismatic V8 racers and some strenuous campaigning in the British Touring Car premier league, and scored their best international result during a night-and-day Belgian road race. And there was more too, including rally sorties and strong outings in the Tour of Britain.

The 'Berthas' define the V8 Super Saloon era

In the early 1970s Vauxhall's Ventora was a slumbering road car, its 3.3-litre inline six-cylinders unstressed to produce 124 horsepower alongside accessible torque and the ability to

LEFT *Tony Strawson's monster V8-motor Capri has just expired as Gerry sweeps on to another 'Baby Bertha' victory at Mallory Park – winning the 1975 Tricentrol Championship.* [Marshall Family Archive]

surpass 100mph. Until the 1973–4 winter fuel crisis interrupted play, Vauxhall had planned to market their sleepy street-car with a wake-up call from a choice of V8 motors in the GM warehouse of fun. To support these plans, a charismatic show-and-go machine – Vauxhall-styled and DTV co-created – appeared for an October 1973 static debut.

A crazy cocktail of glass fibre exterior panels – beautifully realised by Rawlson Plastics – and a spaceframe front were grafted on to the remains of the original steel hull. Frank Costin was chief designer on the Ventora programme, with responsibility for the body structures, spaceframes and integral roll-cage. It carried the 5-litre motor as far back as possible and at the time was claimed to be the fastest circuit saloon car worldwide. The Repco-Holden-sourced V8 was quoted at 495 horsepower, but later research showed a more realistic 460–476 horses, depending on need for a rebuild. The eight mated to a rugged T10S Borg Warner four-speed gearbox and a de Dion rear end.

The completed car was beautifully turned out externally because of its show intentions – four opening doors with proper shut lines – but was as heavy as it looked: over 3,000lb, or 1,375kg, about 200kg heavier than the road Ventora six-cylinder.

The hasty preparation problems – such as the lack of driveshafts in Motor Show exhibition trim – were not obvious to onlookers. Significantly, Britain was in the grip of a three-day working week during the detail construction of the Ventora V8's

hardware, and this led in turn to some early race failures, like the front suspension collapsing when a welded wishbone (needed to stretch inside the heavily offset BBS wheels) failed.

At the back, DTV also had the worry of the de Dion location tubes breaking, but at least that happened in testing, not on a public race day. The steering was so muscular that, years afterwards, Gerry winced at the memory of the effort required to turn the steering wheel on to opposite lock.

When the Ventora ventured to Thruxton, poor Gerry had the indignity of the seat mountings shearing, making him a back-seat driver!

The Ventora's Motor Show and Hilton Hotel press debuts in 1973 were sensational and attracted strong media coverage. 'Big Bertha', as the car was dubbed, endured a late-1973 photo session at Silverstone while she was still literally powerless, lacking driveshafts, and with Gerry aboard had to be *pushed* (hernia time for the gallant half-dozen volunteers) across the frame for snapper Robin Rew – a man with a big Reliant habit – to complete an *Autosport* poster. Gerry quipped: 'It rolled gracefully into camera range with the blokes collapsing, totally breathless and out of the picture!'

As a racing car the first 'Bertha' would fail to deliver its full potential, but as the progenitor of a racing offspring and a tool enabling Vauxhall to promote Gerry's already headline-grabbing car control, it was a major success.

RIGHT *'Big Bertha', presented to shimmering motor show standards, debuted with a win at Silverstone on 31st March 1974. Here the classy 4-door gleams in the paddock with Marshall friend John Pope's white rebuild of one of the doomed Lydden Vivas in the background. Gerry also drove this 'Popemobile' on occasion and won twice at Mondello Park in March 1972, when the reborn Viva was in Shaw & Kilburn 4-cylinder format.* [Lindsay Archive]

ABOVE *Gerry's life was never a dull affair, and here was a definite perky moment, for a studio shoot of the Ventora plugging Vauxhall and Castrol wares.* [Marshall Family Archive]

LEFT *Bank Holiday Thruxton in May 1974. Gerry is strolling across the grid to the Ventora V8, towards mechanic Dick Waldock (facing us in orange overalls) and Bill Blydenstein (back to camera). 'Big Bertha' has qualified second fastest for her third outing, but the race resulted in retirement with the seat collapsing!* [LAT]

1974

Ventora V8 'Big Bertha' ran in six races during 1974 and won three of them, including its 31 March debut in the Simoniz Special Saloon Car Championship race at Silverstone. It won again at Silverstone and Mallory Park. However, it was sidelined by mechanical failures at three other outings, the final failure on 4 August at Silverstone's club circuit costing 'Big Bertha' her very existence and Gerry a considerable accident.

Although 'Old Nail' completed the opening early March races of Gerry's special saloon season, the big and bold silver 'Bertha' was race-ready on the last day of the month at Silverstone. Ian Phillips, editor of *Autosport*, and key Ventora hardware designer consultant Frank Costin, saw the big beast in action, snatching pole position against closest rival Tony 'Strawberry' Strawson's V8 Capri.

Phillips caught this comment from Gerry post-race: 'That was one race I didn't stage, it was really hard work.' The Ventora winner underlined his commitment with a new lap record, a sliver under the elusive 100mph mark, and Gerry was unanimously voted APG Driver of the Day. The award may also have been prompted by what the spectators witnessed: 'The Vauxhall through Woodcote was just something else, Gerry churning the wheel round and still hanging the tail out halfway down the pit straight,' said *Autosport*.

What did Gerry himself think of driving the early 'Bertha'?

ABOVE AND BELOW *Mallory Park on 23rd June 1974. These shots reveal that the Ventora lost some of its gloss in favour of functionality, as we see with the inner 'headlamps' removed to admit cooling air. Gerry Johnstone takes paddock notes (above) behind the big V8, which beat Colin Hawker's DFV Formula 1-engined Capri (below) to win 'Big Bertha''s last victory, although much of its hardware was recycled for 'Baby Bertha'.* [Both Rich Harman]

He had started writing a column for *Motor* magazine during the 1974 season because of a dialogue with staff-man Rex Greenslade, who had been encouraged into the Hamilton Motors Magnum race programme as a driver. In one of his *Motor* columns, Gerry described some of his impressions after the Ventora's first race: 'The car seemed a bit over-cammed, i.e. the power was coming in too far up the rev-range: as the engine was set up by our antipodean friends, perhaps they should have installed it upside down? Never mind. The steering is at present far too heavy, but we have the answer to that one as well. If you can imagine getting a London bus sideways at 130mph through Woodcote, that's what it was all about the last time we were up there. But, unlike a London bus, the road holding once into a corner is very, very good. "Bertha" isn't deflected by bumps; she's very smooth and exceptionally good on directional stability.

'This is a tribute to the suspension and aerodynamics, unlike the Firenza in the early days, which was very twitchy in a straight line.'

It was a great start, but 'Big Bertha' had some fundamental design problems that would lead to worrying unreliability – worrying because Gerry's well-being was threatened by some of the failures…

'Big Bertha' next took that heroic Repco-Holden soundtrack to DTV's home track at Snetterton on 14 April, for a special saloon championship event on Easter Sunday. It was only the second race outing for the Ventora V8, and it showed, in a literally smashing day in Marshall lore with two unrelated

ABOVE *Waiting for the start of an ironic May 1975 debut at the FordSport Day at Brands Hatch. 'Baby Bertha' is surrounded by DTV personnel Gerry Johnstone and Geoff Hall, with media and racing personality 'Captain' Tony Tobias overseeing at the back. Pole position underlined the potential, but a transmission failure forced a retirement just two laps from the finish.* [Marshall Family Archive]

BELOW *Diving through Paddock Hill bend during the May 1975 debut race.* [LAT]

Quids in: 1975–7

As mentioned in the previous chapter, the way in which Gerry was rewarded was changed through 1975–7. On 10 December 1974 Gerry and Bill Blydenstein, writing on behalf of DTV and Castrol, agreed a monthly retainer and testing/race driving fees.

As ever, Bill always appreciated his working relationship with Gerry. In December 1974 he commented: 'I am very happy indeed that you will be driving for us for the eighth successive season in 1975. This is quite a record, I doubt if any other entrant/driver combination has had such a consistently successful and unbroken run.'

For 1975, Gerry would get £250 a month from DTV and £84 monthly from Castrol as retainer fees (annual total: £3,648), plus £50 payable per race, £40 for each test session and 50 per cent of all prize monies. Assuming 20 races and his usual high success rate, Gerry reckoned on some £7,000 total income for 1975, grossed up to £8,000 with expenses that Vauxhall included.

Gerry's predictions proved accurate and his DTV-sourced income amounted to £7,567 in the April 1976–April 1977 span, but almost doubled in 1977 to a gross of £12,120. However, travelling expenses escalated some £1,000 too and the accounted final figure was just under £8,000. That was a bargain salary for such a consistently winning race driver with such a high profile, and Gerry probably earned significantly more outside the professional racing business.

damaged production saloons in the Magnum he had borrowed from his protégé, Jock Robertson, one of four Vauxhall coupés wounded in a fracas started by an errant Ford Capri. No injuries, but the most injured Vauxhalls seen since Lydden 1971.

Autosport's contemporary special saloon 15-lap account revealed that 'even though Gerry Marshall's 5.0 Ventora had only really been finished the night before, it was on pole'. Although a gaggle of V8 Capris had been entered, only two survived practice to provide serious opposition – including a 6-litre weapon for Mick Hill. And those absences summarised the problem with the special saloons of the mid-'70s: there were frequent mechanical maladies amongst the mechanically ingenious hybrids. Snetterton highlighted such carnage, with three leading runners – including the Hawker Capri DFV – eliminated post-practice.

'Marshall had no difficulty leading the first few laps,' commented *Autosport*'s Bob Constanduros, 'but both Strawson and Hill were closing by lap five. But on the next lap the Ventora's Costin-designed suspension collapsed, fortunately with no further damage to the car and its race was run.' This problem was fundamental to the elongated wishbones needed to stretch inside the pronounced offsets of the front BBS wheels, plus a lack of preparation time in consequence of the dual-purpose nature of the Ventora – for appearance counted as much as function to its GM-Vauxhall parents.

accidents. The first was a significant mechanical failure on 'Big Bertha', and the second was one of the largest pile-ups seen in British club racing. Gerry finished up underneath or hemmed in by five

RIGHT *DTV's mechanics are laughing, but here they expose the seriously powerful V8 clockwork under 'Baby Bertha''s one-piece front. This scene is from a later appearance in Baby B's career – Donington 1977. The boys got it all back together for another win of the 20 recorded.*
[Lindsay Archive]

Bank Holiday Monday fell on 27 May, which saw Gerry contest three races at Thruxton and face the unexpected in all of them. 'Big Bertha' battled with the inevitable Hill Capri, but 'before it looked like becoming exciting Marshall headed for the pits,' says a contemporary report, 'virtually sitting in the boot after the seat adjuster broke, a problem which ultimately caused his retirement'.

The other outings were for the 20-strong Droop Snoot race, in which Gerry came second after 'a bull-like charge across the grass on the last lap' failed to dislodge Barrie Williams; and the prestigious Castrol anniversary Group 1 thrash, where he showed Dolomite-baiting speed 'until a wire came off the alternator and he lost much time in the pits – but when back in action,' continues the *Autosport* report, 'Gerry spectacularly fought back to finish seventh in class.'

Not the best day at the races, but Silverstone's June Simoniz round brought better 'Big Bertha' news. In 'atrocious weather' Gerry took the showpiece silver Ventora and it's tinted glass to a near ten-second win over the Hill Capri. As ever Gerry put on a show for damp spectators, 'driving

the beast with typical verve,' wrote reporter Peter Richings, 'holding great twitches in front of the pits as he scored another win.'

That was win number two for the largest 'Bertha'. The final one came at Mallory Park later in June, with a 2.6-second winning margin over the Hawker Capri, complete with a fastest lap just above the 50-second barrier (50.4s, 96.43mph), despite, in Ian Titchmarsh's witty words, 'severe bottoming (of the suspension not the driver!) and a broken exhaust'.

This occasion was made especially memorable for Gerry when protégé Jock Robertson – then helping out as a mechanic on the Ventora – took his first win in the production Magnum, defeating one-time Marshall neighbour Derrick Brunt.

Faced with serious competition from quiptastic Australian racer Frank Gardner in a Chevrolet Camaro at Silverstone on 4 August, 'Big Bertha' qualified third, but the race brought some proud moments before a destructive exit.

Sadly, this renamed 'Superloons' confrontation around the shorter club layout was ruined by

ABOVE *Gerry wheeled 'Baby Bertha' out for this December 1975 Formule Libre event at Brands Hatch. He qualified eighth, but frightened so many of the skinny opposition that he finished fourth overall! Here he chases Philip Guerola's March around Druids, but on another Libre outing he and 'Bertha' beat allcomers!* [Colin Taylor Productions]

Gerry obtaining work satisfaction around Silverstone's Woodcote corner on the Grand Prix circuit. Then photographer Bloxham shows us the crude but effective rear end of 'Baby Bertha', dominated by the necessary capacious fuel tank!
[Both Jeff Bloxham]

the weather. Tempted by the promise of £500 for the winner, an outstanding entry was attracted, including 1971 BTCC Champion Gardner in the 7-litre SCA Freight Camaro and the effective David Howes with 6.4-litre V8 counterpunch in an AMC Javelin. Aside from the Ventora, reportedly 'sporting a new engine', the opposition included Mick Hill, Colin Hawker and Tony Strawson in their very special Capri V8s, Tony Hazelwood's astonishing daffy DAF V8, and the proven Escorts of Nick Whiting and Doug Niven.

In short, the BRSCC Midland centre assembled one of the best saloon car grids of the era, but was rewarded by such appalling rainfall that there were far too many post-practice absentees – and a *Mini* snatched pole position! Now, Peter Kitchen and the Gordon Allen 1.3-litre super Cooper were fine racers, but even they may have had trouble believing practice times that showed them some two seconds clear of the internationally respected Gardner and his successful Chevrolet.

Gerry completed the outside of the front row. The Mini got the initial jump on the big metal from the start, but was swallowed rapidly. For first corner, Copse, the race order read Gardner from Gerry with Hill in pursuit and the Mini fifth. At the slowest hairpin, Becketts, Gerry piled on the pressure, looking for a way past Gardner.

At Woodcote, a contemporary report commented, 'Marshall was making a determined effort to get by Gardner … As the two leaders came into Woodcote to complete the first of 25 laps it was clear that Marshall would do all he could to make a race of it. Grabbing the inside line, he out-braked last year's Group 2 Champion to take the lead out of Woodcote as the two big cars snaked out of Woodcote on a drying track.' A proud moment for Gerry, but good news was scarce for the Big Man and DTV that day.

Gardner retook the lead half a lap later and Gerry ran second at slightly greater distance until 'lap four saw the end of the Marshall challenge,' said *Autosport*,

adding that 'the car turned left into the Armco and everyone's favourite Vauxhall was a sorry mess at the end of the straight.' Gerry was at least saved from major injury by the recently fitted Armco.

'Big Bertha' disgraced herself under heavy braking, as the pads had not been wire-locked in place and simply dropped out. The accident was a large one, but it was a gift to DTV and Gerry, because they would now be allowed to make a proper racing saloon car rather than a hybrid show-and-race item.

'Baby Bertha'

Back at Shepreth the overworked DTV mechanics were not dismayed by the demise of 'Big Bertha'. Gerry Johnstone, Dick Waldock and Geoff Hall – with inspired hands-on assistance from Vauxhall stylist John Taylor – were determined to deliver 'an outright winner, and that's what we needed,' felt Johnstone. 'Gerry M had been too many years without a car to win outright on the faster tracks.'

Basically they resorted to a bigger capacity and higher output powertrain within the smallest and lightest body available, then drew chalk marks on the garage floor to contain the hardware in that smaller package.

Bingo! There was the outline of your compact, bigger power, competition weapon.

For 'Baby Bertha' this meant the iron block V8 of Chevrolet-Holden ancestry, the T10S gearbox and the fundamentals of 'Big Bertha's' Costin

suspension, including BBS wheels and Goodyears, and de Dion rear axle with Salisbury LSD. Those were the hard points around which a cartoon Droop Snoot Firenza style would shrink-wrap. A new propshaft was needed for the Firenza's shorter distance between gearbox and differential.

The glass fibre Firenza panels were fully detachable and covered square tube frames front and rear. They butted on to the reinforced central steel hull of Firenza origin.

'Baby Bertha's' biggest competitive gain over 'Big Bertha' was the predictable boost in her power-to-weight ratio. This baby weighed 784lb/356kg *less* than her predecessor! The original engine weighed in at the same 297kg, but was mounted so far to the rear that it skulked amongst the front bulkheads. The motor also became a lot easier to race, as John Nicholson – famed for his work with McLaren and Cosworth V8s – had looked it over and tidied up the ignition system with Lumenition electronics, eliminating the misfire that sapped 'Big Bertha's' potential and adding 14 horsepower to better manners.

Straight-line performance was exceptional. *Motor*'s independent test featured Marshall laying rubber for the acceleration runs. The fifth-wheel two-way averages blinked out 0–60mph in 4.2 seconds, 0–100mph in 7.8 seconds, and 0–120mph took 12 seconds. The 0–100mph time was virtually half that of the old Viva 2-litre GT and 6.2 seconds faster than the contemporary Lamborghini Countach.

ABOVE *For Americans, 4th July may be a celebration day, but in 1976 'Baby Bertha' suffered an unhappily explosive race on the way into Woodcote on Silverstone's Club circuit.* [Harald Barker]

ABOVE *People person. Bill Blydenstein and influential motorsport film director and creator, Barry Hinchliffe (right) socially surround Gerry. Hinchliffe founded BHP Productions, who brought both saloon car racing (especially the extensive BBC coverage of BTCC) and rallying to terrestrial TV, ensuring the interest of major sponsors.* [LAT]

BELOW *Rare occasion: Gerry got beaten in 'Baby Bertha' by a very special car and driver at Silverstone in 1976, but the car was subsequently banned as too radical even for Super Saloons. 'Marshall, sportsman that he is, came onto the rostrum to shake him by the hand,' reported* Autosport. *We see Gerry standing alongside West Country man Jonathan Buncombe, although his greeting might be construed as a little more robust than a simple handshake. Buncombe drove a concoction nicknamed 'Chimp', a Chevron B21 foundation underneath a glassfibre recreation of a Hillman Imp body.* [LAT]

Other detail changes from the Ventora included inboard operation of the front suspension, part of Frank Costin's suspension-only role on 'Baby B', while the de Dion's triple location links included one new arm. A large water radiator was angled in behind the Droop Snoot, and there was a 24-row oil cooler, rear ducting serving the inboard back discs and the differential through substantial side air-intakes gaping in front of the rear wheels.

Unlike the Ventora there was no wind-tunnel testing – the quartet of hardcore workers just threw away any pretence of leisure time for 11 weeks and smacked 'Baby' into shape. Indeed, they did more than that. The second 'Bertha' proved quick straight out of the box, lapping seconds under the existing Snetterton record.

Unfortunately for the future of special saloon car racing, 'Baby Bertha' and Gerry proved just too good for the formula's health…

1975

The first of 'Baby Bertha's' 24 competitive outings in 1975 – which yielded an astonishing 20 outright wins – was ironically timed to coincide with 22 May's FordSport Day. The newborn 'Bertha' caused a sensation at that Ford-biased Brands Hatch meeting (Walton was there to watch and to race an Escort), but there was no immediate win.

Holding third place, the silver and Castrol-DTV-striped Firenza V8 retired as a driveshaft failed with 23 of 25 laps run. Gerry's only immediate compensation was that his nemesis, Brodie, with a charismatic Capri 24-valve in black, was never in contention. That Ford never did realise its potential, but there were plenty more Blue Oval challengers in the locker…

'Baby Bertha's' winning habit started with one of Gerry's favourite racing weekends: Ireland's Mondello Park, some 25 miles outside Dublin. The County Kildare MC event on Irish Whit Monday offered a brace of 15-lap races – sponsored by Ford's Motorcraft division – and Gerry dominated the proceedings, on and off track.

He arrived for morning practice feeling 'seedy' and asserted 'the crosswinds were so strong we had to land on opposite lock!' On track, he was the benchmark, setting a new lap record after trading times with Alec Poole's pace in Derek McMahon's radical Skoda-BDG. Marshall won both races, his margin nearly a minute on aggregate.

As reporter Brian Foley stated: 'Gerry kept his best performance until much later that day, when he topped off some gymnastic head over heels rolls by carrying the portly Heskethian figure of big Derek McMahon on his shoulders around the Mondello club house.'

Back on the mainland the business of putting wins on 'Baby's' CV continued at speed, but it was not always a popular winner. A backlash developed at July's Silverstone Grand Prix's 15-lapper for Tricentrol Super Saloons. *Autosport* headed their spiky single-page account 'Marshall's monster bore'. The opening paragraph predicted how Gerry's success would lead both the series – and DTV's racing programmes – to extinction. Bob Constanduros wrote: 'Annihilation to the point of boredom is probably the best way of describing Gerry Marshall's win in the super saloon race in the dry conditions at Silverstone on Saturday after the Grand Prix. He had quite a gap after the second lap and thereafter pulled away to win by 38.4 seconds.'

Incidentally, in *Only Here For The Beer* I stated that Marshall was on pole for this GP supporter. Wrong. Our 2009 research reveals that he was third quickest in practice, running only four laps before the rain swept in. His recollection of the event (corrected from the earlier book) states that 'Ian Richardson shot off the line in the Corvair [packing, as we have seen, an enormous 8.1-litre V8 – JW] and he was ahead as we went up to Copse. He braked early and I was through. From that point, I led all the way. I was there to drive, no sideways stuff – besides, the car was suffering fuel starvation, as was pretty obvious to spectators.'

By October 'Baby Bertha', DTV and Gerry had already grasped 13 victories, and between 12 October and 27 December Gerry added another seven straight wins, wrapping up both the Forward Trust and Tricentrol Super Saloon championships.

Although much of 1975 was accounted for by Super Saloon events, busy 'Baby Bertha' and 'Old Nail', Gerry also squeezed in – as in '74 – a significant presence in production categories. More about that in the 'Production racing with Vauxhall' sidebar in Chapter 8.

1976

This was a comparatively slow season for Gerry and 'Baby B', which did not begin until May. The DTV race stars made 13 appearances to score ten outright victories, alongside two retirements and a second overall.

Looking back 33 years, the sheer pace of this '76 combo was astounding. They set six lap records at circuits as diverse as Brands Hatch's slow club twists (48 seconds, 90.37mph) to Silverstone Grand Prix's breezy acres, returning a 113.10mph *average*. All but the Brands lap record posted 100+mph averages. Racers amongst you will respect the compact Mallory record, where Gerry recorded a 47.2-second lap (102.97mph) – not a bad time for

a TVR Tuscan almost 20 years later. Remember too that Mallory includes a 35mph hairpin!

Gerry had raced a dozen times, mostly in the Hamilton Motors Magnum, before the dustsheets came off 'Baby Bertha' for the May 1976 Silverstone 6-Hours meeting – a confrontation between Porsche and BMW that unexpectedly went to John Fitzpatrick/Tom Walkinshaw's Hermetite BMW. Gerry's race was also a surprise. West Countryman Jonathan Buncombe was armed with Chevron B21-formula car foundations on an Imp with a huge rear wing. This hybrid formula car, nicknamed 'Chimp', gave 'Baby B' one of the few genuine wheel-to-wheel races that Gerry experienced in that mighty special Vauxhall.

It was an absolutely fantastic race, real David and Goliath stuff, with the flyweight Buncombe 'Chimp's' 270 horses blasted away on the straights, only to nose back into contention at all but one corner. Gradually Gerry ran wider and wider, and the combination of overheated tyres and minor motor hiccups allowed a 'Chimp' surprise. A contemporary account states that 'a startled Buncombe, who was right behind, swerved past into the lead. The Vauxhall picked up again and, in a very forceful manoeuvre, Gerry showed that there was nothing wrong with his brakes just yet by out-braking the Chimp, for heaven's sake, into the Woodcote chicane.'

Buncombe bit back at Club and the 'Chimp' was through for good, 'a delighted winner … And Marshall, sportsman that he is, came onto the rostrum to shake him by the hand,' concluded *Autosport*'s man after this rare 'Bertha' defeat. Gerry, along with the establishment, never did feel

BELOW *Another day, another Garland! There were a lot more results than originally thought, for Gregor Marshall logged over 30 victories in 'Baby Bertha' appearances from May 1975 to October 1977. The 'If it looks right, it is Right' racing Vauxhall won all the way to its last race.* [LAT]

ABOVE *Rare racing sight. Gerry in 'Baby Bertha' (No 2) leads out Bill Dryden in 'Old Nail' (No 3) to defend DTV honour against ever-stronger Super Saloon opposition at Oulton Park on 28th June 1975. DTV's fears were justified; Alec Poole (Skoda-BDG) won a second successive confrontation after a tough race with Gerry that brought the crowd to its feet. Dryden was fifth, beaten by Dave Millington's private Firenza when a misfire set in on 'Old Nail'.* [Lindsay Archive]

the Imp-Chevron was legal, and it was banned after one more outing – but hell, the spectators and Gerry enjoyed the battle.

It was back to business as usual at Silverstone clubby early in June, although Colin Hawker's pristine DFV-VW eight-cylinders was serious opposition and snatched pole. Walton drove this VW 411 silhouette saloon and fifth-wheel-measured its tremendous performance for *Motor Sport*. This time the Buncombe-'Chimp' alliance was not a threat, finishing fourth behind Hawker and Strawson's now 7.2-litre variant of an ex-Mick Hill Capri.

American Independence Day at Silverstone brought no Marshall-Firenza July joy. 'Baby B' burped horrendous smoke all day, expiring after nine laps to relinquish a third place.

Another retirement came in August at Brands Hatch, when a sizzling pole position lap of 48 seconds was rewarded with a broken de Dion tube weld after 13 of 20 scheduled laps in the lead. Winner Whiting's fastest lap was 49.2 seconds…

However, the rest of the season saw eight straight wins, the last of them an easy run at 26 December's Boxing Day Brands. A second successive Tricentrol Special Saloons title added to one of Gerry's most successful racing seasons.

1977

The last official DTV season for both 'Bertha' and Gerry started slowly, and the legendary combination only appeared at three race meetings. Just five special saloon races, including wins at Thruxton and Donington, separated Marshall-'Bertha' from the end of their DTV careers.

Tricentrol had moved their sponsorship from Special Saloons to the main BTCC series, which became the prime DTV activity for Gerry in '77. He used his Marshall-Wingfield business to back old mate Tony 'Strawberry' Strawson, now with 8-litres crouching in his Capri, at an early March Brands Hatch Century Oils Special Saloons thrash.

A long August weekend saw 'Bertha' and Gerry in a one-off foray to Denmark, where 'Baby B' went out three times on the small Jyllandsringen track – a fun weekend for the Big Man, but ill-suited to his large Vauxhall. The tiny track hardly allowed 'Bertha' out of second gear, and they racked up just a brace of fourth places plus a fifth during two days' racing.

Their final appearance at Thruxton on 30 October was reported in *Autosport* thus: 'There must have been many people at Thruxton who had travelled there solely to see the final appearance of Gerry Marshall at the wheel of DTV's 'Baby Bertha' – and they were not to be disappointed.' However, even 'Bertha' could be caught whilst she slumbered at Shepreth. Nick Whiting's Escort, a 24v Ford-Cosworth V6 replacing the earlier four-cylinders, took pole position. Nick hounded Marshall and 'Baby B' throughout, leading for half a lap when Gerry missed a shift.

Typically, Gerry did not have long to think about that Thruxton farewell, taking the Magnum out for a tough production race and setting the fastest lap in class, only to be sidelined by a puncture.

Gerry's final verdict on 'Baby Bertha'? 'A super, super car. I didn't often have to wring "Bertha's" neck and drive her to the limit, but when I did it was just a question of working away, persisting, as you would in any racing car.'

DTV sold 'Baby Bertha' to Nottinghamshire-based Paul Haywood Halfpenny for £8,500, complete with all spares and a second V8. She has been owned since the mid-1980s by Joe Ward, who has been generous with public and media appearances by 'Baby B'. Today the Firenza sports a Chevrolet F5000 motor rather than the original Repco-Holden, but she is still a crowd stopper wherever she appears.

GERRY AND THE 'BERTHAS' TIMELINE 1973–7

October 1973
London media debut for the Vauxhall Ventora V8 subsequently nicknamed 'Big Bertha'. Not raced until 1974.

31 March 1974
Marshall debuts Ventora V8 at Silverstone with first of three wins.

4 August 1974
After just six races 'Big Bertha' heavily damaged following Silverstone brake failure. Remains serve focussed Firenza racing coupé 'Baby Bertha'.

Autumn 1974
With fourteen wins and ten podiums in 'Old Nail' Firenza, plus 'Big Bertha' Ventora's three wins, Gerry becomes 1974 Forward Trust Saloon Car Champion.

22–25 May 1975
First test at Snetterton for Firenza V8. Under lap record, so debuted at FordSport (!) Day. Fast, but no fairy tale: third lap retirement.

2 June 1975
First two wins for DTV-'Baby Bertha', at Mondello Park outside Dublin.

19 July 1975
DTV-'Baby Bertha' wins Silverstone GP supporting race at an *average* over 110mph!

Autumn 1975
DTV-Firenza wins 18 of 20 races started. Marshall and Firenza V8 scoop five lap records and 1975 Tricentrol Super Saloon Championship.

30 October 1977
Last official race for Marshall and 'Baby Bertha' V8 comes at Thruxton, with a win. The legendary Firenza V8 only appeared at Thruxton, Donington and Denmark's Jyllandsringen during this year.

BELOW *In September 2003, 'Baby Bertha' visited Brighton for a reunion and standing-start run along Madeira Drive in the annual Speed Trials. Meeting many pure sports racing cars in the over 1,600cc class, Gerry and the legendary circuit racing Vauxhall V8 were 12th in class.*
[Marshall Family Archive]

CHAPTER 8

Closing the DTV decade

The 1976 season was particularly busy and successful for both Gerry and DTV, although their best international result came in 1977. To understand what led to that Belgian 24-hour triumph, we go back to 1976. For the 24-hour classic at Spa, a right-hand drive Magnum had been built at Shepreth, and was borrowed back from regular Belgian pilot Michel de Deyne. It was assigned to Tony Lanfranchi and Gerry to contest the Spa 24-hours.

This was Gerry's second stab at the longer Spa race, having retired within an hour of the start of his first appearance in 1972. He commented in 1976 – with a wry reference to his sturdy drinking companion and co-driver – 'I don't want another early exit – I couldn't stand 23 hours of drinking with Tony!' In the event, the pairing got into the top ten before the clutch expired with less than two hours to go.

September 1976, and another step towards 24-hour glory. An unexpected pairing of two General Motors racing legends – Gerry and Australian Peter Brock – entered in a DTV Group 1 Vauxhall Magnum for Britain's oldest motor race cup, the

LEFT *'When I'm old and slow I'll go rallying,'* was a frequent Marshall quip at motoring forums of the seventies, but when he got a taste for the dirtier side of motorsports there was no stopping the spectacular sideways action. Here that is beautifully demonstrated on Gerry's run to fourth place on the 1976 Texaco Tour of Britain with Motoring News editor Mike Greasley co-driving. [LAT]

RAC Tourist Trophy. Although the TT had started as an extremely tough road race, by the late '70s it was an established Silverstone fixture. It had become a BMW playground in terms of overall results, but still attracted a huge entry. In 1976 the TT was special, as Broadspeed debuted their Jaguar XJ-C V12 coupé.

In the smaller capacity classes lurked Marshall/Brock. But what had brought the Oz multiple championship and Bathurst winner to the UK?

In Wayne Webster's book *Peter Brock: How Good is This! – The Real Story*, the Brock UK trip is attributed to have been a courtesy exchange between leading GM dealer teams of Australia

ABOVE *Nasty! This was the fiery first-time result when Gerry's production racing Firenza lost a rear wheel at Brands Hatch in 1972. Stunning commitment and courage from the voluntary track marshals ensured Mr Marshall was safely extricated. Alan Maynell was the 10-stone hero who pulled Gerry out.*
[Marshall Family Archive]

RIGHT *The second time the Firenza lost a rear wheel (look at the back arch!) the consequences were not quite so devastating.*
[Stephen Jones]

and the UK, with some snide comments about Gerry and the poor old poms not understanding Brock speed. Anyone who followed saloon car racing – and there were many in the UK who did that through two weekly sports papers and BBC TV coverage – knew that Brock was a big deal, and both Gerry and the DTV personnel were no exception. Walton and other reporters received courtesy invitations either via Australia's Channel 7 TV or financed their own trips to attend Bathurst, aware of Brock's race pace and folk-hero status.

However, the 1976 TT was not a great outing for the DTV equipe. Gerry and Peter proved well matched, but the regular BTCC Magnum was unused to distance racing and suffered repeated rear brake seizures, leading to small fires and pit stops. Gerry ended up dicing merrily with old mates like Lanfranchi and Williams, but they struggled to finish.

Gerry shared a production Magnum with Colin Vandervell at the 8 May Spa 600-kilometres. Official reports have Gerry 'jumping the start' and front-running in the opening laps, but unfortunately the engine expired before Vandervell could drive. Unofficially the tale was that Gerry jumped the start *and* collected the starter's flag, which was trapped in the window during the opening lap!

The 1977 edition of the Spa 24-hours was a very different story. Again, Peter Brock proved he could pick up a new circuit and set a hot pace. Like Gerry, he was aggressively talented enough to see potential in the traditional rainy interludes for the 2.3-litre/4-cylinder Vauxhall to embarrass bigger capacity cars and established Spa regulars.

So it proved.

The pairing got off to a routine start, qualifying 25th, and suffered a 13-minute delay with a faulty start motor in the early stages of the race. Then they motored fiercely through the night and rainfall. Both gratefully took advantage of at least three leading bigger-capacity Bimmers and Capris crashing out, and Gerry hunted down Vince Woodman's front-running Capri in the closing stages to finish second overall.

It was an astounding result for the comparatively slow Magnum coupé, and a testimony to the talents of two world-class saloon car drivers. They were never going to win outright – the leading BMW had international rally driver Jean-Claude Andruet to deploy their 3-litres effectively, rain or shine – but it was a sparkling strand to add to the legends of both Brock and Marshall, and it gave the Belgian GM-Vauxhall team a lift: they managed to fill two more top-ten slots with Magnums, scooping the prestigious Coupe du Roi team prize.

Gerry commented a year later: 'The truth is that there is a shortage of people who can drive saloons to an international standard over a 24-hour race. I know we would not have had our finishing place at Spa if it had not been for the fact that other drivers tired faster than we did. Both Peter and I were as quick at the finish as we were at the start.'

Jenny Cook reported in 2009: 'The most frightening moment at this race was when Peter Brock spun the car going up the hill just past the pits!' She also remembered these Spa traditions: 'There was torrential rain and the toilets were flooded. After the race the champagne was also flowing, celebrating a fantastic class win.

'On the return journey on the ferry, everyone

BELOW *Vauxhall always took production-based racing seriously. Here Gerry contests the prestigious Access RAC Tourist Trophy of 1974, finishing 6th in class with the 2.3-litre Magnum.* [LAT]

RIGHT *Cheerful enough for their official pictures, but even the flamboyant cap did not help Gerry and co-driver/broadcaster Mike Broad overcome constant punctures on the 1975 Avon Tour of Britain.* [Foster & Skeffington]

Production racing with Vauxhall

Again we are indebted to Rex Greenslade for these memories of his racing relationship with Gerry: 'For 1974 Gerry had influenced Jeremy Lawrence, who was semi-officially running Vauxhall's race efforts at Luton, to support me with a Magnum 2300 in the Britax and Triplex Production Saloon Car Championships. I was working for the weekly magazine *Motor* and we were pretty good friends – he never forgot our first meeting at Snetterton years before.

'Getting this drive was a big step for me and I leant on him for help and advice, which he freely gave. Among his gems:

'"Don't look in the mirror."

'"Always watch the start of another race to see how the starter drops the flag." (This was pre-lights, remember.)

'"Keep your heated rear window on if it's wet."

'"Keep calm."

'"Don't get it too sideways." (Yes, really!)

'At Snetterton in 1974 Gerry was also out in a Magnum. Before the race, we were bullshitting, as you do, in the paddock, and I was trying my best to do an imitation of Gerry's shtick. "Do you take Riches flat?" someone asked.

'"Sure," I replied, not really sure at all.

'The first lap, down the straight Gerry looked across, caught my eye and totally out-psyched me into the Esses. More, much more, was to come. There was a huge accident involving multiple Magnums and a Capri, cars flying through the air, rollovers, and total chaos. The cause of the accident was the driver who'd asked me about Riches. He'd tried to take it flat, of course, and didn't make it.

'So two lessons I also learned from Gerry – neither told, but both clearly taught.

'One – never let another driver catch your eye down the straight.

'Two – never, *never*, try to be Gerry Marshall, on or off the track.'

was in the bar. I eventually headed off to the cabin with the briefcase containing the race winnings – they paid in cash in those days. About an hour later Gerry went to our cabin to find I wasn't there.

'Panic stations, particularly as I had all the money.

'Everyone was searching the ship, and were just about to turn the ship round when they found me in the wrong cabin fast asleep,' said Jenny.

Since the cash was safe, this must have called for another drink all round.

Sadly, Gerry's return match with Brock – a ride in the October 1977 Bathurst 1,000-kilometres of Australia with the freshly formed Bill Patterson Holden Team, in a Torana LX A9X – did not match his expectations.

Australians may recall that Peter Brock had been dropped from the Marlboro-sponsored big league Holden team in 1977 and ran a three-car team for Bathurst. Peter was desperately understaffed and under-funded to field the Holden trio – especially as what GM fans dub 'The Dark Side', *aka* Ford Motor Company, had enjoyed a GM-crushing season with a 1–2 result for their Allan Moffat Falcons and the Australian title.

Ford-Moffat repeated that domination at 1977 Hardie Ferodo-sponsored Bathurst.

Gerry did not drive with Brock, but shared with South Africa's very capable Basil van Rooyen. They qualified 18th, ahead of a third team entry but behind Brock's pole position effort. Gerry and Basil struggled after a seat mounting failure and V8 motor setbacks. They were not classified finishers,

because they found out early why Bathurst's Conrod Straight was such a graveyard for race motors stretched to the limit!

Jenny Cook recalled in 2009 that 'Gerry always felt that the Australian team did not look after him the way Peter was welcomed in the UK and supported at Spa.'

Gregor added this untold perspective: 'Dad invited Peter to stay at Bricket Wood [his home – JW], and had made sure he was busy and involved the whole time. But when Dad got to Oz, he was left to fend for himself and was bumped from his seat. Dad was due to start the race, and when he tested the radio on the grid it short-circuited all the electrics and he was left

stranded. Even in the week he died, Dad commented on his dislike of Peter Brock.'

In 2009 we can understand Gerry's disappointment, especially as Gerry also did not share a number one racecar, as Peter had in Belgium and Britain.

Battling in 1975–7 Britain

Aside from a quartet of Super Saloon championship titles taken outright and overseas excitement, Gerry fought two full-scale BTCC seasons in 1976–7. He also raced abroad in four major events for General Motors in 1976–7, covering Belgium

ABOVE *Crowded pits for an annual Belgian classic that is not a cycle race. Gerry and Tony Lanfranchi shared this British-built Firenza at the 1976 Spa 24-hours, qualifying 26th in a 60-strong field.* [Jeff Bloxham]

LEFT *Into the hairpin just one more time, Gerry steers the emotive Gulf-liveried Vauxhall coupé he shared with Mr Lanfranchi. They were officially classified 27th after a late-race clutch failure put paid to a top-ten result.* [Jeff Bloxham]

twice and Denmark and Australia once apiece. He also brought the Hamilton Motors Magnum to production racing success with a 1976 class points win in the Radio 1 series.

Outside his regular DTV remit, Gerry tackled two rallies in this period as well as the Tour of Britain 1975–6 editions, racking up a creditable Tour fourth overall for Vauxhall with media man Mike Greasley in 1976. Mike recalled in 2009: 'My only firm recollection is Cadwell the wrong way round. Gerry told me, "Don't worry, lad, I know my

effing way round here like the back of my hand." This despite my protestations that the stage was being run the wrong way round the track… When we were at 90° to the apex of one corner, amidst much arm twirling, the great man announced down the intercom: "It is a bit different isn't it?"

'I also seem to recall a layer of slush/snow, but you will tell me that it was June time, so that must have been my imagination. I do remember a lot of laughs though, and a thoroughly enjoyable time. I also vaguely remember a Gerry and Albert

(Roger Albert Clark, Gerry's 1974 Tour team leader) drinking bout at the finish.

'No wonder the memory is shot,' concluded Mike cheerfully.

This adventure was enacted in a 4 DTV-registered Magnum – a registration plate that Gerry hung on to for almost 30 years. Gregor tells me that 4 DTV 'is now owned by Uncle Martyn'.

Although it went through some bleak periods, strange sponsors, and unique rule changes during the 1970s, the BTCC remained the prime British saloon series. DTV was contracted to create the V8 Ventora and Firenza for Super Saloon series in the first half of the 1970s, but recognised Gerry's efforts in the 1976 BTCC, the first UK season that set an upper 3-litre limit to dispense with Chevrolet Camaro domination.

Gerry started 1976 in a Firenza reborn from dealer-racer Tim Stock's 1975 mount. DTV supplied a similar twin Dellorto carburettor five-speed Magnum after the opening round. Equally rapidly, Gerry found the Vauxhall was competitive against class opposition from Andy Rouse (Broadspeed Dolomite) and Dave Brodie (Mazda RX3 rotary). On the shorter tracks – like Mallory Park – Gerry's fast start pace and natural racing aggression brought class wins even against Rouse's race craft. Marshall's five class wins, with one second overall against the literal clash of heavy metal (Gordon Spice versus Tom Walkinshaw) over the Grand Prix layout at Brands Hatch, were amongst Gerry's finest achievements.

I think this quote from the annual *Motoring News* review indicates the brilliant form Gerry attained in 1976, his 15th motorsport season: 'At first Marshall's 185bhp Magnum hadn't the pace of the works Dolomites, but by the end of the season it was not only arguably more reliable, it was also as quick as the "Dollies" with their alleged 200 plus bhp. Ultimately Gerry beat Andy to the Keith Prowse [BTCC] class title primarily because of a better finishing record, but the fact that he did it against all odds, confirmed Marshall as probably the finest all-round saloon driver in Britain today. For that matter, how many other Group 1 drivers were also regularly seen in special and club production saloon racing?'

In 1977, BTCC things got tougher and Gerry's natural rival, Broadspeed's Triumph Dolomite Sprint, found a new lease of life as a solo entry for Tony Dron, who challenged for the championship outright and was capable of outright victories. Gerry also had a potent Vauxhall Magnum class rival, young Jeff Allam – heir to an Epsom Vauxhall dealership and a fine racer. Gerry's results reflected these changes, with no class

wins – he lost one at Donington while leading the class when a half shaft broke.

Motoring News commented on the continuing shift in DTV sporting policy at the close of 1977 BTCC play: 'This year, the Vauxhall simply wasn't quite a match for the works Dolomite, but Gerry and Jeff squeezed every ounce of energy from their machines in their battle against each other and the flying Dolomite. Gerry Marshall is still the doyen of the British "club" racer, even though he has contested a heap of international events on

Magnum force

Gerry used the same poor old Hamilton Motors-sponsored Magnum 2300 from 1975 to 1977, prepared by John Bott. It contested the production series publicised or backed at various stages by Radio 1, Capital Radio and Britax.

Despite many other commitments in super saloons and Group 1, Gerry racked up at least 45 production races in the Hamilton Motors Magnum in that period, and Gregor crosschecked 21 of the 27 class wins that Gerry had claimed by the end of 1977, when the programme finished.

Gerry also successfully drove other production Magnums entered by SMT, and even that of rival Jeff Allam. Best production title season was again 1976, when he took the high-profile Radio 1 class championship.

ABOVE *The 1976 Tourist Trophy saw two General Motors legends from 12,000 miles apart in the first of their driving partnerships, Peter Brock sharing with Gerry at Silverstone. Unfortunately, mechanical traumas intervened and delayed the dream drivers, as you can see in this busy pit stop as the DTV personnel try to calm overheating rear brakes and a gesticulating Gerry.* [LAT]

ABOVE AND BELOW *Gerry often pressed his road cars into competition action. This neat Firenza droop snoot – shown with Mr Marshall and his helmet and in action – sported just one of the many DTV registration plates GM senior acquired (4 DTV is still in the family). 666 DTV won its class in the February 1977 running of the Chiltern Circle & Harrow Car Club annual sprint, an event that Gerry loyally supported.* [Marshall Family Archive]

a thoroughly professional basis for many seasons now. His driving style is as fiery and inspiring as ever, but Dealer Team Vauxhall have been concentrating their efforts ever more assiduously on rallying in the past 12 months. Partly as a result, Gerry has not achieved quite the same results for General Motors as in the past.'

The DTV-Marshall era was ending, and Gerry could see not just the writing on the wall but on a billboard of messages predicting DTV's rallying future. He did his best to stay in the frame with outstanding performances in the 1976 Tour/BTCC and that 1977 Spa 24-hours performance, but the GM-DTV management were set on rally course and Gerry was not part of their plans beyond 1977.

1974–6 rallying adventures

Prompted by Gerry's outstanding runner-up performance in the 1974 Tour of Britain with a Ford, DTV let Gerry out in rallies, a diversion he always said would only occur 'when I'm old and slow'. Actually, most of these outings took place when he was still an outstanding example of a versatile circuit driver, and there were some encouraging results as well as some monster crashes. The worst of the latter was in Chesterfield and DMC's Gearbox Rally in the spring of 1973, when Gerry had his first motorsport-linked overnight hospital stay with three cracked ribs, the aftermath of his Group 1 Firenza embracing 'a large stone wall' which 'materialised where it didn't ought', according to his *Cars and Car Conversions* magazine column.

His most prestigious pure rally result came in 1974, when he took on the best in contemporary rallying on the Manx International and appeared in a Coburn-prepared Group 1 Magnum as teammate to regular DTV charger Will Sparrow. Gerry's co-driver was world-class navigator John Davenport, subsequently competition manager for Austin Rover. Marshall/Davenport had a difficult time with the lack of brakes on Coburn's production-based Vauxhall – it even split a brake disc in two – but they persisted.

This was Davenport's verdict on their second in class (to Will Sparrow's sister Vauxhall), 19th overall result: 'I thought Marshall was a very professional driver. He didn't get flustered by hearing that Sparrow was going faster, he just pressed on at the right pace for himself. Of course he has superb car control, but there's also a brain in there. He drives exactly on the borderline of his abilities. His performances on the Tour of Britain were another example of his talent. I was most impressed by his conduct in a newish branch of the sport to him.'

Unfortunately, Gerry's opinion of Davenport would not always be so mutually warm, but that's another (1979 season) Dolomite story…

In 1975, DTV had Gerry firmly back in the Vauxhall fold for the Tour of Britain. The undignified Chunky Chicken Magnum 2300 in a particularly repulsive yellow (later raced by Jenny Birrell) saw Marshall and top GM co-driver Mike Broad 'trying to destroy the mule so we could get down the pub!' The main problems were punctures and a persistent misfire, but they still finished second in class – just outside the top 15 – to Barrie Williams's Mazda. Williams was in 'the worst car I've ever seen' according to Gerry.

There was also an unfortunate return to the Manx the same year, when he drove a Vauxhall camera car and 'we rolled it on the second stage. It was one of the best accidents I've ever had, but there was more publicity at the time than DTV got all year,' said Gerry, in the case for the defence.

The 1976 outing in the last Texaco Tour of Britain saw James Hunt/Noel Edmonds entered, to gather even more publicity for Vauxhall. In the event Hunt/Edmonds had what *Autosport* described as 'an undistinguished event', marred by encounters with the police, failing lights and an uncompetitive tyre that Hunt was contracted to use. Gerry was right in the zone, fourth overall with *Motoring News* editor Michael Greasley co-driving. Gerry was the only race driver in the top five that year and scored one fastest stage time. His mount was an official DTV machine, carrying the 4 DTV registration that Gerry kept until his death.

He later recalled of the 1976 Tour: 'If it had not

The Vandervell connection

Colin Vandervell – from the (Tony) Vandervell family that created Britain's first World Championship-winning GP Vanwalls in 1958 – shared a fraction of Gerry's racing life. Colin had been known as a promising young charger when he did Formula 3 in the early 1970s, with a likely future in Formula 1.

By 1976 Vandervell had attracted Ford support in a Triplex-funded Capri. In 2009 he recalled that 'the Vauxhalls and Dolomites were no match for the Capri on fast tracks, but on twisty tracks we had some fantastic battles' (with Gerry's DTV Magnum in BTCC). This would lead to a Capri future for Gerry post-Vauxhall.

Gerry had planned to share a couple of Spa outings with Colin in the DTV Magnum 2300. In fact they went to the 12-hour Spa race in May 1977, both men accompanied by their ladies. Colin remembered Carol Marshall as 'very lovely and kind'.

Their race, however, was *not* kind. Vandervell recalled: 'It began to rain at the beginning of the race and Gerry drove brilliantly to move up to second, but then a piston went after 45 minutes before I could drive the car.' They did not finish and other planned DTV outings for the pairing were canned, which indirectly contributed to Gerry famously sharing only with Peter Brock at the 1977 Spa 24-hours.

Vandervell retired from racing in 1977, but has also been seen out driving on Lombank RAC rallies with co-driver and media mover Andrew Marriott.

been for those gearbox changes [two during the event – JW], I really think we could have won. The Magnums were really well prepared and very quick. A great pity, for the Tour was one of the events I enjoyed doing and I was very sorry to see it end.'

Preparing for that last Tour, Gerry had an

LEFT *One of Gerry's longest private associations was with Hamilton Motors and the production racing Vauxhall Magnums. Here he leads two rival Vauxhalls inside the wallowing BMW 3.0CSi in a typical Silverstone fight to the finish. On this April 1977 outing, he finished second in class, eleventh overall.* [LAT]

BELOW *A finer body of men, now sadly all departed. Tony Lanfranchi, Gerry and Tony Pond line up for a group test of their front-running 1976 Tour of Britain machines. Lanfranchi drove the legendary Mayfair Opel Commodore (centre, back), Tony Pond was out in the Leyland Dolomite Sprint (left) and Gerry was fourth in the Firenza (right) that was registered as 4 DTV – a personal plate Gerry subsequently sported on many road cars, now with Martyn Marshall. John Marshall has another interesting registration – NHW 4. This plate was originally bought for Nancy Wingfield (mother of Gerry's business partner John). The winning Ford RS2000 at the front was that of an absent Ari Vatanen/Peter Bryant. Doubtless this trio gave it a fair thrashing!* [LAT]

excellent outing on the Welsh Red Dragon Rally in May in a 1200 Chevette (!), with outstanding road rally co-driver and later GM administrator John Horton on the maps. With John's guidance Gerry did a fabulous job, finishing third overall and snatching a class win. He was awarded a small silver trophy as second 'Expert' home – so the organisers clearly thought of Gerry as no novice to the rough stuff!

There was plenty of media and spectator comment that Vauxhall-DTV had made a huge mistake in dropping Gerry. The man himself was surprisingly philosophical in 1978, saying, 'I couldn't feel bitter towards Bill, we'd done too much together, though I was upset that the rallying obsession should throw out what had been – and still could be – a very successful racing programme. Rallying is a good sport and nobody enjoys it more than me (in fact I even hoped I might be able to take it up with DTV), but to boot out all that racing experience seemed all wrong to me.'

Gerry and GM/Vauxhall nevertheless remained on civil terms into the 21st century. He continued to race Vauxhall products – particularly the Hamilton Motors Magnum – in the 1980s, and regularly arranged for the drivers he backed, like Jock Robertson, to drive the Luton product. In 2001 he was even reunited with 'Baby Bertha' at Goodwood – but that story, along with an account of Gerry's run in a Triple 888 BTCC Vauxhall Vectra, will be found in later chapters.

Gerry's formidable post-DTV competition record is relatively unknown. He earned equal respect and success with Aston Martins, a James Bondish period in a Lotus (an Esprit Turbo the Marshall family say was direct from the set of *For Your Eyes Only*), blue-blooded classics like the Lister Jags, MGs, and full fat V8 sports-racing hardware from Lola. All were excellent rides for big Gerry.

GERRY AND DTV TIMELINE 1976–7

22 May 1976
Marshall contests Welsh Red Dragon Rally with a 1200 Chevette. Wins class and third overall.

9–11 July 1976
DTV contest Texaco Tour of Britain with three Magnums, including one driven by 1973 Tour winner and '76 World Champion James Hunt/Noel Edmonds, which retired in a blaze of publicity. Marshall came fourth with Mike Greasley navigating, and Will Sparrow/Rodney Spokes came third.

24–25 July 1976
Paired with Tony Lanfranchi in DTV-Vauxhall Magnum for Spa 24-hours. Pairing held eighth overall as clutch failed with one and a half hours remaining.

September 1976

DTV contest RAC's TT Tourist Trophy, Silverstone. Special pairing of Marshall and Australian legend Peter Brock is severely delayed by rear brake fires.

Spring–autumn 1976

Participates in BTCC Championship with two 180–185bhp Magnum coupés. Marshall scores three class wins and wins class championship, finishes third equal overall in premier Tricentrol series, tied with Gordon Spice (Capri). DTV 'Baby Bertha' secures second successive Tricentrol Super saloon title; wins nine out of eleven races plus six lap records.

November–December 1976

Gerry Johnstone appointed head of DTV rallying operations. Serious rally development having been devoted by DTV to 2300 HS Chevette, it sports 240bhp 16-valve via Lotus at its debut in RAC Rally: retires after two stages.

March–October 1977

Gerry back to BTCC with Group 1 Magnum by DTV (1976 car). Year of the Dolomite. No class/outright wins.

22–23 July 1977

Marshall/Peter Brock take best international result for DTV Magnum: second overall plus class win at Spa 24-hours, and prestigious Coupe du Roi team prize for trio of Vauxhalls.

LEFT Always happy to oblige the autograph hunters, Gerry between stages on the 1976 Tour of Britain. In the background is rallying and later social friend Roger Clark's RS2000. [LAT]

27 October 1977

DTV announces no racing programme for 1978, but retain Gerry Marshall in 'a consulting capacity'. DTV's thrust switches to a UK-based rallying programme, with greater success for the HS and HSR evolutions (including Pentti Airikkala's premier British Rally Championship title in a Chevette in 1979), and ever more competitive versions of Chevette (HSR 2300). In 1981 DTV merged into the counterpart UK Opel organisation DOT (Dealer Opel Team). In early 1980s General Motors Dealer Sport become parent entrant for GM.

LEFT Some publicity media sessions are more fun than others, and we don't need much excuse to use a PR picture of Joanna Lumley, one of Britain's favourite actresses, posing on a Chevette with Mr Marshall. Earning an earlier living as a model, Joanna was adept at seventies motoring callouts, the defender of the Gurkhas memorably endorsing FPT race overalls for Gordon Spice. [Marshall Family Archive]

CHAPTER 9

Variety – Marshall style

Between 1967 and 1977 Gerry Marshall's racing life outside DTV was successfully varied. From Minis to Lister Jaguars, and even a Morris Marina, Gerry 'would drive almost anything, almost anywhere,' as Tony Lanfranchi observed in 2000.

Ironically, the brand that did most for Gerry's reputation outside DTV over that ten-season stretch, spent driving Vauxhalls great and small, was General Motors' deadliest commercial rival: Ford. Gerry made just two major campaigns behind Ford's Blue Oval in the 1970s, but both brought immense publicity and top results.

We join Gerry in 1967, as he leaves Barnet Motor Co's TVR and Lotus world and the reassurance of a regular wage for Carol and his growing family. Even as he pitches into involvement with Bill Blydenstein's emerging Vauxhall Viva programme, the Mini still looms large in Marshall circuit assaults – not just Bill's own lightweight 850, but also a full-blooded international Cooper 1293S that brought little in the way of results but allowed for some invaluable initial overseas experience.

The story starts with the 1967 Archie Brown Snetterton 500-kilometres European Touring

LEFT *'I spent my racing time avoiding other people's accidents...for a married man with two children, forget it,' was Gerry's verdict on his abbreviated 1969 Formula Ford season for Lotus dealers VRM. In fact, Marshall racked up some fine results including a second overall here at Snetterton in August.* [Ferret Fotographics]

RAWLSON CR7

As driven by Gerry Marshall. Built April 1970. 997 cc Lucas F3 engine, c/w twin 40 IDFI Webers Mk 5 Hewland 5 speed LSD c/w, spare ratios, 8½in x 10½in rims fitted YB11s. Just been rebuilt for next season. New discs, pads, rose joints, etc. Resprayed yellow/blue but will spray to choice. Will take FVA or FVC. Reason for sale, 2 litre car on the stocks. Offered complete at £1,500 ono or might split. Would take road car in exchange. Many spares still for sale. See last week's advert.

MIKE RAWLINGS,
28 Castle Street, Dover. Tel: Dover 2611 (10 am-5 pm)

RIGHT AND BELOW
Sports cars figured in Gerry's 1970 racing life, including multiple entries and isolated race appearances in the rare Rawlson (Autosport advertisement – right). There was also an unexpected May 1970 outing in this Brabham BT8 (below) at Spa-Francorchamps for the 1000-kilometre sports car championship event. Gerry attended Spa to drive the Viva GT and finished fourth in it having sensationally qualified second fastest. Here in the neat Brabham he qualified 30th, but the BT8-Climax was retired from the race itself.
[LAT/Marshall Archive]

Car Championship event, where he had won the class in 1965. Gerry's wisecrack way of describing his search for a competitive Mini there began, 'I bullshitted this American [Rexford Finnegan – JW] into thinking I was the guarantee of success, just sitting in the car. I practised it some 12 seconds a lap faster than him, which doesn't tell you anything about my driving, but does say a lot about his!' This Mini, a tidy 1275 Cooper S prepared by John 'Rollbar' Aley and subsequently tended by Blydenstein, quickly retired during Gerry's opening

stint when he was running 11th overall: 'The Diva bush went and oil seeped on to the clutch, and that was our race run.'

American USAAF man Finnegan was game for other Mini adventures with Marshall, rolling up to races in a blushing blue Mustang. The pairing took in a number of 1968 European Championship events, including the opening March round at Monza. Gerry remembered: 'The car was good but we suffered this overheating problem. We did a head gasket in the end, but I had a super start

to the race. I was keeping up with Rhodes in the works Mini.' Here Gerry paused for thought, and added with the benefit of ten years' hindsight: 'In retrospect I now realise I was trying and he wasn't! It was a four-hour race after all.'

The biggest race of all – the *Grosser Preis der Tourenwagen* at the Nürburgring – also ended in retirement, but for a different reason, as Finnegan put the Mini off at the beginning of his stint. The Mini was entered under the American Competition Enterprises banner at a final Snetterton '68 fling, but the partnership never did score a finish.

However, that did not mean Minis were a failure for Marshall at home that season. Gregor has identified at least four class wins in the Blydenstein 850, and Gerry scored a tight race victory at Snetterton in June with the 850. *Autosport*'s Simon Taylor reported: 'The fight for 850 honours was, if anything, closer, although Roger Williamson held off Charles Aveling, Gerry Marshall and Paul Hughes until lap 5, when he coasted into the pits with his head gasket blown and his race run. After much door-to-door stuff, both Marshall and Hughes got past Aveling, though 0.6 sec covered the three of them as they crossed the line.' Gerry's class-winning reward was a silver cigarette box, and the useful mention in the UK's established motor racing weekly.

In the smaller capacity classes of the late 1960s his increasing ties to the Blydenstein Viva dominated Gerry's racing life. In fact, the Viva was his ride for all 1968 saloon car events. But in 1967 Gerry was also reported out in an Alan Fraser Imp – the hot ride in the 1-litre category – for a one-off that ended in retirement when well-placed.

However, Gerry did score one anecdotal victory during the 1967 Nürburgring racing weekend, the only time we can trace the Big Man taking on the long-circuit 'Ring. Gerry recalled beating fellow Mini ace Gordon Spice in a running race that weekend. 'I don't think I was ever forgiven for that!' Later an accessory shop and Capri king, Spice took up the tale in 2009: 'I was never a great mate of Gerry's and we normally only met in the bar when we were both pissed. On these occasions we became best buddies and I'd tell him how I admired his exceptional car control (which was true). He'd tell me how he thought I was the quickest man in saloons (also true). At that stage we'd run out of conversation.

'At the Nürburgring, we were drinking at the Wildenswein Hotel at Adenau. Gerry could hardly walk and somehow we got into a challenge match over who could run faster over 50 yards. I thought it would be a doddle – Gerry being overweight, unfit and very pissed. There was a big local audience for the sprint and serious money was bet on the outcome.

'Gerry absolutely thrashed me – he ran like a bull with enormous strides and unbelievable acceleration.

'I learnt later that I was not the first to be "had",'

BELOW *'I shouldn't be driving a Ford, it's against my religion,' was Gerry's 1971 mantra, but he appeared in a Blue Oval mount, this 1970 3-litre Capri, for a July Brands Hatch Production Handicap race. After practising so fast he had to start from scratch, the Ford was sidelined by a race puncture. Look at the Capri's cramped rear accommodation and you'll see a large teddy bear came along for the ride!* [David Turney]

ABOVE *Story of 1971 – Marshall beats Ferrari's 1979 World Champion! Young Jody Scheckter came to Britain from South Africa to shine in Formula Ford and be fast-tracked into the world of Formula 1. The Ford-backed entry in their Escort Mexico series did not run totally to plan. Here, Gerry started from pole position and led Jody's battered Mexico at London's Crystal Palace.* [Marshall Family Archive]

reported Gordon, with the wisdom of financially painful hindsight. 'It was one of his regular party tricks and no one had heard of him losing!'

Tony Lanfranchi also recalled this adult sprinting talent of Gerry's, but revealed that the distance run was critical: 'My 100-yard course really came to only about 55 yards, because Gerry was not as young as he used to be.'

Tony's 1980 book, *Down the Hatch*, summarised this extraordinary talent. 'Gerry, notwithstanding his bulk, is incredibly quick over about 60 yards as a sprinter. This won much money between us, because it would be hard to find anyone who looked less of a sprinter.' These comments came after Gerry had beaten a trained athlete in another pub contest, and fit lady ski-racer Divina Galica, this time on a bicycle!

Amongst many memories, Lanfranchi also recalled a North London pub confrontation. 'A huge man butted up to Gerry and said words to the effect, "Come on you asterisk, let's see how strong you are – you talk a lot…" And, boom-boom, Gerry beat him twice. So they brought another tough guy in from the next pub down the road, and Gerry beat him, twice!'

John Llewellyn added: 'The headstands and cartwheels were another trademark of the Big Man. I used to win plenty of beer in pubs betting locals who disbelieved what he could do. There was one occasion where we were in the pub at Silverstone on the main road [probably The Green Man – JW], and there was a group of army guys in there. We took them on at everything, darts, spoof, and running races up the main road.

'The final challenge was headstands. They didn't believe Gerry could do that! From the car park there were quite a few steps up to the back door to come into the bar. Gerry decided to perform his headstand against this door, just as someone opened the door – Gerry went spilling out into the car park!'

Jenny Cook recalled of his public-house forays: 'Gerry loved talking with people, especially over a pint [his glass always with a handle, reports Gregor] in a bar. His favourite drink was a pint of beer with a splash, or a double gin and tonic [Gordons and Schweppes – JW], ice, no lemon. He found it very difficult to refuse a drink and hence usually had several rounds to catch up on!

'After a race we were usually the last to leave the paddock bar when it shut. We would all go on to the bar, especially the Silverstone club bar. Gerry would go to meet up and have a drink with some of the marshals and locals. Or we would go to a local pub.

'Sometimes, Lanfranchi and Gerry would take on the locals at darts, arm wrestling, spoof, drinking a yard of ale, or the infamous 100-yard sprint. On one occasion we had been to a meeting in Barnet and were in a pub in the town afterwards. Jeremy Lawrence from Vauxhall was there and Gerry was taking on various people at arm wrestling.

'When we left and got into the car, he turned to me and said "For God's sake get me to the hospital, I think I've broken my wrist!" Fortunately a couple of hours later in Casualty we discovered that it was not fractured.'

1969

As 1968 was an all-Vauxhall affair for 30 Marshall races, we now take a look at the 1969 season's departures from the Blydenstein squad.

Unexpectedly, Gerry raced a single-seat Lotus 61L Formula Ford (the L standing for large, not lightweight) with Victor Raysbrook's Lotus dealership. Gerry joked: 'That 61L was the first Lotus ground-effect racer, of course. With me on board it was permanently attracted to the ground.'

Gerry was entered in or demonstrated the Formula Ford eleven times that we trace between May and August 1969, but did not start, or retired, on four occasions. A fourth showed as the best result up to 10 August. Then the Big Man topped that with his best Formula Ford position, a creditable second overall on the familiar Snetterton

ABOVE *August 1971 and Gerry has become a benchmark among the ambitious Mexico-series drivers. Wet conditions at Castle Combe assisted another Marshall victory.* [John Gaisford]

LEFT *Gerry and Jody Scheckter chat at a later seventies winter racing car show. Gerry Johnstone and Bill Blydenstein of DTV are in the background, ensuring that Mr Marshall does not defect to the dark side!* [Marshall Family Archive]

ABOVE *Fruits of victory. Gerry taking cash from a Ford executive while 1971 Escort Mexico owner Larry Sevitt (centre), of Tiran Auto Centre, stands in front of the Championship-winning Ford. Carol Marshall attended a more formal prizegiving when Ford Advanced Vehicle Operations boss Ray Horrocks handed over a new RS1600 registered PPU 240K. Gerry subsequently had the 16-valve swapped for a then-flagship Ford Zodiac that a customer wanted. By 2010 unmolested RS1600s fetched circa £30,000…* [LAT]

circuit on 24 August 1969, at an event organised by Romford & DMC.

Yet the repetitive racing accidents got through to him. 'I really enjoyed driving on Firestone 100s, provided I was a long way away from the other lunatics and assorted hooligans,' he said years later. 'I spent my racing time avoiding other people's accidents – for a married man with two children, forget it.'

In what would become a Mini tradition, Gerry drove Robbie Gordon's 970S at Mallory Park on Boxing Day to close the year with a class win. The Marshall name was also twice attached to Hugh Denton's bigger capacity Mini Cooper 1293S without a result, but he scored a third in class early in the season with an unidentified Group 5 S-type that was entered in the prestigious Guards 500km event at Brands Hatch in April.

So Minis and Marshall were far from finished, even two years after being hired by Bill Blydenstein.

1970

Gerry's 58 competition appearances in 1970 were dominated by the Blydenstein Viva programme, but he also drove some fascinating machinery outside the Vauxhall fold. Most obscure award goes to the Rawlson CR7 sports racer, but a Brabham BT8 outing would not spring naturally to mind in association with Marshall arts either. Robbie Gordon's Healey 3000 and a return to Mini magic also featured in that busy season.

Built by Mike Rawlings, then based in Dover, the pretty glass fibre-bodied Rawlson sports racer then sported a 997cc Formula motor (Ford Anglia block), a pair of Weber downdraught carburettors and a Hewland five-speed. There was also a limited slip differential, and 8.5in/10.5in rims carried slick Firestones, so there was a surplus of grip over low-speed horsepower. Gerry was entered in the yellow machine at least five times that season, but the only concrete result Gregor could find outside a string of non-starts was a second in qualifying for the 15 August weekend of *Motoring News* and Special GT racing over Silverstone's full-length GP layout. Rawlings's abiding memory of the outing is Gerry overtaking a GT40 on the outside of Woodcote – in the wet!

Ian Titchmarsh reported for *Autosport*: 'An interesting combination was that of Gerry Marshall in Mike Rawlings's neat Rawlson but, after a good practice time, the car needed a push start and then lost all its oil pressure.' The Rawlson was later advertised for sale at £1,500 'as driven by Gerry Marshall'.

The Brabham BT8 was a bigger deal and appeared at the Belgian World Sports Car Championship round at Spa. Gerry and BT8 qualified 30th but failed to finish the 30 May 1,000km event. This was the Belgian trip that saw Gerry accrue export publicity for GM with a brace of Viva GT appearances at Zolder (13th) and a fine fourth at Spa.

At the August Silverstone meeting where he practised the Rawlson, Gerry also drove a Mini again. In this one-off with a car from Ian Blaunt, Marshall qualified it second in class and finished third in the category.

The Marshall Mini reunion of the season came at the end of the year. Boxing Day at Mallory Park in Leicestershire saw one of Gerry's proudest and subsequently saddest racing memories, when he beat local ace and subsequent Tom Wheatcroft protégé Roger Williamson, who made it all the way to Formula 1. Roger died tragically in 1973 at the Zandvoort GP, Holland – a scandalous and obscene death for a major British talent so significant that he was in line to replace Jackie Stewart at Tyrrell after the Scot's winter '73 retirement, all fully documented in David Tremayne's masterpiece *The Lost Generation*, published by Haynes in 2006. As it happens I was later privileged to drive the Formula 3-engined Anglia that Roger used in that Boxing Day epic against Gerry, and can confirm that this 123bhp flyweight was a worthy match for Roger's absolute commitment.

In 1978, Gerry recalled of that epic win: 'I also put in a rare performance that day because

I actually managed to beat Roger on his home circuit. I think that may have been the only time he and his Anglia were beaten fair and square.' Williamson had managed to beat a lot of properly-driven bigger capacity opposition in that Anglia, so the victory was an especially significant entry on the Marshall CV.

In 2009 the owner of the Mini that Marshall drove, Robbie Gordon, recalled that 'it was the ex-Rob Mason Group 2 Mini with some excellent Don Moore parts, which were the best bits normally reserved for the BMC-Cooper Car Company factory entries. We had a good relationship with Moore up in Cambridge and he sold us the parts BMC had forgotten at wonderful prices!'

Another Robbie Gordon racer also appeared in Gerry's hands – DRX 258C, an ex-Abingdon works Healey that had been club-raced by Lionel Mayman. Robbie recalled: 'Peter Jackson normally drove my cars by this stage. We'd had a Lotus Cortina that raced against Gerry in the Viva era and an Elan 26R. The Elan often raced against Gerry in the Barnet Elan and was in similar silver-grey colours, so they could be confused in a black and white picture. Anyway, Gerry really wanted to have a go in this car, not just because it looked like his sort of hairy-chested natural choice, but also because he wanted to beat a certain Mr Gott. Now John Gott was chief constable in Northamptonshire and king of the racing Healey 3000s, especially at Silverstone. Gerry took him on up there and made my Healey go faster than ever before. We got within 0.5 of a second of Gott's lap times.'

Unfortunately that was not quite enough, and Gerry only took third quickest in practice and second in the Healey-dominated category of this late-August Bank Holiday meeting. Gerry persuaded Robbie to field the Healey again in early October around the shorter Silverstone National track. The result was a runner-up spot again. A sad footnote is that John Gott GM, MBE, was killed at Brands Hatch in 1972 when a wheel collapsed on his very special Healey 3000. The authors will remember Mr Gott with respect for his medal-winning gallantry and motorsport exploits, from Brooklands to BMC Team Captain.

1971: Marshall-the-Mexico beats '79 World Champ

Gerry Marshall was exceptionally busy in 1971, receiving 30 guineas (£30 30s of old money) for his July-contracted column in *Cars and Car Conversions* monthly magazine. This would prove by far the funniest of Gerry's three major motoring columns in the 1970s, but he certainly had plenty

to talk about right from the start, tackling 66 races in 1971. His season that year was neatly split between Ford and Vauxhall, but his main contract did see 13 Vauxhall wins racked up, including borrowing John Pope's 2.6-litre version of the S&K Viva.

Gerry dealt himself into a Ford Escort Mexico series to contest against apprentice 1979 World Champion Jody Scheckter and some familiar faces, such as Barrie Williams and *Motor* magazine's Roger Bell.

The first Rufforth race on that bleak Yorkshire ex-airfield went to Williams from Bell, Gerry on the sidelines supporting his friend Larry Sevitt. Marshall saw that this well-promoted and rewarded series was going to be a major attraction. Split-second racing featured from a variety of Tin Top heroes, including rally ace (and subsequent DTV driver) Chris Sclater and one of the Mexico's key creators, Ford Advanced Vehicle Operations engineer Rod Mansfield.

Despite frequently protesting 'I shouldn't be driving a Ford, it's against my religion,' Gerry swiftly became a major challenger for the first Mexico title hunt in his flamboyant Tiran Auto Centre example in Esso gold. Tiran and the Mexico belonged to Larry Sevitt, who had raced the Ford in the first (Rufforth) round without success. So Gerry took over the small Ford from the second (Snetterton) round onwards and, as he reported, 'won after a big dice with Squeaker [Williams] and Rod Mansfield'.

ABOVE *Gerry in happy mode with the prospect of two Hexagon pedigree classics to play with. In the foreground is the Lister Jaguar, with the Maserati Birdcage in the background. Gerry scored an historic victory with the ex-Bruce Halford Lister, winning the last full-circuit motor race at Crystal Palace… just!* [Marshall Family Archive]

Ivan the Paralyser

Renowned Bugatti restoration and sales specialist Ivan Dutton was often called the 'The Paralyser' by Gerry. Gregor asked him, 'Why the nickname?'

Ivan answered with inimitable confidence. 'I was asked by a sponsor if I was going to win. I told him, "Win? I'm not going to win, I'm going to paralyse them!"'

Ivan recalled: 'The first time Gerry and I met was in 1972 at Brands Hatch, when I was racing my Escort Sport in only about my eighth ever race [Gerry wrote about it in his diary on 3 September 1972 – JW]. My two main rivals that year were John Lyon and Jeremy Walton in matching cars. John couldn't make this round so Gerry was lined up to drive. I didn't know who he was, I didn't really know who anyone was back then.

'Anyway, everyone kept winding me up before practice, saying that Gerry was going to blow me away. When it came to practice I really went for it, tried my hardest and I was one second a lap quicker – it was only my second or third time at Brands!

'Gerry came to find me after practice and said how well I'd driven, but pointed out the disadvantage he had with his weight, new car etc. Gerry said "Right, lad," ("Lad? Blimey, I'm older than you," I thought) "for the race, why don't we just have a gentle start, make a race of it and make a name for yourself?"

'Everyone said Gerry was sand-bagging in practice, that's what he did to all the new boys, and he was still going to blow me away in the race. I thought, "Bugger this," so at the start I shot off into the lead and drove my absolute hardest and managed to win by six seconds. After the race Gerry came off and said, "Bloody hell, Ivan, you shot off like a startled rabbit, I struggled to keep up with you!"

'We had a drink in the bar afterwards and became friends from then on.

'Career and business-wise, Gerry helped me out many times over the years.

'One of my biggest achievements was winning the Peter Collins Memorial Trophy in 1973 as the best newcomer. It had never been given to a saloon car driver before and Gerry was on the awarding committee. No one wanted to give it to me but Gerry fought my case and said, "This bloke has come out of nowhere, won 18 races, what more do you want? If you don't award it to him I'll resign!"

'Luckily Gerry did have a lot of sway and they awarded it to me…'

Ivan also told the next tale, which we haven't seen published previously: 'At the end of the 1973 season I was really struggling financially. I had a huge overdraft and lots of debt and decided to sell my Escort racer. We had a bit of a get-together, end of season do, I can't remember everyone there but there was certainly Gerry, Tony and Alan Foster [former MG ace and proprietor of London Sports Car Centre on the Edgware Road – JW].

'We were at the Chequered Flag, drinking the place dry. Then we went on to another club in London, and there was music and girls. Alan Foster played the piano and everyone was having fun, except me.

'I was really down about selling my racer and Gerry said to me, "C'mon, Ivan, what's up with you?"

'I told him about the my overdraft and worrying about paying the bills. And that I was going to sell the Escort.

'Gerry said, "How much do you want for it?"

'I told him a thousand pounds and he said, "Right," whipped out his cheque book and wrote a £1,000 cheque there and then. "Now cheer up you miserable sod!" was all he said.

'I couldn't believe it – it cleared my overdraft and a bit extra. It was so useful and he really helped me out.

'Saying that, I don't know how he ever did business. Whenever I'd ring him at Marshall Wingfield he was never there, he was always off at a circuit testing or racing, but he always had an eye for a deal no matter where he was.

'I'm sure if he had concentrated on the business more he would have made a fortune,' concluded Ivan.

Incidentally, Gregor checked Gerry's sales ledgers and 'on the 13th November 1973 Dad did buy an Escort Sport from Ivan (RMF 22L) for £1,000, and sold it on for £1,100.'

Gerry tried getting some sponsorship from Castrol – now firmly in bed with Vauxhall – but they turned him down in favour of Scheckter, Ford's Chosen One. Gerry then turned on his most persuasive charm offensive and secured Esso Uniflo, then backing Ford's factory rallying programme in Britain with Roger Clark's 'Old Gold' Escort.

The Tiran Escort – with its blueprinted motor, outstanding Keith Tillbrook preparation and the one-make slick racing tyres installed – was a neat drive. Walton drove it at Brands Hatch post-season and found it obedient and a potential winner against the absolute best. Marshall's Mexico was the equal of Andy Rouse's obviously talented counterpart car built at Broadspeed. Gerry said in later years that he wished he had the talent for sorting out a car transferred from his closing seasons to life as a young charger. Walton can only say that in 1971 – when Gerry had only just turned 30 – the Tiran Mexico proved GM's sorting talents in association with Tillbrook, also famed for his preparation prowess on the Bevan Triple BTCC championship-winning Imps. Another factor was Marshall driving neatly and intelligently whilst 'wild man' Scheckter provided more lurid action sequences.

Gerry won a quartet of the ten Mexico races he contested in the 12-round series, albeit the August Silverstone round was cancelled. Marshall backed those four wins with single second and third places, plus a couple of fourths, an isolated sixth and one retirement. Most personal satisfaction came from the Oulton Park round, where 'I out-braked Jody at Esso and won'. Gerry changed the first-prize Escort RS1600 into a Ford Executive Zodiac barge, which proved financially more rewarding!

There was controversy, but when was there not with one-make racing saloons?

After a last-round victory at Brands Hatch Club, the Tiran car was transported straight back to its base when required in the Brands Hatch scrutineering bay. It was inspected just prior to JW's track test for *Motoring News* and was found legal. Marshall was declared Castrol Escort Mexico Challenge 1971 Champion from J. Scheckter (the 1979 World Champion for Ferrari) and Williams.

Just as some Tin Top men never return results outside their roofed world, Scheckter struggled to win Championship Mexico races.

1972

The 1972 season was just one Marshall event down on 1971, with 65 races completed but in a wider variety of non-Vauxhalls. These included a classic Maserati Birdcage sports racing classic, fleeting

BELOW *Two tummies and a wristwatch. Gerry, along with employee and friend Brian 'Slim' Atthews (centre) are merry, while Ivan 'The Paralyser' Dutton reads through the timesheets and sports his first wristwatch after consultation with Gerry on the merits of having a timepiece to calm startline nerves. Renowned as a Bugatti specialist, Ivan was behind the construction of the brilliant Alvis Grey Lady racer that thrilled 2004 Goodwood Revival crowds in Gerry's hands.* [Motor/LAT]

reappearances in Ford Escort and Mini, plus a much-valued outing in a Lister Jaguar.

Through his GM contacts, Gerry's first experience of the Spa 24-hour Belgian classic came in 1972 with a 2.8-litre Opel six-cylinder, where he renewed his acquaintance with preparation specialist Vic Hylens. Here's how Marshall recalled that outing for *Autosport* readers seven years later: 'I did (briefly) drive a Commodore at Spa in '72 that made a wonderful noise. It dropped its propshaft in the middle of the Masta Kink at enormous speed. This resulted in the car coming

Post-GP rescue

Motoring writer and classic auction expert Ray Potter wrote to us in 2009 with the following illustration of Gerry's extraordinary helpfulness.

'Imagine the situation. British Grand Prix, one of the last to be held at Brands Hatch in the late '70s. Because of the inevitable traffic jam on the A20, long after the racing had finished, my wife Viv and I visited the Kentagon Suite, a well-known Brands watering hole for so-called VIPs, officials and competitors.

'Our Kentagon company included Gerry, "Squeaker" Williams and the like, from the support races. Around midnight, the car parks were emptied and we were all about to leave. To my horror, the headlights of my new Datsun 260Z lit up for just a brief moment before dwindling to a glow equivalent to a toaster element. The Z had been peppered following an overloaded ballast lorry, and close examination revealed both sealed-unit headlights were cracked.

'As Hertfordshire residents, Gerry suggested to Viv – who had elected to drive after the inevitable imbibing – that she followed his car very closely on the streetlit route to his house. We would then swap cars, and be able to complete our journey into darkest rural Hertfordshire with no streetlights. A generous offer.

'We left in tight convoy until, a couple of hundred yards outside the circuit, traffic ground to a halt. The Datsun stopped right by a cop, controlling the impatient home-going crowd even at midnight. The policeman indicated he wanted a word and politely said, "Dipped headlights on, Sir – safer for everybody."

'"Of course," I replied from my slumped passenger position. I leant across to the headlight stalk, pretending to turn them on. He repeated his request, but this time put his head through our open window to watch this useless exercise. Gerry, watching in his mirrors, grasped the situation: he allowed the queue to move off. Then he accelerated, us following in hot pursuit, leaving the astonished foot cop looking puzzled.

'The remaining journey was hazard-free. At Gerry's house, we took his BMW road smoker, arranging that Gerry took the Datsun to work to have new headlights fixed by his "friendly" electrician, just in time for a lunchtime pint.

'A call to Gerry in the morning confirmed that the job was all done, and the Datsun back at his Temple Fortune showroom. With his Bimmer returned, and the bill settled – at basic cost I should add – Gerry suggested a suitable hostelry for lunch. Not having driven the latest 260Z, he wanted to take it for a spin.

'In just a few yards, there was the most terrible shaking and rumble from the front end.

'We both leapt out to find that the nuts which held on both front wheels, recently removed to fit the new headlamps, hung by a thread, not even finger-tight.

'"I'll have his guts for garters," Gerry exploded amongst other Anglo-Saxon oaths. Gerry rushed back to his office to phone the electrician.

'"Where's the Datsun?" Gerry demanded.

'"I left it outside your office," was the reply.

'"It's not now," says Gerry, "my friend has just gone through a local supermarket window, pinning a little old lady underneath – with the wheels hanging off," he added.

'"I'll come straight down," the erring sparks man offered. "Which shop is it?"

'Gerry nominated a shop, right next door to a pub in Golders Green Road. We arrived to see the flustered man examining the unbroken shop window, trying to find the Datsun.

'Gerry smartly led him straight into the pub, demanding that the drinks were on him! Those were just for us two, as Mr Sparks was dispatched, armed with the necessary jack and wheel brace, to tend to our Datsun.

'The incident illustrated Gerry's aptitude to resolve problems with great alacrity, combined with a wicked sense of humour,' concluded Ray. 'I will remember it for his instant and generous offer to help out a friend, just when roadside rescue services would not be best pleased to struggle to post-GP Brands after midnight.'

BELOW *Classic car collector and auction expert Ray Potter had cause to be grateful for Gerry's patient assistance after a Grand Prix meeting at Brands Hatch.* [Potter Pix]

RIGHT *Mighty man and machine combination. Gerry drifting one of the Mathwall prepared BMW Concessionaires team 3-litre BMWs at Brands, an equipe managed by a certain Mr Lanfranchi that 1973 season. Sadly, this March outing was a one-off, Gerry taking third overall. Gerry scored a sixth place with a BMW 2002 later in the season after qualifying quickest.* [Motor/LAT]

BELOW *Gerry is not in the Vauxhall! Rarity value here as Mr Marshall conducts the Chrysler UK factory-built Hunter at Thruxton in pursuit of an ex-works Capri in October 1974: long time friend Derrick Brunt gives Vauxhall chase.* [Motor/LAT]

to a sudden halt from what seemed like a million miles an hour. I think I had to throw those overalls away!'

The Maserati Tipo 61 (*aka* 'Birdcage', after its spindly tube chassis) deal came through Paul Michaels at North London BMW dealers Hexagon. Michaels was a great racing supporter who lent considerable backing to John Watson up to Grand Prix level. Gerry drove Hexagon's Maserati at a Silverstone round of the JCB championship (6

August), but avoiding spinning Hexagon teammate Nick Faure in a downpour saw a retirement posted. Gerry then took on Hexagon's WTM 446, an ex-Bruce Halford Lister Jaguar, at the last Crystal Palace meeting of 23 September. The opposition was intense, with JCB title prospect Willie Green (Maserati Tipo 61) and seven Listers on the grid, Marshall's Hexagon teammate Faure opting for their Maserati.

Faure led for five laps before he reportedly

'fluffed a gearchange in the Glades, had a moment and Marshall was through into the lead'. Green finished second to take the '72 JCB title and the fairy-tale ending was that Gerry won by just over a second. He commented: 'We had a super race – it really was a tight one, but I just managed to hang on and win the very last race on the circuit.'

1973

Not quite such a busy season as the previous two, but still 58 entries made for G.D.R. Marshall and 22 victories recorded in a season extending over the full 12 months from January to December, with wins – including class victories – recorded from start to finish. Outside the contracted Vauxhall world, Gerry drove some unusual – some would say unique – machinery in '73. For example, there was a Hot Rod Escort, a Clan Crusader, a Morris Marina, a Ford Consul GT and a luxurious BMW 3-litre flagship. He did quite a lot of test miles and managed a third overall in the BMW 3.0Si for Tony Lanfranchi, who had almost accidentally become team manager of the BMW Concessionaires production racing team that season. Gerry did not race another BMW (again a 3-litre saloon) until 1976.

Much more regular was the reconnection with Lotus agent Victor Raysbrook (VRM), who had provided Gerry's earlier Lotus Formula Ford season and a very smartly turned out Elan for '73.

Unfortunately this promising partnership rarely finished. A typical outing at Silverstone in March saw Gerry quickest in practice, only to lose his race lead when the throttle linkage came unclipped. Gerry told *Cars & Conversions* readers in July 1973 that the VRM Elan-Marshall record now stood at four starts, four pole positions and an equal number of retirements. Gerry commented: 'The tragedy of it is that it's probably the smartest and best-prepared Elan extant and most of the problems have been minor ones,' this after another race-leading performance ended with a gearbox failure at Cadwell Park. They did record a class second placing during the year, but even then the jinxed VRM Elan suffered a puncture.

The Morris Marina is easily explained, as it was a social and trading friend – Alan Foster of London Sports Car Centre – who loaned that hapless '70s coupé from the house of doomed British Leyland. Alan was well respected as an MG ace in his driving days for Dick Jacobs, and lent the Marina to Gerry as much for laughs as with any serious intent to steal points from class rivals. Gerry did give it a skid at a wet Silverstone – we have the pictures to prove it – but the duo non-started at a second Cadwell entry in the Britax series.

The Clan Crusader – the Hillman Imp-powered baby GT that worked as a road car – was subject to the Marshall tricycling technique at the 750 Motor Club's September 6-Hour Relay at Silverstone. Gerry was part of a three-car team and was an

LEFT *In the enemy's den! Taken at the Boreham airfield Ford Motorsport base, before the 1974 Avon Tour. It brought Gerry a lasting friendship and a startling result, here talking team testing with Roger Clark (left) and Ford team manager/co-driver Tony Mason.* [LAT]

agent for Clan at the time. In this outing he found the seat too small for sustained three-wheeling interludes on opposite lock, and handed the Clan over to a teammate whose more modified example had destroyed its motor: Team Clan finished 21st at best, 25th in one class. 'Never before have I driven so hard, for so long, to finish last,' was Gerry's contemporary comment.

The Consul GT belonged to an ill-starred Ford-financed celebrity series that injured some notable drivers – Richard Longman and Tony Pond in one race – and was a one-season FordSport Day wonder. Gerry qualified one of the big Fords on pole at Brands Hatch, but left it to Barrie Williams to win with in the afternoon, as the sore ribs that were the legacy of a rally accident persuaded the Big Man that this was a painful event too far. Gerry

was entered at the Castle Combe destruction Derby that shook even second-place man Roger Clark and winner Andy Rouse, but we can find no trace of a result, or a mention, for Gerry that day.

Later in the season, Gerry also recorded a one-off class second in a factory-backed Hillman Hunter at Thruxton, this in a tactical effort to boost points for regular driver Bernard Unett, a dour but exceptionally talented driver more usually derided by Gerry in print for not buying his round at the bar!

A one-off in the Hot Rod Escort started badly with Gerry having to squeeze his 'sylph-like frame' in through the side-window aperture, as the doors are welded shut in this category. Electrical troubles curtailed his first and final outings in the Rod, but he did manage one heat victory, and his ace starting

LEFT *Well it's a rally isn't it? Got to get sideways now and again. In fact, Gerry was generally a lot neater than the opposition on the 1974 Tour and this Cadwell picture simply reflects the fastest way through this section of the challenging 'mini-Nürburgring.* [LAT]

technique took the regulars longer to overcome than anyone expected.

Gerry also scored a Shellsport Celebrity win in the popular Ford Escort at a December Brands Hatch outing to close a season that confirmed his enthusiasm was undimmed after a decade of racing.

1974

Gerry's entry-to-win rate this season saw 57 events on the slate and 20 class and outright wins recorded. However, it was a second place on the second Avon Tour of Britain in a Ford Escort RS2000 that brought a new friendship and attracted most publicity. It also prompted DTV and Marshall to take Gerry's rallying ambitions seriously, as

the only man to beat Gerry in '74 was the UK's contemporary undisputed master of the rally stages, Roger Clark. Roger was Ford's fastest home-bred driver and the UK's only winner of the World Championship RAC Rally since 1959 (he won it again in '76). The silver-haired charger was also capable of winning pace around a track too, though he always told people that he found racing 'dead boring'.

Like Gerry, Roger was no stranger to a bar, nor shy in the presence of plentiful pints. A born sports competitor, he grew to enjoy Gerry's company and the two often got up to high jinks once they had sorted the important business of who was buying the drinks…

Sadly, Roger died before Gerry, in January 1998, but he was one of the very few to beat Gerry and

BELOW *Gerry did many sales and a few racing deals with Pete Hall, better known through his ICS company and backing Andy Rouse. Here's Gerry on a one-off outing at Thruxton in 1976, where he took the second-generation Capri to outright victory and a new lap record.* [Jeff Bloxham]

found a strong friendship that extended to other shared competition cars.

That Tour of Britain 1–2 Clark-Marshall result, with Clark just 16 seconds ahead after three days and a night, has been widely described. A full account can be found in both editions of *Only Here For The Beer*, so here I recap only the less obvious aspects. The 138hp Escorts Marshall and Clark used – accompanied by brave co-drivers Paul White and Jim Porter on all but the circuits – were not the most powerful cars in the event. They could be beaten on the track, but their agility and pace ensured that only Gerry's old mate Lanfranchi, in a classy coupé from BMW, stood any chance of interrupting their progress to a winning result.

Here's an extract of what shrewd Tony L. felt about that Tour result in 1980: 'We had a ball. I won every race we did – the car ran like a dream. But it and I were no match for the little Ford Escorts on special stages. Roger was superb, as you'd expect, and Gerry learnt very quickly. On the third day of the event I had a 27-second lead. But Eppynt and three or four other special stages were coming up.

On one they took 36 seconds off me, and that was that.'

Gerry commented in a *Motor* column of 1974: 'Roger and I seemed well matched at Mallory and that's how things continued for the rest of the event, since it all seemed to keep the crowd on their toes, and we weren't actually intending to drive into each other. Honestly!' Certainly, neither RS2000 showed any contact damage. The other constant post-event public query was whether Gerry had been told to let Roger win?

Neither the Ford contract letter to Marshall of 5 June 1974, nor Walton's attendance at the event (for Ford Motorsport), revealed any master plan. Financially, so far as can be told, Gerry's only cash benefit in the totally factory-financed entry was £15 per day expenses allowance. The idea was that an outside sponsor would pay Gerry's unnamed driving fee, but the only backers were the usual trader suppliers, including Dunlop tyres.

Over 35 years later, Roger Bell vividly recalled that Tour display: 'Then there's that 1974 Tour of Britain epic in which Gerry and Roger Clark gave a three-day masterclass in car control. I remember

BELOW *This was a famous and relevant media shot – Gerry and James Hunt (1976 World Champion) making up after a minor fracas at the BRDC Ball*
[Chris Harvey]

admiring them at Mallory Park, where the two cars seemed to dance together, so close was the action.'

More praise came Gerry's way from an independent source when he was present at a Snetterton testing tragedy. I quote from Peter Evans – Secretary to the Clubman's Register – in a letter to *Autosport*, published 6 June 1974: 'May I, through your columns, take the opportunity to express sincere thanks to Gerry Marshall for the part he played in organising the rescue attempts on the sad occasion of the recent fatal accident to Gavin Scott whilst testing at Snetterton. Gerry took complete charge of the rescue operation and, in the words of those present, was a real tower of strength.'

There was more in a similar vein, but personal experience tells us that Gerry often did get involved in such trackside accident aftermaths, right from the time of his father's inversion of the family MG Magnette back in the '50s. Walton remembers that it was Gerry who raised his hand from his production racing Vauxhall's window at Brands Hatch in 1972 to warn the following pack

that his inverted Ford lay ahead, its apprehensive occupant trapped within.

Other 1974 Marshall outings included the stark contrasts of a 5.6-litre Chevrolet Camaro at the Mallory Park Castrol Anniversary opening round of the BTCC, and a class-winning production Hillman Avenger. The ex-Martin Thomas 1973 season Camaro qualified third quickest in the wet, but failed to complete the race, for its oil pressure plunged soon after another of Gerry's demon starts had netted second overall in his debut Camaro drive.

Ironically the Avenger subsequently got written off by an errant Camaro after Gerry had scored a class win with it, which, he said 'cost him my no claims bonus'. So that was probably on some kind of road-car insurance deal.

1975

There were few non-Vauxhall outings this ultra busy 75-event season, when 'Baby Bertha' was in her prime. A solo Ford appearance resulted in a

BELOW *Gerry always loved Jaguars. Here he is on the way to a win in March 1977 at Silverstone with a Coventry-registered 2.4-litre Mk2 saloon.* [John Gaisford]

pole position and overall victory for the Marshall-conducted classic 2.5-litre Zephyr, entered by fellow motor trader Bill Wykeham.

There were also two successful weekends in Bob Saunders' Triumph Dolomite Sprint. They returned a class win and a second overall in production trim. Those Triumph experiences led to a much heavier involvement for Gerry and Triumph in post-1977 production and BTCC categories.

A Capri win and an Opel sacking

Ex-racer Pete Hall recalled the following regarding the Marshall-Lanfranchi incident at Thruxton: 'I've always been really unlucky at Thruxton. Every time I've been there something has always gone wrong with the car, and I just don't like the place. But Gerry loved it. He was always super-quick around there, and there was one event in August 1976 [on the 8th], where I was entered in the Capri.

'Gerry was there but only spectating – I think he had a few cars entered in other races. Anyway, he had itchy feet, wandering around the paddock. Gerry said he was surprised to see me at Thruxton, knowing my dislike for it. He suggested I let him drive and he'd win in my Capri!

'I thought. "He's right, I don't like this place and it would be an honour to have him drive." I said that if he could sort it out then he could drive. At the time Thruxton was like a military camp, run by Sidney "BARC" Offord, who no one seemed to get on with. Sidney didn't seem to get on with anyone either – other than Gerry: they had a good relationship.

'They let Gerry take my place and he qualified second, a second or two behind Tony [Lanfranchi] in the Opel Commodore. Tony was the class of the field that year. The Commodore was superbly prepared by Gerry's team, as it was his car. Gerry employed Tony to race it under the Marshall Wingfield banner.

'Come the race and Tony shot off into the lead, with Gerry second, and Tony had about a seven- or eight-second lead until he started lapping people. Even so, he had a good cushion and on the last lap he was about two seconds ahead of Gerry.

'Gerry could sniff a win and was flinging the Capri about. Going through Church on the last lap Tony must have had a good second or two lead, but Gerry wasn't giving up and threw the Capri through Church and on the run down to the chicane was catching Tony. The Capri didn't like corners, but was quick in a straight line. They closed on some backmarkers and Gerry jinked one way, which forced Tony in behind the backmarkers, who were trying to avoid the leaders. Tony had to lift and, with the loss of momentum, Tony and Gerry arrived at the Chicane nose to tail, Gerry just in front. On the run to the line Gerry just managed to cross first, literally by the length of the front wing.

'On the presentation rostrum Tony was being interviewed and said it was the most unsporting bit of driving he'd ever seen and Gerry should be penalised. I think Tony was annoyed at himself for having had a commanding position, only to be caught out by Gerry.

'When the microphone came to Gerry he said he thought Tony was a better and more sporting person than that. Tony had the championship wrapped up, so it didn't affect that. Anyway, the Commodore was his, and Tony was his employee. He was therefore sacked!'

1976

Gerry attacked 60 events and won a personal season's best of 34 class or outright victories. These results included hard-fought events in production-based Vauxhalls as well as the more predictable V8 special saloons from DTV. Which is ironic, because DTV was the backbone of such a record, and yet they were steering towards a rallying future without Gerald Royston at the helm…

Star turns beyond a busy DTV-Vauxhall schedule saw Gerry steering an ex-factory Sunbeam Tiger Le Mans, securing one class win amongst the classic race events at Silverstone in July, a silver cake slicer his tangible reward!

The following Brands Hatch GP weekend, Gerry was voted into a Celebrity Ford Escort, but posted a race retirement with a sick engine, as did best mate Lanfranchi. However, another Ford delivered a single Thruxton win via the ICS production racing Capri, a result that would influence Gerry's post-DTV racing life.

He also did the deal that put Tony Lanfranchi in the Mayfair Opel for the '76 season and they were best pals again. But then came a rather public falling-out at Thruxton. Tony Lanfranchi takes up the story: 'I was leading the race with Gerry and Derrick Brunt and a few others all around as we came up to the last lap. And at the chicane was a whole heap of cars upside down, and yellow flags were being waved everywhere.

'I thought, "Great, I can't lose this. There's a yellow flag here and a yellow flag there, and there isn't a green all-clear flag until after the chequered flag, which denotes the winner. So just cruise in." As I cruised in, Mr Marshall cruised past me to win the race… Of course, I was a bit annoyed, not to say incensed. But Gerry never will agree that he passed under the yellow flag. Anyway, the thing that really niggled me was that they made him Man of the Day or something equally bizarre. So we had a great shouting match. What got Gerry, in turn, really annoyed was that when I got out of the car, all dithering with emotion, I was opening my big mouth, shouting over the public address loudspeakers. "I didn't think you could overtake under the yellow flag!" Gerry was upset; enraged, in fact, although no blows were exchanged on that occasion, which was just as well, for Gerry doesn't half throw a good right-hander!

'That soured our relationship for a time – we don't stay mad at each other for too long. But when 1977 came I was no longer driving for Mayfair and Gerry Marshall.' Protégé Jock Robertson, who Gerry had known since DTV days, got the Commodore drive instead and did an excellent job.

LEFT *Gerry's disappointing outing at Australia's classic Bathurst race in a Peter Brock Holden Torana was no fault of South African ace Basil van Rooyen (left). A poor repayment for Gerry's shared TT and Spa drives with team owner-driver Peter Brock.* [Mike Harding]

1977

Despite increasing pressure in his home life (Gregor was born this year), Gerry contested over 50 events, including multiple results for one Spa meeting and the disappointing trip to Australia to race the Holden Torana, described in the preceding chapter.

Beginning with his traditional participation in Chiltern & Harrow CC's Sprint – driving his contract road car, 666 DTV – a class win opened the season. He finally closed the competition yearbook with a November win, by which time he knew that the DTV decade was over. Just 15 assorted wins were recorded, mostly class results in a thinner season.

As in the previous two seasons, DTV-Vauxhall

BELOW Billed as the Battle of the Sexes, Gerry (inside line at the chicane) squeezes by former ski ace Divina Galica on the last lap at Thruxton in September 1977. [John Gaisford]

six-hour serious international race were Lanfranchi and Williams, one of the few times all three raced the same innocent victim sorry, motor car. The big Monorep Bimmer belonged to Don Abrahams, the immensely loyal backer for Lanfranchi: the three 'musket-beers' rented it for £250 apiece. Back in the day, Williams told the best stories about this outing, these including Gerry managing to hit a turbo Porsche 'up the arse' in practice (Gerry reckoned it was in the way!), a team tactics meeting devoted to whose drinks round it was – and a race start which saw Gerry out and repairing a fuse after just three laps. Unfortunately these tales don't appear in the Williams book – I found them in *Only Here For The Beer*, so we will not repeat them verbatim here. The tortured BMW (Tony used to club-race it as well) finally finished 21st, but was not officially classified.

A brace of Jaguar drives came in the Classic Saloon Car Club series, with TVC 254 securing outright wins at Silverstone and Thruxton. Gerry was nominated in an old friend, an Austin A35, for a late season appearance. This car was a winner with Andy McLennan, and Gerry's brother – Martyn – would later drive it with Andy until it blew an engine in 1978 at Thruxton.

In the next chapter we shall explore Gerry's traumatic 1978–9 Triumph Dolomite seasons, in which consistent success was balanced by the biggest accident and most disappointing season of his career, against a backdrop of domestic strife.

ABOVE AND RIGHT
Superb Marshall Archive shot of Tony Lanfranchi (get those cowboy boots!) and the Mayfair Opel at its 1976 presentation and in action. The Opel competed from 1975–77, honourably completed a Tour of Britain in the hands of former World Champion Denny Hulme, and won nearly 50 races over those three seasons in Tony's hands. [Marshall Family Archive/Jeff Bloxham]

still provided the overwhelming majority of drives, but Marshall posted three entries and a brace of overall wins in a 2.4-litre Jaguar Mk2, additionally contesting Silverstone's World Championship for Makes round in a rented BMW 3.0 Si. There was also a scheduled drive in the Debenhams Escort series, but no result after a particularly vicious race.

The legendary outing was in an Americana Jeans-backed BMW, and Gerry's cohorts in this

OPPOSITE *Happy chappy! Gerry gives a good interview at Oulton Park in 1980.* [Alan Cox]

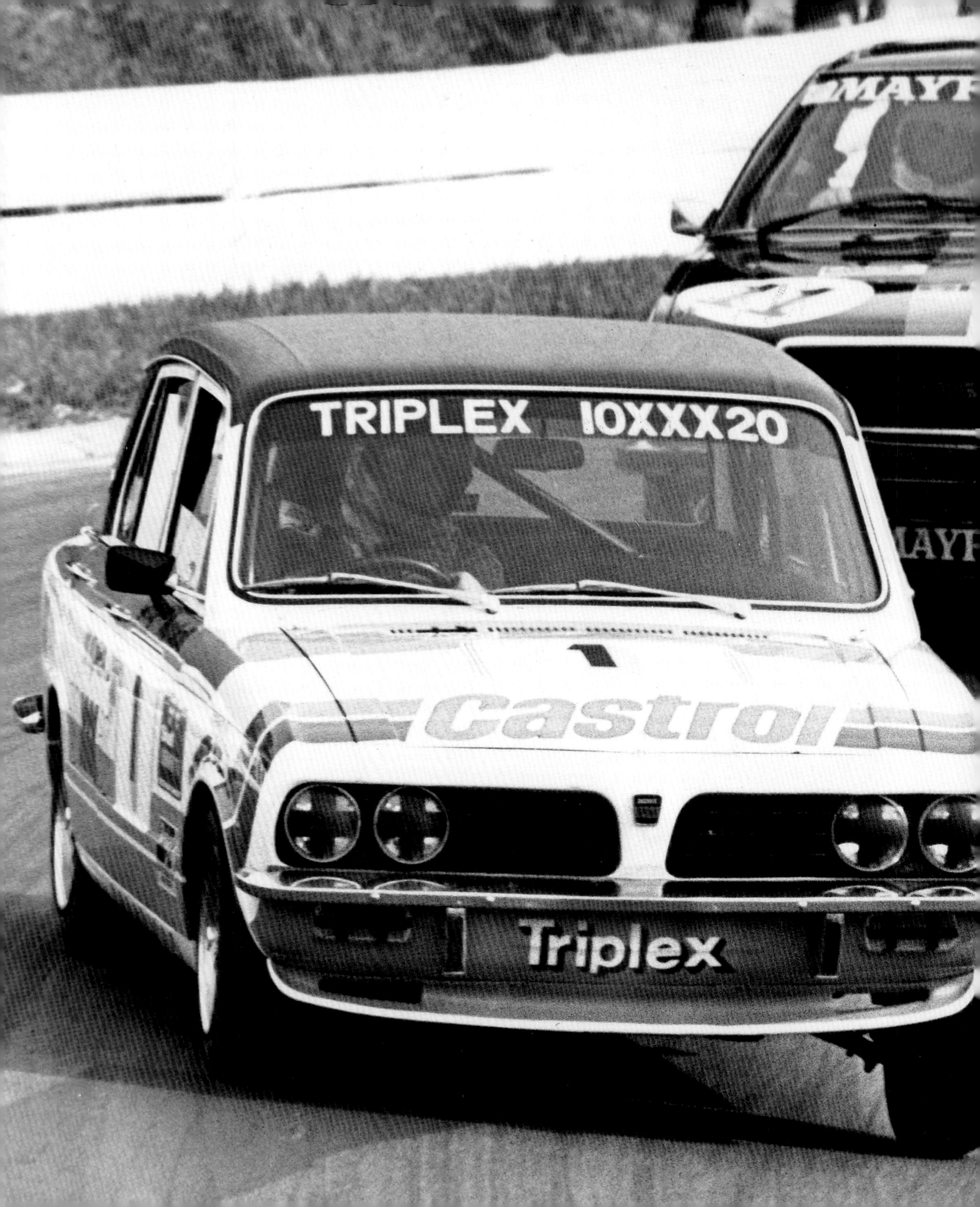
TRIPLEX 10XXX20
Castrol
Triplex
MAYF

CHAPTER 10

Life with Dolly

O ver 30 years after Gerry found there was no future for him at DTV, I asked his first wife, Carol, if the Big Man became a big pain to live with after that decision. 'More difficult, perhaps?' I asked tentatively.

Carol threw her head back and laughed loud and long before she spluttered, without a trace of malice, 'Gerry was always difficult to live with, it made no difference at all!'

Professionally it *did* make a major difference to Gerry's life. Now he would no longer receive a regular retainer from DTV, although there was the fee for his retention in a 'consultancy' capacity.

Through 1978–9 Gerry was far too busy to look back at the DTV period, entering more than 90 races and running his own Gerry Marshall Racing (GMR) team as well as his North London car sales company. Of that enterprise Gerry commented, in May 1979, 'Marshall Wingfield Ltd in Finchley Road, purveyors of swift horseless carriages, takes up most of my time. Since my partner John Wingfield died in his formula car at Thruxton, Mrs Wingfield has taken a large interest in the business and has been a magnificent and loyal partner. Racing can be a cruel business, but this kind of support makes sense of the whole thing.'

He would suffer a horrendous accident himself in the 1979 Silverstone saloon car supporting race,

LEFT *Employer showing employee the way!. Gerry leading Tony Lanfranchi at production play in the Dolomite and Mayfair Opel in a mid-season Mallory Park encounter.* [Marshall Family Archive]

RIGHT AND BELOW
Gerry faced two
years of personal
and track drama
through 1978–9, but
his driving remained
as spectacular as ever!
These racing seasons
were dominated by his
appearances in Triumph
Dolomite Sprints for
production and (1979)
premier-league BTCC
Championships.
[Both LAT]

and undergo every emotion, at home and on the track. On a happier note, 7 May 1979 saw Brands Hatch boss John Webb back the 'Gerry Marshall Benefit Day Races'. Gerry told *Autosport* readers: 'What it meant was that I had to stand and talk to Neville Hay for a new UK racing drivers' all-comers record. Or smile while Big Tone [Lanfranchi] and Whizzo [Williams] slagged me in front of the sunbathing spectators…I didn't feel like me at all! That several thousand people came along to see the day's attractions was quite heart-warming. I left

feeling it has been an honour to be singled out in this way.' More about that memorable week in the sidebar entitled 'Confessions of an errant author' (page 148).

Right from the start of the 1978 season, Gerry got stuck back in at the sharp end of saloon car racing, albeit he began with a Vauxhall reminder. In February he turned out for his local car club sprint – the Chiltern Circle & Harrow Car Club – with a then sparkling Chevette HS2300, the base for Vauxhall's future rallying programme! He won his class and got a silver tankard as a memento.

Vauxhall was really a memory, though, at least as a consistently funded adjunct to GM-Vauxhall ambition. Gerry would return to the marque, but only as a privateer and to demonstrate his more famous racers into the 21st century. More often than not he would return to his roots, entering others in Vauxhall descendants of the Firenza coupes that had given him so much success.

Gerry's weapon of choice for 1978 was a Triumph Dolomite Sprint in production trim for the Shellsport Derwent and Britax series, which foretold his Triumph involvement in the British Touring Car premier series in 1979, utilising ex-Broadspeed factory-backed Dolomites – a case of triumph followed by near tragedy, pun intended. As with the ex-Colin Vandervell Ford Capri campaigned in the 1978 premier league British Touring Car Championship, the Triumphs were backed by Triplex, sponsorship that extended to 1979 when two cars were run with auxiliary sponsorship from *Motor* magazine, their road-test

ace employee Rex Greenslade proving an extremely able teammate to Gerry (see the sidebar by Rex on page 146).

Former Standard Triumph experimental and competition division engineer Roger Dowson explained in 2009 how the link with our hero came about, one that evolved into a racing partnership for Roger in Gerry Marshall Racing: 'Bob Saunders had been racing a Dolomite that we had prepared in the 1977 production series. Bob could not make one race and gave Gerry the drive. Anyway, Gerry

liked the car and he bought one himself and brought it to us to prepare and enter for the 1978 season.

'It went really well and we ended up winning both championships.' Indeed, Gerry was rarely beaten in the class and took a trio of overall wins against the larger-capacity opposition. The only problem Roger remembered was with 'the scrutineers, they were convinced we were cheating'. Roger chuckled as he recalled how Gerry had solved that problem at picturesque Cadwell

ABOVE AND LEFT *The combination of Roger Dowson's Downie Racing preparation and Gerry's spectacular speed brought immediate results in the 1978 Shellsport and Britax national championships for production saloons. This (above) is their third appearance, which brought a fine outright Thruxton victory: just in March '78, they scored three class wins in four outings. From the same early '78 period, we have a fine action study (left) at Brands Hatch.* [John Gaisford/Marshall Family Archive]

Park in Lincolnshire: 'It was always a father and son team of scrutineers up there. Gerry took them out to the pub and got them bladdered! The old boy was in such a state he had to use the fence around the scrutineering bay to hold him up!'

On 5 March, a month after his warm-up 1978 outing in the Chevette, Gerry debuted the Dolomite at Brands Hatch. It would be a typically intense season, 27 Britax or Shellsport Derwent Production Saloon Car Championship races tackled, to bring three outright victories and 23 class wins.

Roger remembered one Marshall winning run at Donington in the production Dolomite particularly well. 'It was a typical ten-lapper and Gerry was miles in the lead. On lap nine he came into the pits.

'"What's up?" I asked.

'"Nothing, just wanted to let the rest catch up,"' quipped Marshall, before tramping off to rejoin the race and score another win!

Graham Scarborough – fast becoming a driver that Gerry respected – remembered this Donington racing charade too. Graham told Gregor in 2009:

'The first time Gerry and I really came into contact was my fourth race at Donington in the April [on the 30th]. Practice was very wet and I managed to qualify third overall, on the front row!

'Gerry was on pole with Derrick Brunt second in the BMW. Gerry came and found me, asked me a few questions.' Gerry knew about my Mazda and was obviously intrigued. Graham continued: 'I remember the race vividly. The track was still damp but it was drying. Gerry just disappeared, leaving all the bigger cars behind him.

'On the penultimate lap, for whatever reason, Gerry came into the pits with a "problem". Apparently there was much gesturing from Gerry and posturing from Roger Dowson, who took off a bit of duct tape from the front of the car and off Gerry went for the last lap.

'Obviously it was a bit of a ploy of Gerry's to keep everyone entertained, but it backfired as he came out in third place on a now dry track! Anyway, he did manage to win, but I know from speaking to him after the event it wasn't planned like that.

'I think to a degree he had been slightly embarrassed that he'd been so far in front!'

Those with strong DTV racing memories will remember Gerry doing much the same thing at Thruxton. All to such good affect that Murray 'Trousers on Fire' Walker's commentary box practically exploded in the face of the barrage from the legendary commentator.

That Triumph campaign would have been enough for most, but Gerry also tackled the major league Tricentrol British Touring Car Championship in 1978. Armed with the ex-Vandervell 3-litre Capri prepared by subsequent Dowson and Williams Formula 1 technician John Westwood, Gerry was in his spectacular sideways element, with plenty of grassy moments from the start.

It looked like it would be an excellent year when Gerry finished second overall in the rain-sodden opening round of the '78 BTCC at Silverstone, but this was not an accurate portent of the Capri-Marshall season. Unfortunately, the crowd-pleasing

BELOW *The fourth round of the 1979 Tricentrol BTCC series was at Thruxton and produced this fine Gaisford action picture. The opposite-lock is particularly impressive, as Marshall is out on the fastest section of this quick track, perfectly placed on the kerb at over 100mph.*
[John Gaisford]

ABOVE *Burnout! September 1979 Oulton Park and we see the onset of the rear-tyre problems that often delayed Marshall with race pit stops during his harsh BTCC season.* [LAT]

combination suffered some non-starts and non-finishes. Gerry completed the BTCC season with a final-round appearance in a borrowed Alfa Alfetta GT, but that failed to finish too.

A Ford 3-litre V6 recipe Capri also served Gerry in his attack on a brace of prestige European touring car races that season. At the late July Spa 24-hours there was little chance of repeating his 1977 Vauxhall success, as intense warfare between top Capri teams (mostly British-based) and BMW's Belgian, British and German-sourced 5-series four-door saloons disputed the honour of winning the last long-circuit (8.1 miles) layout day-and-night Spa classic. The top-scoring Capri driver in the UK, Gordon Spice, sharing with Belgium's Teddy Pilette, put the Ford into the history books. The race pace was hot and the Marshall Capri was one of the many retirements. There was some compensation in the Marshall-backed Jock Robertson Vauxhall Magnum managing 12th overall, shared with Karl Jones and Andrew Major.

Silverstone's senior league RAC Tourist Trophy is another established European classic event. In September 1978 the weekend included a race run to Diners Club rules, but Gerry's Capri failed to finish that as well.

1979

Looking back over a tremendously busy '78 season with strongest success coming consistently from the Dowson-prepped Dolomites, Gerry might have been forgiven for thinking 1979 should be a Dolly doddle back in the BTCC big

time. It was memorable all right, but for all the wrong reasons…

Gerry's fabled dealing skills were stretched to also cover tasks previously tackled by Bill Blydenstein, DTV or Vauxhall management. Yes, Gerry had the skills to manage others, as he demonstrated in the '60s and would echo in the '80s, but not whilst in the middle of marital strife and battling a machine that did not respond to his increasingly desperate efforts to outpace his teammate. It would end in tears.

Finally, Gerry did assemble a truly significant deal for the 1979 season. Negotiating with then British Leyland Competition Director John Davenport was a frustrating exercise. John remains one of the most intelligent of beings, but that huge brain can be obstructive. That may sound like a backhanded compliment, especially to former Au*tosport* rally reporter and leading international co-driver John. For Gerry in pursuit of a deal, and especially of keeping that deal into the '80s, the Davenport factor was just one more straw that threatened to break the Marshall bank.

Having to tread a tightrope between sponsors who delivered publicity (the now defunct weekly *Motor* magazine) and cash (Triplex and Esso) was not easy. Add in a teammate who peddled with increasing speed and the background marital battlefield, and you have the combination that many contemporaries associated with the Big Man's troubled 1979. For Gerry had reached a crossroads in his marriage to Carol and his now seven-year-long relationship with Jenny. One insider associated with fielding the Triplex Dolomites every racing weekend observed: 'The Jennifer-Carol thing had reached a peak and I just don't think his whole mind was on the racing job.'

Roger Dowson recalled how the GMR team picked up the brace of Dolomites that would be raced by Marshall and Greenslade in 1979: 'It was late in 1978 when all the decisions were made. Ralph [Broad] had given up motor racing [after the European Jaguar fiasco and the death of his daughter in a road accident – JW] and he packed up to retire to Portugal. So, we had to collect the Dolomites from Broad's place at Southam in Warwickshire. It was snowing and a hard job was made worse by those dreadful Leyland Sherpa vans; they weren't great in the dry, but in snow with full loads aboard it was a struggle, I can tell you.'

The vans may have been horrible in a Ford Transit-ruled world, but the pedigree Dolomites were a winning credit to Broadspeed's last hurrah. Racer-journalist Tony Dron took five outright victories and was tied on points with

1977 title winner Bernard Unett, who had a clear run to the title as he dominated a comparatively uncompetitive class with a Chrysler Avenger GT.

Roger Dowson reported: 'I think you could see which way things were going when we did our first wet test. Gerry went through a set of wet-weather Dunlops in ten laps. Just rooted Dunlop's brand new tyres.' With the benefit of 30 years' hindsight, Roger added: 'Aside from the emotional time Gerry experienced, I think the season also went badly for him because the car didn't suit his sideways style. Rex was that bit neater and it paid off.'

The March opening round of the '79 BTCC was anti-climactic, being snowed off at Donington. Just a weekend later battle commenced at a Silverstone international meeting, and the omens for class or overall honours were not good.

The Ford Capris had broken out into a class of their own – it was 1980 before the Rover SD1 V8 put a stop to such Ford dominance – and even in

the sub-2,300cc class the Dolomites faced tough opposition. Stretching the rules in his creative way, Tom Walkinshaw and Mazda had persuaded the ruling bodies that the rotary motor RX-7 was just the sort of machine you'd think of first when defining a touring car!

Tom and his recently created TWR (Tom Walkinshaw Racing) team had the rotary spitting out ear-splitting power and had the advantage of a low roof, lowered centre of gravity compared with an upright saloon, and Tom (as this writer knew from Tom's earlier 1970s employment at the Ford Competitions department) was a world-class Tin Top conductor. Tough, utterly uncompromising, and with a gift to inspire his TWR team engineers to think laterally, upwards, sideways, anyway that would gain an advantage from subtle to blatant regulation manipulation. Tom – and later the fabled Winston Percy – would be the hardest of RX-7 acts to beat, as even the Capri guys were to find in the class above.

For Roger Dowson and Big Gerry, the 1979

BELOW Hectic production racing life continued in 1979, as this Brands Hatch shot demonstrates. Gerry leads a lot of larger-capacity cars after one of his sharp getaways on the way to an overall win and becoming Demon Tweeks Champion in the Production Saloon series. [LAT]

pointers to the season were there from the start. Walkinshaw practised a clear 1.5 seconds faster than the Dollies, and Gerry was a bitterly unhappy third in class for practice, Greenslade pipping him by 0.01 second. True, they had not enjoyed much pre-season testing – a stark contrast to TWR's hard pre-season regime in search of a car Tom couldn't break – but the race just confirmed Gerry's worst fears.

Rain swept in, but it was not Gerry's saviour this time. The Big Man had shredded a Dunlop wet in his warm-up lap (!) and would retire in the race with steering and tyre woes, hating the 'Dunnies' as much as some of the Capri men, who had to trail behind Goodyear-attired Gordon Spice, Chris Craft and Vauxhall graduate/Epsom dealer Jeff Allam in another Ford. Ironically, Barrie Williams beat Greenslade in the remaining Marshall-Dowson Dolomite. That hurt – Barrie 'Squeaker' Williams was in one of Gerry's obsolete DTV Magnums!

The Easter double-header weekend in April saw Gerry start his '79 BTCC points with a second in class at Oulton Park, despite a rupture amongst the seat belts. Gerry was beaten by Walkinshaw's Mazda, Rex by the scrutineers, who decided the anti-roll bar on his Dolomite was illegal. As ever in saloon car racing, the scrutineering sessions produced as much argument as the races themselves.

When the BTCC squabble arrived at Thruxton for the traditional Easter Monday's European Formula 2 meeting, Walkinshaw continued his class success at a shattering 91mph average and Greenslade took a reportedly 'inspired' second in the class, this despite a spin on the second lap at the fast Hampshire track. Gerry? Retirement with

BELOW *Aftermath of the July 1979 smash at Silverstone's Grand Prix's supporting race. The Dolomite injuries are obvious, but Gerry had 10 days in Northampton General Hospital and the legacy of his injuries led to further health complications in later decades.* [Marshall Family Archive]

a shredded rear tyre again, which *Motoring News* reporter Ian Bamsey described as 'a legacy of his sideway style'.

The Silverstone and Donington rounds of the premier British saloon car championship saw Gerry at least finishing, but each time it was a third in class result, Walkinshaw so far ahead he was fighting for podiums overall amongst the Capris, whilst Rex Greenslade consistently out-raced his team boss.

Going into the prestige BTCC round of the year, that supporting the Silverstone Grand Prix, Gerry was not a happy man. And an unhappy Gerry would vent his feelings on all those around him. Unfortunately, it got worse.

Here's how *Motoring News* reported the biggest crash in Gerry's career, and one that required a ten-day sleepover: 'Entering Club for the second time it appears that Walkinshaw and Marshall had a slight collision, which sent the Dolomite into the dirt. Somehow, it tripped up and went into a sickening series of cartwheels, which left the car virtually destroyed, and Marshall lucky to be alive. He was taken to hospital with head injuries and cracked ribs.'

I was at Silverstone that day and heard the incident discussed by all concerned – and by distant onlookers and web sages for 30 years afterwards – without ever getting a definitive version. I was out on the fastest section of the circuit, where the accident occurred, and the Dolomite certainly rolled on to the elevated spectator protection fencing. Both Gerry and Tom were tough racers, Tom behind at this stage with Rex Greenslade leading both. My impression was that there were some heavy race impacts before Gerry finally went off.

This was Gerry's account in a contemporary *Autosport* column: 'At the end of the first lap my Dolomite was up with Rex and Tom. I was able to get past both of them coming out of the chicane. At Copse, we caught a Capri – Vandervell's I think – and I lifted off. Rex went by, but Tom was still behind in the Mazda. I followed Rex down to Stowe with Tom right in, virtually under my back bumper, trying to keep up with the unusually down on power RX-7.

'We went nose-to-tail along from Stowe to Club. I remember thinking that, when we got to the slightly uphill drag from Club through Abbey, the Dolly would pull away, because it had a little more torque than the Mazda, and I had an especially good unit in, [so] Club is now a top gear corner. That means you must approach at about 120mph, lift, dab the brakes, and settle the car around the corner under power.

'Tom was right with me and a Dolomite is not renowned for its braking powers. Tom's intention was clearly to out-brake me on the inside. I lifted off and braked, but Tom didn't expect me to do that so suddenly and so early. Eye witnesses tell me that the resulting collision between Mazda and Triumph lifted the rear wheels of my car clear from the ground.'

'Not unnaturally, the Triumph got very sideways as I piled on the opposite lock. I don't really remember too much about the next few seconds, as the World went mad. The car must have rolled sideways and cleared two layers of catch fencing, before going end-over-end and attempting to vault the 15-foot high safety fencing, coming down on its back.

' I am told I gave a better display than the Red Arrows, but the finish wasn't quite so polished!'

Not so amusing were the injuries sustained in those aerobatics. 'Assorted head cuts, three skull fractures, cracked ribs and assaults on my jaw, teeth and kidney. Mugged by a Dolomite Sprint, I ask you,' quipped Gerry. Although he could be loudly volatile over apparently insignificant incidents, he rarely complained about his hospital spells.

Jenny Cook recalled: 'I went from the pits on the little monkey bike to the scene of the accident. I went with him in the ambulance to the hospital and sat with him. By that time he was quite OK, despite terrible facial wounds. He had to have about 70 stitches in his face. I think the number has increased as the story has been passed on.

'Gerry made a very speedy recovery,' she added, 'and whenever I visited the room was usually full of cigar smoke and visitors!' But it was not much fun. Jenny confirmed that 'it was helluva time in his life. The big accident took a lot out of him and any money was getting gobbled up in the racing. He never complained about the hospitals or the operations in later life, he was very brave in that respect.'

A look over the twisted Dolomite betrayed just how severe the accident had been: it was the worst in Gerry's long career by a big margin. Technically, accident investigators found that Gerry's helmet had been forced off in the impacts (with the chin strap still fastened). The roll-cage absorbed the 'immense force of the impact extremely well,' in *Autosport*'s words, and the doors could still open and shut, whilst the windscreen remained intact, but the mountings of the racing seat broke. A doctor later confirmed that he considered Gerry's back would have been broken if the seat mountings had *not* sheared.

Rex Greenslade had a good rear view and clear recollections of this monstrous accident, which would subsequently lead to a major back operation for Gerry. You can read his account in the 'Rex Greenslade: 1979 teammate' sidebar on page 146. It should be added that Rex managed to beat Tom that dramatic day, a rare and fine achievement.

Gerry was out of hospital at the end of July, and visited the Brands Hatch saloon car festival to see

ABOVE *Mallory Park always delivers close competition action. This looks like the 1979 Tom & Gerry show, but appearances are deceptive. As Rex Greenslade won the class on a tyre chosen by Gerry, Chuck Nicholson drove the Marshall Dolomite in this August 12th BTCC round, substituting for the injured Gerry after the Silverstone accident. Tom Walkinshaw in his TWR preparation company Mazda RX-7 that usually dominated the class in 1979, robustly retains the inside line at the hairpin. Chuck prevailed against his later Jaguar racing partner and took third in class, 6th overall ahead of Walkinshaw. Vandervell won outright in the Capri Gerry raced the following season.* [Rodger Calvert]

Writing from his American base 30 years after he spent the 1979 season driving the ex-Broadspeed Dolomites, Rex Greenslade recalled: 'Gerry, having got a contract from BL to take over the Broadspeed Triumph Dolomite Sprints and run them under the "Triplex Racing with Esso and *Motor*" banner, had three priorities for 1979.

'Clearly he needed to establish himself as a team owner. Second, he needed to win. And third, he needed to gain credibility with BL and get the Rover contract everyone knew was coming for 1980. All this caused him enormous personal conflicts – he was the archetypal winner but now had to prioritise winning as a team owner over winning as a driver. Gerry dealt with two mega motor-racing egos: one off the track – John Davenport of BL – and one on the track – Tom Walkinshaw of TWR and his RX-7. Davenport liked to play mind games – riddles, statements with double meanings, and his selective availability for discussions. All were tactics Gerry found frustrating in the extreme.

'Gerry viewed Walkinshaw as his nemesis, campaigning a car that most competitors thought shouldn't have been allowed in the series (an RX-7 a *saloon*? Gimme a break). Gerry thought (with justification) the RX-7 was blatantly illegal, race after race.

'Enmity broke out into total war at the supporting race to the British GP at Silverstone. Walkinshaw punted Gerry's Dolomite up the rear coming into Club Corner, triggering a most sickening series of end-over-end rolls. I was leading the class and, exiting Club, glimpsed a flurry of movement out of corner of my eye in the mirror. Next time around, I arrived at Club with a solid lead, but found Gerry's helmet in the middle of the track.

'"God, his head's still in it," I thought. It wasn't, thankfully, but the shock triggered my involuntary lift and Walkinshaw caught up. That I went on to win the race was huge consolation to the team and to Gerry. As long as I knew him, Gerry believed that Walkinshaw deliberately caused the accident.'

Rex reflected on a sometimes strained Marshall relationship. 'At the beginning of the season we got on well, but this deteriorated as it became clear that the Dolomite suited my driving style better. To be beaten by his teammate was something Gerry had never experienced before and it tore him apart.

'Roger Dowson – who prepared and ran the cars – ensured that right to the end the two Dolomite Sprints were as identical and as good as they could be. Even though it reflected well on Gerry as a team owner to be competitive and have wins (we got two), he couldn't deal with not beating *me*. In hindsight, I had spent three years in Alfasuds, finding ways to turn horsepower into mph. Gerry spent ten years finding ways to tame excess horsepower (such as in "Baby Bertha") and a lack of traction.

'I didn't expect to beat Gerry and was more than surprised when I did. The car suited me so well – there was no shortage of oversteer, but you had to make sure that it wasn't accompanied by too much opposite lock. The Dolly repaid absolute smoothness so that you could carry the speed through the apex of the corner, while conserving the tyres and the brakes. It wasn't a car to wrestle or fight: often GM would charge off from one of his flying starts but soon fry the tyres and have to let me through.

'The irony was that the prize we really all had our eye on – the Rover 3500 deal for 1980 – would have probably suited him far better, with the power/traction ratio much closer to his comfort zone. Gerry became increasingly frustrated that Davenport wouldn't talk to him about the Rover contract for 1980. Gerry suspected I knew more than I was telling him – which was true, but only marginally. Ultimately he didn't get the Rover deal and I did, driving for David Price Racing. Our friendship went into a cold freeze, understandably.

'It was a shame that 1979 didn't work out for Gerry. Perhaps it would have been better if he had simply been a team owner and not one of the drivers.

'For me, 1979 was the best race year of my career. For Gerry, it was probably the worst.'

BELOW *Happier post-accident times. Rex Greenslade (left) and Gerry at Mallory Park in August 1979.* [Marshall Family Archive]

Chuck Nicholson drive the Triplex production Dolomite to ninth overall in the Derwent series. Gerry returned to his earliest racing apprenticeship role: 'While I was not racing, it was enjoyable to watch Chuck and Rex in our Dollies, and I managed the team at Donington and Mallory. Naturally I attribute Rex's win and Chuck's third place at Mallory to my tyre choices on the grid.'

Shortly afterwards he was back in harness, contesting production races in the Triplex Dolomite with class-winning success at his 5 August comeback. But the BTCC season still went to hell. Post-crash, the BTCC points recorded Walkinshaw leading the class, with Greenslade second, and Marshall tied at third with Barrie Williams in Gerry's old DTV Magnum! The Dolomite held fifth position in the Manufacturer's tables. Not the results the Big Man wanted to read.

The remainder of that BTCC season saw Walkinshaw's class dominance so securely established that Tom seized second overall in the series to points champ Richard Longman's final British Touring Car Championship win for a Mini. At the August Donington round, Tom Walkinshaw won outright – causing a lot of rumblings about the legality of the Mazda in the Capri camp – but Gerry did not drive, preferring to return to a role as team manager for the Triplex squad, which was made up of Greenslade and Nicholson. Greenslade took another second in class, eighth overall, underlining the massive gap 'twixt RX-7 and conventional Triumph.

The following weekend at Brands Hatch saw Gerry return to the BTCC Dolomite and he picked up second in class, one of his best results of the season, but it wasn't all good news. Gerry commented: 'It's nice to be back in the Triplex Dolly, especially in such a friendly formula. My comeback was the August Bank Holiday at Brands, where they had 11 protests – 10 from Tom Walkinshaw!'

Brands exacted a toll on the Dolomite's handling, especially in practice when 'a rear axle bracket decided to detach itself,' observed Gerry at the time, 'giving me a very exciting moment at Westfield. I found the combination of front and rear steering axles too much for me.' Rex Greenslade was eliminated in the first lap Brands race traffic. Gerry led the class for much of the race, but was finally passed by Barrie Williams in that ageing Vauxhall. Oooh, the pain!

Thruxton in early September saw Gerry return to form on a rapid circuit he always loved. Holding a place on the fourth row, little adrift of Walkinshaw, it looked like this was to be Gerry's best BTCC result of the troubled year. Rex was out early, with a front wheel departing (!). Described as 'a burly motor trader', Gerry's driving was

described as 'with bags of brio', but it all went wrong when the gear lever snapped. He returned to the action, but neither of the Triplex Triumphs scored their due ration of points that promising day, Gerry finally fifth in the class having held a top ten placing prior to the gear lever failure.

Not in the BTCC schedule, but perhaps the largest grid assembled for Group 1 saloons in the UK in 1979, was the 15–16 September RAC Tourist Trophy. Gerry was also racing at Oulton Park on the Saturday practice day for the 500km Sunday TT, so he flew in by helicopter with some 20 minutes to spare before his session. That weekend he would share with rally legend Roger Clark (reportedly the nearest pubs had their beer stocks replenished overnight!), who also had to travel in late as he was contesting the Manx Rally for Ford. Gerry and Roger were well matched, as you would have expected of the 1974 Tour of Britain duet, their TT race lap times being less than 0.3 seconds apart.

ABOVE *Gerry and Tony Lanfranchi had some bust-ups in their volatile friendship, but they remained mates through some of Gerry's harshest times in the later seventies.* [Marshall Family Archive]

RIGHT *Barrie Williams and Gerry in pre-race conversation before a 1979 Marshall outing in the soundly prepared Roger Dowson Dolomite.* [Tim Tyler]

Confessions of an errant author

During 1978–9 co-author Walton was involved in Gerry's business life, as they had concocted two books together – *Only Here For The Beer* and the lesser known *Competition Driving*. Jeremy recalled: 'I was also intermittently ghosting Gerry's *Autosport* column. I traded the occasional high-performance Ford through Marshall Wingfield and appeared in some of the same races between 1972 and 1991. We last appeared in the same event in 1991, when Gerry thrashed the rest of us in a two-part TVR race at Mallory Park; I was an enduring sixth.

'We had mild fallouts, and one of these became public in May 1979. In a footnote to his 'Marshall Art' *Autosport* column Gerry commented, with uncharacteristic restraint: "We seemed to have entertained the journalists and some VIPs here at the test days held at Donington on the Wednesday and Thursday after the benefit day. Ironically, my book on competition driving came out in time for these sessions, for I was actually passengering most of the time while my Triplex sponsor struggled to find the right diagram in the book!

"One of the better journalist drivers and I were also nearly wiped off the face of the earth by the man who helped me write that book: he appears to have found the joystick option offered within a BMW 528i, but no smooth way of landing the plot."

'I had not seen this reference before 2009, so I looked up the offending diary date and found the following 9 May note of shame: "Win a bottle of champagne in Ford Formula Finesse – long moment in BMW GB's 528i when the brakes faded going into the chicane. Tony Scott of *Motor* was driving the Triplex Dolly, when I shot by on two wheels, brakeless! No crash, but I don't expect Mr Scott will offer me that rally job we have been negotiating…"

'I had no idea Gerry was in the car with Scott until 2009. I am amazed there was not a blazing row on the spot.'

Greenslade was assigned Chuck Nicholson, but practised both Dolomites. Both Dollies were trouble to restart when hot and the Clark/Marshall Triumph ate pads and tyres, so neither brought home great glory, and Gerry fared no better in the Lister Jaguar he was also scheduled to steer that Silverstone weekend.

Back in the BTCC, battle resumed – or would have done if the Triumphs had not been 'outlawed' from participation in the penultimate Snetterton night races. That was because of original front and rear suspension tweaks disclosed by a former Broadspeed employee to TWR, including front suspension ball joint reinforcement (recognised for rallying) and relocation of the rear shock absorbers in the original Broadspeed specification. Some of the leading Capris and Tom's RX-7 had been found illegal on other counts, both sides protesting and counter protesting *ad nauseam* that season. Tom's Mazda was ejected from the Brands Hatch results in August for running no fan and oversize wheels, and the Dolomites suffered in the protest fallout from the Gordon Spice Racing Capri team versus TWR-Mazda.

So the Triumphs did not feature on the Snetterton grid for the evening race start – a break from BTCC routine that also saw a trio of the leading Capris absent, although Tom Walkinshaw and his much abused Mazda were present, battling with Marshall protégé Jock Robertson's borrowed Capri. Jeff Allam, inheritor of Gerry's Vauxhall Magnum racing crown in BTCC, had graduated to Capris and won this unusual darkened BTCC round.

The Oulton Park final round was a cracker, and once again promised Gerry more than the results finally revealed. He led both Walkinshaw and Greenslade after one of his demon getaways, but the tyres went off after just six laps and he had to let both past. Subsequently third gear kept jumping out of engagement, and he retired from the last BTCC of the season with the small compensation of knowing he was as fast as ever, having broken Tony Dron's 1977 Dolomite lap record by 0.2 seconds. Rex rescued second in class from the final Oulton results, Walkinshaw recording yet another class win.

That '79 Oulton was significant as the last appearance of Gerry Marshall as a BTCC regular. But he did drive in 1980s BTCC events on a one-off basis and must have had one of the longest career spans in the prime British saloon series. Yet the Triplex-Dolomite experience marked the end of an era for the British motorsport legend.

Gerry's memories of 1979 were particularly bitter. On the personal front, a divorce from Carol became inevitable. He also never forgave Tom Walkinshaw for what he saw as blatant rule-breaking, an opinion shared by the leading Spice Ford Capri team. Spice and team manager Keith Greene took things all the way to an RAC Tribunal over those oversize RX-7 wheels and won their case. The winning Capris were consequently allowed to complete their seasons with acknowledged illegal strip welding, so Tom did not have it all his own way.

The tough Scot was squeezed out of the BTCC title that year; but the TWR RX-7 returned in 1980 and won commandingly with Winston Percy aboard.

Gerry's verdict on the season some 21 years later makes poignant reading. 'That was the culmination of my front line career,' he told *Autosport* in 2000. 'I had everything sunk into that – my own team, works support and backing from Esso, Triplex and *Motor* magazine. Everyone wrote me off, but I bounced back.'

The remainder of the 1979 season demonstrated the usual Marshall recipe for racing variety, from a production Ford Escort to an entry in a Scottish-owned Chevrolet Camaro.

The Escort ride was in the hotly contested Debenhams Escort Challenge – a descendant of the Mexico series Gerry won in '71. He enjoyed the traditional paint-polishing battle in the pack, disputing fourth before 'I could only get half throttle'. He fell back to seventh, but finally finished fifth after a couple of cunning late race moves.

Gerry was entered in the Lloyds & Scottish

Historic Sports Car Championship during the year. Silverstone's GP supporter was an obvious non-starter after the Dolomite's major accident, but sadly there were no other top results in Listers that season.

In total, during 1978–9 Gerry contested 94 races in production Dolomites, BTCC and production Capris, the Group 1 Triumph of 1979 and the Lister Jaguar, never mind the Escort one-offs and a quartet of runs in the Porsche 924 Championship. And that was just two seasons in his four-decade career, pursued vigorously despite recurring problems with his back and the 1978 emergence of a hernia.

An aborted record run in the Gordon Lamb dealership Porsche 924 that Gerry raced regularly in this period led to some chuckles amongst a veteran crew assembled at Snetterton in September 1978. They included the inevitable Tony Lanfranchi, Barrie Williams, the first BTCC champion Jack Sears (who later raced Gerry's production Dolomite intelligently), and 1960s British Saloon Car champ Roy Pierpoint. 'Gentleman Jack apparently spent some of the time helping with the harvest at his nearby farm,' according to Gerry. But harvesting was probably the last thing on anyone's mind when the attempt to wrest back the Commanders Cup trophy from an early '70s Ford Granada team (yes, really) was abandoned in thick fog.

BELOW *Champion chat. Multiple championship winner Gerry and triple British Saloon Car Champion and friend Win Percy (right). Win won titles with the TWR Mazda RX-7 that Gerry frequently faced in Tom Walkinshaw's hands.* [LAT]

CHAPTER 11

1978–85: The best and worst of times

L ate 1970s racing, outside the Dolomite shunt saga of our previous chapter, became a relief to everyday life for Gerry Marshall. Huge emotional, health and financial worries lay ahead, and though Gerry survived the '70s he would continue to face multiple troubles through the next 27 years. However, he did meet a racing saviour in Geoffrey Marsh, who owned some fantastic Aston Martins amongst a collection that also included competitive Lolas. Marsh and Marshall would enjoy (albeit with explosive interludes) a 26-year racing relationship that would see over 61 wins recorded, mainly in Aston Martins but also including a famous Lola T70 Victory in Dubai's self-styled GP.

Despite the termination of the DTV decade, Gerry started 1978 in traditional Vauxhall style at the Chiltern & Harrow Circle Sprint around Brands Hatch. This delivered a class win in his 4 DTV-registered Chevette HS2300 (sold, minus personal plate, straight after the event) and an outright win for 'Old Nail', detailed earlier.

Anyone who thought that Gerry's competition presence would wane post-DTV was totally wrong. Our man completed 57 events that first privateer season, taking 29 victories. Many of these were class victories in the Dolomite Sprint, the subject of the previous chapter, but Gerry was also a threat for outright wins in the ex-Colin Vandervell Capri

LEFT *Acknowledging the August 1981 Brands Hatch crowd after another win in the Aston Martin DBR4 within the Lloyds & Scottish series.*
[Marshall Family Archive]

RIGHT *Gerry entertains at one of the many forums where he took a central role. Here, left to right are: Roger Willis (Castrol Competitions); Gerry and the moustache of John Foden (effective media/ marketing man and perpetual Christmas quiz front-runner). Beside John is Peter McBride of Magard (who distributed DTV and many other performance parts) with Roy Cook furthest right. Roy was a significant Vauxhall engineer, the liaison for many years between Luton factory and sub-contractors.*
[John Lakey]

for major league BTCC. The Ford now featured a Mk3 body conversion from its Capri II origins.

Gerry also drove a Porsche 924 regularly for Gordon Lamb's dealership in the one-make series, and in a Commanders Cup endurance record attempt. Barry Simpson owned the Lister Jaguar that Gerry drove once, and there were singleton appearances in Jon Dooley's Alfa Romeo GTAm and differing Celebrity Escorts.

The significant results came in the Vandervell Capri. Colin totally lost interest in racing, honourably transferring the Capri and spares

that Ford had supplied. This car came with Triplex sponsorship, attracting outstanding media coverage. *Autosport*'s cover picture on 10 August 1978 displayed the Triplex livery and the fact that Gerry's broadside style suited the fast Ford.

Gerry memorably described the Vandervell Capri deal in his July *Autosport* column. 'Colin Vandervell, that well-known tycoon and happy smiling man about town, had been with them [Ford] for about six years, but owing to business commitments could not do a full season. So he has bequeathed (you meet a nicer class of word in this

RIGHT *A drenched Silverstone GP circuit in March 1978 saw Gerry improve from seventh in qualifying for the BTCC round to continually challenge for the lead. A number of grassy adventures saw him take second overall in the ex-Vandervell Capri, beaten by an inspired Tony Dron in the works Dolomite.*
[John Gaisford]

column!) the sponsorship to me. To sign the deal up was a last minute affair before the Silverstone round, when Colin and me had to meet the man from Triplex – Mike Beard, it turned out to be – on platform 12 at a London station. He was coming down from the frozen north to meet us and catch the next train back. However, Colin had never met Beard, and Beard had never met Colin or me, so all sorts of wild recognition plans were tried. Can you imagine me wearing a pink carnation? Or Colin wearing a wild rose in one ear?

'Anyway,' Gerry wrote, 'the deal was done in the palatial premises of a British Rail canteen.' Unfortunately Gerry and Colin did not part on the best of terms when the Capri was later resold, Vandervell being unhappy with Gerry's profit.

The first 1978 Capri result at a soaking Silverstone was the best of the season, although there were a couple of overall fourth positions elsewhere amongst multiple retirements. Finishes usually revealed a top ten placing, but the outstanding run came in the opening round of the Tricentrol BTCC Championship. Around Silverstone Grand Prix track in full wet conditions there were many offs, Gerry included. He persisted and careered to second overall and a class win, behind Tony Dron's Broadspeed Triumph Dolomite, one of the Ralph Broad racers of the type that Gerry acquired in 1979.

Besides the Dolomites and Capri, the Porsche 924 was a regular ride, with six scheduled entries. Some results we could not locate, but a third overall and two pole positions were revealed.

The 1959 Simpson Lister Jag brought a third overall at Donington against pedigree single-seater

ABOVE *Gerry's three offspring gathered around the Triplex Capri at Silverstone in 1978. Tina is on the left, Gregor is the toddler on Gerry's shoulder and Justine is on the right. This picture was taken by Carol, Gerry's first wife (now Mrs Carol Hutton), and was carried on the funeral service booklet in 2005.*
[Carol Hutton]

BELOW *The ex-Vandervell Capri at Marshall work for the Brands Hatch Grand Prix crowds in July 1978. Despite these heroic efforts, the results did not match his usual top-ten pace. A 12th position in practice was followed by a panel-bashing race start (look at the rear bumper) which eventually punctured a rear tyre and demanded a pit stop after running as high as fifth overall. [LAT]*

opposition, a meeting that saw Gerry compete in three events despite a reported hernia. The Capri was sixth overall and Dolly enjoyed a class win and fourth overall. Gerry and the dark blue Lister held second on two occasions, but affable fellow motor dealer Bobby Bell got by in his 1958 Lister during the last lap.

In May Gerry took a fifth overall in a Brands event for Escort Sports. Another Celebrity Ford rounded off the Marshall season with a second overall, this in a November Brands race for instructors – no pressure there, then – during the Formula Ford Festival. Winner was David Watt, just

0.9 seconds ahead of Gerry. Our man had to be satisfied to beat Lanfranchi, who started at ninth slot on the grid.

There was another late season date, attending the relocated Birmingham version of the British motor show, primarily to fulfil contractual obligations for racing sponsor Triplex and Vauxhall. Gerry told *Autosport* readers: 'This year I did four days without remission for good conduct. There were two weekends amongst them where I worked from 3 to 6 pm signing things for sponsors and generally doing a roaring trade. Whether it was my magnificent body, or that of my Dolomite Sprint … or even the new improved and totally wonderful Triplex stickers [advertisement] I do not know, but either way we were surrounded by the PST [Proverbial Seething Throng] and I have now found out what my right arm is not for!

'The crowd was definitely different to that of a London show. In Brum it was all rally jackets, jeans and turbans. In Earls Court it is all high heels and Hooray Henrys. Incredibly, there were 108,000 there on the first public Sunday … And I think they were all on my stand, together!'

1979

This was the year that Gerry met Geoffrey Marsh, the most important figure in his post-DTV racing life. Some 30 years later Geoffrey described how they came together and the epic results of their 26-year alliance, which centred on some quite fabulous Aston Martins – albeit their working relationship began with a very special Lister Jaguar sale.

LEFT *YCD in Marsh Plant colours at a Silverstone Aston gathering. Note the one-off Bulldog showstopper in the background and company demonstrator AM V8.* [Marshall Family Archive]

BELOW *Gerry clears the pack – including Richard Bond in the second-position Marsh DBR4 – through Paddock Hill bend at Brands for the Lloyds & Scottish supporting event to the 1980 British GP. He finished second in class after qualifying fourth overall.* [Marshall Family Archive]

Geoffrey told us in June 2009: 'I first met Gerry late in 1979 when he had the Costin-bodied Lister Jaguar for sale. We negotiated a price. He then asked who was going to drive it?

'I said at that stage I did not know and asked "Why, are you interested?" So, we renegotiated a lower price. I said [that] if he did not damage the car I would give him the balance of the full price at the end of the season. During 1980 he drove the car with success.'

Gerry did not damage the Costin Lister. Geoffrey takes up the story again: 'We were also running the Aston Martin DBR4 Grand Prix single-seater with another driver. At the end of the season I felt we needed a change of driver. Anthony Bamford [JCB] had brought out Stirling Moss to drive initially his 250F and later the Ferrari Dino.

'I decided to have a test at Goodwood at the end of the season and first of all had Mike Salmon down first thing in the morning. He circled for about 30 laps and achieved a best time of 1 minute 32 seconds.

'Then came Roy Salvadori (age 60) who was instantly in the 1 minute 30 second times.

'Gerry arrived at lunchtime and in the afternoon instantly achieved 1 minute 28 seconds. Roy said to me "Gerry's got to have the drive." Roy remained an ardent fan of Gerry's abilities in such thoroughbreds, and was extremely generous in his praise of later race outings from Gerry against proven historic racing aces like Willy Green.'

Geoffrey Marsh concluded with quiet understatement: 'I enclose a copy of our racing successes, which show Gerry as winning 61 races overall with other class wins that are not recorded.'

RIGHT *September
1980 and Gerry is out
in class-winning form
with Barry Simpson's
well-engineered Lister
Jaguar. The combination
finished fifth overall.
Gregor commented;
'This was the Lister
Dad raced to victory at
the last race at Crystal
Palace and now, in latter
years, it is the Lister
Coupé (WTM 466) raced
by Justin Law and Andy
Wallace.'* [John Gaisford]

BELOW *Although he
had entered a Dolomite,
Gerry took over Pete
Hall's Capri II at
Donington in April 1980
and raced it to second
overall with this classic
chicane attitude to
entertain us.*
[John Gaisford]

Marshall made 44 entries in 1979, and some of these were outside the usual Dolomite production and BTCC season, often bringing retirements or non-starts. Sadly this applied to the Lister Jags that appeared three times in Gerry's hands that season, only to score an equal number of retirements, whilst the Dollies did the business with 18 class wins.

However, there were Lister bright spots. In Gerry's first outing with the Equipe Esso-backed machine a troubled practice saw him qualify on the third row. *Motoring News* wrote of his race: 'He immediately darted up the pit wall [I don't think they mean he became a pedestrian! – JW] as the green light came on, taking third place at Copse behind Hoole and [Bobby] Bell. He gradually dropped down the order

with some engine malady, retiring to the pits after five laps of highly entertaining driving. Which had the crowd cheering wildly.'

A scheduled second appearance with the Lister was a non-starter because of Gerry's huge Dolomite accident at the Silverstone. A third scheduled Lister Jag appearance, at the supporting race to the September Silverstone TT, saw another non-start for Marshall in one of his favourite rides.

Just how strongly Gerry felt about the Listers was summarised for Walton in a 1999 interview covering Lister Jags that he had owned or raced for others in bewildering deals. Here is a typical example from the 1979–81 period: 'I owned my own Lister, one of the nicest, straightest, quickest of them all. I gave £5,000 for it, including the trailer. I sold it on for £22,500 and an additional £2,500 bonus if I raced it for the season without damaging it. Not only did I get the additional £2,500, but I also didn't have to sell the trailer,' Gerry exclaimed, with an expansive gust of laughter.

At the close of April Gerry was scheduled to reappear in the European Touring Car Championship, but the Jim Paterson-owned Camaro based in Scotland was absent after an unsuccessful test-day on the Friday. That left a period BMW walkover for the few Brands spectators present.

High-stress '80s

The 1980s would bring every financial and emotional stress known to modern racing man into Gerry's seesaw life. Financially it was pretty grim – Marshall Wingfield went out of business in the later '80s – and the formal partnership with Roger Dowson was dissolved. Marshall Asquith Racing was a respected race preparation specialist and entrant, but much of Gerry's trading from the late 1980s was without premises, or racing-based, with consequent shorter periods of stability as sponsors came and went.

There were also health issues, with a hernia to be operated on after it became painfully obvious at race meetings. Emotionally, Gerry was formally divorced from Carol in 1981, married Jenny in 1983 after having known her for 13 years, and was divorced from her by 1988. In 1984 he lost his driving licence for 18 months. Yet he raced – or entered others to race – throughout most of this turbulent decade, albeit missing out much of the 1984–5 seasons as a driver in consequence of his driving ban.

Jenny Cook had finally married Gerry on 16 February 1983. Looking back, she commented: 'It was hard for Gerry – and for us as a couple – through the '80s. I'd say money was one of the prime reasons we divorced. Just everything would go on racing, he would literally spend his last penny on the sport.' Jenny said this with a surprising lack of bitterness, as the Marshall family remember the couple quarrelling after Gerry spent cash sponsoring another driver that should have been used to settle an electricity bill!

The 1979 termination of the official Leyland-Dolomite deal was not the end for the Marshall-Dowson working relationship. Silverstone-based Dowson was a full partner in Gerry Marshall Racing, bringing all his workshop equipment and facilities to GMR, but the early 1980s were not a happy time for Roger. 'All I can really remember is working my balls off on too many cars to keep Gerry in racing from 1980 onward.'

Marshall had multiple production racing Capris. The first recalled by Roger was 'bought in from the rallycrosser, Hugh Wheldon. That was a 3-litre Essex V6 and our first test at Snetterton showed me why this car wasn't winning before, or doing the times we expected with Gerry driving. Basically it came down to the front springs getting coil bound, and we were able to sort that out and a few other problems reasonably quickly.'

Mk1 Jaguar – 'The National Debt'

In Autumn 2009, established racing entrant and former racer Pete 'ICS' Hall added this perspective on Marshall lore:

'Gerry had a fantastic Mk1 Jaguar (220 LPE) and the story was that it was Mike Hawthorn's car, ordered by Mike before his accident. It was a lovely car, very original, showing 4,000 miles on the clock.

'Like most of Gerry's favourite cars, it was the best in the world and wasn't for sale – but as it was me he'd let me have it!

'We agreed on a price, £9,000, which was a lot of money then. I said to Gerry I couldn't quite afford it, and he said "No problem, just give me some money every time I see you." So every Friday, I'd ask my secretary to raid the petty cash and give me whatever was in there, whether it be £10 or £200. I never checked, and she would hand it over in a brown envelope. I'd see Gerry at the track and I'd hand over the envelope … This quickly got the nickname "The National Debt"!

'Gerry never counted it in front of me, we just relied on my secretary to get it right. After a year of seeing Gerry almost weekly, I had paid for this car. It ended up in my Jaguar museum, still with Gerry's BRDC badge on it. That was part of its charm, even though it was frequently photographed for magazines and books, which would refer to the BRDC badge as being Mike Hawthorn's!

'Over the years I bought a few cars from Gerry and always found they were genuine cars. Sometimes the stories behind them weren't, but the actual cars were. I never had any problems with any of them and I don't think we ever even haggled on the price either.'

ABOVE *There were plenty of Willhire 24 hour races and podiums on the Marshall CV, but this Eric Cook owned Ford had the most co-drivers. Shared by Mark Thatcher, Cook, the Scarborough brothers and Gerry, the 3-litre Capri delivered front-row qualifying (No 10 closest camera) and went on to a second-place finish.*
[John Lakey]

Gerry started to win from the March 1980 off in that Capri for the Monroe and Wilcomatic Production Saloon championships. A later move to an ex-Ford press fleet freebie 2.8 injection model, backed by Autoplan Warranties, was not so well rewarded. As Roger recalled, 'That 2.8i injection Capri motor wasn't good for racing and Gerry started to get beaten by Graham "Skid" Scarborough in the older 3-litre. We did try Neal Brown [ace Lincolnshire engine builder] and I went back to a top-notch motor engineer then working at Ford. Neil could not get the power predicted out of the motor – and the Ford guy said it was no good for our purpose!' Reportedly the cylinder head was pretty hopeless, and, looking back, Roger felt that there was 'not enough water jacket around the heads either'.

That 2.8i lethargy afflicted all the top Capri teams, and the older 3-litre remains the best bet in classic events today. Semi-retired from 2007 onward, Roger Dowson recalled building 'a lot of Capris to pay for Gerry's racing from 1980 onwards. Then I was in my Unit 10 Silverstone premises, and we also worked on a Mk2 single-headlamp Capri and a twin-headlamp later one, plus many more for customers.'

Roger Dowson and Gerry parted in 1982, when Gerry formed Marshall Asquith with technician Richard Asquith. Roger revealed they had run a lot more than just Capris, and their association continued on an intermittent basis with a Lola T222 – 'Gerry beat John Foulston's mighty McLaren M8 in that,' said Roger with justified pride. Roger also recalled a Lister Jaguar that 'detonated itself to death'.

Dowson was the engineering force behind Colin Pearcy's E-type too, which Gerry was to share with the young Bobby Verdon Roe on one occasion in the 1990s.

1980

This season saw Gerry earning increasing professional respect as a supremely versatile racer. Competing in significantly less events (42) than his DTV heyday, Marshall's success rate soared, with nearly half the events he entered returning a class or outright victory. Those 19 victories were won in machinery varying from production racing Dolomites (eight wins) and Ford Capri (seven wins) to Historic racing Lister Jaguar (three wins). There was even a one-off victory in a BMW 3.0Si. Not so successful was a celebrity outing in a Fiesta (ninth overall), and a fourth recorded in Paul Everett's Commodore.

Gerry made it look too easy in the Lister for some tastes. Here's what *Motoring News* reported of his Lloyds & Scottish Championship outing at a wet Oulton Park in June. This quality event at the Cheshire venue was honoured by the presence of Stirling Moss, but spoiled by heavy rainfall. *MN* commented of Marshall's professional win: 'Gerry Marshall dominated the processional Lloyds & Scottish sports car race…His Marsh Plant Hire Lister Jaguar never challenged. It won at 72.9mph, headlamps blazing.'

The newspaper also noted that Gerry beat fellow Lister men Michael Bowler (twice European Champion) and Barry Simpson. Additionally, Gerry 'set the best lap time, equal to 73.87mph'. That report was signed by B.L.O.B., which JW recalls as Bill Boddy's pseudonym when writing for poor relations at *Motoring News*.

Another seasonal highlight was a second overall in the Willhire 24-hours with an astonishing variety of co-drivers. Backed by JJ Veneers, Eric Cook's 3-litre Capri was primarily assigned to Gerry, but was also steered by Mark Thatcher (mother Maggie had swept into office as Prime Minister the previous year), the Scarborough brothers Graham and Trevor, plus Jenny Cook's Dad, Eric.

In 2009 Jenny Cook described how 'I went with Gerry when he met up with Mark Thatcher in a restaurant in London to discuss arrangements for Mark to drive in our team. Mark actually drove OK at Snetterton, at least he kept it on the track! Mark went back to the hotel and was to return in the morning to do the last stint. However, we were in with a very good chance of winning and it was obvious we needed the quickest driver in the car.

'It was therefore decided that when Mark returned I should be the person to tell him that Gerry would be driving instead of him,' revealed Jenny. 'He actually took it very well!'

This assorted crew finished second, some two laps behind the winning Opel, although lap-scoring controversies and the demotion of a front-running VW marred those 1980 results.

For Gerry, one of *the* Snetterton memories was battling Stirling Moss in a Mayfair VW Scirocco that also featured Marshall mate Lanfranchi on board. That rapid VW managed to lead for much of the event, but was dropped out of contention by an accident for Big Tone and a Steward's post-race decision. Also in the star-studded entry list was 2009 BBC Grand Prix commentator Martin Brundle, racing a Toyota with Dad John and brother Robin.

Jenny added: 'I was renowned for my accurate timing skills in those days and I was convinced that we won the race. Unfortunately the officials didn't agree and placed us second.

'My brother Martin was a mechanic for my father's Capri in the team and he remembers Gerry

Accident at Oulton Park – and a show of emotion

Former saloon car racer and entrant Pete Hall recalled in 2009 that 'Oulton Park was one of my favourite circuits and I could be quite quick round there. We were running quite a professional team, to the point where we had different tread depths for different conditions. We had a tyre-cutting machine and about eight sets of new tyres with various levels of tread in the van.

'Practice had been wet and I hadn't judged the conditions, or the tyres, very well. I was down in seventh or eighth, with Gerry on pole – he was always a master in the wet.

'The race started, and I had chosen the right tyres. I made up positions left, right and centre, running third; Gerry was leading and Skid [Scarborough] was second.

'I caught Skid and got a run on him out of Lodge and dived down the inside of Old Hall to out-brake him. Skid took a wider line into Old Hall, as it was drier than the inside. As I went down the inside he moved over and watched me merrily aquaplane/understeer off the track and into the Armco on the outside of the track!

'I rolled once or twice and then slid down the middle of the circuit towards Cascades, still on my roof. No one collected me and I managed to undo my belts and run over to the marshal's post and recover.

'I was just getting my wind back when I saw Gerry. He'd seen the yellow flags and my blue car on its roof. Gerry-style, he slowed down, saw where he could park his car on the grass out of the way, undid his belts and leapt out of his moving car, which ended up perfectly parked!

'He sprinted over to my car shouting "Pete, Pete, don't panic, I'm coming!"

'Gerry dived in, only to find I wasn't in the car. He then shouted out for me. I'd sort of got my wind back and shouted "Over here, Gerry."

'He came running over. "Cor, I'm glad you're okay, Pete." He picked me up, bear-hugged me and started jumping up and down saying, "Pete, I'm so glad you're OK, you're my mate!"

'I'm not sure what winded and shocked me more, the accident or the show of emotion. It was a huge gesture by Gerry – he could easily have lost the race, as it hadn't been stopped at that point. Yet he was more concerned about his mate than the race.

'As an aside, the race was then stopped and given to Gerry on count-back – so it worked out OK in the end!'

LEFT *A sunny feeling. Participating in a high-speed parade in a thoroughbred single seater. Gerry takes a bow in the Marsh DBR4 in Dubai in December 1981, the meeting at which he won the Marlboro Cup Super Sports feature event with the Lola T70.* [LAT]

coming past the pits waving the gear stick out of the window. It had snapped off, but we were able to borrow another from a car in the car park!'

Graham Scarborough also told us about that second-place run in 2009: 'To be asked to be in the same team as Gerry Marshall, and with the Prime Minister's son in the team, well, it was a huge coup for me. Even to this day I still think we won the race – I know Jennifer is now part of my family, but back then she was not. She was well known for her timing.

'The main reason we got Jenny to tell Mark he couldn't do the final stint (other than the fact we were all too scared!) was that we knew we could win with Gerry in the car. I remember watching the prize-giving with Gerry, and they only let each class winner on to the podium. Gerry said something along the lines of "F—k me, we've driven our arses off and don't even get on the podium!"'

However, 1980 remained a fine Marshall season of consistent success.

1981

This was another rewarding year, especially in terms of prestige. After 48 race entries, Gerry had won three British championship titles – Lloyds & Scottish and both Production racing series, Monroe and Wilcomatic – plus the BARC President's Cup. Having proved himself virtually unbeatable in the Dowson-prepped Capri, with 24 confirmed wins and three possibles, the BARC Cup recognised not just an astonishing winning rate but also some fabulous victories with exotic classics. It was his most successful season for Geoffrey Marsh, with eight outright victories recorded, most in the Grand Prix single-seat Aston DBR4, but there were also two excellent wins in the Marsh Lola T70.

In the Aston Martin DBR4 of (Geoffrey) Marsh Plant Hire, Gerry scored six confirmed wins on the way to the Lloyds & Scottish title, including *the* supporting event of the season at the British GP, in which he blitzed a quality field. This is what he told Walton about that fabulous race 18 years later: 'I think some of the best memories are associated with Geoffrey Marsh and his racing collection, particularly the Aston GP car [DBR4]. We contested the Lloyds & Scottish title twice in the '80s, but I particularly remember a 1981 GP support event at Silverstone. The front row featured me in Geoffrey's Aston, Willie Green in the Ferrari Dino single-seater and Robs Lamplough in a P25 BRM.

'It turned into a wheel-to-wheel fight with Willie, with some nose-to-tail interludes. Even in GP cars you could hear the huge crowd shouting for more. That win was special, and so was Roy Salvadori's filmed comment on our performance in the '80s that we would not have disgraced ourselves in the Grands Prix of years ago.' Gerry said this with a warmth that suave Salvadori reciprocated and publicly acknowledged in respect for Gerry's driving capabilities.

A Lola T70 3b-Chevrolet V8 hurled Gerry past the chequered flag first in Dubai and at a later Silverstone. Like the Aston, this Lola was the property of Marsh Plant Hire, and like the Aston it was a pedigree winner. Gerry did have an early season retirement with the T70, but at Silverstone in October he was in majestic form. He swept the Lola to pole position, seconds faster than the talented John Brindley in an open T70 Spyder, and scored a second victory – not over Brindley, but over the fabled Ferrari 312P of leading Swiss-based collector Albert Obrist, which started from the back with a ten-second penalty.

For the self-styled Dubai GP, Gerry mopped up most publicity in a last-lap win with the Marsh Lola. This time John Brindley came armed with a mighty

LEFT AND BELOW
High point of the 1981 season was Gerry's hard-fought victory over Willie Green in the Lloyds & Scottish support races at the British GP, Silverstone. Here we see the winning Aston-Marshall combination.
[Both LAT]

Can-Am McLaren M1D, formerly property of John Foulston, the Atlantic Computers multi-millionaire. Andrew Marriott (A.R.M.) handled ITV *World of Sport*'s commentary, and wrote for *Motoring News*: 'At the start, Brindley got a flyer and Gerry gave hot chase. But the McLaren seemed faster on the straight and, though Gerry sneaked by on lap seven, he was immediately re-passed by Brindley. Going into the last lap the McLaren still led, but had a slight misfire. Gerry took full advantage of this and – as the flag dropped – was ahead by inches after a superb overtaking move.'

One Dubai story that remained a rumour, until Gregor and Jenny confirmed it in 2008, was the post-race party antics that so nearly cost Gerry his most prestigious and rewarding post-DTV drives. Jenny explained: 'After Gerry won the Marlboro Cup Race at the Dubai GP in 1981, he threw Geoffrey Marsh into the swimming pool! They didn't speak for ages after that. As time progressed, Geoffrey and Gerry grew to have a great mutual respect for each other.' Considering the atmosphere that must have followed that incident, Geoffrey Marsh was quite generous to allow Gerry some fabulous racing opportunities in the best of British machines.

By contrast, most Marshall Capri wins were easy and he occasionally resorted to hamming it up with Lanfranchi and Williams to entertain spectators. This happened at Thruxton, where he also drove a Sunbeam Talbot hatchback in a Celebrity thrash and finished second in a torrid event to Formula 3 hot shoe Tommy Byrne. *Motoring News* had an outstanding reporter at the June scene in Michael Lawrence. He not only dryly observed how Byrne took the lead from Gerry by cutting a corner out on the grass, but also explained that 'Although Stirling Moss's lap record remained intact, three other records were set. The most cars going side by side into the chicane (five); the most cars going side by side into the complex (three), while the car having least wheels on the ground and still getting around the corner (one) fell to Nick Baughn.'

Gerry was scheduled to appear in an AMX Pacer (think glassy alien blob) with former British BMW competition manager and Lotus 30 driver John Markey. Unsurprisingly, they did not make the Silverstone start in the undeveloped US import, which was probably a Good Thing.

1982

At 31 races entered and 14 confirmed wins, this was a shorter season than most Marshall campaigns. Again, the 3.0 Capri was the backbone for Gerry's results, recording seven wins, but he also ran the Autoplan/Ford-backed 2.8i version, which was just not so quick as the obsolete 3-litre.

Glamour choice of the year was a Lotus Esprit Turbo carrying the Hethel factory registration OPW 679W. It reportedly came direct from the film set of *For Your Eyes Only*, a Roger Moore 'Bond' movie. Its role was apparently as a sister to the star's, in blue rather than the metallic plum of the Bond Esprit (OPW 678W), which featured ski racks. The movie's other Esprit outline (OPW 654W) suffered an explosive Bondesque termination. The Marshall Lotus can now be seen at the Haynes Motor Museum in Somerset, painted black, complete with incongruous rollcage within the luxurious rolls of leather trim, plus BBS wheels and race suspension.

Gerry scored another second overall placing in the annual Willhire Snetterton 24-hours, this time with a late substitute vehicle. Teamed with Scotsmen Hamish Irvine, John Clarke and Andrew Jeffries, Gerry shared an ex-BMW County Championship 323i in a race that attracted just 20 entries and was dominated by a fast and light Morgan Plus 8. Interviewed in a rowdy bar, Marshall was complimentary about the 2.3-litre BMW's reliability and pace, and raced a 323i again in 1983.

Speaking half an hour before the finish of the 1982 day-and-night race's conclusion, Gerry made some intelligent comments on the state of saloon car racing and the lack of manufacturer support at this level. Barracked by the other occupants of Snetterton's crowded bar, he explained: 'This car was a last minute deal and I'm very impressed with the BMW, it's run flawlessly. I doubt if I've driven 40 non-British cars in all the races I have done, but this one has been good as gold over the 24 hours – and it's only being beaten by a 3.5-litre hybrid sports car.' Incidentally, Gerry added little to that foreign-car total to 2005.

The charismatic Lola T222 thundered Gerry to a brace of outright wins, and he netted an AMOC award for his 4 DTV-registered Aston Martin V8. Gregor recalled in May 2009: 'That concours trophy was for Dad's road car, which meant a deal with Aston boss, the late Victor Gauntlet. Dad had an immaculate red DB6, registered 666 DTV, which was his pride and joy, appearing in various mags and calendars. Victor saw it, and wanted it. So they did a deal and Dad bought the ex-press V8 Oscar India and put his 4 DTV plate on it.

'That V8 was Dad's pride and joy for nearly 20 years. I remember I was never allowed to wear a seat belt in it: no one was, you might wear them out! Dad would occasionally remind us what he could do in a car with the V8 … And as a memory of Dad, the V8 was always his car; it always smelt of leather and cigars. He always managed to thrill [I think that's a polite word for scare! – JW] us all in it.'

To illustrate the point, Gregor showed Walton a local Hertfordshire lane with narrow chicane and sturdy steel poles that threaten slim saloons. 'Dad used to come through here full bore – how he got

the Aston through unscratched I'll never know,' muttered Gregor, this as Walton trickled gingerly between the poles at 15mph in a Mini.

Another Aston connection was a class win in the extraordinary Aston V8-engined Viva that neighbouring farmer John Pope tenaciously and ingeniously constructed from the wreckage of a Lydden Viva.

Most prestigious event of the 1982 season was an outing in the supporting event to the Brands Hatch GP. In searing heat, the 'immaculately restored' Lola T222 of Nigel Gibbs proved a bit of an unknown quantity on its Marshall-Dowson debut, snapping an elderly throttle cable in practice. Gerry described it as 'magic to drive' and finished fourth overall, second in class, after a ferocious scrap with Nigel Hulme (Lola T70) and Ted Williams in the monstrous March 707 Can-Am car. Ray Mallock (Lola T70) won after Mike Wilds led in a Can-Am rarity, the BRM P154. Mike spun off when plagued with mechanical hassles.

Gerry tackled two more HSCC Atlantic

BELOW *Just singing in the rain! Record runner 3.0 Capri in 1981 with (left to right), David da Costa, Tony Lanfranchi, Graham Scarborough and Gerry. They took an ICS award for their speed during 2000 Snetterton kilometres over 24 hours. It was the last time the older, longer circuit was used. Gerry and this Autoplan-backed Ford won 27 times in production races, making it one of the most successful cars over a season that Gerry ever campaigned.* [LAT]

ABOVE *Respect! There were many epic 1982–83 production saloon battles like this Mallory Park hairpin Capri confrontation between Gerry (car No 1) and Graham Scarborough. Ford support for Gerry's 2.8i did not help it overcome the older 3-litre used by Graham (and Gerry for previous seasons), so the Marshall monopoly on Capri class wins was broken.* [John Gaisford]

Computers rounds in September and won both, outright. At Oulton Park only five cars took the grid, but the quality was high with Foulston and Ted Williams in quick Can-Am machinery that Gerry cantered away from in the T222. The later September date at Brands Hatch brought a more convincing 11 big bangers out to contest the Atlantic race, part of that computer leasing company's own race day. Gerry had the Lola working well from his usual prompt start, although he had to trail Foulston in one of Can-Am's most successful cars – McLaren M8D – until the second lap. Marshall was never headed and set the fastest lap around the shorter Brands Indy circuit at a giddy 46.6 seconds/92.98mph.

Gerry did not drive the emotive Lotus Esprit until autumn, but continued to rack up results with it in 1983. Dubbed the 'Bond Lotus', it was inherited from a Pete Hall-financed, Andy Rouse-built project to race an Esprit in the production sports cars category under Industrial Control Services sponsorship from Hall. ICS boss Hall did drive it, but was persuaded to let Gerry out in it too. The Lotus suffered from excess weight and the inboard location of rear disc brakes, which were hard to cool.

Gerry bought the Lotus the following season, to celebrate his wedding to Jenny on 16 February 1983. The smart black car was already extensively modified to meet the challenges of the race circuit. It featured a Rayvic-modified 2.2-litre turbo yielding 270 horsepower.

Gerry commented that 'it won every time it finished,' but sometimes this could be a fiery experience!

The first race for Gerry and the Lotus that we have logged was a supporting production sports and saloons event to the Shell Oils 1,000-kilometres at Brands Hatch on the weekend of 16–18 October. It poured down and Gerry couldn't stay with Big Tony Lanfranchi in the Porsche 924 Carrera GT, despite setting pole. However, he did secure a strong second place, so assertively that he was hit with 'naughty boy' flags for using unauthorised parts of the circuit!

Gerry got his revenge almost exactly a month later at Brands when he won overall with the Lotus. At a typically British 'clubby' that was terminated when bad light on a damp day curtailed the programme, Gerry was in his element – and so was the ICS Motorsport Esprit. Marshall scored a flag-to-finish win. He set fastest lap at 56 seconds (77.37mph), whilst the main Morgan opposition fell away.

This 21 November result was sufficient encouragement for Gerry to get financially involved with the Lotus for the following season. Gerry had also made a friend who would trade race-drives and cars through the next 23 years: builder and property developer Colin Pearcy. He was an avid MG collector and owned one of three fabled iterations of the Jaguar E-type registered CUT 7 – not the chassis that Gerry had tested back in the '60s, but still a legendary mount.

1983

Although this 44-entry season looked normal by Gerry Marshall's enthusiastic standards, it would end in turmoil on public roads when Gerry lost his road licence for 18 months in a post-Beaujolais wine run incident during November. For details, see the sidebar 'After the wine stopped flowing' on page 162.

However, there were also celebrations on- and off-track, with his pre-season marriage to Jenny, plus 16 class or outright victories backed up by second places in the charismatic classic Lister Jaguar and Lola T222.

Gerry reverted to previous tradition and started the season early with a February outing at Brands Hatch for the Chiltern Circle & Harrow Car Club sprint. This time he deployed a VW Scirocco that had already tackled the Snetterton 24-hours and enjoyed a 1,600cc class win some nine days before his second marriage.

Now prepared by Marshall Asquith Racing, Ford Capris took the majority of Gerry's 1983 results. There were a dozen class or outright wins

and he took the Monroe production saloon car championship again. For this season the Fords regularly appeared in Chelmsford Car Auctions or London Martin Construction colours. Gerry also scored a Monroe win in Eric Cook's Capri at Snetterton and a second overall result for the Uniroyal series in loyal friend Martin Mulchrone's Capri at the same Norfolk venue.

Now owned by Gerry, the ex-factory ICS Esprit worked harder. It appeared in both BRDC and Uniroyal races open to production sports cars. That campaign started in March and saw the first outright win for the Lotus-Marshall duo in late June. Racing around the Brands Indy layout, Gerry qualified quickest and won the ten-lap event at a canter from Tony Dron in that year's Willhire-winning Porsche 928. This Uniroyal result was ironically recorded at a GM Dealer-sponsored meeting before 2,000 corporate guests. There was the added satisfaction of beating the only proper GM car in the race, Lanfranchi in the Mayfair Opel.

The Esprit took Gerry to three wins this season in just seven outings, and promoted him to fifth overall in the Uniroyal series. Published legend

BELOW *'Magic to drive,' was Gerry's verdict on this beefy Can Am challenger. The Lola 222-Chevrolet V8 was wheeled out for a GP-supporting Atlantic Computers event at Brands Hatch in July 1982. Gerry was fourth overall, second in class this time, but took two wins with the Ian Gibbs Lola during the season.* [Chris Davies]

RIGHT AND BELOW
*Glamorous choice in
1982 was this ex-factory
Lotus Esprit. Originally
campaigned by Pete
Hall in ICS colours
with Andy Rouse
preparation, Gerry took
it over and had some
success with it between
fiery outbursts. The car,
not Gerry! Today it lives
in the Haynes Motor
Museum in the black
coat of paint it adopted
after Gerry's ownership.
Our second picture is
of Mr Marshall bullying
a moped (shades of his
teenage years) outside
Snetterton scrutineering
bay. The guy on the
right with an ICS Esprit
T-shirt is Peter Hall.*
[Both Marshall Family
Archive]

has it that Gerry won a race with the Lotus at
Silverstone, even after a pit stop to put out a
small fire. We haven't been able to confirm that,
although we did find one July weekend at Brands
Hatch where Marshall won the prodsport race

comfortably against the Porsches of Lanfranchi
(928) and Colin Blower (911). On the same day,
Marshall was demoted to sixth from third in the
Capri after a jostling match with Tony in the Opel
and illicit use of the Paddock Hill Bend slip road!

Over the weekend of 6–7 August, Gerry won
a Uniroyal round with the Lotus at Oulton Park,
setting a record lap after having practised *two
seconds faster* than the nearest Porsche 911. That
was Saturday. By Sunday he was out in a Capri
brawling around Lydden with the Lanfranchi Opel
again. The best mates/worst of enemies finished
third and fourth (Marshall ahead this time), whilst
their race was won by ex-pat Kiwi Norris Miles – a
valued contributor to this book – in an Alfa GTV.

The Lola notched up a second and two
retirements. That second overall was around the
full-length Silverstone circuit, where Foulston's
McLaren M8D could gallop energetically into the
early October distance. Sadly the Capri was not on
form that day and sank to a fourth in class finish.

At the annual Willhire 24-hours Gerry failed
to equal his previous hat-trick of second places.
Sharing with Andrew Jeffries, Eric Cook, and Martin
Mulchrone, the injection Capri with Gerry aboard
certainly fought for second place in the opening
laps, but sadly it demanded a fuel tank in the third
hour and that lengthy job demoted them outside
the top six finishers. They did, nevertheless, record
a third in their competitive class.

1984–5

The November 1983 post-Beaujolais run incident
(see page 162) dominated these seasons, as

Gerry fought legal battles for as long as possible to preserve his licence. Inevitably there were repercussions on the way he did business and participated in racing during 1984 and 1985. Just 24 entries were logged in 1984, and some of these called for further research on our part. What we can see clearly is that the majority of entries came between March and August 1984, with no personal race appearances at all in 1985 and just five class or outright wins in 1984.

It was during this period that Marshall Asquith Racing became prominent as backers of promising drivers, such as the phenomenally fast Karl Jones (Fiat Abarth TC and Escort Turbo), former Mini racer Barbara Cowell and others.

The Capri 2.8i kicked off Gerry's personal '84 results with a win at the traditional February Brands sprint. His first drive in friend Colin Pearcy's machinery saw a 3.9-litre MGB GT V8 return a clear win. This triumph came over two Porsches around the Silverstone club layout during a March Intermarque Saturday event. On Sunday, Gerry was at Silverstone again, fulfilling his GM Dealer contract, fielding one of three competitive Opel Monza 3-litres: Lanfranchi and future double BTCC champion John Cleland drove the others. Gerry fought the punchy turbo Colt Starion of Colin Blower throughout, sneaking ahead on occasion but finally finishing second ahead of Cleland and Big Tone.

Most Marshall race miles came in 19 events in a Kendal Computing-backed Opel Monza, gaining him a wooden trophy as a seasonal reward! There were no other trophies in 1984–5. The three wins with the Monza all came in April, but it was

a consistent front-runner for Gerry's abbreviated Monroe season. Spring came in with a vengeance for Gerry that season, featuring another April win, this time in a Celebrity Escort XR3i.

At the Willhire there was no result. There was no way anything but the late Bill Taylor's 'Bandit'-plated Porsche 911 was going to win – by a staggering 17 laps!

An extreme '80s Mini fan writes…

Alastair Mayne is the top tech magician for Graham Good Racing (GGR) in Leicester. He is renowned for his hard-headed track and street expertise on full-house Subarus and Focus RS, via the inevitable Sierra Cosworth generations.

He revealed an unexpected affection…

'Gerry was always my hero, being a Vauxhall fan from an early age. So much so that, when I raced a Mini Se7en (in 1982–3), I painted it Vauxhall Starfire Silver (the Droop Snoot Firenza colour) with a red roof. I even fitted a Griffin badge to the bonnet. As a joke I wrote "Vauxhall" as the engine make on entry forms!

'At a Modified Saloon Car race at Mallory, there were only two cars in the up to 1,000cc class, so I was guaranteed second-place prize money. I remember Gerry was racing at the same meeting. I took my mate, who'd spannered for me, to the clubhouse for a beer after the meeting. Gerry was there in the bar, surrounded by an entourage, telling stories.

'I really thought I'd made the big time. Not only was I racing at the same event, but now I was also drinking in the bar "with" my hero.

'The last time I saw Gerry was at the *Autosport* Show a few years ago. He was in typical pose, sitting in the bar with an entourage around him, hanging on every word whilst he was telling stories.

'He was a truly big man in every sense, in and out of the car. His personality just overtook whatever he was doing, or wherever he was.'

OPPOSITE, ABOVE AND BELOW *A truly versatile professional. Gerry at work in successive March 1984 weekends at Silverstone. Above in Colin Pearcy's MGB GT V8 on the way to an outright win among the Morgans. The equally professionally presented No 1 Opel Monza, streaming past the old BRDC clubhouse, was third on the sodden track.* [Both John Gaisford]

Following an eighth place qualification at the usual Snetterton venue, Gerry and teammates Roger Clark, Sean Walker, and late recruit David Sears got off to a reasonable start: Gerry held eighth in the opening hour with Lanfranchi for company in another Monza.

The Monza's front tyres couldn't stand the pace with Sears at the wheel, and it became the race's first retirement as the wounded machine slammed the barriers at the challenging Coram swerve. It had completed 157 laps, versus the winning total of 952.

1984–5 was not all grim reality, however. Racing compatriot and friend until the end of Gerry's days John Llewellyn recalled: 'In 1984 I was an official GM Dealer Team driver along with Terry Nightingale, Gerry, Tony Lanfranchi and John Cleland – Gerry only for part of the season, as he lost his driving licence and Andrew Jeffries took over.

'At the last Snetterton round, after the race and

Time for another…

'After a big accident, at Snetterton in a March Sports 2000,' John Llewellyn told us in 2008, 'I decided that saloons might be safer, so I went and bought Tony Lanfranchi's VW Scirocco from Gerry Marshall Racing, and had it prepared by Eddie Jordan.

'After practice for a 1982 prod saloon race at Oulton Park, we all went down the pub in Little Budworth. It was a summer's day and the pints were going down.

'Tony Lanfranchi looks at his watch and says, "Christ, it's 1:45 and our race starts at 2!" Gerry looks around the bar, and replies, "Well most of us are here and they can't start without us, so we may as well have another pint," which we did.

'Arriving back at the circuit we were in deep trouble, our cars waiting for us in the collecting area, engines running. On to the grid, I'm on the third row, on my left is Tony, and the three-minute board is displayed. I look at Tony and he's licking an ice cream…

' I look forward, and there's Gerry, belts undone and having a piss against the Armco…'

in the bar, Bill Cleland [John's formidable Dad – JW] was there as our GM Dealer Team manager. Gerry said how upset he was not being able to race because he had no licence. Jeffrey then told us he had no licence either. I then announced that I too had lost mine!'

Gerry observed that Bill's good eye spun round 'like a Catherine wheel'!

LEFT *Originally captioned 'that famous rear end,' an affectionate portrait of Gerry investigating the Marshall Asquith Racing Fiat Abarth Strada 130TC after it had been heavily kerbed. The Marshall posterior is accompanied by kerbing offender Eric Cook and Martin Cook. In the background (right of van doors) is preparation specialist Richard Asquith chatting to Karl Jones (red jacket). Karl drove the fast Fiat and became a star performer.* [Jenny Cook]

CHAPTER 12

1986–9: The roller coaster ride revived

During the second half of the '80s, Gerry's life remained as colourful as ever. Jenny remembered: 'Gerry was a real wheeler-dealer and loved to clinch a good car deal, but on one occasion he branched into property. We were at a concert in Drayton Beauchamp church, which wasn't really Gerry's cup of tea. During the interval, he got chatting to a local builder and by the end of the concert had bought an almost derelict house in Pitstone! It needed a lot of work, but we moved in during December 1986.'

Gerry's later life saw less time roistering around bars and restaurants with his racing mates. Jenny commented: 'Gerry had a great reputation for drinking but rarely drank at home unless we had visitors. We had a cabinet full of drink, which was years old. He was very much a social drinker, thankfully.' Gregor added that 'I only saw Dad drink at home twice, and one of those times was with me!'

There were some quieter moments. Jenny explained that Gerry 'had this fantastic book collection. I could also ask him to spell any word from the dictionary and he always got it right.'

Though they were divorced in 1988, Jenny and Gerry stayed in contact right up to the time of his death.

LEFT *Comeback 1986 season. Gerry in full-lock Thruxton practice action with the Teroson-backed Monza. He qualified second overall, but was unable to start the race.* [John Gaisford]

ABOVE *This last-corner side-by-side session at Castle Combe, with the Istel Rover of Marshall protégé, BTCC Champion and 2009 ITV commentator Tim Harvey, yielded a fourth-in-class result.* [John Gaisford]

After Jenny, Gerry swiftly married Penny Dealey, who says he 'bowled me over, head over heels in love'. She had a son (Ben) by a previous marriage, a teenager of much the same age as Gregor. Though by 1995 this marriage would also be annulled, Penny retained warm memories of their time together when we spoke to her, 14 years after that final divorce. She pointed out that 'I'm still the only one of the former Mrs Marshalls who kept the surname!'

How did Penny and Gerry meet? 'We met through friends who owned some land where people – including Jenny – kept horses,' she told us in 2009. 'It was something of a whirlwind affair from February of '89 to May. Then we split up, because Jennifer was back on the scene. But by

November of that year we were married. Gerry always wanted to be married to his loves and, Jennifer apart, I was not convinced that he was the great womaniser of his reputation, at least not to my knowledge, during our time together.'

After his eventual divorce from Penny, Gerry spent the late '90s living alone. He had a few girlfriends but kept them at arm's length, then spent the final five years of his life in the new millennium with 'constant companion' Gwen Howard, about whom more in later chapters.

Although Gerry enjoyed supporting the efforts of Jenny's father Eric Cook it was no substitute for being behind the wheel himself. It was in the

RIGHT *Gerry racing happily with protégé Patrick Watts (Fiat Uno Turbo) in pursuit at the Mallory hairpin, prior to a major incident.* [Alan Cox]

Fiat Abarth registered C29 FBH that Gerry made his 1986 comeback, appearing at the traditional February Brands Hatch sprint organised by the Harrow & Hampton Car Club, with snow still laying trackside. The Brands Fiat result for Gerry was another class win, one of five class or outright victories taken in 1986, each with a different car.

Motoring News commented: 'The Fiat Strada Abarth in Gerry Marshall's hands is a pretty quick beast and the "Big Fella" (2m 12.8s) had little trouble in mopping up the 2-litre class after his enforced lay off.'

Through the mid-'80s, Gerry also entered and backed former single-seater ace Karl Jones and Barbara Cowell, who came from front-running in Minis. In 1985 they used a powerful but wayward 2.0 Fiat Abarth 130 TC. Another Marshall driver who joined his 1986 production racing stable was former Mini and Metro top man Patrick Watts, who usually steered a peppy Fiat Uno Turbo,

Gerry's 1986 winners in 35 outings were headed by an Opel Monza prepared by his Marshall Asquith team, backed by Teroson. Then there was an Escort XR3i in a celebrity race – and big brother RS Turbo Escort racked up another GM win (this Ford – B276 XVX – is pictured in Walton's book *RS Fords*). Marshall also took an unidentified classic Lotus Cortina to a fine result at Oulton Park, overtaking a Mustang V8 on the way to win for entrants Pipeline Induction in the pre-'65 event.

ABOVE *The Opel Monza was regularly replaced from June 1986 onward with this Escort Turbo, an ex-Ford Motor Company press vehicle. Still backed by Teroson, the fierce Karl Ford was usually well placed in its class and won on occasion, but also suffered its share of retirements.*
[John Gaisford]

One of the most satisfying wins came in the Easter Brands Celebrity race. As rain and hail greeted a quality field in near-showroom XR3i Escorts, Gerry was in his element and 'Marshall drove serenely to the flag', according to a contemporary account. Strong opposition included rallycross winner Graham Hathaway, who gave Gerry's regular Abarth driver – the promising Karl Jones – a shove into the ditch on the way. Result, Gerry wins, Karl fourth – but Jones set fastest lap.

Talking to us after a day race-instructing at Thruxton in July 2009, Karl had warm memories of Gerry's generosity and humour. From 1984 to 1986 the Big Man backed Karl's promising career in the Fiat and Escort Turbo, both of which won Production Championships after some hair-raising outings. Driving Gerry to his regular role as a BMW Day instructor in one of the many Marshall Jags also stuck in Karl's mind.

The Opel was Marshall's most regular '86 mount, with 14 appearances in production races up until June. Then an Escort RS Turbo, also running Teroson sponsorship in both Uniroyal and Monroe championships, replaced it. The large Opel Monza coupé was strong and reliable, but its aged straight-six was simply outpaced by an incoming turbo generation.

In the UK, Mitsubishi Colt with BF Goodrich sponsorship pioneered the Starion's turbo coupé speed, as did old Marshall mate Andy McLennan and respected rival 'Skid' Scarborough. Ford had a turbo Sierra coming, but for 1986 that winner would not be homologated until later in the season. Many Blue Oval runners opted for the baby

brother Escort RS, which won the 1986 Willhire 24-hours.

Ah yes, the Willhire. Though JW wrote how reliable the Monza was, it consistently let Gerry down in the 24-hour hardy annual. Walton drove a Sierra 4x4, gambling on rain – and it was the sunniest edition yet! The chance to observe Gerry's participation first-hand was reduced to watching running repairs, as the Opel suffered an overheated engine. An overnight cylinder head replacement saw the Monza stuttering into the race half a lap behind.

Sharing with Tony Lanfranchi and Ian 'Formula 3' Khan, *Motoring News* reported: 'Marshall had been causing a few missed heartbeats as he roared through the field, but his fun was curtailed by clutch trouble, which eventually ended the car's race after Tony Lanfranchi briefly took over only to pronounce the car undrivable.'

Gerry's only compensation was that the Marshall Asquith Fiat Abarth, with Jones/Watts and John Llewellyn aboard, performed magnificently. From a class pole position, the now *Autocar*-backed Fiat romped through the field, holding third overall in the night and improving to a fabulous second in the morning. Sadly, a split fuel tank delayed them badly, and a collision occurred within sight of the finishing line. They finally finished ninth overall – creditable, but not the same as their top three pace could have delivered.

By the end of the season, Karl had scooped up the Monroe production saloon car title for himself and Marshall Asquith, Gerry's second British championship as an entrant. This Fiat was a credit to former Ford Competitions Centre technician Richard Asquith, his preparation notably superior to less reliable rival Abarths.

A single outing in the glorious Marsh Plant Aston DBR4 around Silverstone Club for the St John Horsfall meeting brought a fourth overall.

Gerry was out in the established RAC Tourist Trophy in September, but in an unfamiliar small class Toyota Corolla 16-valve. The Japanese coupé was shared with owner Geoff Kimber Smith. It qualified third in class but was in trouble as the race started, fuel leaking from the tank, and soon became a retirement.

A brace of interesting classic rides came Gerry's way in late September. In the HSCC John Scott Endurance Race over 50 Snetterton laps he took an eighth position finish in Colin Pearcy's MGB, but we could not find a result for the other posted outing in a Sunbeam Tiger.

Into October, and Gerry had an exceptionally competitive car to share in a four-hour production saloon endurance event at Donington. Old Capri

rival Graham 'Skid' Scarborough had opted for a Mitsubishi Starion in 1986, and it was planted firmly on pole for this new event. Graham led off, and headed the race securely for the first two hours. Just after the halfway mark, Gerry took over the turbo coupé and led all the way – then this happened. We quote from a contemporary *Motoring News* report: 'With a few minutes left to run, the leader did not come past the pits. Marshall had suffered terminal brake fade at the Old Hairpin and put the Starion into the wall.'

Some 23 years later, Gregor talked to Graham Scarborough, who became part of the extended Marshall family after having married Jennifer's cousin, Lindy, and Gregor asked him about this heartbreaking Donington incident, which was still emblazoned in Scarborough's memory. Animatedly, Graham said, 'I really could have killed him that day! We'd qualified fastest and we knew we were a little marginal on brakes and fuel. I calculated we had two hours ten minutes' fuel, so when I came in at two hours to hand over

Norris Miles, a New Zealander who spent 28 years in the UK, arrived as a motor racing champion at home and ran two motor trade businesses from the late '70s into the '90s. In 2009, in a series of phone conversations – often made in the early hours of the NZ morning – he let us have this appreciation of racing against Gerry, up close and very personal.

Norris first met Gerry at a Snetterton production race (probably in 1978), where Gerry was sharing paddock space with Jenny and Eric Cook. 'I thought I was a bit of a gun in my 3-litre Capri, but I hadn't even buffed the tyres down. In practice, I think I'm going pretty quickly into the slowest right-hander, slipping and sliding with a bit of opposite on. Then, *BANG*, I get hit quite hard up the rear by Gerry.

'Afterwards he comes up to me acting all aggrieved. Asks me, "What did you run into me for?"

'Now I'm the new kid on the block and I'm not sure what this bloke is all about, but I can see the three-inch dent on the back. I had it signwritten *Gerry Marshall* and it stayed on for a few more races until I had a bigger accident. Gerry obviously hated it, because he came up to me after the larger crash and said, "I'm glad that sign's gone!"

'Gerry was pretty aggressive on or off the track, and he didn't need to be. Gerry was a very special person, literally head and shoulders above the rest. Trouble was he got nasty sometimes with people who could help him, and that didn't help his career.

'Sometimes Gerry's performance was so dominant that the rest of us may as well have gone home. I arrived at Thruxton one day for a meeting in driving rain. On track for practice, it seemed that Hamish Irvine and I, in Opel Commodores, were the fastest out there. We were drafting each other in the wet at what seemed like a quick pace. Exiting the complex after the pits, Hamish had just slipped past me. I was tucked in behind when I noticed – over my right shoulder – a tidal wave approaching from behind. A couple of corners later, the wave became Gerry in a plain white Capri. He passed me almost immediately and took Hamish around one of the fast sweepers. We tried to stay with him but he drove off into the distance.

'Gerry was a master in the wet, or when things got difficult. On a dry day, on a circuit they knew, a good driver could match him, but as soon as the going got tough, nobody could match him.

'He was also the consummate racer and a difficult man to have on your tail – like a terrier. At Silverstone, when I was in the Capri, I was passed by the very fast and well-prepared BMW 3.0Si owned by Macmillan's grandson. Gerry was up ahead in the Dolly and the BMW hauled him in. But Gerry wasn't having any; he absolutely stuffed the BMW guy's race. Even when the BMW went

to Gerry and refuel we definitely had enough to reach the end, never mind our lap-and-a-half lead. I had noticed for the last 15 minutes the brakes were going off, and I did have to pump the pedal a little.

'I told Gerry, "Just be careful with the brakes."

'Gerry drove a great stint, extended our lead to two laps but, with about 30 minutes to go I could see he was having to press the brake pedal halfway down the straight into Redgate … With less than ten minutes to go, he decided to overtake old Piggy Thompson (James Thompson's father) round the outside of the Craners. Gerry was off-line into the Old Hairpin and just went straight off into the gravel and the barriers.

'I just couldn't believe it. The £500 prize money would have settled a load of bills for me, as the most I'd ever won was £30 to £40 – so it was a big amount! Luckily, there was little damage to the car, but I was so annoyed with him. But then I'm sure Gerry was probably more annoyed with himself than anyone else could have been,' concluded Graham generously.

1987

Results for this year were harder to clarify, with just 26 entries able to be confirmed and three more under investigation. We know there were six wins, three of them outright in the Aston DB4 registered 455 YYC that Gerry drove five times in the course of the season.

That Aston had an astonishing history, as recalled by Gregor: 'The first Aston Martin that Dad raced for Geoffrey Marsh and Marsh Plant Hire was rescued from the bottom of a quarry. They had been looking for a DB4 for some time – even in 1992 DB4s were still very valuable. Dad managed to get wind of a wrecked DB4 at the bottom of a working quarry in Denham. So one sunny day Dad and I set off for the quarry near Harefield [Middlesex] to try and locate the car.

'Dad took his Mercedes Benz diesel estate places where it should not be able to go, including overtaking several massive caterpillar construction vehicles in the mud. After more driving around, he actually asked a couple of the workers if they

past, Gerry fought back, hurtling into Woodcote with all four wheels on the grass, lights on, right up with the BMW: it just couldn't get away, with Gerry biting at its back bumper. Even though it had proved capable of lapping 1.5 seconds a lap faster than any of us, the BMW still finished with the Marshall Dolomite all over it, the guy obviously scared to death of Gerry's antics.

'Everyone said his car control was fantastic, but not many were there at close quarters to see *how* fantastic. I was drafting him at Snetterton once, both of us tucked up oh-so-close in Capris. Slipstreaming along the back straight, an Alfasud spun right in front of Gerry. I thought, "This is it – I'm going to see Marshall have a real big accident."

'Gerry goes this way and that – virtually loops the loop – turns the Ford sideways and ploughs along on the grass and muck on the way into the right at the end of the straight. Jesus! I don't how he did it, but eventually the poor old Ford slews back from the outside spraying muck and bullets everywhere – and Gerry's back in the race!

'Gerry Marshall was an absolutely and total special case. His talents and his personality were such that he simply and undeniably *made* club racing in the UK.

'I was very, very, sad to hear of his passing.'

ABOVE AND BELOW *A tale of two TVRs. Gerry reunited with the marque which established his reputation outside saloon cars. The 420SEAC (above) fielded by David Gerald Sportscars gets some last minute attention in 1987. Below, Gerry stands by the Tuscan 4.5-litre, also entered by David Gerald, in 1989. This was twice a winning TVR for Gerry in 1989 and secured outright podium places that season.* [Both Marshall Family Archive]

knew anything about the possible whereabouts of the car. Eventually one of the older guys said there were the remains of a car at the bottom of one of the quarries. But it was "virtually unreachable" and definitely wasn't salvageable.

'Eventually, peering right over the edge of a 90-foot drop, I spotted a couple of tyres poking up through some brambles. Now it was a case of working out how to get to it. Due to my small size at the time, I led the chase through the brambles. After an hour of getting through about 1,000 metres of rough stuff, I set eyes on this upside down wreck of a car.

'On closer inspection the car had been painted red but was now a little bit rusty and singed round the edges. It had been used in a Hammer House of Horrors film. The engine and gearbox had been removed and it had a petrol-filled oil drum inserted in the cabin. This was remotely detonated when the car was pushed off the cliff as part of the film.

'The Aston had lain at the bottom of the quarry for some 20 years. As Geoffrey Marsh owned Marsh Plant, he managed to get one of his large cranes there the following week, when it was winched out from that resting place.

'The task ahead looked enormous, but Geoffrey got to work. After several months of hard work by all those at Marsh Plant, the car was finally ready for a Brands Hatch debut. Even though the Aston was still in primer, my Dad stormed off into the lead and was a good ten seconds in front first time out. With only a couple of laps to go he pulled over on the bottom straight, because he'd run out of fuel!

'Geoffrey made sure this never happened again!

'In some ways this was a good test session for the team, as the race probably had come a little too soon, so it was off to Silverstone for round two of the AMOC Thoroughbred series and to try again. Dad was his usual flamboyant self – and quick. He put the car on pole, and led from start to finish.'

We should pay tribute here, incidentally, to loyal Marsh racing engineers Martin Bachelor and Chris Lawman, who wrought miracles on the fabulously varied Marsh Plant Astons that Gerry conducted over so many seasons.

There were more fine classics for 1987, including a Ferrari GTO for three days on the 25th Anniversary Cavallino International Rally, for which a small silver trophy was awarded. Gerry took a 1,840cc MGB, plus another similar B (registered 189 DMO), and appeared nine times in that brace of Bs during the season. The most popular of Abingdon's MG classics became a potent performer – and often a commercial deal success – for Gerry over the years.

In 1999 Gerry related these '80s MG motor trader tales for Walton to retell in *Classic & Sports Car*. 'I heard an owner cursing his luck with a B that I had raced successfully. When the owner-driver said "If it breaks down again this afternoon, I'll sell it," a disorderly queue of traders assembled. The MGB duly broke down again: Gerry muscled to the head of the queue and grabbed it at a well-haggled £8,000. Just three days later it resold at £17,500.' A competition MGC fared even better. Gerry recalled: 'This time I bought it and sold it in the paddock that afternoon! It would be fair to say I made a perceptible profit.'

Walton gathered that it was important to ensure that a certain amount of alcohol primed any deal, and it helped if the potential vendor named a ridiculously low price.

Despite his DTV fame, Ford was never far from Gerry's racing life, now evolving from the Capri to the Sierra Cosworth. We found four entries for such turbo Fords in '87, three in a car owned by Tony 'Strawberry' Strawson (formerly a Super Saloon rival) and one in a car owned by Jerry Mahony. Gerry was also entered in a Thundersaloon Escort Mk2 with Cosworth 16-valve power, owned by Joe Ward.

The season started in February with the traditional trek to Brands for a sprint, although this time it was billed as the Brands Kentagon event. Gerry appeared in two reported class winners, the MGB and an Escort Turbo. We could not check the B's appearance, but a wooden 50p trophy was awarded! The Escort won, with this mention from Dud Candler in *Autosport*: 'The unlimited class contained a varying entry, but when GDR

Marshall is entered, the others have a real fight on their hands. The big man didn't disappoint his followers, being over 3 seconds quicker than the hard-trying Derek Wileman, whose Sierra Cosworth looked a handful.'

The resuscitated Aston DB4 was the best steer for Gerry that year, winning outright on two successive late May weekends at Silverstone and Mallory Park, beating experienced and effective driver David Heynes and his DB4 on both occasions. At Mallory Gerry was pole for the AMOC Thoroughbred Sportscars ten-lapper by a solid two seconds. *Autosport*'s Paul Lawrence reported: 'Although he won by almost 20 seconds, Marshall never eased up and kept the crowd entertained in his usual style.'

On 20 June, Gerry was back at Silverstone for the Thoroughbreds race and again caught the media's attention. Graham Rowan reported for *Autosport*: 'No race in which Gerry Marshall competes could be boring. Driving a DB4 rescued from a quarry, where it's film stunt crew abandoned it, he dominated the SKF Thoroughbred Sportscar race with a breathtaking display of car control. The smoke from Gerry's four-wheel drifts obscured a fine contest for second…'

For all the Cosworth-powered entries made that season by 'Strawberry' Strawson, we failed to turn up any results, but thanks to Simon Lewis and a black and white photograph we know Gerry drove the black Ford at Brands Hatch. We also hear that the Ford was apparently meant to be used by Mr Strawson's wife! On occasion 'Strawberry' also raced the Opel Monza driven by Tony Lanfranchi in 1985 and Gerry in 1986.

In October, Marshall shared a Sierra Cosworth with another Jerry (Mahony), and they qualified fourth overall for a four-hour prodsaloon race at Donington. However, their successful Sierra was unhappy that day and the engine management wouldn't allow more than 4,500rpm, disliking the health of the turbocharger. They were out after running as high as second. Gerry also shared the Toyota Corolla GT16 with Geoff Kimber Smith again. This time the pairing took a 12th in qualifying amongst some heavy BTCC metal at Oulton Park, turning that into a satisfying ninth overall, third in the smallest capacity class.

Gerry also tackled three early Saab Turbo rounds. The car was entered under the auspices of Beechdale Saab dealership and had been raced by Jonathan Collet-Jobey, nicknamed 'The Rev'. When he died in 1988, Beechdale wanted the car employed, so Gerry raced it on virtually no budget with Vincent Cyril Higgs as the mechanic, and son Gregor changing wheels. Vince is remembered by Gregor as 'one of Roger Bunting's protégés and Steve Soper's best mate – until he kept beating Steve when they both raced A35s! Vince stopped racing and became a mechanic. In the mid-'80s, he worked for Colin Pearcy looking after the MGs, but he also built Dad's MGs and is an MG specialist. However, Vince did help me with my Firenza and is a typical old-style mechanic – a good bloke,' Gregor summarised.

Gerry's best Saab result that season was a fifth overall at Silverstone, followed by a sixth at Brands. There was a fastest lap at Thruxton in April, but Marshall was excluded in post-race scrutineering as the excess boost light triggered.

ABOVE *Gerry and the Ford Sierra Cosworth were never strangers, but this was a Brands Hatch one-off in friend Tony 'Strawberry' Strawson's example. Apparently, Mrs Strawson did wonder what had happened to her shiny road car…* [Simon Lewis Transport Books]

THIS SPREAD *The astonishing rescue and revival of what became the winning Marsh Plant-Gerry Marshall Aston Martin DB4 is documented in these before and after pictures and* The Times *cutting of the former Hammer House of Horror film victim. We also have a contemporary shot with Gerry and Gregor either side of the reborn thoroughbred. Debuting at Brands in primer paint it famously ran out of fuel (Geoffrey Marsh never allowed that to happen again). Pictured at Silverstone (bottom left) the No 74 pole-position Aston was a winner. This DB4 raced six times in Gerry's hands and won four of those events, before it was sold and exported to the USA.* [All Marshall Family Archive]

1988

This was the year of classic racing results for Gerry, with such disparate machinery as the blue-blood Aston Martin DBR4 Grand Prix monoposto and a variety of MGBs. There were 28 confirmed Marshall entries, with three awards given recognising class-winning success in two cases; these suggest 30 events were tackled. The win rate also went up in '88, with 13 victories recorded.

Most prestigious ride was in the Marsh Plant Grand Prix Aston, which scored wins or top-three

THE TIMES SATURDAY JUNE 6 1987 ★★★★★

The rescued Aston Martin DB4 with Mr Gerry Marshall, the racing driver, and his son, Gregor (Photograph: Harry Kerr).

Cliff plunge car races back to form

By Ruth Gledhill

A car which once plunged off a cliff for a Hammer House of Horror television series is the hot tip to win the thorough-bred sports car championship at Brands Hatch tomorrow.

Earlier this year, the 1959 Aston Martin DB4 was a rusted, crumpled and over-grown wreck lying forgotten at the base of an 80ft cliff.

But now it is back on the road and has already won in two out of three race outings this season, at Mallory Park and Silverstone.

The stunt involved the car being hurled over the almost

The wrecked stunt car as it was found at the foot of a cliff

inaccessible cliff top near Rickmansworth, Hertfordshire.

The car, now worth £40,000, was wired to explode once it hit the bottom of the quarry.

The burnt-out shell was forgotten by all but Mr Richard Williams, the Aston Martin dealer who supplied it.

Mr Gerry Marshall, a champion racing driver, said:

"He knew we were looking for an Aston Martin to turn into a racer. He went to look for it himself but could not find it."

Last Christmas, Mr Marshall and his son, Gregor, conducted their own search and after struggling through farmyards, undergrowth and deserted quarries, they found the wreck, 60 feet away from the base of the cliff.

Using a specialist all-terrain crane supplied by Mr Geoffrey Marsh, a business-man and race sponsor, the car was lifted out on January 8, a day that was so cold that video cameras which were to film the event froze.

placings in all three starts. The aristocratic Aston also returned award-winning results in the AMOC/HSCC pre-60 Historic Championship.

It was also a year of returns, because Gerry appeared in a Vauxhall twice and fielded a Saab 900 Turbo with more success than before, including a win and front-running finishes.

It was late March when Gerry started his '88 season with a brace of Brands outings around the Brands Hatch shorter (Indy) circuit in the Thundersaloon series. He was entered in a Rover Vitesse and the Transpeed Droop Snoot Vauxhall normally driven by Tony Davies. The Vitesse was no more than a class contender with so many 600hp Thunderloons about, but the Vauxhall got on to the leader board before a puncture demoted it down the overall order, finally taking second in the sub-2,500cc class as compensation.

Gerry also appeared the following weekend in the Transpeed machine at the Snetterton Thundersaloons round on April Fools' Day. A tremendous performance saw the agile Vauxhall up to third overall and looking at the second-place Vauxhall V8 senator, which was 'under attack from the relentless Marshall,' according to a contemporary report. Sadly, Davies and Gerry lost third position and a likely class win late in the race. In 2005 Davies revealed that Gerry had a 'robust tussle' with the late David Leslie's Manta, 'which involved the Firenza getting ahead and the Manta taking to the grass'.

A month later Gerry drove the shorter Brands track for a European Championship event with the single-seat DBR4, one of just four such Astons constructed, a machine that had demanded every ounce of Geoffrey's commitment to the marque, requiring a new cylinder block to be cast during its restoration. Gerry seized a class win, but even better was to come over the Grand Prix Brands Hatch layout during the series of HSCC historic events packed into June weekend.

The Aston won comfortably after a rare bogged-down start caused 'a few anxious moments'. Gerry was also out twice in an MGB that Brands weekend, beating the similar car of friend Colin Pearcy, aka 'Silly Bollocks' in Marshall-speak. That was during the HSCC Saturday event, with a separate class for metal-bodied MGBs. On Sunday Gerry was a fine third overall in the Pearcy B, this despite starting last with a ten-second penalty, as Colin had decided after practice the car was no good! Gerry monstered through the field behind a well developed Healey 3000 and John Young, an excellent driver, in a Jaguar E-type. Vintage Marshall art in a quality FIA European Championship weekend.

Marshall also took the six-cylinder MGC to a class win at Donington, so it was a very good MG season all round, enough to make Gerry's Dad proud of the example he had set his son in that 1950s MG Magnette.

Gerry had not lost touch with contemporary front-drive cars, for the Saab brought an outright win at Snetterton in September, beating Champion-elect Charles Tippett. That turbo result was followed by a second overall at Thruxton in the final October round, where he had set pole-position time.

This account from fellow competitor John Llewellyn tells us why there were few Saab encounters that season. 'Gerry did a few Saab

RIGHT *Variety was the key to Gerry's post DTV racing career. This turbocharged front-drive SAAB from Nottingham dealers Beechdale was campaigned by Mr Marshall in 1987–88 on an extremely tight budget that saw young Gregor on pit-crew duty.* [Marshall Family Archive]

races, as I did in the 1987–88 seasons, winning both Championships. At one memorable Thruxton [1988], it rained in monsoon style. I was on pole and Gerry fifth: we disappeared, leaving the others miles behind. Gerry led with me in pursuit, but not close. As I rounded Church on lap six, I lost it and rolled it into a little ball.

'They stopped the race, although I was fine. I got in the back of the ambulance. We headed off back but stopped at the chicane. The back door opened and there stood Gerry, He looked at me and said, "What the f—k are you doing here?"'

'I asked him the same question. Apparently, Gerry had gone straight on at the chicane into the Armco. More upsetting was that the race was won by Andy Dawson, who Gerry called "Turbo Gob",' chuckled Llewellyn.

Gregor added this footnote: 'Vince and I were at that Thruxton. Dad had told me to watch on the outside of the Chicane and he crashed right at my feet. He could see me as he was aquaplaning … And even though he was quite winded, he thought he'd better get out so that I knew he was OK!'

Walton also saw Gerry being thrust into an innocent Suzuki Swift Gti at an early '88 season one-hour prod saloon race around Oulton Park. The Gti practised OK, but did not finish, possibly because they were having difficulty closing the driver's door on the Big Fella.

1989

Race entries this season stayed right on the late '80s Marshall average at 32, but the number of outright victories was exceptional. Gerry took eight overall wins in a radically redeveloped Aston Martin V8 for Geoffrey Marsh, plus two victories in the charismatic TVR Tuscan challenge, his Rover V8-energised mount in the bellowing one-make series provided by David Gerald.

Dubbed 'Silver Dream Racer', the Aston V8 formed the backbone of Gerry's racing for several seasons, and the TVR series became a regular hunting ground for Marshall wins in the early '90s. Gerry should have won the overall championship, but for mechanical unreliability and some rides in celebrity cars ineligible for points.

During 1989 Gerry also drove a Manta with Pontiac V8 power that should have been a good ride in Thundersaloons, plus a classic Ford Anglia that performed above expectations and a BMW M3 he shared with John Llewellyn.

Built with Intermarque racing in mind under liberal regulations, 'Silver Dream Racer' was the first of two V8s Gerry would race for Geoffrey Marsh in the 1990s. Each season saw more radical redevelopment of the 450 to 500-plus horsepower heavyweights (from 1,220kg/2,684lb).

ABOVE *A June 1987 chance to mix with the Ferrari elite on the 25th annual Cavallino gathering. Gerry tastes the delights of Nick Mason's appropriately registered 250 GTO. Rock drummer and established historic racer Nick indicates to Gerry (carrying helmet) the LHD entry to any enthusiast's wheeled paradise.* [Marshall Family Archive]

ABOVE *Gorgeous! This unusual angle on Silverstone depicts Gerry in winning June 1988 action at the wheel of the stunning Geoffrey Marsh DBR4.* [Gary Hawkins]

Most famously, subsequent input on the Aston's dynamics came via loyal Williams engineer Jock Clear. Jock was best known for his GP association with Jacques Villeneuve's 1997 world title season, and he was prominently 'hands-on' in the Marsh Plant pits.

The bulky Aston began Gerry's 1989 campaign with a proper result at Brands Indy layout on 30 April, seizing an overall win. The annual AMOC fixture delivered the appropriate dream debut for the Aston and its 'rumbling V8'. That Aston was never beaten in the rest of that season, but failed to take up its grid position on a second outing at Brands that April day, having practised an indecent seven seconds faster than the nearest opposition!

RIGHT *The fabulous Stars and Stripes paint of Nick Oatway's Opel Manta with Pontiac V8 power takes time out at Zandvoort, Holland, for some PR duties. It delivered some exciting Thundersaloon outings for Nick and Gerry. Best result was a second at Oulton Park, but here at Zandvoort promising qualifying sessions (third and fifth) were followed by troubled races.* [LAT]

The TVR reunion was rekindled almost by accident, long after the Martin Lilley era. Now Peter Wheeler was the owner-boss at Blackpool. Peter loved not just imprinting the production TVRs with inspired style, but also the hurly burly of racing his accelerative but tricky products – lusty and light V8s, perfect for Gerry's talents. Sadly, Peter died as this book was being written.

The David Gerald TVR deal was not competitive at the opening Donington round in May, that race being won by young Marshall Vauxhall sparring partner Jeff Allam. Neither did the Gerald TVR qualify at its second appearance. However, by June's Brands Indy circuit TVR date a transformation had brought pace. Gerry fought for the lead from the start with all the claimed 400hp present. Allam took the verdict again, but by just 1.1 seconds after some frantic jousting that saw Gerry second with future Tuscan double champ Mark Hales in third place.

The Gerald and Gerry TVR remained a front-four runner until September and the longer GP layout at Brands, where Gerry scored its first victory. It was a close thing, though, with spins galore and a 0.2-second margin over second man Steve Cole, but immensely satisfying in the carnage of an abbreviated race in 'descending gloom'.

For the rest of the season, bar the last TVR Challenge round, Gerry never finished lower than second in the dealer TVR – one that was far from works specification, when many had the absolute latest tweaks.

The '89 season also witnessed more Marshall adventures at the Willhire, Thundersaloons and yet more races in a career that already spanned more than 25 years. The Manta – owned by co-driver Nick Oatway – with its 5.7-litre Pontiac punch, entered five Thundersaloon Championship races with Gerry aboard. Best result in the Stars & Stripes Opel V8 was a second overall in the

BELOW *Gerry's 1989 Snetterton 24-hour mount was this David 'Jess' Yates-owned Sierra Cosworth. It qualified in the top ten, but retired in the June endurance race.* [John Lakey]

To Gerry —

I thought you should remember the season by this picture but you still won both races! Many thanks for six wins — Geoffrey.

RIGHT AND BELOW
Front air dam absent, the Silver Dream racer brings home the garland of victory at Brands Hatch in April '89 for a justly proud Gerry. It also earned a handwritten 'thank-you' for Gerry from Geoffrey at the end of the Gordon Russell Inter-Marque Championship in 1989 with six wins recorded. [Marshall Family Archive/Steve Jones]

second round at Oulton Park, where Gerry took 'a blinding getaway to lead into Old Hall' according to a contemporary report. He led for the opening stint in this 24-lap/66-mile event, but fading brakes and an uncooperative differential slowed co-driver Oatway to finish behind the winning Mazda V6.

That promising performance was followed by a troubled 15th and subsequent 16th over a twin-race weekend sortie to Zandvoort in Holland – which was disappointing, as they had qualified third and fifth respectively for the two races.

The 1989 Willhire promised a reasonable result. Sharing with David 'Jess' Yates in one of the inevitable Sierra Cosworths, they qualified eighth but failed to finish.

Another Ford, this one the potent JTM Racing Services Anglia, gave Gerry pole position at Mallory Park in early October. Teammate Phil Wight blasted his Mustang into Gerrards first and Gerry finally succumbed to the attentions of fellow Anglia man and legendary hot-rod ace George Polley. Polley bravely took the Mustang around the outside of Gerrards' elongated right-hander to win from Wight. Marshall's 1.8-litre Anglia, now reportedly suffering a misfire, took third.

At the same Donington weekend as he drove the TVR, Gerry had the welcome task of sharing John Llewellyn's BMW M3 in the BTCC one-hour event. Despite a full 30-car grid – and the presence of the official factory-backed Prodrive M3s – the friends made a fine seventh overall. Only Frank Sytner and the late Will Hoy in the surviving Prodrive Bimmer beat them.

In the summer of 2009 Llewellyn told us that 'the BMW was prepared by Roy Kennedy Racing. Other co-drivers were suggested to partner me, but imagine the grief I would have got from Gerry if I had chosen someone else.

'The car was on Dunlops, and the Prodrive cars and Forrest's M3 were on Pirellis, which were a good couple of seconds quicker. Don't know what went wrong in qualifying, but I do remember everyone hanging over the pit wall, looking up to the first corner to see how sideways the Big Man could get the M3!

' I did the first stint and Gerry the second. You always knew when he was really trying: he was very neat and tidy, no sideways driving evident. It was a great result, and close to being perfect.

' Celebrations did go on somewhat, that's why I cannot remember too much. He did enjoy the race, but didn't rave on about it – Gerry felt there wasn't enough power in the car, so it didn't suit his style I guess.'

Rebonding on track

Graham Scarborough told us this revealing tale of a seesaw Marshall relationship:

'After 1987 I didn't have my own car any more and raced sporadically. It was also around this time that Gerry fell out with me – even to this day, I don't know why. I never had an issue with him but he just ignored me at the track and we didn't speak for over a year. The only thing I can think of was that I was married to Lindy, who was Jennifer's cousin, and Gerry and Jennifer were going through a pretty messy divorce – as I was now part of Jenny's family, I was lumped in with the enemy.

'One day I was at Snetterton for a media or charity day. I was on track, going past the pit exit, and I could see this car coming out. After all our side-by-side racing, I knew it was him. I knew instantly it was Gerry, you could just tell if Gerry was driving, due to a car's stance.

'Gerry obviously didn't know I was coming around the outside but as he pulled out he and his passenger noticed. His passenger turned to acknowledge me, and it was Tony Lanfranchi, who gave me a wave.

'We then spent the next three laps going at each other hammer and tongs. I'm not sure who was more scared, Tony or my passenger, but it was great.

'We got back to the pits and Gerry came bounding over and said, "Cor, Skid, what a good little race, just like old times!"

'From then on we were friends again; nothing was mentioned about the fact that we'd not spoken for over a year...'

ABOVE *Graham Scarborough enjoys an outing at Spa years after his Marshall Capri era.* [Scarborough family]

CHAPTER 13

1990–2000: Success in adversity

A third and final divorce beckoned during this decade, this time from Penny when they had completed some six years together in 1995. When we spoke to her in the summer of 2009, the third Mrs Marshall was amazingly buoyant and philosophical about her life with Gerry. 'He really was the love of my life,' she began. 'and that is one of the reasons I've kept my name as Penny Marshall. I never have found anyone to match him in the 14 years since we divorced and – at 62 – I probably never will … It was an experience I would not have missed. He was simply a unique man and we parted as friends. I spoke to him most days for the rest of his life and the thought that he's dead still makes me want to cry.'

We were slightly overwhelmed by this reaction, as life with Gerry was not easy financially. Penny began her married life in Thespians Orchard, the Pitstone house that Gerry and Jennifer had bought. 'I knew it was Jenny's house, so I was not very happy with that. I bought a bungalow less than ten miles away, but things were never financially easy during my time with Gerry.' A small pause for thought regarding the years that had diminished her housing assets significantly, reportedly by borrowing against her bungalow. Penny then agreed with the wives' consensus opinion that 'Gerry

LEFT *An enjoyable way to celebrate the start of a new TVR season. In a Tuscan owned by Martin Crass, Gerry qualified fastest and won the May Thruxton round of the Mobil 1-backed challenge, despite losing fifth gear.* [LAT]

would spend everything he had – and more – on racing; often the cash went to promising drivers.'

Although she worked for a computer company and did not retire from work until long after their divorce, Penny was committed to Gerry's social and racing life. She commented: 'I don't think I missed a race in our time, and I certainly drove back on all occasions so he could drink!' Penny particularly valued Gerry's wide circle of friends, especially David Yates and Bob Sherring.

Penny was spared Gerry's immediate health problems that came before – and especially after – their marriage, but observed (as did Jenny on many occasions) that Gerry bore all his medical issues courageously and with 'no fuss'. Having met the lady socially during 1991, Walton thought that Penny also made light of what was often a tough relationship. Her effervescent spirit triumphed over what he had expected to be a tense conversation.

Through peals of laughter, Penny reported that 'Gerry told me I was the oldest woman he ever went to bed with.' Then we knew this lady had possessed the right blend of humour and resilience to cope with Marshall life.

Although second wife Jenny Cook and Gerry had divorced back in 1988, they stayed in touch for over 20 years, until the end. Gerry even stayed at Jenny's house with his final companion, Gwen Howard.

Friends and family tell us that Gerry met Gwen – who had only recently moved into the area – whilst lawnmowing, but a wickedly observant offspring added that Gerry also had an eye for Gwen's sister! Whatever the truth of that, Gwen 'was his steadfast companion' for the last five years of his life.

Simon Allen, Officiant and Celebrant, Non-religious rites of passage, added this significant testimony at Gerry's May 2005 funeral: 'I heard from his children that Gwen has quietly looked after him and ensured that he could get to the track and get to see the fans that wanted to see him. Gerry was not

the type of man who made a song and dance about his affections, but it was clear to his children that he worshipped her, and that she was a vital part of his life. During the time that his health was closing in on him, she remained stoic.'

Jenny Cook recalled of the decade: 'There were a lot of health problems through the '90s and right up to the day before he died. Gerry experienced a very difficult time but rarely complained, despite being in a lot of pain. There were many operations.

To my knowledge he had surgery for a hernia, prostate, hip and two knee replacements. Then of course there was the major one, a quadruple heart bypass in November 1996. It was amazing how quickly he recovered from this. He was determined that nothing would ever stop him driving a car and going motor racing.

'In 2000 he was diagnosed with PMR, polymyalgia rheumatica, which is an inflammatory rheumatic condition which made all his muscles

and joints ache and made him very tired. In true
Gerry style he had a book about medication and
did his own research on the tablets the doctors
were giving him.'

Jenny added: 'Gerry was diagnosed with PMR
in July 2000. I know because I have just found a
birthday card that he sent me from hospital for my
birthday on August 2nd. He signed it "From Stoke
Mandeville incurable ward"!'

1990

We have 25 confirmed race entries and one
spectacular demonstration on record for Gerry's
start to the '90s – 'spectacular' because Mr
Marshall showed just what the V16 BRM could do
in the sound and fury stakes, in front of an April
Silverstone crowd who still talk about the display.
Back in 1990 *Autosport*'s Nik Phillips waspishly

LEFT *Three sons and a motorcycle. Gerry with son Gregor, third wife Penny Dealy's boy, Ben, and John Rhodes's son at Mallory Park with a Harley Davidson for company and Chris Meek's hospitality.*
[Marshall Family Archive]

commented of the 21 April meeting and Gerry's dream drive: 'The VSCC assembled a superb array of machinery from 1908 Napier to 1960 Cooper, to entertain the tweed-clad classes around the National Circuit on Saturday. The unique sound of the V16 BRM was also on hand as Gerry Marshall put Nick Mason's car through a handful of hairy demonstration laps.'

Nick Mason confirmed in 2009 that this was the V16 he subsequently sold to Formula 1 supremo Bernie Ecclestone. The Pink Floyd drummer and president of the Guild of Motoring Writers added: 'As usual it needed another rebuild after Gerry's ride. No criticism – it needed a rebuild after every trip!' Originally, the idea had been for Gerry to demonstrate the Meyer-Drake Offenhauser Indycar that Fangio once qualified for America's great race, but it was unreliable, as Gerry confirmed.

LEFT *As a warm up for its first Grand Prix, Magny Cours hosted some British historic racers. Gerry was among them with this Aston Engineering DB5, which duly took an outright win at the fresh French track. The major Marshall memory was of 'the enormous kerbs!' and being 'in the middle of nowhere!'*
[F'Autodelta F Haase]

In a subsequent *Autosport* interview on the contributory reasons Mason let him out in the BRM, Gerry asserted that 'the worst [car] I ever drove was an old Indycar of Nick Mason's which kept breaking. So he let me demonstrate his BRM V16 at a VSCC Silverstone.'

1998 Vauxhall reunion

Walton refereed an October 1998 close encounter between Marshall and the Vauxhall marque, courtesy of 2009 Vauxhall Racing Team and multiple BTCC title winners Triple 888. Published in the now defunct *Cars & Car Conversions* in January 1999, this report included these scene-setting period references:

'There are still echoes of the past, like Gerry's enduring 4 DTV registration plate – now on a Nissan 200ZX – and the man himself, truly a legend in his own lunchtime. Gerry is still a big man with not a lot of hair, and the one-liners are as cutting as ever. Yet, the past twenty years would have been enough to make any smaller man whimper. There have been three wives, the financial roller coaster ride offered by motor trading, and GM has been no stranger to hospital wards. Spend 40 minutes in GM's company and you discover his encyclopaedic memory for track and trade life is accompanied by a curiosity to explore the current 1998 front-drive BTCC Vauxhalls.'

I also mentioned that Gerry was then 57 years of age and reckoned to have 'won 587 class and outright victories'. There would, of course, be more Marshall wins yet, despite increasing medical obstacles in the last seven years of his life. But for now, back to that sunlit 1998 day at Snetterton.

The £200,000 Vectra Gerry drove boasted the usual click-clack instant Xtrac sequential gearbox of the period, but was on a limited 275bhp at 8,100rpm for media appearances. It was a good 25 horsepower down on the usual 300 horses from a front-drive 2-litres. Hardly a recipe for traditional Marshall pleasures.

Gerry still got within four seconds of a proper BTCC time at the Norfolk track, and appreciated all but the limited motor power: 'That's literally a Super Car. It's so well engineered you would not know it's front-drive … If you compare a TVR Tuscan I was driving last week with one of these things, they both do similar times. But they get the job done a very different way. A Tuscan has another 150 horsepower, so the cornering and braking from these Tourers is phenomenal.

'This is where we switch to the Vectra things I loved…

'First off, the gear change is absolutely superb – so fast, so accurate. I never had a bit of bother with the system and it's obvious it doesn't need the clutch on the move. The second big impression came from the brakes. It takes ages to understand just how good they are, and I never thought I'd explored all their potential. Which brings us to the heart of what makes a good Super Touring driver: you've just got to take those Big Brave Pills before a qualifying session!'

Gerry's words of wisdom for aspirant professional racing drivers still ring true in the 21st century. 'I still don't think saloons are the way to go if you want a top-line professional career. Sure, you can earn a much better living than we did in the 1970s, but you're not going to get to the very top via BTCC – it teaches you some terrible driving habits!'

Simon Lewis remembered the event as well. 'Hats off to Nick Mason for giving him the opportunity and, for those of us who saw it, an unforgettable memory. I thought it was fabulous, especially screaming flat through Woodcote.'

An unexpected Lewis insight was of Gerry before the BRM demo: 'I saw Gerry coming out of the BRDC suite that morning in TVR overalls and cowboy hat, clearly charged up and quite animated. Gordon, the BRDC gatekeeper, asked what he was driving that day.

'Gerry rubbed his hands like Arkwright [a TV sitcom character in BBC's *Open All Hours* – JW] about to make a big sale: "Gonna drive the V16!" he said.

'There was a massive grin on his face. He was a kid about to be given free rein in a sweetshop…' concluded Lewis.

Less exotic racing dates that season were dominated by a determined 11 TVR Challenge outings in the David Gerald-owned Tuscan. Sadly, there were seven retirements, and it was not until Gerry borrowed the Celebrity Tuscan that he got a suitable result, winning at Oulton Park at the back end of the season. In terms of results, the best bet was the wonderful Marsh Aston DBR4, which maintained a 100 per cent winning record for Gerry, winning three out of three outings to take the SKF Historic Car Championship.

The 'Silver Dream Racer' V8 Aston Intermarque projectile also did its job, taking three wins, a brace of second places and more in just seven entries. Gerry collected a silver platter as an AMOC Championship winner.

The Willhire served up dramatic surprises too that season, the winning Mercedes disqualified for being underweight. That left two BMW M3s to beat the troubled Nissan GT-R of Janspeed's Keith Odor. Meanwhile, Gerry had a torrid time sharing with Richard Cabburn, Roger Bennington, and Porsche Turbo brave man Chris Millard. Entered by SKF Engineering Products in the familiar Jess Yates Sierra Cossie, they finished twelfth, fifth in class, having led the race at 9:00pm. Cabburn had to complete a double stint as Gerry rushed back from a Silverstone commitment.

A Snetterton race in the TVR did no better that weekend, another retirement being posted.

It was not the luckiest of seasons, the emotional pleasure of being reunited with a classic TVR Griffith V8 (Ronnie Farmer's example) being tempered by two July retirements at Pembrey and Donington. At Pembrey the Griffith's differential overheated as Gerry led the opening laps of the 100-mile Classic Car Trophy, while at Donington

later that month he set fastest long-circuit lap (1m 52.54s/79.97mph) before a second failure intervened, again whilst he was leading, this in a field that included a winning AC Cobra.

Gregor particularly remembers the Donington race, as it was all 'my fault apparently, as I was timing him every lap, which Dad said was bad luck – the first and last time I did it!'

1991

The 1991 season marked 30 years since Gerry had made his sprint debut at Brands Hatch. It saw him enter 30 events and return with a fine TVR Tuscan racing record, one that included ten outright wins in the brutal one-make challenge courtesy of a privateer entrant, Martin Crass. He also took three

RIGHT *The old Tyrrell Formula 1 transporter reappeared for Marsh Plant to support the racing Aston Martins of Geoffrey Marsh. Here we see the earlier Silver Dream Racer (closest to transporter) and the mighty evolution V8 that had ground-effect aerodynamics and a substantially larger V8.* [Marshall Family Archive]

Coronation upset!

Malcolm Hamilton, National Car Control Centres director and erstwhile E-type racer, drove an awesome V12 built by marque specialist Rob Beere against Gerry in hard-fought Intermarque events. He recalled the following unique story for us:

'Before one of our 1999 Races at Brands, I stayed with Gerry on a Saturday night at his home at Tring. Gerry was fully aware that the race would be contested between him, myself, and Win Percy. I think Gerry saw this Saturday night out as an opportunity to incapacitate one of his main challengers, so we spent the night in virtually every pub in Tring. We ended up in Horace's Night Club, which as far as I can remember was based in someone's front room.

'However, my drinking capabilities (although never a match for Gerry's) were enough to ensure that on the Sunday morning of the race I was up and ready for our battle. We set off late to Brands in an E-Type Gerry had scrounged.

'Our race was the first race, therefore practice was at 9:00am. I was worried that we had an hour to complete a one and a half hour journey. Gerry drove at breakneck pace: after we had travelled more than half an hour, we had pulled back quite a bit of lateness.

'I was beginning to believe we might make it in time.

'I was beginning to relax and make plans for the race as we sped nearer and nearer to Brands. Just as I had convinced myself we were going to make it in time, Gerry's face turned ashen ... A look of abject horror spread over his face. He stood on the brakes, locking the Jaguar's wheels and bringing us to an abrupt standstill.

'Gerry was almost crying and moaning, "Oh no! NO!"

'I sat there shocked and bewildered, frightened to ask Gerry what awful problem he had remembered, one that could cause us both to miss the race at Brands. Seconds passed into minutes, Gerry shaking and looking terrified.

'After what seemed a lifetime of deliberation, Gerry turned to me and said "I'll have to go back!"

'At that we turned round and sped back even

second-places and a glass bowl for the trophy cabinet. Indeed, he would probably have won the TVR title that year, save for a closing race collision and the fact that he twice raced the 'null point' Celebrity car. He also appeared in a classic Griffith V8 in his last race of the season, at Snetterton, where he recorded a third place.

Outside the world of TVR, Gerry made three appearances in the 'Silver Dream Racer' Aston (two wins and one non-start), and there was a one-off winning appearance in the delectably valuable DB5 at the first Magny Cours race meeting. He also drove a Van Diemen Multisport, Richard Cabburn's Porsche Carrera RSR – the only time he raced a 911 – plus an assortment of Vauxhalls, including Tony Lanfranchi's effective Monorep production racing Astra GTE, the Transpeed/Davies machine, and even a Vauxhall-powered Caterham.

faster than we had been travelling in the other direction.

'What could this problem be? I thought perhaps it was an imminent death in the family. Did Gerry need to administer some life-saving drug? Or perhaps he had left something on in the house that was going to burn it down?

'The problem was obviously so serious there were no grey areas. We were going back to Gerry's house, some 35 minutes' drive away. I was terrified to ask what the problem was. We both sat there silent and grim-faced for around five minutes.

'Gerry drove us back at near racing speeds, until he had composed himself enough to speak.

'Finally he said: "I forgot to put the f——g video on to record *Coronation Street*!"

'That tragedy rectified, we eventually arrived back at Brands.

'Gerry got a big bollocking from his Aston owner, Geoffrey Marsh. And I've hated *Coronation Street* ever since.

'...And I won the race!'

RIGHT *More stars and stripes and more litres for the Marshall man. The Hal Danby 7.2-litre Corvette lurks in its June 1994 Brands Hatch pit prior to a second-place finish in the HARA TransAm Challenge race.* [Marshall Family Archive]

BELOW *The 1994 season was the last one that Gerry contested at all regularly, but it was an unlucky year. The Giles Cooper/TVR Centre machine suffered multiple retirements and was never the anticipated front-runner.* [Marshall Family Archive]

His outstanding TVR season began at Brands on April Fools' Day, Gerry racing in the Celebrity Tuscan. Dud Candler wrote in *Autosport*: 'Bobby Sands and Jimmy McRae fought a mighty battle in the TVR Tuscan race, until the latter spun at Paddock. Sands then had to withstand a late race charge by Gerry Marshall, who nearly snatched it at Druids on the last lap.' In fact Gerry finished less than a second behind Sands and set fastest lap (49.18s/88.13mph) around the shorter Brands track – not bad for a man who had made his sprint debut 30 years earlier! Jimmy McRae was a multiple British Champion rally driver and father of 1995 World Champ Colin, who also appeared in Tuscans.

Walton has good cause to remember Gerry and
Penny Dealey (then the third Mrs Marshall) at a
late May Mallory Park TVR round, where Gerry was
in the Martin Crass example of the 4.5-litre Tuscan
breed. JW was in the Celebrity TVR, while Gerry
had already racked up a win in the Crass car at
Snetterton. Mallory was unusual as it was in two
ten-lap parts: Walton had to run from his Sierra
RS500 in the preceding Fast Ford race to join the
Tuscan circus, but it was worth every puffing yard.

There was a lot of official pre-race talk about
clean starts and accident avoidance, but JW
nevertheless remembers showers of glass fibre as
the grid departed, with the midfield apparently

ABOVE AND OPPOSITE PAGE *Three scenes from the successful 1999 campaign with Max Rostron's Lotus Cortina in the FIA Championship for historic saloons. Clockwise from above, Max (left) and Gerry pose with the car at Paul Ricard in April, take a break under the awning and occupy second slot on the podium at Zolder in August.* [Max Rostron]

intent on an orgy of TVR recycling. Gerry was long gone and dominated both races, although local Colin Blower 'made him work hard in the first', according to a contemporary report. Gerry set a record fastest lap (49.10s/98.98mph) – some pace for a short track that features a second-gear hairpin!

And Walton? Some 29.47s behind in sixth place on 20-lap aggregate. More interesting was that JW experienced fizzy Marshall life post-race. Following Gerry's large outline planted precariously on a diminutive Honda Monkey Bike, buzzing around the closed circuit on a fine summer evening, started the laughter. We went over to circuit owner Chris Meek's place, memorable for its position on the middle of the Mallory Lake and for Gregor's 'anti-clockwise ride around Mallory on the back of Meek's Harley, ridden by Dad'.

Dinner followed at classic saloon racer and local factory owner Bob Sherring's home. At the long table were Penny, her son Ben and then-teenage Gregor.

A great day's racing and socialising, but uneventful by earlier Marshall senior standards.

19 October at Oulton Park closed the TVR series. Gerry arrived as series leader over Steve Cole, and qualified second to guest driver Derek Higgins. The scene was set for a dramatic finale.

Autosport reported that 'as the lights changed, Marshall and Higgins briefly touched to let Colin Blower emerge through the dust at the front. Two

corners later, at Cascades, Marshall and Higgins inevitably clashed, leaving Gerry to fume at the side of the track for the rest of the race, while Derek continued.'

Blower easily won, but Cole stayed out of trouble to finish fifth and take the title. Gerry felt he had been robbed by the guest driver, and successfully protested him out of an eventual third place.

There were three other awards to collect at the end of the season, but the respected TVR title was not one of them.

A large silver Trophy from Caterham race specialists Hyperion testified to Gerry's unexpected performances in a Caterham 7. He appeared three times in the flyweight racers that season, taking a Cadwell Park victory and a third overall.

The Cadwell win was in a 100-mile endurance event, where Gerry shared with Caterham heir Robert Nearn. As ever there was drama, and Lawrence Foster filed this for *Autosport*: 'Poleman and perennial crowd pleaser Gerry Marshall dominated the first half of the race with a virtuoso performance … Marshall scattered the field behind him as his lead built to an incredible two thirds of a lap. The leader stayed out late as the flurry of pit stops commenced, finally coming in bang on half distance to perform a surprisingly graceful changeover.' Short of fuel and pursued by the talented Alec Poole, Nearn nursed it home to finish just 2.7 seconds ahead of Alec.

Beerey tales

Coventry-based Jaguar specialist Rob Beere contributed this reminiscence from the early '90s, when Beere customer Malcolm Hamilton raced a V12 E-type against Gerry, who was armed with Marsh Plant's Aston V8.

'The first time ever I talked to Gerry was in the Paddock Bar at Silverstone, this after our 1990 first victory against him in a close on-track battle. I got a firm tap on the shoulder by a walking stick and a loud voice said, "Mine's a bitter, Beerey," which I rapidly ordered.

'We had a few more "Beerey Bitters" and congratulations on our win from Gerry. His Marsh Plant brigade had long gone, with long faces and no congrats received, but Gerry and I met again in the toilets.

'Gerry came straight over and said, "When I was a lad, my Dad always told me that to be a racing driver you needed big balls." Whipping them out, he added, "What do you think, Beerey?"

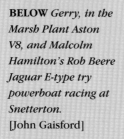

'Well, what could I say? I was presented by what I can only describe as a pair of ginger tennis balls!

'Some years later I was at Silverstone again, sat on the hill opposite Copse corner. For some reason I was spectating at an old XJ race.

'Only months before I had seen Gerry looking very poorly.

'Feeling the now famous "shoulder tap" I heard, "Beerey – take a look at my new knees!" Gerry all but started dancing around, clad in a new haircut and looking very well!'

Carl Taylor in turn – Rob Beere's business partner – was prompted by Malcolm Hamilton to tell this tale. Carl reminded Malcolm what they did to honour Gerry during 2000–1.

'As we all regarded Gerry as *the* Driving God, we created a shrine to him in our transporter. Everyone at race meetings was invited to worship!

'Our shrine consisted of a big picture of Gerry with a daft hat on. Either side of the picture we had lighted candles mounted in holders made from Jaguar Group C valves and springs and a pint pot and a bottle of rum and a chest wig (we know not why!). All insiders were asked to come and worship at The Shrine and write a short letter of worship about Gerry in our visitors' book, and now we have a lot of signatures in the book including Geoffrey Marsh.

'Gerry loved The Shrine. He used to say, "You're taking the piss out of me," with that special glint in his eye.

'The Shrine is still intact in our transporter, which is at the back of Rob Beere's workshop. We still have the Book of Worship. Gerry used to have great fun in our transporter, looking through the book.

'He couldn't quite work out what it was all about, but he enjoyed it.'

The Astons, meanwhile, racked up wins for Gerry that included, as already mentioned, a sortie to Magny Cours in central France for a one-off in a DB5 (358 DLW) at the start of June.

Another one-off involved a Multisport Van Diemen drive at Mallory in May, which must have reminded Gerry of his Formula Ford forays: a contemporary report stated that 'the first race stoppage came in the Multisports event on lap 2, and the number of damaged cars by the end of 12 laps was amazing.' Apparently even the winner crossed the line with its rear body panel missing. Gerry was fifth, some 36 second adrift.

1992

A quieter season than before, with just 17 events entered and singleton overall and class wins returned. However, Gerry's return to the TVR in Graham Nash's Tuscan was deeply impressive, with an outright win, a second, a third and two other top six placings – all in just six outings!

Other promising forays included Mike McGoun's Ford Sapphire Cosworth. The turbo Ford returned a brace of pole positions and a racing fourth, which gained Gerrry a trophy at Castle Combe right at the end of August.

ABOVE *Things did not always go to plan for Gerry and the Marsh Plant V8 Astons! This is just part of a long sequence showing a clash with Richard Chamberlain's Porsche 911 Turbo. Over the same June 1999 racing weekend in Derbyshire Gerry racked up another brace of victories in the Edd Sharpe Aston DB4.* [Linzi Smart]

LEFT *Awesome sight. Gerry in the second-evolution 6.1-litre version of the Aston V8. The car was a front-runner, but I think you can see why this 1999 Silverstone race was cancelled after the mighty combo had practised second quickest.* [Alan Cox]

An Aston DBS V8 (DRY 840K) gave him a class win at the St John Horsfall during the annual Marshall pilgrimage to Silverstone.

1993

Fewer events still, but a marvellous win-to-race ratio with eight victories recorded in just 12 events. The Marsh Plant Aston Martin V8 with 5,340cc punch cleared five overall first past the flag results and a couple of class wins.

However, perhaps the prestige result of the year came with a June win in an Austin Healey 3000 at Brands Hatch, as that race was for the Donald Healey Memorial Trophy.

Colin Pearcy's passion for MG and Rover saw Marshall out in a Bastos-liveried TWR Vitesse to close the season. That was in October at Oulton Park, where it showed well until, in Pearcy's words, 'the gearbox blew'.

1994

A busier season than the previous two, with Gerry tackling 26 events for sure, and possibly more. There were ten wins, half of them within the Intermarque series in the evolving Marsh Plant Aston Martin V8. However, there were also another five successes in the pedigree Aston DB3S sports racer, three wins in the DB4 model and a class-winning outing in a DB4 offering higher power Vantage specification (registered CJB 949B).

A one-off ride in a 7.2-litre Chevrolet brought back a second overall in a HARA Trans Am event around Brands Hatch Grand Prix circuit in June. Ted Williams took 'a cosy win from Gerry Marshall, who was guesting in Hal Danby's awesome Chevrolet Corvette', according to *Autosport*. This classic 'Vette and another cheered Gerry's driving life, as well as those of spectators.

The following June weekend saw Gerry at Silverstone for a particularly successful Sunday. He won in the 3-litre Aston DB3S and the 5.3-litre DBS V8, and achieved a class win for a standard road-going DB4 Vantage. These were not easy wins, as a 5.3-litre AC Cobra in the Intermarque event twice beat him off the line. Hmm, very unusual for Gerry – must have had a clutch problem! But Gerry 'returned and controlled the Aston Martin and Prewar sports car race from the front', according to a 16 June copy of *Autosport*, while his nearest challenger spun.

The TVR series was revisited but was not a success, as the Giles Cooper example suffered seven retirements in ten outings and its best result was barely inside the top ten. A cruel contrast to previous front-running seasons.

Incidentally, Giles Cooper still runs a motor trade business from the old BarMoCo site in Barnet, and had traded with Gerry back in the 1960s.

1995

There were just a dozen entries this season, but the win rate was astounding, with nine taken in a predominantly Aston competition year. The exception was a late July Grand Prix circuit performance at Silverstone.

Gerry took one of the seriously focused Austin Healey 100S breed. Registered RWD 323 and owned by Robert Waterhouse, this well-known machine secured a class second for Gerry in the Donald Healey Memorial race.

Over that same Silverstone weekend, Colin Pearcy's flourishing MG collection provided Gerry with two Coys of Kensington rides. On both occasions the Marshall mount was an 1,860cc MGB, but we don't have confirmed results for either outing.

The Marsh Plant V8 contested Intermarque and the Goldsmith & Young Thoroughbred Sports Car series, with five victories at Silverstone, Brands Hatch, and Thruxton. The Brands success was scored at one of Gerry's best hunting grounds in powerful sports cars, the longer GP layout, where he had won outright with the original TVR Griffith some 30 years earlier.

Yes, immediately after his under-the-weather wedding night!

BELOW *Race banter after another John Rhodes encounter. September 1999's Goodwood Revival saw Gerry and Rhodes renew their wet-weather rivalry. John took his traditional Cooper S mount and Gerry was armed with the Rostron Lotus Cortina. Gerry won again and now his victory totals nudged the magic 600, finally hitting 600 wins in an Aston at Snetterton in August 2000.* [Marshall Family Archive]

1996

This was an understandably restricted season – Gerry had major heart bypass surgery in November – with just five confirmed entries made. All outings were Aston-mounted, the Marsh V8 run at least three times. It was also entered at a major Brands Hatch meeting in July, but no qualifying time or result has been discovered. The balance of events were entered in a DB4.

As ever, the strike rate of results to outings was impressive: an outright victory supported by a brace of seconds.

The win came despite a ten-second and back-of-the-grid start penalty when the V8 Aston missed its practice session. Reporting the ERF Intermarque race at Brands Hatch, Dud Candler wrote: 'Gerry Marshall stormed through from the back of the field.' He beat two Porsche RSRs, including that of *Financial Times* staff man John Griffiths, to set fastest lap at 49.61s/87.36mph. In June 2009, now freelance *FT* contributor Griffiths commented that he had, in turn, also managed to beat Marshall at Brands. 'But it did need a bit of bodywork rubbing to get by the widest Aston I've seen,' said jovial John.

Gerry's failing health dictated that the last appearance for him in 1996 was at Mallory Park in August, where he turned out twice in the 4.2-litre DB4, finishing fourth in class within the Intermarque struggle and topping that with a second overall in the Postwar Aston dice. *Autosport* reporter Richard Wright revealed a supplementary

reason for not winning: 'Guessing right with a back marker helped [Ronnie] Farmer [DB5] regain the lead from Gerry Marshall [DB4].'

1997

Following his major heart surgery in the closing months of 1996, Gerry made just one appearance this year, in the Marsh Aston V8 at Donington in October. Now sporting over 6-litres, it dragged him up to third overall, behind a brace of Porsches.

1998

Now back in better health, Gerry tackled 14 events to secure nine top-three placings on a class or overall basis. The 6.1-litre Marsh Aston took the brunt of the revived Marshall assault and thundered to one outright win.

Class wins went to the David Heynes DB4 Gerry drove at Brands Hatch and a loaned E-type Jaguar (registered PFO 416). The Jaguar started Gerry's season in May, at Silverstone. He also drove a Lotus Cortina and a 3-litre Capri during this comeback year.

1999

In his strongest season since the early part of the decade, Gerry featured in 25 events to take ten overall wins and one class victory. His Aston Martin links were maintained with 13 entries, and he sprinted again at a special Crystal Palace revival.

BELOW *The André Bailly Jaguar E-type provided a battling race for Gerry at the September 1999 FIA Cup event for historics. After a spin and an off-course trip, the determined Mr Marshall emerged 4th overall.* [Marshall Family Archive]

A major motor dealer and consistent racer, Nick Whale sent Gregor these memories of Gerry. 'I first met your Dad when I was 13, at Mallory Park on a school trip. I told him I was the son of a Midland Vauxhall dealer. To my amazement, he remembered my family Vauxhall connection and me every time I saw him. He had an incredible and exceptional memory for faces and names.

'He soon became my hero and I had a picture of him with "Big Bertha" and some topless models above my bed, throughout my teens.

'Subsequently, as a Volkswagen salesman, I visited Silverstone and GTI Engineering to see Gerry and Roger Dowson at their Silverstone unit. I was hillclimbing and your Dad kept telling me to get on and race – which I didn't have the bottle to do until 1987, aged 24. That was at Mallory and Gerry was there, propping up the bar as usual, and giving me stick for driving like a wimp.

'He became much more impressed when I sold my Mallock and bought a prod saloon BMW M3 for the 1988 season. Gerry competed in proddies, and we shared a lot of time together at the circuits: he became my driver coach.

'We became firm friends again when I started historic saloon racing in 1997, a friendship that lasted until the end of his life.

'We had our best race against each other in 2000 at the Revival at Goodwood when we were both in Mustangs. We finished very close, first and second – the only time I would ever beat him.

'I had much the better car!

'Another Gerry memory comes from 2000, after I had contested and won the British Historic Rally Championship. My car was sealed after the last win and inspected by the MSA officials. The gearbox ratios were not as per the homologation papers.

'Unless I could prove that this was the case in the period (1973), my car would be declared illegal and I would be stripped of the title. I was mortified.

'Next day I rang Gerry: I just knew he would recall the rules of Group 4 cars from 1973. Sure enough, he did, and Gerry had an FIA Yellow Book from 1973, which said that gear ratios were free. Brilliant!

'All I had to do was drive to Saffron Walden and he would give me the Yellow Book. In return, he would meet me at a pub of his choosing and I would treat him to a few beers and lunch.

'"Fair enough," I said, very grateful.

'When I arrived, I noticed someone painting inside the pub, but thought no more about it. We sat at the bar and had a couple of pints and a good

He also drove Dave Methley's Marcos 1800 GT to a one-off outright win at Silverstone to close the year.

But for a man who loved to meet people and travel, this dream season centred on an excellent drive in the FIA European Championship for Historic Cars. That meant travelling to Paul Ricard in France, Italy's historic Monza, Zolder in Belgium and Holland's then longer-tracked Zandvoort.

The six-race FIA programme, which also included a British round at Donington, was courtesy of Motor Auctions company director Max Rostron, with whom he regularly raced during 1998–2001 and also in 2003. They contested the FIA championship in 1998–99 and 2001. Looking back on his Marshall seasons in 2009, Max remembered that 'they were by far my most enjoyable times in motor racing and my whole family loved Gerry to bits'. Max had a very well-developed 1963 Lotus Cortina, and Gerry would later share a Mustang with the Yorkshire-based businessman. The twin cam Cortina had lightweight race engineering that even Colin Chapman could not have imagined in his Lotus heyday.

The civilised FIA season started in the April warmth of Southern France, with the Cortina

at Ricard. The venue brought a top-three class qualifying result in a field with plenty of V8 iron: the Cortina came home second in category. A couple of weekends later Gerry was out in friend Bob Sherring's Mustang with a chance of an overall win at the HSCC Donington classic race meeting. The V8 qualified up front, but a period report reveals that it 'spat its propshaft out on the warm-up lap'.

Back on the FIA international trail with the Cortina, Gerry and Max were at Zandvoort in May. They suffered another disappointment with a race retirement following a top-three class qualifying session. Later that month the Cortina appeared at Monza and finished an encouraging fifth overall.

The results improved radically from the Zolder round onward. In Belgium's August humidity they returned a fabulous second overall, but better awaited them. On home soil at Donington, they fought with a fellow Cortina crew for third, but eventually had to settle for fourth in class, as they had to make a second pit stop. Gerry also had an eventful Donington outing that September day in André Bailly's Jag E-type, battling TVR associates Rob Schirle's Griffith mightily for third until a spin.

laugh. We then went to order some food and I stood up to go to the loo.

'I collapsed on the floor and passed out!

'I came round to find Gerry pissing himself laughing, on his mobile to John Llewellyn saying that Nick Whale couldn't take his drink, and that two pints had finished him off!

'Actually, the smell of the paint had caused me to faint.

'They made a huge fuss of me, propped me up at a table. Gerry thought it was all hysterically funny and kept ringing people to tell them what a wimp I was and how the Brummies couldn't take their beer.

'The final straw for Gerry came when I went to pay the bill as a thank you to him for the Yellow Book and all his help and I found that I had forgotten my wallet!

'Gerry couldn't believe it and started ringing everybody back again to tell them not only was I a complete wimp, but a skinflint as well!

'He never let me forget that day.

'I admired your Dad hugely,' Nick concluded, 'and was totally in awe of him as a driver. He helped me find my first E-type, CUT 7 [ex-Colin Pearcy], and he helped me sell my Mustang, both hugely helpful at the time.'

Gerry persisted and re-passed, but another minor off left him fourth. Never say die!

The final 1999 outing with the historic Rostron Ford was a wonderful weekend for Gerry. At Goodwood for the September Revival meeting, he commanded media attention again. Pictured with his winning garland, the *Autosport* caption read: 'Gerry Marshall notched the 593rd win of his career in the saloon car race.' Marcus Pye, respected warehouse of motor racing knowledge, Goodwood

ABOVE AND BELOW *Back in Edd Sharpe's yellow DB4 prepared by Aston Engineering. At Donington in October 1999, Gerry repeated his brace of outright victories in this very successful racing Aston, registered 991 YBF.* [Both Alan Cox]

commentator, and loyal *Autosport* associate wrote: 'With the track awash, veteran saloon car aces Gerry Marshall and John Rhodes provided a heart-stopping Lotus Cortina versus Mini Cooper S encounter to rival the BBC's 100 Great Sporting Moments thrash at Crystal Palace, in which Marshall also starred. Big Gerry just nicked it to score the 593rd victory of his career.'

Contributing most to his winning score lines that super season was not the evolving 6.1-litre Aston, but the quick Edd Sharpe-owned DB4 registered 991 YBF. It took a perfect seven out of seven races entered score, including a two-part event at Brands Hatch to start the season. An eighth scheduled DB4 drive resulted in a race cancellation after qualifying on pole.

Gerry also won with the Methley Marcos at an October Silverstone for his penultimate race of the season. *Autosport* coverage of this outing was strong, with a picture showing Gerry leading a trio of similar Marcoses (Marcii?), and the main headline: 'Marshall triumphant in frantic classic encounter.' Marcus Pye awarded his Star Drive accolade to Gerry, who, he reports, 'took a borrowed Marcos by the scruff of its neck to victory'.

Unusually this Marcos result did not feature one of Gerry's famed fast starts. As the opening paragraph explained, 'Gerry Marshall was seventh into Copse, having mistakenly put the Marcos Volvo in reverse at the start of a frantic *Classic & Sports Car* encounter.'

Gerry was also a winner (class) in an Escort

RS1800, at a Sevenoaks & DMC club revival of the North Tower section at Crystal Palace. As winner of the last race at 'The Palace' in 1972, Gerry did his best with the immaculate red second-generation Lyons Escort. He 'won his class, but was edged out of the top six overall', according to a contemporary report.

2000

This was another decent season as Gerry looked to his 600th win, a landmark that was achieved – appropriately – in a Marsh Plant Aston. He also appeared at Goodwood in the Robert Waterhouse Healey 100S and Max Rostron's Mustang, both finishing second overall, and there was also a return to Spa. In total he had nine wins recorded, three of the class variety (one in a TR6), after attacking 19 events.

By his own calculations, Snetterton on 6 August saw Gerry's landmark 600th victory. He took that result in loyal supporter Geoffrey Marsh's Aston DB4.

John Llewellyn remembered some of the post-race partying: 'His famous 600th win at Snetterton meant some of us went along to watch in the hope that he would accomplish this magnificent feat. Of course, there had to be a drama, he loved a drama, and made an uncharacteristically bad start, and left it until three laps from the end before taking the lead and that 600th win. My God, did we sup some ale that night!'

John added: 'A few weeks later I organised a lunch for him at Silverstone to mark the occasion.

BELOW *'This is one Aston that is not yours, Geoffrey.' Geoffrey Marsh quizzes Gerry before a June 2000 outing. Contesting the Feltham Aston Martin event at Silverstone's St John Horsfall meeting, they were third in class.* [Marshall Family Archive]

I got TV footage there of him at Crystal Palace and other racing outings, his old Astons were there, "Old Nail", and all his family, including a new grandson.' Daughter Tina Lynch's proud contribution to the family tree appropriately carried the forenames Harry Gerald.

'The place was packed,' John continued, 'a proper sit-down lunch, after which we passed the microphone round so guests could tell a few stories about Gerry. Old rival Brodie told some fantastic ones.' That tells us a lot about generosity amongst the former bitter racetrack rivals and Harrow locals.

September 2000 was a glorious racing month for Gerry, with Spa-Francorchamps and the Goodwood Revival to tackle, both Mustang-mounted, with the Waterhouse Healey 100S as a Sussex Revival bonus. Spa's one-hour Top Hat classic saloon car thrash received minimal media coverage. However, we know that Gerry finished in the Mustang, officially fourth in class and out of top-six contention.

Goodwood Revival 2000 brought better fortune, Gerry chasing home friend and contributor to this chapter Nick Whale, both Mustang-mounted, in the St Mary's Trophy. (See the sidebar on page 206). Gerry did well to dispel memories of his practice session, when his Rostron-owned Mustang shed a wheel!

The Healey 100S went well at the Revival meeting too, beaten only by an agile Lotus Elite. The sleek Lotus was less than a second ahead at the close of the ten-lap Fordwater Trophy.

A couple of weekends later Gerry was busy at Donington, driving the DB4 to hard-fought overall victory and taking a Triumph TR6 to a class win in the half-hour 'endurance' race.

Unusually Gerry got beaten away from the start of a ten-lapper for Astons of all ages. Ronnie Farmer's well-prepared and recent DB7 was quickest away, albeit with – as Peter Scherer put it in *Autosport* – 'Gerry Marshall's DB4 nailed to its boot lid, and Roy Stephenson's DB4 and Malcolm Young's DBS V8 threatening to join in. Marshall grabbed the lead on the second lap.' As the race developed, 'Young edged ever closer until he spun backwards at Coppice. Marshall was left with a clear run to the flag.'

A rain-soaked Snetterton closed October and Gerry's lusty 2000 season with an outing in the 50th edition of the 750 MC's six-hour Relay. Marshall was scheduled out in an RX-7 Mazda, but it expired in practice. Fortunately CSCC Hot Shoes team came to the rescue with a ride in Steve Cripps Escort RS2000. The race itself only lasted five of the scheduled six hours because of the weather. Having passed his personal 600-win landmark in August, Gerry commented: 'The wins seem harder to come by these days, but I keep trying.'

Teaching Marshall arts

Gerry took the role of race instructor/driver coach more frequently as the seasons rolled by. Karl Jones recalled plenty of Gerry's amusing 1980s encounters with fellow instructors at BMW driving days, in the heyday of BMW's 6 series coupés.

Many benefited – all sorts of people, from new performance car owners to celebrities, appreciated his hands-on approach. Most famously, star musician Chris Rea described Gerry as 'My Hero'. Serious motoring man Rowan Atkinson of Blackadder/Mr Bean fame was also a Marshall racing pupil, appearing in the '80s crash-and-bash Renault 5 series (which also featured Andrew Ridgley of Wham!) as well as at Goodwood, the latter in the 21st century with some upright classics such as the larger Jaguar saloons.

When Gerry died, some Marshall-the-instructor memories surfaced – such as these TVR-related items, the first from Brands Hatch 1999: 'He took me on a fast lap in my then fairly newish Griff. Overtook everything. Fezzas [Ferraris], Caterfields [Caterham 7s and Westfields], Loti, you name it. Really opened my eyes to what the car would do. Highly enjoyable and shit scary at the same time. Then he instructed with me driving on a few more laps. A thoroughly top bloke.'

Another Griffith owner posted this: 'I spent one of the most terrifying laps ever with Gerry instructing me in the Griff. We had agreed, on the lap before, that I would not brake at the end of the Revett straight until he told me.

'As I passed my normal (*ie* mere mortal's) braking point, willing my right foot not to lift, I glanced nervously at Gerry, who yelled, "Not yet!"

'The next 50 metres or so, before he decided I should hit the brakes, were the longest of my entire life…'

ABOVE *This was the devilish black TVR device that Gerry employed to train novices, plenty of them vividly remembering the experience in internet tribute after his death.* [Marshall Family Archive]

CHAPTER 14

2001–4: Full-on final seasons

Although Gerry's life had less than five years to run, he packed in as much motorsport as possible alongside a refreshed personal life with Gwen Howard. Because of Gwen's unobtrusive personality it has been difficult to write a proper recognition of her importance to Gerry in those closing years, but we can gain some insights from friends and family.

Gwen was close to Gerry's now adult offspring, his 2005 funeral arrangements being made primarily through Gwen, Gerry's daughters Tina and Justine and his son Gregor. Other close family had inputs that we will discuss in the final chapter, but Gwen was obviously pivotal to Gerry and his relatives during that final five years.

There is a temptation to think that because of ill health and financial worries, Gwen and Gerry had a convenient relationship and not much more. Gerry's daughter Tina put us right on that one. 'Dad and Gwen came to stay for two days with me just four weeks prior to his passing away, and they were talking about marriage...' Gerry was apparently adamant that nothing was 'going to spoil what he had with Gwen,' according to several members of the Marshall family.

How did Gwen and Gerry meet?

This story seems agreed amongst family and friends. Loyal Marshall cohort Colin Pearcy

RIGHT *Hard work holding off the silver DB5's pursuit, its front panels and grille already scarred. Gerry scored two outright victories over this May 2003 racing weekend at Mallory Park to add to his 600 aggregate.* [Mary Harvey]

ABOVE AND BELOW *A fantastic 2001 Goodwood outing netted Gerry a Driver of the Day award for his wonderful win in the St Mary's Trophy. He drove the Chris Sanders Lotus Cortina, which is seen centre of the front row and behind owner Chris in the paddock celebration picture.* [Both Marshall Family Archive]

Son of Blydenstein

Gerry did a lot of race instruction over the years. One recipient of his race lore was Bill Blydenstein's son, Ben, who told us in May 2009: 'My own memory was of testing the Mini Cooper for the John Cooper Challenge at Silverstone in 2002. Gerry overhauled me at considerable speed on the straight in an Aston Martin, slowed, waved cheerily, and then accelerated away.

'Subsequently in the pit lane Gerry, Peter Baldwin (who helped me with set-up during testing) and "Whizzo" Williams were all together in my pit garage. They had a good chat about events past and present and drew quite a crowd.'

Ben added: 'Incidentally, I came third at the Silverstone round and got fastest lap.' So all that advice was not wasted…

explains: 'Gwen lived opposite the second house Gerry had in Pitstone. My understanding was that they met when both were mowing their lawns!' Colin paused for merriment at the thought of this epitome of high-speed panache chatting up his lady neighbour. Actually they struck up a friendship in which Lloyds bank administration manageress Gwen Howard – who had moved into Pitstone less than a year before – effectively ran a separate Marshall household, becoming a constant companion and facing with him the multiple health problems that clouded Gerry's 21st-century years.

Late in 2009, Gregor expanded on these. 'Dad's back problems started after the Dolly shunt at Silverstone in 1979. Years of driving un-servo-assisted braking systems and non-power-steered cars, along with Dad's large frame, took their toll. It was around 2000 that Dad started to use sticks and had to use a buggy to get about. That was a combination of bad back (he had a cancerous growth on his spine removed and a couple of vertebra fused) and having severe arthritis in his knees. Both knees required replacement surgery. Unfortunately about six weeks after that surgery, Dad tripped and fell, and broke his hip. That put him back on sticks, and having to use an electric buggy again. Finally, he got his hip replaced and then he was back on two legs again!'

Gerry showed considerable courage when confronting the repetitive hospital and electric buggy spells that his health latterly dictated. Both Pearcy and AC Cobra owner Kevin Kivlochan subsequently confirmed that when driver changes were demanded in longer 2001 and 2004 races, Gerry asked that they simply haul him out of the car and leave him lying on the ground, to be picked up at their convenience, when the Cobra departed!

John Llewellyn commented of Gerry's changing life with Gwen: 'In Gerry's last few years, when I had moved to live in Tring, we used to meet several times a week for a quick drink … which never was quick, of course! I've often said that GM's passing has lengthened my life expectancy by many years, as I don't drink anything like what I did when he was around.

'Regularly he would drop Gwen off at Tesco and come round for a cup of tea. We have a wicker chair that – because of the way he sat in it – we named *Toad's Chair*.

'And it really was tea, nothing more!'

John also recalled a hospital story that has echoes of Gregor's separate memory of an earlier hospital stay.

'The Gwen years were also the ones that Gerry was most poorly,' said John. 'However, he would always drive himself to hospital, and home again, no matter how serious the op.

'In the Royal Orthopaedic Hospital, Stanmore, he met and got on well with the guy in the next bed. They decided one night that they would tell the nursing staff they were going to the TV room to watch a film. Instead, they escaped in their pyjamas and dressing gowns down to the local pub in Gerry's car. When they got back it was late and the front door was locked: they couldn't get back in! They had to keep ringing the bell until Security came to let them in.'

'Imagine their faces when they opened the doors and saw Marshall stood there, well-inebriated, in his pyjamas,' said Gwen. 'Gerry was always escaping from hospital. I used to see him most evenings, but he'd always say he was happy to see me go by early evening as he wanted to get off down the pub with his new mates!'

The similar incident recalled by Gregor saw Gerry befriend a group of bikers in hospital, young bloods with obvious injuries that included missing limbs. This time he drove a small party out to the pub, where they attracted a lot of interest with their restricted hospital dress, missing limbs and high-profile bandaging.

Gerry got them all back inside the ward without a fuss that time.

Now it's time to get back to motor racing, and some remarkable results recorded in Gerry's final four seasons, 2001 to 2004. Backbone to his competition forays was Geoffrey Marsh, and particularly his Aston Martin DB4. Although Gerry

ABOVE *Gerry was reunited with 'Baby Bertha' in a 2001 move initiated by General Motors and former Triumph Dolomite teammate, Rex Greenslade.* [Glynn Williams]

'Baby What?'

Rex Greenslade explained how Gerry was reunited very publicly with 'Baby Bertha' at the Goodwood Festival in 2001.

'Gerry and I reconnected in 2001. My company had been awarded GM's worldwide heritage communications business and we were looking for suitable personalities and cars for the Goodwood Festival of Speed. Top of my mind was Gerry and "Baby Bertha".

'"Baby *What*?" the suits in Detroit said, not knowing Gerry's charming habit of giving his cars quaint names. The win sheet and Gerry's popularity soon persuaded them. I managed to track him down through the BRDC.

'We did the deal for Goodwood and through it rekindled our friendship. I found him a changed person. Quiet, reserved, thankful beyond belief for this chance to parade his stuff with the car that was closest to his heart.

'Gerry brought up 1979. It was an "awful year", he said, because of dealing with Davenport, Walkinshaw and all the technical wrangling. And, of course, dealing with me. But he said it with a smile, showing that any long-term animosity was gone forever. I'd managed to produce a large blow-up of the rock-ape style caricature that *Motor* used for his column in the '70s and got it placed in "Baby Bertha" when he wasn't looking. He positively beamed with the surprise.

'By then, I'd been retired from racing for 20 years and in the United States for 17. I'd seen the stories about his "600" wins, which amused me greatly – I was a Gerry fan first, race rival second, after all. But I had heard that his other contemporaries had been upset by what they saw as grandstanding, using figures that they didn't believe. I know that this caused some bridges to others to be burned irrevocably.

'Apparently, there was a distance in his relationship with Vauxhall. Perhaps they wanted to emphasise the future, not the past, an attitude we ran into all the time on heritage communications. I'd like to think that the Goodwood programme helped to reconnect him with GM and Vauxhall.'

the seriously powerful competition cars he loved, including a Chevrolet Corvette and a Ford Galaxie that exceeded 7-litres, and he was reunited with 'Baby Bertha's' V8 firepower too. He also appeared at least four times in an excellent AC Cobra, travelled extensively in Europe to race the Rostron Mustang, returned podium places in a well-known Healey 100S, and had a headline rain-master tussle with Cooper S legend John Rhodes, successfully employing a Lotus Cortina to win this Goodwood battle of British saloon car racing legends. We also have the rib-tickling 2003 tale of how Gerry's pole position and winning co-drive in a Mazda RX-7 defeated a 500hp Jaguar.

Recognition of his efforts during these closing seasons included a Driver of the Day award from Goodwood in September 2001 and a BARC Gold Medal in 2002 to mark his outstanding contribution to British motorsports and a lifetime of personal achievement.

2001

This season was a remarkable one, with half a dozen overseas events to relish alongside plenty of the big banger drives Gerry adored. These covered the biggest of them all, a 7.2-litre Corvette, plus a 7-litre Galaxie, regular rides in the Rostron Mustang, a brace of outings in a superb AC Cobra – and an emotional reunion with 'Baby Bertha' at Goodwood.

The year started well with an April class win in the Aston DB4 at Brands Hatch, a result he equalled in September at Donington to complete a two-out-of-two 100 per cent class-winning record in the classic Aston.

ABOVE *Gerry back at work signing autographs at Brands Hatch. Many of those in the queue for signatures had DTV memorabilia in hand, including portraits of 'Baby Bertha' to be annotated by their hero.* [Marshall Family Archive]

enjoyed some serious overseas competition at legendary tracks, these seasons are particularly notable for the wealth of comment we had from those who shared their cars or racetrack adventures with him.

The Goodwood Revival and Festival became important diary dates in the Marshall year and he continued to entertain and return results in Lord March's consistently dazzling displays of our motoring heritage.

Nostalgically, most Goodwood spectators will remember the unlikely sight of an Alvis *Grey Lady* – superbly re-engineered by Ivan/Tim Dutton's famed Bugatti craftsmen – seizing second in the St Mary's Trophy of 2004. However, during this quartet of motorsport seasons Gerry also drove yet more of

RIGHT *Another aspect of DTV reunited, Gerry, Bill Blydenstein and 'Baby B' get back together.* [Marshall Family Archive]

Kevin's Cobra tales

Cobra owner Kevin Kivlochan wrote in February 2009: 'I first met Gerry briefly at one of the Goodwood Revivals, just for a few moments, when I had a photograph taken of me with him. The following year, I was driving through the paddock at Donington Park in a Toyota Landcruiser when he jumped out in front of me waving his walking stick. I wound the window down and he asked me for a lift to the other end of the paddock. He got into the back seat of the car and explained that his legs were not what they used to be.

'I said that I would on one condition – and that was that he would do a race with me in my car.

'He said "Yes" straight away … Then asked what the car was!

'I told him that it was an AC Cobra. Gerry asked my name.

'When I said Kevin Kivlochan, he said that he had always wanted to meet me as he had heard so much about me. I was initially flattered, soon realising that he probably did not have a clue who I was, but that did not matter. If it had been anyone else saying this, it would have been a piss-take, but Gerry was a charmer and meant every word.

'We did many races together and they were the best and most enjoyable. Not because we won or anything like that, but he knew how to live life to the full. He would always take the time to introduce me to his friends and include me.

'A mate of mine, Adam, would often come to the races to help spanner and watch. Gerry would always talk to him and include him. It might seem a strange thing to remember, but sadly not all people are like Gerry. Adam was a young lad who could offer Gerry nothing materialistic, only his friendship. For Gerry that was more than enough.

'Sadly, there are many in the paddock that measure friendship by the size of wallet, but not Gerry.'

'Gerry wrote me a letter following our race at Castle Combe. He thanked me for giving him the chance to celebrate 40 years of racing and told me how it helped to give him his confidence back. Castle Combe pictures in *Autosport* showed we had to physically help him out of the car at the driver change. It was a kind of joke for us at that time.

'Gerry was always faster than me in the car (apart from once) and I would jest with him how I could walk faster … Incidentally, I was never sure how he got his race licence at that time. [Journalists were still commenting on that in 2009! – JW]

'The one time that I did a better lap time than him he was genuinely gutted, but he also took it as an opportunity to make a big thing of it to all his mates. He would make up excuses of how he was not feeling well etc. I am sure that he used this as a way to thank me for the drive, as he knew that it would make me feel good.

'We had to have Gerry start every race as it just took too long to get him into the car, but once he was in there was no stopping him. For the driver changes, he would ask the team just to haul him out of the car as quickly as possible, even if it meant throwing him to the ground! Gerry was no marathon runner, so it took some doing to hold him up, and at Combe he almost collapsed in the pits.

'But hell, he was fast once he was in the car.'

'The Snetterton race [October 2001; they took fifth in class – JW] was a period when Gerry was in his electric wheelchair. We spent the night before in the clubhouse at Snetterton. Gerry had us in stitches of laughter, mock racing his buggy around the tables, crashing and banging into everything.

'My races with Gerry were the most serious fun I ever had in historic racing. He was a true inspiration to me in both racing and the art of living life to the full, and still is to this day. It has been years now since Gerry died and I guess the best way to show what he meant to me is that I still have his mobile number registered in my phone.

'A picture of Gerry and I at Donington Park takes pride of place on my desk at work, along with the rest of my family…'

Gregor commented in 2009 that 'Kevin Kivlochan has been great at keeping in touch, and Dad did love racing his Cobra. Kevin recently bought Dad's Land Rover; I tracked it down for him, as Dad had tried selling it to him before he passed away. Kevin was disappointed, so he pestered the guy Dad sold it to, and has now bought it.'

May saw the beginning of the heavyweight stuff with a brace of weekend outings at Donington in Kevin Kivlochan's Cobra (see the 'Kevin's Cobra tales' sidebar on page 215). Gerry also made his 2001 debut in the Rostron Mustang.

Auctioneer Guy Loveridge gave us this unique view of Gerry's run to second place in that Cloth Cap Top Hat Donington event: 'I was on the back row of the grid in my MkI Sprite, alongside Simon Hope of H&H Classic Auctions, my employer and the series' sponsor.

'When the flag fell I accelerated hard and found, thanks to the Sprite's nimbleness and everyone else's caution, that I could carry on flat around

Original values

Guy Loveridge has a recollection that dates from the Goodwood Festival of Speed Press Day in 2005, the year Gerry died: 'I had finally found a *really* good condition copy of Gerry's earlier biography, *Only Here For The Beer*. So, with David Brazil, an old mechanic of Gerry's, I went to seek him out.

'As I approached, he smiled, recognised me, and asked, "Are you sharing your Sprite with my mate's daughter again this season?"

'"No, Gerry, not this year."

'"Ah well, not to worry. Not such a top driver." He paused. "Great tits, mind!"

'We laughed, and I handed him my book to sign.'

'"Do you know, one of these sold on eBay last week, signed, for 85 quid?"

'I said I didn't know.

'"Wasn't signed by me, mind you, for some reason it was signed by Pentti Airikkala!"

'Gerry duly signed my book and was about to hand it back when he looked at me quizzically, and said, "Is this going straight in one of your f——g auctions?'

'"No, Gerry. This is for my personal library."

'"OK then." He wrote in something else, handed me the book and started a conversation with Lord March.

'I walked from the house out into the spring sunshine, and opened the book to read *To Guy, with all best wishes, Gerry Marshall. P.S. This book is now totally devalued!*

'Not a chance Gerry, not a chance.'

Guy also remembered the Snetterton paddock at another Top Hat meeting.

'I took around a copy of the 1964 Motor Racing Register for drivers to sign. Gabriel Konig, Jack Sears and more, all duly signed.

'I took the book to Tony Lanfranchi. He signed his name, and then looked up at Gerry, who was sat opposite him at a table.

'"Oi, look Marshall! I've got 14 lines, you only rated two!"

'Gerry held his hand out, looked at the register and winked at me as he signed it.

'"Yes, Tony, that's because you had to pay to be a member, and I was spending my money on cars..." He handed me the book back, and added, "...And girls, of course!"'

Red Gate and down the Craner Curves. I made up about 12 places.

'Naturally, as we hit the long straight the more powerful cars overtook me, but it gave me some self-belief. I was able to press on and enjoy the race. After less than five laps, the leaders were catching me up to lap the smaller capacity Sprite. So I was looking as much in my mirror as I was at the track as I came down the hill on the GP loop to the Melbourne Hairpin. I looked back again, and there was Gerry in Kevin Kivlochan's Cobra.

'"Yikes," I thought, moving to the left of the track. I pointed for Gerry to pass me on my right, inside. As he went past, I looked over and Gerry eyeballed me and gave me a quick thumbs-up with his left hand, and then blasted off uphill.

'I was gob-smacked, and tried to follow him. Failed, of course.

'In the paddock afterwards, at the prize-giving, I apologised ... had I slowed him at all?

'Gerry said, "No, not at all," and thanked me for the courtesy. Quietly he explained, away from the others, how he felt I could improve my lines around Donington.

'I was both flattered and mesmerised.

'Gerry was driving one of the fastest cars out there, fighting for an eventual second place – and yet had time to critique the driving of one of the slowest. What a hero!'

The Mustang FIA historic season with Max Rostron covered Monza, Zandvoort, Zolder, Nürburgring, and Dijon. There were class wins at Zandvoort in Holland and at the August Nürburgring Oldtimers meeting.

Friend and rival Mustang driver Nick Whale particularly remembers the German weekend. Nick got so drunk in Gerry's company he could not race – much to the disgust of his sons – but Gerry's top-three result was noted in the *Autosport* report: 'Gerry Marshall netted a popular career win number 604, relaying Max Rostron's Mustang to third overall [first in class – GM Jr]. It was a close thing, as the faster Gerry Wainwright/Allen Lloyd machine was right on its tail at the flag despite no fewer than three Stop-Go penalties.'

Another seasonal highlight was the reunion with 'Baby Bertha' at Goodwood, an event visited by a record 123,000 people on that three-day weekend. The background to this occasion can be found in the sidebar 'Baby *What*?' on page 213. Gerry was second in class, and there was a great picture of the heroic V8 Vauxhall in *Autosport*, captioned: 'Big man, big talent, big power – Gerry Marshall in Baby Bertha.'

Gerry starred again at the September Goodwood revival. This time he shared quick West Countryman Chris Sanders' Lotus Cortina (registered 828 CDL). *Autosport* said it all: 'Gerry Marshall may not currently be able to walk unaided, but by Jove while he awaits surgery to fix his damaged back [a legacy from the 1979 Dolomite accident – JW] can the burly saloon legend still drive. Spectators all around the 2.4-mile circuit were whipped into a frenzy as Marshall hurled Chris Sanders' Lotus Cortina around in an absorbing dice with Justin Law, exercising his considerable car control in the ex-Albert Betts Jaguar Mk1. Time after time, their order changed as they jinked and danced their way through the St Mary's Trophy back markers in an awesome display of precision motoring,' ran the breathless prose. Less imaginatively, the Jag started to smoke.

Gerry went on to win over three other decent Lotus Cortinas, including drivers of such talent as Jackie Oliver and the late David Leslie. Poignantly, Gerry took a prestigious Goodwood Driver of the Day trophy – a large silver car – for his triumph over the opposition and obvious health issues. It would be his penultimate major award.

Our hero had less luck in the RAC TT Celebration event at Goodwood, the 7.2-litre Chevrolet Corvette he shared with John Young ending up amongst the 'beached Jags at Woodcote', the race being stopped at three-quarter distance because of the accident rate.

That was not the end of Gerry's 2001 Cortina competition mileage. He also took on a brace of outings in October at a then new Rockingham track, originally built with oval racing in mind but with a widely used infield loop for conventional road racing. Gerry managed a close (less than two seconds in it) second overall to Chris Sanders in the Cortina Gerry and he shared at Goodwood, and was credited with a second in class for a separate outing on the same date in the same loaned Ford.

2002

This was a comparatively low-key season, with just a dozen events entered and four wins. Yet the variety of vehicles and the warmth with which Britain's biggest winner was greeted, particularly at Goodwood Festival hillclimb and the Revival race meeting, kept Gerry firmly in the public and motoring media eye.

'Baby Bertha' rumbled at the Festival again, officially winning her class. Gerry won a coveted Karl Bloechle Trophy for his efforts and also enjoyed a personal battle across the classes, setting very similar times to a Ford NASCAR stocker driven by Ron Huber.

Owned by Boysie Thurtle, whose father, Arthur, was also an Aston racer, an Aston V8 took Gerry to one class win at Brands Hatch in May. That marked a double for Marshall at this Aston historic meeting, as he also won with the Marsh DB4. In May he won

Rotary victory

Stacy Vickers is a multiple Classic Touring Car Championship and Britcar 24-hour class winner. He now races in his faithful Mazda RX-7 in Toyo Tyres' saloon series and continues to take wins. He sent us these witty racing memories:

'The final 2003 round of the Group 1 Championship was at Oulton Park. We had the championship wrapped up, so Gerry was a guest driver in the Mazda RX-7. I would test the car on the Friday, and Gerry would arrive Saturday morning for qualifying.

'Friday passed without incident, though it did look as though Gerry might not make it, suffering heavily in the aftermath of intensive medical treatment. Our RX-7 was great, and we were packing up ready for race day when the phone rang. Gerry said, "I can be a retired racing driver any time, but I don't want to be a retired racing driver yet. Can I come up?"

'The weekend was back on.

'Gerry entered the paddock just after scrutineering to sign on, and there was a tangible buzz. He was clearly the visiting celeb. Paperwork completed, Gerry tried the seat for size. The bum was lowered, the belts pulled over, and then he realised that he had room to spare – I was a bigger chap.

'"Blimey, you're a fat bastard aren't you?" he grinned.

'With the banter flowing he made his way out to qualify, and came back ten laps later with pole position, ahead of the 500bhp Jaguar XJ-S that had dominated the series for years prior to our RX-7.

'"Understeers terribly, Stacy," he said. This was a surprise, because Yvan Muller had driven the car a few weeks previously and told me it oversteered too much!

'We loaded up the data logger and downloaded Gerry's session to see how it differed from mine. A few seconds later Dave Warner – mechanic extraordinaire – called me over. He had loaded up Gerry's throttle trace. "It's like a bloody hacksaw blade!"

'Seemingly, the understeer at Druids, the fastest corner on the lap taken in fourth gear at circa 100mph, was too much of an irritant for Gerry. He was arriving at full speed and loading the car up in the corner, fully lifting the throttle before mashing it back down again to kick the rear out. Repeat this as many times as required before the apex. For most people, including me I suspect, it would have resulted in a disappearance backwards through the tyre wall and a landing in the nearest town, Northwich.

'At the very least, you'd have needed tickets to get back in, and would be very late for tea.

'The wait between qualifying and the race was also punctuated by a visit from the marshals' representative. Gerry had been given a Mintex Award for the person most obviously trying hard in qualifying by taking pole. The marshals just adored him, and it doesn't take too much thought to see why.

'The race was no less entertaining.

'I chatted to Gerry in the collecting area suggesting that – if the XJ-S did get in front from the lights – he needed to dispatch it very quickly indeed. The Jag was a big old car, and could be made the widest Jaguar ever, prodigious straight-line speed making up for lower corner speeds. The Jag also had uprated brakes, which no longer faded at the tail end of a race. Although the rival XJ-S in second place on the grid put its power down well, its driver was always nervous on cold tyres. I told Gerry this was his best bet – harass Jag Man and get it done by any means on the first couple of laps. Otherwise, it could be a long race staring at the back of a Jaguar.

'The Jaguar did indeed out-drag the little Mazda into the first corner, and the first lap seemed to take a very long time indeed. Then Gerry came round and we breathed a sigh of relief. However, we noticed that the Jaguar XJ-S hadn't made it, and worse, there seemed to be the slightest ripple on the nearside wing of the RX-7.

'At the same time, the red flags came out. Hmm.

'Gerry parked the car on the grid and I wandered over. The slight ripple was a big knock on the nearside front corner, and I opened the door to see what he had to say. "You weren't lying about cold tyres, he came to a bloody standstill! Sorry…"

'Apparently, Gerry had tracked the Jag into the fast Druids corner, when the inevitable happened as the Jag's anchors went on early. Gerry had given it a punt and it beached up on the gravel.

'Oops.

'It was clear we were not terribly popular! Still, I did say by any means, I suppose.

'They recovered the Jaguar and the restart took place. This time, though, the RX-7 was unchallenged, as the Jaguar driver seemed less keen to race. This left Gerry with enough time to set a new lap record, which stood for some four years, and win by a comfortable margin.

'In the bar post-race Gerry held court as only he could, and the weekend ended up with fish and chips on the way back to the motorway, with a bottle of champagne from the back seat.'

from pole at Brands Hatch, again in the Marsh DB4, this as Boysie Thurtle was penalised ten seconds for a yellow flag incident after an apparent win.

One of the best results came in the Kivlochan Cobra (this time COB 6008), which qualified third in its class but won outright at Donington. (See 'Kevin's Cobra tales', page 215.)

Goodwood Revival was Gerry's busiest weekend, with three rides arranged. RWD 323, the Waterhouse Healey 100S, gave him another great race, finishing second overall. He equalled

that result in Justin Law's Mk1 Jaguar 2.4, the Jag restricted to much smaller capacity than for 2001. A return to Chevrolet and the Corvette was an attractive proposition, but it qualified only 15th and finished 11th.

The Aston Martin marque and the Marsh connection was not forgotten in 2002, Gerry winning an outright and a class victory in the DB4 while closing his season at the AMOC Silverstone meeting in September. Graham Read wrote for *Autosport*: 'Boysie Thurtle got the better

ABOVE *The Waterhouse-owned Healey 100S (numberplate RWD 323) gave Gerry terrific Goodwood Revival races. Here he battles a Morgan at the 2002 event, to take second overall.* [LAT]

LEFT *The racing friendship continues into the 21st century. Gerry and Tony Lanfranchi share another pit counter, this time at Goodwood Revival in 2002.* [Linzi Smart]

of polesitter Gerry Marshall when the lights went to green at the start of the Aston Martin Championship race, and remained in front of the pack to the close. Marshall's DB4 closed on the victorious V8 in the later stages, but had to settle for the runner-up spot ahead of a recovering Arthur Thurtle [in the family's second V8 – JW], who had earlier spun out of second at Luffield.'

BELOW *Sensation of Goodwood Revival 2004. The saloon car event for the St Mary's Trophy featured the Ivan Dutton-created Alvis Grey Lady. Gerry qualified fifth and finished a fabulous second, leaving a lot of more conventional saloon car racing machinery in his wake.* [Glynn Williams]

Incidentally, Geoffrey Marsh did not count class victories in the total of 61 wins attributed to Gerry's efforts in the Marsh Plant Hire records supplied to us in June 2009. From these statistics, we can also see that Gerry had more outings for Marsh than any of the other drivers Geoffrey employed to wheel his collection of Astons, Lolas and the BRM P25 between 1977 and 2008. Between them, Richard Bond, Robert Lamplough, Mike Salmon, Ray and Michael Mallock, Gary Pearson, Malcolm Young and Anthony Reid won 25 events, Bond taking eight wins and Ray Mallock recording six.

Gerry's best season for Marsh – 1981, in the DBR4 and Lola T70 – saw him equal Bond's total tally in a single year!

2003

Gerry Marshall returned to full throttle this year, appearing at 22 events. Over half of these sorties were in Aston DB4s to rack up five outright victories in the Marsh Plant example and a further win, plus a class victory, in other loaned DBs. There was a memorable Oulton Park defeat of a 500hp Jaguar with an RX-7 (see the 'Rotary victory' sidebar on page 218), plus a Silverstone one-off in the Rostron Mustang that yielded a pole position and second overall late in the season.

There were also demands for Gerry to complete demonstrations or sprint runs in 'Baby Bertha'. The V8 legend appeared at Brighton Speed Trials, and was officially placed 12th in a racing car class, but what a spectacle! A Vauxhall Centenary Celebration at Shelsley Walsh hillclimb saw Gerry and 'Baby B' out again, and at the tenth Goodwood Festival the following July weekend, where the records show an official fourth in class … but so long as 'Baby Bertha' ran, and Big Gerry was aboard, none of the record 158,000 crowd cared much about the result. At the end of August DTV personnel, Gerry, Bill

Blydenstein, and 'Baby Bertha' were reunited for some Brands Hatch demonstration laps at a BARC Championship meeting.

Once again, September's Goodwood Revival offered a variety of race rides. Unfortunately, a return to the Chris Sanders Lotus Cortina allowed just a fifth in practice for the St Mary's Trophy, followed by a race retirement when a water hose split. A contemporary report denies that Gerry raced, but a superb Jim Houlgrave grid picture shows Gerry blasting off inside 828 CDL in a sea of Ford Falcons, headed by Barrie Williams in a Cooper S registered 10 NOB. Barrie took third and set fastest lap amongst the larger motor metal – not so knobby after all!

The John Young Corvette did not qualify for the TT Celebration race, but was allowed to race at the Revival from the back. Gerry cracked tenth place eventually in the Chev shared with John, amongst a field full of finely honed E-types, Ferraris, and AC Cobras.

The extended Aston DB4 season brought drama in October when Gerry snatched a late victory in a 15-lap encounter at Brands. Here is a taste of the excitement and sportsmanship on display from a contemporary Dud Candler report: '"Who *was* that? He didn't put a foot wrong and I'm sorry about beating him." Those were the words of prolific race winner Gerry Marshall, who snatched victory in the final seconds of a most incredible Thoroughbred Sports Cars race.'

That opening paragraph led into a description of tricky conditions that left the track wet under strong sunshine. The pole position man stalled and MGA driver Mark Ellis seized the initiative to lead from Wyndham's E-type whilst Marshall made 'alarming progress, his Aston Martin DB4 spinning its wheels even in a straight line! He was up to second by lap three, but locked in battle with Harry Wyndham's well-driven E-type. After 15 laps, Marshall caught Ellis within sight of the chequered flag to claim the last lap victory,' read the contemporary account.

There was more at that meeting, for Gerry also completed a Brands 14-lapper for Aston Martin Championship points in the DB4, this time versus the V8 power of Arthur Thurtle. Thurtle won after an early spin, Marshall was second and a class winner, along with famous former pupil Rowan Atkinson, who sported a Vantage.

2004

All but four of Gerry's 2004 season races were in Marsh's Aston DB4, which had adopted a 4.2-litre motor by autumn. In total GM tackled 14 events, scored podium positions in half of them and secured two overall wins, plus a single class result.

Racing beyond the Aston world saw Gerry in the most extraordinary Goodwood mount for the St Mary's Trophy race at the Revival meeting. Ingenious Ivan Dutton and his team of fabled craftsmen – known throughout the Bugatti restoration world – concocted a unique Alvis racing saloon.

Ivan bought a '50s Alvis TC21, known as the *Grey Lady* series, from a widow at a garden fete in 1999–2000. Chuckling Ivan paid £800, but this would be no bargain basement conversion, for a custom crankshaft demanded over £3,000. With a wary eye on Goodwood's preferences for a period interior and exterior to invited competition cars, modifications were subtle in respect of appearance, radical in fundamental engineering.

The wooden flooring went, the body now carried on outriggers and bolted on to the chassis, a tailor-made Safety Devices cage increasing stiffness significantly. They reworked the suspension, enabling adjustable competition castor

Monaco celebrity

John Llewellyn told us this story in February 2009:

'I always wanted Gerry to come down to my place in the south of France, and persuaded him to attend the 2004 Historic Grand Prix.

'Gerry and Gwen came down for a week and stayed on board. He wasn't very able at the time, and my crew had to help him up and down the *passarelle*, until after lunch when a few glasses of wine had gone down. Whenever he saw someone walking by on the quay, he would shout his or her name then sprint down the same *passarelle* completely unaided!

'I had my new yacht moored stern to, just before the chicane.

'On the Saturday night, we had a few guests for dinner. My skipper came to me during the main course, which we were having on the fly bridge, in full view of people walking by. Skipper said, "John, have you looked out over the back of the boat lately?"

'I said "No" and looked out. It was amazing, there must have been 30 or so people standing there pointing out Gerry Marshall.

'Just two days after the Historic I took him to the Monaco BRDC lunch, hosted by Henry Taylor. Held at the bar/restaurant on *Rascasse*, everybody was so pleased to see him. Behind us, Henry had draped a full size BRDC flag.

'As we sat down for lunch, Gerry turned to me and said, "John, we are getting slow in our old age."

'I said, "What do you mean?"

'Gerry replied, "We would have had that flag away half an hour ago!"

'Needless to say, come evening the flag was resplendent, hanging from the back of my yacht!

'It has now become a tradition that I nick it every year: it's expected.'

Gerry's favourites … and a few regrets

Asked the inevitable 'What's your favourite car?' question in 1999, Gerry replied, 'I owned an Aston V8 for more than ten years, so I obviously liked that as a road car. On track, I also had a Lister Jag of my own which was a favourite.'

When, after his 600th win in 2000, Gerry was asked the same question specifically about racecars, he answered, 'I love big hairy cars. So I remember the Lister Jaguars, Aston Martin DB4s, a Lola T70 and "Baby Bertha" fondly.'

Asked about racetracks in the same August 2000 *Autosport* interview, he rated the rapid circuits like the old (long) Spa, Thruxton, and Snetterton as his favourites. Agreeing with Tony Lanfranchi's earlier verdict on his fast track pace, Gerry explained, 'I don't like slower corners because I am untidy in them. [He chuckled.] I try too hard.'

Although Gerry drove an astonishing variety of competition cars, he did have regrets. In 2000 he stated: 'I've never done enough historic stuff, which I find frustrating. I've never raced a Maserati 250F. Or ERA, for example. That's a gap I'd love to fill.'

He also expressed personal reservations about his life. 'I wish I hadn't upset so many people. And that I'd known then what I know now about sorting a car. I must have been incredibly naïve to get away with some of the things I did, but have always been incredibly loyal to my teams. I passionately believed that Vauxhall was the best in the '70s, and the company is still brilliant to me.'

and camber settings. The unlikely Alvis was now substantially lower thanks to the remounted body resting on a strengthened chassis, which hosted another cross-member.

Gerry commented 'It's an easy car to drive fast,' after the quick Alvis recreation shocked onlookers with its front-running pace in such an unlikely and upright outline. It had an estimated 140hp, replacing the 1954 showroom 101hp.

Gerry seized second overall in his heat of the St Mary's Trophy. Ivan secured a fifth in his Sunday outing, placing the Alvis third on aggregate.

Talking to us in 2009, Ivan added: 'When it came to building the Alvis there really was only one person I could ask to drive it with me, Gerry. During practice a half-shaft broke, which meant I didn't get to practice. I just had to do my three laps to qualify it.

'When Gerry raced it, he did drive it superbly as the old girl wasn't actually that quick. We had terrible problems with overheating, but it handled perfectly straight out of the box. I thoroughly enjoyed my race in it.

'The car had taken longer than I thought to prepare, so it was remarkably standard engine-wise, just [upgraded] rods and pistons, but standard carbs and exhaust. I reckon there was another 40bhp to come from the engine but I think

Goodwood knew that too – hence why it's not been invited back since Gerry and I raced it!

'I had to sell it – it was too depressing having it sitting in the workshop unraced and knowing how much time and effort I'd put into it. I didn't get much for it when I sold it, £17k, nowhere near what I effing spent on the thing!'

Other Goodwood weekend ventures were not so successful: the Waterhouse Healey 100S finished third and an exotic Ferrari 330 LMB galloped to eighth for Gerry in the TT Celebration race. He stated in one of his last interviews that the Healey race was probably one of his best and the Ferrari was a big disappointment. That was due to a bump at the start with eventual winner Dickie Attwood, leaving the Ferrari with a slow puncture that had to be changed when handing over to Peter Hardman. Gerry did well to keep it as far up the grid as he did.

The 14-event season had started for Gerry in July with four DB4 races, followed by another September to October sequence of five DB4 entries that yielded a brace of outright wins for the Marsh equipe, three podium positions and a class win. There was more Aston action with that 4.2-litre in the regular Marsh DB4, which returned a retirement and a second place.

The season and Gerry's racing career closed with a November outing in Michael Steele's Lotus Cortina, which qualified 16th for the British Racing Driver's Club members' race at Silverstone, finishing 15th. Gerry had been made a lifetime member of the BRDC back in the '70s.

As we prepared this book for press, Gregor revealed that he had discovered more than 1,400 motorsport entries and over 450 trophies and assorted awards logged to his father's credit. These included more than 400 assigned trophies, mementoes and cups that could be attributed to championships or seasonal recognition of Gerry's achievements, plus 13 other awards that could not be linked to particular events.

If you want to see some Marshall memorabilia, the Donington Collection (www.Donington-park. co.uk/grand-prix-collection-museum) has a sizeable chunk, including trophies, overalls, helmet, a fine montage by Andrew Kitson of some of Gerry's most successful cars, and the 'Old Nail' Firenza. All are gathered in a corner of the world's finest historic display of Grand Prix hardware.

A full listing of Gerry's astounding racing record – surely the largest to be documented in the UK – is found at the back of this book, and led to Walton wanting this book to be titled *Britain's Biggest Winner*.

LEFT *In the 2004 Goodwood Revival Paddock, Gerry is flanked by Grand Prix and international sports car legend Richard 'Dickie' Attwood (left) and current Audi ace Alan McNish. Alan also tasted Formula 1 with Toyota.* [Glynn Williams]

BELOW *The Marsh Aston DB4 continued to deliver pole-position pace in Autumn 2004, gaining a 4.2-litre engine update during the season.* [Marshall Family Archive]

CHAPTER 15

The end: 2005

Talking to us in 2009, Gerry's final companion Gwen Howard said, 'It's true what his friends have told you. Gerry did live right opposite me; we did meet doing our gardens ... And I still live at the same place, because it has many happy and loving memories for me. Although, as we speak, Gerry's house is about to sell for a second time since his death.'

Conveniently, Gerry and Gwen kept their separate houses in Pitstone, but how did their relationship develop?

Gwen laughed, and said, 'I moved in during 1999, but it was some time before we went out together. He tried to set up a meeting with me through my sister and her partner first. My sister knew he was famous in motor racing, but I hadn't got a clue – it came right out of the blue when I realised just how well-known he was, because I did not follow the sport. When that set-up with my sister didn't work out, then Gerry told me my brake lights were not working on the car ... then he couldn't fix one of them! So he had to get somebody else in to do that, but by then he had asked me out. We went to the Chequers at Weston Turville for an evening meal in May 2000.'

It was not all cheery pub meals.

LEFT *Gerry and Roger Clark were an extrovert double act at BRDC Balls in London and a frequent race-weekend social duo for more than 30 years after their memorable 1–2 on The Avon Tour of Britain. Roger Albert Clark MBE died before Gerry, in January 1998.* [Marshall Family Archive]

Gwen quietly and strongly looked after many of Gerry's daily needs, and stayed supportively in the background for racing weekends. Most significantly, she saw him through some of his worst medical problems.

Gwen recalled: 'The main hospital time was spent on back surgery at Stoke Mandeville to tackle a spinal growth, and repairing both knee joints at separate intervals over three months or so. Some of the knee work was done at a private hospital at Great Missenden in Buckinghamshire and some at Mandeville, but there were some typically Gerry snags.

'The first knee operation went to so well he was ready for the second, but you have to understand this was against the odds, as Gerry was told not to drive for six weeks. Nobody was ever going to stop him driving, and as soon as he was out, he was at the wheel! The second op went well too, and Gerry was so glad to be out of the pain that he bore so well. Unfortunately, he fell and cracked his hip shortly after the second knee was done … that meant a hip replacement operation.

'Always, he was exactly the sort of determined

BELOW *Gerry's pristine 1930 Model A Tudor Ford, originally restored at the Lakeland Museum, affordably satisfied his collector lust in later years.* [Jenny Cook]

and fast-recovering patient that they hold up as an example to others,' recalled Gwen.

In a totally separate incident, Gerry got 'one of those little electric things to scooter about [a two-wheel Go-Ped – GM Jr]. This was just before Goodwood Revival, and I was out at work when he fell off and cracked his head and suffered quite a lot of facial cuts. Most people would have said, "OK, I'll give the racing a miss," but nothing would stop him, and he raced so well. Even if he couldn't walk and felt lousy on the way to a track, the adrenaline of racing again would carry him through the pain, and he'd race so well. He lived for it.'

Gwen recounted how Gerry cared about his fans. 'The first Goodwood Revival we went to, Gerry could still walk, but we couldn't go two feet without somebody asking for an autograph. It didn't matter if it was a child or an old man, Gerry took time for them, and he'd stop and have a quick word. He was really good like that, totally unassuming about his fame.'

Similarly, Gwen remembered that life with Gerry was utterly different to that predicted for her by friends. 'Funny…' She paused for thought. 'Gerry

was quite different to what I had been told about him. He still liked to go out for a drink with Colin [Pearcy] or John [Llewellyn] – any excuse and he'd be out for a glass [sometimes of wine] with them as part of the "Three Musketeers", but he was nothing like the drinker and party person I was warned about by so many.

'By then Gerry was a very thoughtful, loving and caring person, he'd slowed down socially, but he still loved his racing, and he was just so good at it. I had lived a comparatively a quiet life, I just didn't realise about his popularity until we went out racing. I did most of the British meetings, but only one abroad. That was to Zandvoort in Holland with Max Rostron, but I felt a little left out over there when Gerry was with all his mates, and I didn't go racing overseas again.'

We asked about Marshall's blunt approach to overcoming disabilities during driver changes at longer races, especially those shared in the Kivlochan Cobras. 'Oh it was true – he just told the crews to pull him out as fast as possible, didn't matter what happened to him … Just get the other driver in as fast as possible, even if Gerry was lying on the ground!'

Incidentally, there was unique coincidence in Gerry's and Gwen's names. Remember Gerry adding a 'Royston' to his birth certificate names back in the 1960s – a name subsequently entered on his passport? Well, Gwen's Christian names really *did* include Royston. She did not find out that Gerry had added the Royston part until after his death. Destiny calling?

Gwen retained the Royston element in 2009 as part of her regular contact address.

The last 24 hours

'The lunchtime on the day before he died,' recalled John Llewellyn, 'Gerry and myself met at the Swan in Buckinghamshire, a regular meeting place for us. Usually Colin would meet us here too, but – unusually – he was not there that day.

'Gerry was in a very sombre mood.

'At the end of our session, we decided it was time to go. Gerry was going to the doctor about a lump on his elbow [a painful abscess he was fretting over – JW]. I was going home to pack, as I was on the early flight to Monaco next morning.

'We lingered for a while in the car park, just waiting for one of us to say "Come on, let's go to so and so for another pint," but we didn't. Very unusual.

'As I was talking to Gerry, he came closer, put his arm around me and said, "Look after yourself, son," and off we went.

'It was if he knew something was going to happen.'

Silverstone final

It was a death so appropriate that no Hollywood scriptwriter could have matched it for sheer professionalism. Around 3:30pm on 21 April 2005, Gerry was driving a borrowed 1972 Chevrolet IROC specification Camaro, originally built by Roger Penske's legendary operation for the equally famous NASCAR star Richard Petty. Gerry always wanted to drive beefy 'Yank Tanks' and he tackled the shorter Silverstone club circuit with gusto. However, Marshall access via a driver's door window space (the doors being welded shut in many US categories), and a shortage of fuel, were obvious setbacks.

Tina remembered being told about an understandable moment of confusion at Silverstone that day.

'Dad had been testing for a few laps in the Camaro and it ran out of petrol. This marshal went over to see Dad and he explained what had happened. Dad duly drove off. A few laps later, Dad pulled over again (next to the same marshal). The marshal went over to Dad and said something along the lines of, "Gerry, I can't believe you have run out of petrol again," and Dad was dead.

BELOW *Gerry with John Llewellyn at the 1986 Willhire 24 hours. John gave a moving summary of Gerry's life at his funeral and was with Gerry through the good and bad times of Gerry's 21st century life.* [Jenny Cook]

Personal effects

In July 2009 Guy Loveridge – 'author, racer, auctioneer, long time mate of Gerry's' – gave us this insight. It tells how much of Gerry's personal racing memorabilia dispersed.

'Working at Goodwood as Superintendent of the Revival Runners, I knew of Rose Gibbs; I knew, peripherally, that she had something to do with one of the star drivers at Goodwood Revival. I had probably not listened when she said it was Gerry.

'One year, after the end of the meeting on Sunday, I saw Rose trying to get over the pit wall, but failing because of her police uniform skirt [Revival attendees wear appropriate period costumes – JW].

'I asked where she needed to go.

'Rose pointed at Gerry and a lady in a Naval uniform. I picked her up and carried her over to Gerry, in his buggy along with Rose's sister, Gwen Howard. They were enjoying a glass of champagne.

'"Think this is for you, Gerry!" I said as I sat Rose down next to them.

'The next time I met Gwen was at Gerry's wake in Tring. I had gone with Rose and her husband Mac, meeting Julius Thurgood, Spadge Hopkins and some other friends. We all stood at the back, discussing Gerry, remembering the good times.

'At the hotel Rose and her other younger sister – Sharron – made sure that they stood me in front of Gwen. I expressed my sympathies, and somehow managed to leave her with my card, then scuttled off to a pint. Gerry had taken an interest in my automobilia auctioneering when I was with H&H, so I felt I ought to offer assistance.

'A few weeks later, Rose telephoned to ask me to go to her sister's house, where Rose was staying to keep her company. I could meet Gwen properly and discuss the collection. I went, had tea, and Gwen took me over the road to Gerry's house, right opposite her place.

'I was able to make a few comments about the trophies, race suits, helmets and library of books. I wondered if I would hear anything more.

'Gerry's daughter, Justine, then telephoned me. Over a few more calls, we arranged that I would come back and do a detailed valuation and report of the items in the house. I went three or four times, taking a few hours over each visit, and catalogued the trophies. Early on it was decided the trophies would not be sold, along with some books in the library, a few older race suits and a jacket or two.

'As I worked through the piles of loose papers, and catalogues, books, and files, I'd find things that were clearly personal, and so they would go to Justine. We might chat about them for a bit, and I'd go back to cataloguing. She kept me fully supplied with tea and biscuits, which is about all a bloke needs under those circumstances.

'Once I had done the listing, it was decided that I needed to meet Tina and Gregor and for a discussion on selling the collection. I remember that as I was typing out six copies of my proposal for a sale, my printer ran out of black ink and I ended up handing everyone rather green printed documents.

'The sales meeting took place in Gerry's house,

'That poor marshal was a big fan of Dad's and terribly upset about the whole thing,' she recalled.

Eyewitness accounts added that ultimate pro Marshall managed to switch the engine off before he died. He cut not just the ignition, but also clicked off the fuel pumps. Gerry was within sight of the BRDC premises, a club that he had been so proud to join. There was no question of losing control, and Gerry had been happily power-sliding the Chevrolet seconds before he died…

The cause of death has been frequently cited as heart-related illness. This was true, but we now know that the death certificate issued after a post mortem listed the specific causes as acute chronic myocardial ischaemia and severe coronary artery atherosclerosis.

For more than 20 years Gerry and property businessman Colin Pearcy were friends, their relationship interwoven by many racing miles and frequent bouts of car trading. Gerry had raced a half-dozen of Colin's MG collection, and Colin was at Silverstone on the April day that Gerry died.

Gwen said, 'I didn't know Gerry was going to Silverstone on the Thursday he died. Friday was planned, I knew he was testing then, but on Thursday he went off with Colin Pearcy.

Gregor explained: 'Dad took Colin in his new Vauxhall Signum.'

Here's how Colin recalled that April day four years later: 'That day, Gerry and I travelled together in a Vauxhall up to Silverstone for an HGPA [Historic Grand Prix Association] open test session. He was going to drive anything he could scrounge, and I had my Frazer Nash up there.

'We went our separate ways while I got on with the Nash, which is quite small and light.

with us all around a table. I answered a series of quite severe and serious questions ... and became utterly convinced that I had not a chance of getting the collection to sell. At that moment, Gregor told me that he had spoken to both H&H and Bonhams. Both said that I was "probably the best in the auction industry" to handle this type of motorsporting library/collection sale.

'At the end of this meeting, it was left that I would be selling the collection at *Classic Cars Live!* at Alexandra Palace in London; H&H would sell some of Gerry's cars in Buxton.

'I began promoting the event through the early part of 2006. Mick Walsh gave it some good coverage in *Classic & Sportscar*, as did Phil Bell in *Classic Cars*. *Motor Sport* made mention, and I started to get enquiries for catalogues. We had a professional photographer come and do the catalogue pictures, and I was confident of achieving a decent result.

'The only issue I had was over one client, new to my company and knowledge. He wanted to bid on the telephone for the vast majority of items, those that were not books. I made a point of telephoning this man and trying to work out if he was genuine or not, as the last thing I wanted was to be left looking stupid with a great number of "Sold" but unpaid-for lots.

'My concerns were, as the results show, clearly misplaced.

'This gentleman, from Wales, a former motorsport professional himself, would *not* be beaten on any lots he wanted. Even though he was hung-over from a birthday celebration the night before, he bid, and bid, and bid again. I had asked my father to be on the phone to him, and they built up quite a repartee.

'There was one particular lot that stands out in my memory: Gerry's DTV rally jacket. He is pictured wearing it, and a clown mask, in the book *Only Here For The Beer*. There was a pair of twins in the room, Mario and Edmund Lindsay, long-standing ultimate fans of Gerry, especially his DTV career. They had announced that they *were* going to buy this jacket. As I opened the bidding, I knew they were already picturing themselves wearing it, presumably in turns, at "Droop Snoot" events.

'My Welsh friend was having none of it, however. We went up by £10s, £20s, then £50s and hundreds, until, with visibly breaking hearts, the twins dropped out and "That Welsh git on the phone!" ended the sale considerably poorer, but with all of the helmets, suits and race gear to his account.

'We sold a couple of small items to John Llewellyn and Colin Pearcy as well, and a large number to many of Gerry's fans. As a gesture to commemorate the event we produced a facsimile "Marshall Wingfield" compliments slip, stamped "Loveridge Agents & Auctioneers" and marking the sale date. Our slips went into each book, magazine, helmet, jacket, and race suit purchased that day.

'The 19th March 2006 was a very important day in my career. I was able to do what I felt was a good job, for someone I had been proud to know. I hoped that we did his memory a service after he had gone.'

'Next thing I know, he's come up to me and said, "I'll drive that next."

'I said, "You'll never get your arse in there … look at it."

'Somehow he wriggled his way in there, but I said he couldn't possibly drive it; his legs were hard up against the steering wheel.

'Gerry buzzed off then and he ended up taking that American Chevrolet out. We all noticed when the session was red-lighted and I was pretty sure it was Gerry out on the circuit, but didn't think too much of it.

'After three-quarters of an hour Gary Pearson told me they were asking for me on the loud hailer system. I went over to the media centre and they told me the circuit doctor wanted to see me.

'I gathered that something had happened to Gerry and I asked the doctor, "Is it serious?"

'"Quite serious," he replied, "in fact very serious."

'"Very serious as in…?" I asked, not wanting to say outright "Has he died?"

'"Yes," the doctor confirmed, answering my unspoken question.

'I waited around 30 minutes, identified the body and then got on the phone to Carol and others I could reach, those who had to know. Luckily, I caught Gwen at home.

'I ended that awful day driving that Vauxhall of Gerry's back to his house in Pitstone, right opposite to Gwen's place.'

Gwen remembered that 'I didn't know what had happened until much later in the day. Not many people appreciate what Colin did for Gerry that day. He was a true friend, but he was not the first to get hold of me.' John Llewellyn's partner, Gilly Bryant, broke the news of Gerry's death to Gwen – 'Because she kept trying on my mobile until I switched it back on at the end of my working day,' recalled Gwen.

that many people visit Dad's house in all the years he lived there. The neighbours must have been more annoyed with him than ever … He always had loads of cars (for selling) in the cul-de-sac he lived in … Now that he was gone there were even more cars clogging up the road!'

Tina recalled a family pilgrimage to the scene of her Dad's death. 'A few days later, Silverstone and the BRDC let us (Gwen, Jus, Greg and myself) spend the day there and relive his last hours.

'We went on a minibus (like Japanese tourists) and were taken round the track to where he pulled over. We watched a recording of the testing in the control room to the point where Dad pulled over: they stopped it there so we didn't see him being worked on. We were taken to the emergency centre and met the paramedics who worked on him and went where the Camaro was impounded, so we could see it.

'I actually climbed into it as I was intrigued how Dad would have managed (as entrance was through the window), and I struggled. Plus the bucket seat was so restrictive, I don't know how he managed it.'

Gregor recalled that 'it took me about ten minutes to get out of the bloody thing! Tina then decided she wanted to get in. I'm six foot four inches and she is five foot three inches, built for racing. But even Tina struggled to get in and out. I subsequently found out it had taken three people to help Dad to get into the car … And when they had

ABOVE *May 6th 2005 cover to the* Celebration of Gerald Dallas Royston Marshall's Life. *Hundreds attended with standing room only the order of the day for many at the West Herts Crematorium, Garston. Also on hand were some of the significant cars in Gerry's life including the Alvis* Grey Lady *and Model A Ford.*
[Gary Hawkins]

She concluded: 'That was around 5:30pm. Gilly was great, because she had already told my manager what had happened and arranged for me to be driven home.'

Gregor recalled the next day (Friday) as 'a bit surreal, as everyone started turning up at Dad's. Family, friends – I don't think there'd ever been

RIGHT *September 2005 Goodwood Revival, the St. Mary's Trophy presentation is made to period saloon car race winners Alan Jones (1980 F1 World Champion) and Leo Voyazides (leading historic saloon car racer). Left to right: Gregor, Jones, Lady March, Voyazides and Gerry's daughters, Justine and Tina.*
[Marshall Family Archive]

to extricate him it took eight. I'm not surprised.'

'It was a very surreal day to say the least,' said Tina four years later, 'but it did help, and the day was actually filled with lots of comical moments.' She also reminded us there was talk of renaming that bend 'Marshall Corner', but 'that never happened'. She felt 'it would have been a huge honour and it is a shame they didn't.'

'I think we went to Silverstone the Tuesday after it happened,' recalled Gwen. 'They were helpful. As Tina says, we were driven round the track, the car stopped where Gerry had pulled up and we were allowed to get out and spend a few minutes by the side of the track and place some flowers there. There were sad moments but also some things that made us laugh.'

Gregor commented on the flower arrangements: 'Justine had brought a beautiful tulip which she lay where Dad stopped. Me, being a typical bloke, hadn't brought anything – but we all picked up some bits of gravel from where Dad had lain. I picked a couple of daisies which I kept until his funeral service – it's amazing what you try and hold on to sometimes.'

Gwen resumed: 'I remember we were amazed at the whole Silverstone set-up, from the amount of information that could be checked in the control room to the amazing medical centre. I'm not sure any of us realised that it was like a mini-hospital.

'It was good to see the film of Gerry driving round the track, as it showed that he had been driving normally and at some speed right up to when he pulled the car up,' said Gwen.

Gregor added: 'One thing I really wanted to see – but also didn't want to see – was any footage of Dad in the car, as I knew there were cameras all around the circuit. I wanted to see if he had passed away peacefully, or if there was something wrong. There were so many stories doing the rounds as to what had actually happened that any footage would dispel.

'They had captured the last few bends, the Complex.

'Gary Dearn, Track Operations Manager, took us to the control tower. I'd not been into the main part of the control tower before and it was all a bit of an adventure for us. There was a wall of TV screens; there must have been about 60. The camera was positioned somewhere near the BRDC and the Brooklands suite, on the outside of Brooklands corner. Dad came thundering towards it, turned into Brooklands with a lovely four-wheel drift around the left-hander, straightened up slightly on the brakes, and turned into the double apex right-hander of Luffield. Then, as he exited Luffield he slowed down, pulled to the outside of the track and stopped. There was no spin, no going off, no drama, and no fuss.

'It was all controlled and, if anything, peaceful.'

LEFT *Also a frequent sight at that Goodwood Revival and BTCC rounds following Gerry's death were 'Only Here for the Beer' logos. Although this is a picture of the official signwritten text on a Triple 888 factory-backed Vauxhall, you'll see they actually left it reading 'Only here for he Beer!' Perhaps it was deliberate? Anyway the move to carry these references to Gerry's original pre-'78 racing biography was touching, and is still widely copied among historic and saloon car racing ranks.* [LAT]

The funeral

In the aftermath of Gerry's sudden death, Gwen, and Gerry's three adult children, bore the brunt of organising a funeral, which was held at West Herts Crematorium at Garston, Watford, at noon on 6 May. Then aged 89, mother Ruby's vigorous memory and practical assistance from brothers John and Martyn proved invaluable. The ceremony became an appropriately big occasion, one that generously bubbled beyond natural sadness amongst family, friends, and fans.

Over 550 paid their respects at that suburban crematorium.

Decorated with a winner's garland, BRDC stickers, racing roundels carrying number 1, and a chequered flag, the coffin was carried by four men: Gregor, John Llewellyn, Richard Cabburn, and Simon Pratt, Gregor's best drinking buddy. Apparently, Gerry was amused that his son's mate was a policeman!

Colin Pearcy carried Gerry's racing helmet, whilst *The Entertainer* played.

John Llewellyn pungently revealed that 'when we carried him into church, I cursed him all the way. What a bloody weight. I thought my neck and head were going to burst!'

Interesting motorcars attended in abundance. Gregor arranged Dad's Model A Ford, the Ivan/Tim Dutton Alvis *Grey Lady* and 'Mum's Mini Cooper with Miles Hutton [Carol's second husband], Keith Eggers [Justine's husband] and Brendon Lynch [Tina's husband] inside. They were my back-up for when the Model A would go wrong, as it had been having charging problems…' Gregor remembered that 'it did stop on the A41 between the cremation and the wake!'

Humanist Simon Allen conducted the service. Allen did his homework at a 'quiet and good humoured evening' with Gerry's close family. Allen prefaced his Marshall remarks with: 'The first things I learnt about him were humour and motor racing. Or was it motor racing and humour? The two were always linked for this rumbustious character. And that is the problem for today. When faced with such a remarkable individual, one who was capable of turning a stranger into a friend in seconds – or, of course, driving them away saying they never wanted to see Gerry Marshall again in their lives – how do we start to make a tribute to him?

'Sometimes I stand at this lectern and hardly know what to say, whereas now I hardly know where to start,' said Allen. He selected slices of Marshall life that had eluded us previously.

'By the time he came to his first race that was televised, the commentator was so amazed by the show that he turned to his notes on this new driver, wondering what job he did.

'In the form for the race, under "Employment", Gerry had written "Unemployable"!'

After an appropriate pause for laughter, Simon quipped, 'For once his father agreed with him!'

Simon Allen commented of Gerry's marriage to Carol that 'the residents of Sudbury Hill in Harrow must have been very glad when Gerry stopped racing up and down their road at night … Carol talked of the times she had been driving with him and said she was never frightened. She was more irritated by his inability to arrive anywhere in anything like a punctual manner.'

Allen continued: 'Gerry's children arrived and the next phase of his life had begun. Tina, Justine and Gregor are here, with the next generation as well. To say they spoke enthusiastically of their parent is to put it mildly. They understood what made him tick and had long ago accepted that family holidays were just something he did not do!

For Gerry could never have sat around – and so they took holidays with their mother.'

An unsung sadness of Gwen's bereavement was that she had managed the impossible. She and Gerry were booked for an apartment holiday in Spain later that month.

The ceremony also included a period for quiet reflection, the chorus and three verses of *Heavy on my Heart* by Anastacia, a personal recollection of outrageous and touching anecdotes from John Llewellyn, a reading by Gregor of Canon Henry Scott Holland's poem *Death is nothing at all*, of which Gerry had kept a copy on his desk after it had been read at close friend Mike Bennion's funeral. Then came committal of the coffin, the epilogue, and a second musical outburst – this time from Willy Barrett – of the wartime ditty *Wish me luck as you wave me goodbye*, one of Gerry's favourites.

Outside that request for fellow Pitstone resident Wild Willy Barrett to sing, Gerry left no specific funeral wishes for Gwen and the junior Marshalls. They did an amazing organisational job under huge emotional pressure. They assembled not just three ex-wives and a fine non-religious ceremony for the departed, but they also made it a joyful occasion, one that Gerry would have relished – especially the wake at nearby Pendley Manor, Tring, on a fine May day.

Pendley Manor Hotel's gracious ballrooms, near to Gerry's modest home in his final years, echoed to our toasts and increasingly unlikely tales of a

ABOVE AND LEFT
Jason Plato, Triple 888 Vauxhall-backed BTCC driver, the 2001 British Champion, was prominent in celebrating Gerry's life. Overshadowed by a giant portrait of Mr Marshall, we see Jason signing autographs (above). On the left, Jason is holding a tankard alongside Gregor, sister Tina and her boys. The tankard is one of eight 'Gerrys' awarded to celebrate the 50th Anniversary of Motorsport News. [LAT/ Marshall Family Archive]

mischievously merry life. All underlined Gerry's impact on the vigorous UK racing community. His death drew together many who had not seen each other in years, yet conversations from motorsport events of the 1960s to the new millennium segued seamlessly.

'I arranged for "Old Nail" and "Baby Bertha" to be at the wake,' said Gregor. 'Both were parked in the disabled bays at Pendley Manor, adjacent to the ballroom entrance. Pendley advised me that they had suffered traffic wardens issuing tickets, so I gave Joe Ward Dad's disabled badge for "Baby Bertha". "Old Nail" we left alone: as the Vauxhall press department said, "Who were they going to issue a ticket to, Vauxhall?"'

At one end of the airy upstairs reception rooms a film of the Big Man hustling around Oulton Park was shown, all sideways action from the DTV era. The other side of Gerry's character as a family man, amongst the latest of his grandchildren, was portrayed in extracts from family albums – snapshots that domestically contradicted his public image.

Daughter Tina told us: 'As a Grandfather, he was the best. I could not fault him, as a mother of three little boys who adored him. Even when he was suffering and in lots of pain, he would attempt to get on the climbing frame, get on the floor, play, and spend hours looking at car magazines and listening to them. He had much more patience and tolerance than I have ... He was not the Dad I wanted as a little girl, but he was the Grandfather (just like his Father) that I adored.'

Gwen recalled: 'I travelled to the crematorium with Ruby, Justine, and Tina – as Gregor drove his Dad's Model A up there. We could all see this was going to be a bigger occasion than I thought. There was just a continuous stream of cars going in for the service ... and when we got there, it was just a surge of people. The funeral director was very good and ensured that we could get into the crematorium directly.

'It was the same at Pendley Manor, and the whole day is just a blur to me now. I spoke to dozens of people, as we all did, especially Ruby, who was just so with-it that day. It was Ruby who told me that Gerry had adopted the Royston name – I was not aware of that before.'

Aftermath

Life after Gerry was certainly changed, for both family and friends. The initial obituaries and Internet tributes were overwhelming and came from overseas as well as via the massively loyal UK following. His fame spread through 44 years of motorsport, show attendances, two books and public forums. He was also the subject of Vauxhall, DTV, and Castrol media campaigns, had Thames TV connections, and three columns for national motoring magazines. All ensured that there were few enthusiasts, never mind thousands of motor trade dealers and acquaintances, who had not heard of Gerry Marshall.

Many Internet and obituary comments appeared in the tribute edition of *Only Here For The Beer*, so what follows is a more personal and thoughtful cross-section of memories, provided in hindsight by family, friends, and passing acquaintances.

Looking back on life after Gerry, Gwen Howard reflected: 'I was floored, it just came out of the blue.' When the hectic rush of arranging the funeral and the wake at Pendley Manor with the junior Marshalls subsided, Gwen had major life decisions ahead. 'I did not do much for about a year and I retired from the bank with over 40 years' service in 2006.'

Friends and family asked frequently if Gwen wanted to move house, as Gerry had literally lived opposite. She felt the happy memories outweighed the sadness, so Gwen was still at the same address when we talked in 2009.

As executor of Gerry's Will, she worked closely with Gerry's brother, Martyn. As you saw in the sidebar entitled 'Personal effects' (page 228), Guy Loveridge auctioned much Marshall memorabilia, Gerry's daughter Justine aiding him as he catalogued the mass of material.

By 2009, Gwen had enjoyed some holiday cruises and had 'moved on' personally. However, she still had abiding memories of Gerry: 'He was a very thoughtful, loving and caring person. He gave me a lot more confidence in myself and I appreciated life in a different light after being with him. I suppose I had had a quiet life and didn't realise his popularity. So I then got used to being out, with people popping up everywhere to talk to him. I stayed in the background, but some of that being in the public eye was bound to rub off on me, and that's maybe what increased my self-confidence.

'I will never, ever, forget what he gave to me in a warm and loving life,' Gwen said finally.
Tina Lynch (née Marshall) left us with this thought: 'He was not a conventional father in any form, but

OPPOSITE *Marshall memorabilia, including Gerry's favourite Marsh Plant race overalls, gloves, trophies, original Andrew Kitson montages, glassware and 'Old Nail'. All on display at Donington Museum during 2009–10.* [Both Gregor Marshall]

Because Justine – Gerry's second daughter – was expecting the most recent addition to Gerry's grandchildren as this book was being written, we asked her for some special memories at a more convenient time! This is what she wrote for us in September 2009:

'Like most daughters, I idolised my father. I was well aware of his faults. Yet I was protective of him, especially in later years. I dreaded anything happening to him. Like others, I thought Dad was invincible – dying was something other people did. He had been in and out of hospital regularly after a heart bypass in 1996 and it was awful to see him suffer. I was terrified that he would die in hospital, or, worse still, at home on his own.

'However, his death was as dramatic as it was unexpected. Even the obituaries editor of the *Daily Telegraph* commented: "What a colossally good death your father had." And it was true. We drew enormous comfort that Dad died in such a fitting way.

'Prior to having children I worked for one of the largest recruitment agencies in the world as a website officer, then in PR and marketing in the London head office of Harvey Nichols. My husband and I now run our own gas engineering and renewable energy business, K25, in Hertfordshire.'

Justine has three children to add to Gerry's seven-strong grandchild collection, which seems to grow annually. Justine's contribution comprises four-year-old Madeleine (born 10 December 2004); then Edward, 'who has definitely got his grandfather's genes – a real extrovert and totally fearless' (born 3 September 2006); and most recently Meredith (born 22 July 2009).

'I have endless memories of Daddy,' wrote Justine, 'so where to start? My early childhood seems appropriate. Unforgettably, Daddy taught Tina and I to sing *Supercalifragilisticexpialidocious*, from the Mary Poppins film, and he once threw us both into the bath fully clothed! He told me off for standing on the running boards of his Armstrong Siddeley, and I recall my sister and I had a crafty puff on his cigar, carelessly left in the ashtray of his Jensen. We also put a lump of joke dog excrement on the floor of our home in Bricket Wood and freaked my mother out! Then there were the plastic ice cubes we embedded with cigarette butts and flies for our guests' party drinks, and Daddy's face when Gregor rode his mini motorbike for the first time (aged approximately two!), never mind my mother's expression!

'Daddy bought me a much-loved red Panasonic Toot-a-Loop bangle radio, and my sister some plastic glasses with working windscreen wipers…'

'Growing up in the motorsport world meant endless early starts, circuit breakfasts, hanging around in clubhouses, and late-night meals, usually at an Indian restaurant. Most vivid memories of him are of watching him race, and glowing with pride when the commentator spoke about "the legendary Gerry Marshall".

'Everybody knows how competitive Daddy was, and how he would consistently up the ante over anything. He could also be hugely embarrassing … without exception, he was always the centre of attention and loved to put on a show. Had he not been such a skilful driver, then I am sure he would have been on the stage.

'Returning from race meetings we would stop to have a curry. He would, without warning, perform a cartwheel in the middle of a crowded restaurant, often full of fans who had attended the race meeting – understandably thrilled and amazed in equal measure to see this big man putting on an acrobat show! On more than one occasion he split his trousers…

'Daddy was a formidable father and father-in-law. My husband, Keith, took time to feel comfortable in his company. However, they found common ground – a beer – and would

BELOW *Gerry's daughter Justine (left) and her Eggers family. Left to right: Madeleine, Meredith, Keith and Edward, taken in September 2009.* [Justine Eggers]

share a drink in the many clubs or pubs in Hertfordshire. I don't think Keith will ever forget when they arm-wrestled in a local Indian restaurant, Daddy won, of course!'

'He was proud and excited by his first granddaughter, Madeleine, born in December 2004. He referred to her as "a little pudding". After her birth Daddy visited us regularly, which was unusual. I joked that I should have had a baby years ago. Having a baby brings into sharp focus the loss of your loved ones all over again. I know Daddy would have been hugely proud of his little grandchildren with their inherited personalities, some similar to his own.'

'There is a lot of information in the public domain about Daddy – however, there was a side that not many knew about. Not long before he died he had attended a pain rehabilitation clinic and painted a glass jam jar for use as a pen pot. Who would have believed it? Gerry Marshall painting a jam jar! At the same clinic he managed to escape with some of the patients and visit the nearest pub.

'Daddy was a complex, fascinating man. He was capable of many things – rescuing a man from a burning racing car and running to the assistance of other competitors. Generous to a fault, he would, quite literally, give you the shirt off his back – but we never knew his talents stretched to painting jam jars!

'Controversial, affectionate, witty, intimidating, exciting, emotional, and at times an exasperating but a wholly unique father. The antithesis of boring.

'I was aware from an early age that he was very different from other fathers. Everything we did with Daddy was an adventure – some good, some not so. He was always in a hurry and packed ten lives into his one extraordinary one. The party never really started until he arrived, and you never knew if he would turn up.

'I loved him very much and miss him every single day. It's no exaggeration to say that his death has left a huge void in our lives.

'Sadly, I haven't inherited his talents. I failed my driving test three times. However, there is one family trait that I have inherited, and that is a poor sense of time-keeping. Which brings me neatly to a close – amongst Daddy's possessions we found a book of quotations by Oscar Wilde.

'One apt quote stood out: "Better to be expected than to arrive…".'

he was incredibly loving and also very generous when he was about. Don't get me wrong, we had ups and downs, but I never doubted he loved us, although I always knew his job came first.

'He would do *anything* for any of his friends, and some took advantage of that.

'Now I have brilliant adult memories of Dad and am so proud of his achievements, because I know now [that] had he been a better father, he wouldn't have accomplished what he did … And I can appreciate that now.'

We were unable to talk very much to Gerry's second daughter, Justine Eggers (née Marshall), as this book was researched and written, as she was busy producing her third child! However, we know from other family members' recollections that she was an equal partner in her father's affections, and played a touching and effective role in the aftermath of his death. Happily she has since been able to provide some recollections of her own, as set out in the accompanying sidebar

Gregor summarised what his father had meant to him: 'I couldn't believe he was gone, he was so strong and such an important part of my life that there couldn't be any way he was gone. Even now, typing this in summer 2009, I still can't really believe it.

'We did have an up-and-down relationship, but more because we were very similar. We were best friends rather than father and son – he'd always been my hero, but later in his life we seemed to be much more on level terms.'

Nick Whale wrote Gregor these simple final words: 'I was massively fond of him and miss him loads, and can imagine you do too.'

Martyn Marshall delivered a powerful final testimony, almost four years after Gerry's death: 'There were two very powerful males in my life, my father and my brother … But Gerald was my hero and my friend, as well as my brother.

'If I was in trouble, I'd always ring Gerald, not Dad, because Dad could be negative, but Gerry would fix anything.

'His mind was just so fast. I still miss him terribly in my life.'

Affordable Model A classic

Jenny Cook carries a blazing emotional torch for Gerry even today; some of his prized possessions, like his beautifully preserved 1930 Model A Ford Tudor (registration SV 7994) are still with her in East Anglia.

'Gerry loved cars,' she said, 'whether it was a Ford Prefect or a Farmall A tractor. He enjoyed washing, polishing and most of all touching up any little chips so they didn't get any worse. Unfortunately, in his latter years he couldn't afford an expensive collector's car. Then he discovered the vintage Model A Ford that could be bought relatively cheaply, was simple to run and maintain – and a pleasure to own. He found a lovely car, a Tudor (two-door) that had been restored and then displayed in the Lakeland Museum in the 1980s. He managed to buy it and it really was his pride and joy.'

Jenny continued: 'Amazingly – shortly after this – we discovered another Model A Ford in Suffolk, where I live. It was a Phaeton (four-door convertible), and Gerry convinced me that I should try and buy it because it was such an original car.' Jenny did buy the Phaeton a year later. 'When Gerry's car went to auction [after his death] I knew that I had to try and buy it. I used telephone bidding, which I had never done before. Both cars now live happily together in Suffolk.

'Gerry would have been proud of me!'

Marshall as a cool dude

Octane magazine and Jenny Cook prompted us to recognise the 'coolness' of Gerry's mindset. Jenny highlighted that Gerry had long been ranked amongst the global greats recognised for their indefinable but apparent 'cool dude' status. An article in *Car* magazine in April 1997, for instance, named him among the 'all-time Top Ten car dudes'.

Jenny explained: 'They were, in no particular order, James Dean, Steve McQueen, Luca Di Montezemelo, Gerry Marshall, Paul Newman, James Hunt, Keke Rosberg, Graham Hill, Jacques Villeneuve, and Dale Earnhardt.'

Writing in the June 2009 issue of *Octane*'s dedicated 'Cool Issue', Tony Dron asked readers: 'Was Gerry Marshall cool? It did seem that way when he left scores of his fellow BRDC members wondering how to top such a startling career move.'

Dron senior outlined Gerry's death and his opinion of him as follows: 'Testing an IROC Camaro at Silverstone on April 21 2005, Marshall slowed safely to a halt in the sand trap right in front of the BRDC Clubhouse, finding time, in a moment of supreme self-discipline, to switch off the engine before he died of a heart attack.

'Better suited to the Merry Olde England of the Wars of the Roses than the 20th century,

the mighty beast known as Gerald Dallas Royston Marshall, Champion of St Albans, would have shown no mercy to anyone suggesting he was cool. Cunning and strong in battle, off the field he was a jolly ale-swilling hard man. With his loss the wimps run free – but how did he get through the stress-related ECG in the MSA Medical in the first place?'

Gregor commented that this could have been because 'for a National B licence you don't need a medical, plus the MSA would personally visit Gerry and check on his well-being.'

No, you sign *mine!*

Mike Wilds, former BRM Grand Prix driver and later commercial aeroplane and helicopter pilot, wrote this deeply sincere – and typically modest – message to Gregor in March of 2009:

'I knew your Dad for around 30 years off and on. I got on with him really well apart from the times he was worse for the drink; then he used to be quite rude and aggressive to me. It didn't matter though, because it was all forgotten by the next time we saw each other.

'My fondest memory of Gerry was the last conversation I had with him only weeks before his sad and untimely death. I walked into the BRDC Suite at Silverstone and saw Gerry sitting at a table reading a book.

'I went over to say hello and see how he was getting on, as we all knew about his illness. He looked up at me, and smiled.

'"You drove for BRM, didn't you Mike?" he said.

'"Yes," I said, "but only in two Grands Prix."

'Gerry then handed me the book he was reading, which was about BRM. It was a very surreal moment for me because Gerry asked me to autograph his book.

'I couldn't believe this motor racing legend was asking *me* to sign his book!

'I never saw Gerry again after that day. It was so nice to have my last memory of him as a smiling, happy friend, sitting enjoying his day, among many friends in his Club, on the racetrack that he loved.'

Classic tribute

In 2005 Hugh Poston, editing the Classic Touring Car Racing Club magazine, wrote an editorial about Gerry that spoke for many. Here are some extracts:

'I am sure, like me, many of you were truly sorry to learn that Gerry had died and like me have specific and vivid memories of Club Racing's most successful and entertaining driver.

'Apart from televised races, my first memory is of Big/Baby Bertha exiting Thruxton's Club chicane totally sideways, just avoiding the old footbridge and charging into Allard Corner without any form of "lift", truly awe-inspiring.

'Obtaining his autograph in the paddock at Thruxton, accompanied by my then young family, Gerry said, "I must go, I think they are calling me." He casually pulled up his overalls and climbed aboard 'Baby Bertha' to win. He inevitably attracted attention in the paddock but had time for everyone.

'At Brands Hatch, he raced a Group One Capri, which expired early on. I managed to win the baby class and was stranded in the pit road, so I grabbed a ride back with Graham Scarborough, who had won his class, but not the race.

'Gerry greeted us in the paddock by yanking the door open and berating his old friend Graham for not having won the race! In more recent interviews, Gerry rated Graham as one of the most talented drivers he had raced with or against. A view most of us share, but real praise from a man who won over 600 times.

'My last meeting with him was in autumn 2003, when at Oulton Park he drove Stacy's Mazda to Group One victory. He was enthusiastic, despite being unable to walk without his sticks.

'A true giant of motorsport, but first and foremost an enthusiast who just loved to drive and to entertain.'

Brands' eye view

Arthur Benjamins, established artist and former Brands Hatch marshal, told us in June 2009: 'To me, Gerry Marshall was the embodiment of British club racing at its best. As I had moved to the UK in 1974, he also became an immediate symbol of my own new life in a foreign country.

'Becoming a BRSCC marshal at the local track, Brands Hatch, provided me with a new view of 1974 British motor racing at its best. Paddock Hill Bend, Post 3, offered the best vantage point I could have dreamt of. Behind the relative safety of two crooked tiers of battered Armco, I saw Gerry Marshall for the first time.

'Gerry exited from the almost perpendicular pits exit and on to the track, past us. It was immediately apparent that he was not of the usual racing driver mould. Unlike all other drivers, Gerry seemed to fill the complete interior and saw away at the wheel when negotiating Paddock bend. No other driver handled the car like he did.

'Out of the car, Gerry's shape was unmistakable. I never saw him being able to walk from A to B without stopping to talk to people.

'During my marshalling years, Gerry's cars came and went. Some were prettier than others, but the characteristic driving style remained. He was invited to pilot nimble single-seaters – and we always uncharitably wondered just how he fitted in them! At an historic race, Gerry seemed swamped by a Can-Am car. For the very first time Gerry looked positively puny.

'The view of Gerry inimitably sawing away at the steering wheel when negotiating Paddock will remain in the forefront of my mind. Although we may have exchanged only a few words, I was one of the many who still has his footprint on their souls.'

Watch it!

Ivan Dutton recalled how he lost his wristwatch virginity: 'The best bit of advice Gerry gave me was to buy a watch – I'd never owned one in my life.

'I found that before a race I'd get really nervous waiting. I'd sit in the car on the grid, put it into gear, take it out of gear, several times. I just couldn't judge the time from the four-minute countdown. It was affecting my starts, and I'd always seen Gerry and Lanfranchi so cool and calm before a race.

'I would wait until I saw Lanfranchi get in the car, he was always calm, but I still found on the grid I'd panic. Finally, I asked Gerry what he did.

'"Just relax until you see the minute board go up, look at your watch for 30 seconds. Put the car into gear and then wait, as very rarely is the delay a full minute," he said. "Just be careful you don't get caught out – it isn't the golden rule, but will work 95 per cent of the time."

'Of course, he was right and it worked perfectly.

'I have the Omega that I bought back then, and it's still the only watch I have!

'It's funny,' closed Ivan wistfully, 'as I'm talking about Gerry it reminds me of all the times he helped me out. He was incredibly good like that.'

John Llewellyn added this watching postscript: 'Gerry bought a Rolex watch and I had always admired it, and told him so. For 20-odd years he had told me and everyone else that when he was gone it would be mine.

'My God, I wish I wasn't wearing it now!

'There was many an occasion when he wasn't feeling too well that we would joke about it soon coming my way. The day Gerry died, I rushed back from Monaco and got to Gwen's house early evening, to drive the family up to see him.

'As I entered the door the first thing Gerry's brother Martyn said was, "You've got the Rolex now."

'I have left it to Gregor in my will, and I wear it every day.'

GERRY: THE COLUMNS

FROM THE VERY HOT SEAT

BY GERRY MARSHALL

YOU MAY HAVE HEARD I HAD QUITE a good burn-up at Brands last month. There I was, ambling along quite happily in the lead on the seventh tour of a ten lapper, having whittled a good 2.2 secs orf me own lap record, when I decided to slow down a bit to play with the other lads. Well, Bernie Avenger's Unett and Alan Mexico's Wilkinson had just crept up to me when the nearside rear wheel of my Firenza decided to set up a splinter Vauxhall component group well divorced from the rest of the car — me wheel fell off. 'Ahah,' thinks I, 'this hasn't happened to me since 1967 when I lost six TVR wheels in eighteen months' (yes, really). Being Mrs Marshall's brightest offspring I immediately realised that something must be wrong, and my suspicions were confirmed when the car fell over. Several times. Not content with a simple roly-poly, the errant wheel removed the filler neck from the petrol tank, which then commenced to light up the proceedings in the biggest possible way (thought for the month: is a man who escapes backwards from a blazing car called an arsonist?).

Anyhow, stopping only to switch off the ignition, pull on the handbrake, put the gears in neutral and retrieve the Whiter Shade of Pale tape from the stereo, I picked up my handbag, undid the belts, and tried to get out. Alas and alack. Me big head had jammed itself twixt seat back and roll cage. What is more, the whole front part of the roof had collapsed, leaving minimal clearance for my lithe form to wriggle through. Confirming this with the Nomex tape measure that I always carry in my overalls, I decided that the only means of escape would be through the back screen, so in no time at all I twisted myself lengthways in the car and started beating furiously at the glass, while humming tuneless strains from the Firebird Suite to calm myself. Big and butch though I am, my flexing pectorals and rippling biceps had little effect on the stubborn screen, and things were getting a trifle warm, with great spurts of flame and smoke everywhere. 'Oh Smit!' thought I, 'me favourite fornicatorium is going up in smoke, and Marshall G. is about to be rendered down to a sort of motor racing Flambé.' At that moment a voice, which I was sure came from my Maker, cried: 'Stop effing about and I'll drag you out.' 'Funny,' I thought, 'didn't know he used words like that, perhaps I'm going to the other place.' However, the firm grasp of hands round my ankles revealed that help was coming from a more earthly source, and with much grunting and heaving, and scraping of my fore parts along the tarmac, I popped out of the driver's window like Bernard disappearing from the bar when someone tells him it's his round. Scrambling to my feet and stopping only to retrieve my handbag from the pyre, I galloped off to the other side of the Armco to sit and admire my handiwork.

It turned out that the guy who dragged me out was marshal Alan Maynell, who had galloped all the way down Druids hill to get to me. When he realised that I wasn't Gillian Allaskew-Thomas he almost turned round and ran back again, but thought that as he was there he may as well do something about extricating me. Great bloke Alan. It's fellows like him who keep British marshalling at the top of the list — and keep this particular British Marshall from not collecting his old age pension.

Although I was okay you couldn't say the same about me poor old Fire-enza, which succumbed to its injuries after only its second race and was buried with full military honours (four crates of light ale and a membership card to the Holtsberg Stripperama in Hamburg) in Bill Bly's back garden.

At the moment we're galloping around building a replacement car (this time with full roll cage) for the Bank Holiday weekend. By the time you read this you'll know whether we were successful or not.

The Brands fracas was a great setback to our plans as it stopped all our development work both financially and timewise. The reason for the accident was a chance in a million: it was caused by a flaw in the halfshaft where it faces on to the hub. As we've been using the same type of hub for the last five years with 10in wheels and over 200bhp without a single failure, you can see that we have no cause for alarm.

Incidentally, the date was the thirteenth of the month — and they have the cheek to laugh at me because I'm superstitious.

The week before Brands, by way of a busman's holiday, I was driving your actual ex-Dan Gurney, Stirling Moss, Edgar Jessop Maserati Birdcage Tipo 61 at Silverstone in the JCB Hysteric car round. This car is the property of Hexagon of Highgate, and is usually driven by Nick Faure. In official practice we qualified for a very lowly grid position owing to a valve shim having moved, therefore reducing us to a very meagre two laps.

However, all will be well on the day, we thought. But of course it wasn't. For a start it was hissing down with felines and canines (cats and dogs to you), but unperturbed I took my place at the start humming excerpts from the Eton Boating song. Don't know if you know, but the Birdcage Mazzer has this bloody great bubble of a windscreen, and as soon as I dropped the clutch about 97 gallons of finest 100 per cent pure aqua gushed back over the screen, soaking my visor and facemask and running down my body to dampen my ardour. Ho ho. Somewhere around halfway through the first lap I found myself in third place behind Neil Corner in the Maserati 250F and my team mate Nick Faure in the Hexagon Lister. The conditions were really atrocious and all this became too much for poor old Nick, who had himself a spin (he actually managed three spins on the first lap). Fortunately he revolved harmlessly in the middle of the track, but taking avoiding action I boated across a river which suddenly appeared, causing me to gently smite the bank with the rather phallic tail of the Mazzer, so I decided to call it a day and retire to the paddock, as did Nick. I forgot to mention that we were both on dry tyres as someone had left the wets at home.

Nevertheless, happier days are in store because Hexagon have asked me to drive the Lister at Crystal Palace before that super circuit is closed forever. I'm really looking forward to this as the Lister is an ex-Le Mans streamliner designed by me old mate Frank Costin.

With all these tales of woe it's nice to be able to relate that the day before my Brands incident I won the Forward Thrust race at Oulton Park by a clear 34secs from Tony Strawson in the ex-everybody Falcon Sprint.

There was a very unfortunate pile-up on the first lap when about seven cars settled for a slogging match at Old Hall and the rest of the race was run under a perpetual yellow flag. A great shame.

All Mick Hill's fans will have to be disappointed this month as he doesn't seem to have done much — so I won't mention him. Sorry.

I see Brodie has managed another accident (road) and I hear rumour that Victor Raysbrook has taken out a mortgage to cover damage to the Elan at Cadwell Park — reputedly £800 worth. Apart from that I can't think of any more embarrassing inside chat, so that's it.

PeeEss, I'd like to thank Alan Wilkinson for putting me back in the hot seat by lending me his Mexico for the Britax round at Brands seven days post-burnup, even though the cooling system didn't.

And that's really about it. Yours, **Gerry.**

. . . "a better display than The Red Arrows, but the finish wasn't quite so polished. . ."

The 1979 British Grand Prix was going to be the highlight of my racing year. I had two good rides, the Triplex Dolomite for the Tricentrol round, and my Lister for the Lloyds & Scottish race for historics.

As you all know I ended up in hospital — but my Dolomite certainly followed Formula 1 fashion, ending up the day with real ground effect! In fact the roof and other panels showed traces of gravel effect, a phenomenon that even Colin Chapman has yet to exploit fully.

Because it was practice for the GP meeting we had freshly rebuilt Moore engines in the Triumphs. Mine was down on compression for one cylinder, so another unit was put in for the second session. With full tanks and race tyres I was a touch slower than Rex Greenslade and Tom Walkinshaw, but I really wasn't worried as the new engine was "a beaut."

On Hangar Straight, it was 300rpm up (7600 in top) on my previous best, which may have had something to do with our substitution of Lucas Opus ignition for another well known brand. The engine was giving a good torque spread by Dolomite standards, too.

I had an unusually bad start. In the Triplex Group 1 Dolomites, we have close-ratio four-speed boxes with an enormous first gear. You must use 7000rpm to get away, just dropping the clutch, but I couldn't bring myself to do it. In the production saloon Triumph it is a different story. With a standard first gear, those Dollies just fly off the line.

So I dropped 50yds at the start. At the end of the first lap my Dolomite was up with Rex and Tom. I was able to get past both of them coming out of the chicane. At Copse we caught a Capri — Vandervell's I think — and I lifted off. Rex went by, but Tom was still behind in the Mazda. I followed Rex down to Stowe with Tom right in, virtually under my back bumper, trying to keep with us in the unusually down-on-power RX7.

We went nose-to-tail along from Stowe to Club. I remember thinking that, when we got to the slightly uphill drag from Club through to Abbey, the Dolly would pull away, because it always had a little more torque than the Mazda, and I had an especially good unit in. Club is now a top gear corner. That means you must approach at about 120mph, lift, dab the brakes, and settle the car around the corner under power.

Tom was right with me and a Dolomite is not renowned for its braking powers. Tom's intention was clearly to outbrake me on the inside. I lifted off and braked, but Tom didn't expect me to do that so suddenly and so early. Eye witnesses tell me that the resulting collision between Mazda and Triumph lifted the rear wheels of my car clear from the ground.

Not unnaturally, the Triumph got very sideways as I piled on opposite lock. I don't really remember too much about the next few seconds, as the world went mad. The car must have rolled sideways and cleared two layers of catch fencing, before going end-over-end (arse over tit is the technical expression) and attempting to vault the 15 ft high safety fencing, coming down on its back.

I am told I gave a better display than the Red Arrows, but the finish wasn't quite so polished!

I was unconscious, for my helmet came off on the vee of the roll cage — which stood up magnificently to the impact. The seat sheared its runners, and I went backwards into the untrimmed rear compartment. The roof peeled off, leaving a lot of jagged edges, How I kept my head I'll just never know. The doctors told me that, if my helmet had not come off, I would probably have broken my neck instead. Charming . . . .!

Regular readers will know that my years spent practising keep fit with no alcohol or late nights have been dedicated ones. I am glad to say it all paid off, the doctors said a normally fit person would take a week to regain consciousness, but I came to within half an hour.

Imagine the scene. Marshall starts to register again, and finds he has the dubious honour of being the first customer for the new BRDC medical centre at Silverstone! Chris Buckingham, the chief among doctors for the RAC (among other titles) said he was glad to see I was at least a BRDC member!

After putting a big turban around my head (I'm auditioning for the part of Ali Baba at the next Doghouse Panto; the girls will never find out until it's too late. . . .) and giving me an injection, I was floated to Northampton General Hospital.

A consultant, Dr Vanhegan, then addressed himself to the problems presented by assorted head cuts, three skull fractures, cracked ribs and assaults upon my jaw, teeth and kidney. Mugged by a Dolomite Sprint, I ask you! Naturally I owe an enormous thank you to those that dealt with me at the circuit and the hospital, but I would especially like to say what a fabulous cosmetic job they did on the cut right beside my eye at Northampton. All the staff were super, but a special thank you to the delectable Sister Booth and her team.

One thing I remember is a chap called Tom, a porter, asking me for an autograph on the first night. I wondered if he thought it was not worth waiting until morning! Perhaps he knew more about hospital catering than I did?

The hospital were very tolerant, though even they raised their collective eyebrows when Mike Beard at Triplex sent me a case of Scotch medicine: to be taken intravenously? Seriously, the Scotch was kept for visitors only and I must say how gratifying it was to have so many visitors, especially BRDC members. I can't mention any names without leaving out some of the many who bothered to come, so I will just say I really appreciated their support, and the expensive gifts (books and so on) that many brought.

There were an awful lot of Greetings Telegrams too. How the GPO brought themselves to publish some I'll never know! Star efforts here came from Colin Folwell of Corbeau Seats who mentioned what could be done with ladies in black stockings, and Gordon Lamb's Porsche outfit who told me that I had "Cattle-Trucked" my car! Billy B and the DTV boys sent flowers, but I could not decide whether to get married or buried, though I appreciated the thought. . . .

What with Nigel Stovin Bradford ogling the nurses, Squeaker Williams squeaking and a 'get well soon' letter from the RAC (an in non-joke I'm afraid), a good time was had by all.

I was out in 10 days, my ideas of a long rest quickly shattered by 6am "wakey-wakey". Once dressed and washed there was nothing to do, except nasty exercises and to ogle the aforesaid nurses, knowing that one can do nothing about it, despite the advice of Alan Foster et al.

Yes, they soon had enough of me on the George and Elizabeth Ward, (named after George and Liz Smith of Silverstone circuit management?) I had the same room that Jochen Mass once occupied and it was the same ward as David Purley was in. Such is the price of fame. . . .

I would like to say congratulations to Rex Greenslade for his fabulous drive at Silverstone, keeping out the Scottish invader to the end, and commiserate with Martin Crowther. Martin changed the engine on my Lister through the night at Silverstone. Of course, I was unable to drive the car in the event.

Still, after 15 years this is the first time I have put myself in hospital through motor racing. I did have a brief stay after a rallying foray once, but that doesn't really count.

I had a super card from all at Vauxhall which said, "Gerry! Your car will be finished in a couple of shakes! — And ready when you are — enjoy your pit stop, best regards" from Wayne (Cherry, the styling chief, and many, many others). I am ready, now where's my customised Sportshatch?

A comeback? Certainly, I will be at Brands on August Bank Holiday Monday, I hope, with the Equipe Esso Lister and the Dolomite for the Tricentrol round. See you there?

Cheers. Gerry. ■

You can tell it's a Triumph because it says so on the side . . .

GERRY MARSHALL

TIN TOPS
On tour the hard way

If only I hadn't thought I knew Knebworth after rallycrossing there last year, those 20-odd seconds I lost might have helped to put me ahead of Roger Clark on the Avon *Motor* Tour. The final margin between us was only 16 seconds, which must be about as close as you can get after three days and one night of concentrated dicing. Still, as Roger said ruefully, "three spins at the silly little Norwich Showground cost me more than Gerry's nonsense at Knebworth."

So, even the mighty make mistakes. Interpreted my way, the results of the Tour indicate that the racing men trounced the rallyists this year. Roger is the exception to every rule, of course, but then few people realise just how good a race driver Roger is—and could be—if Stuart Turner wasn't paying him so much to stick to the rough stuff.

Looking around *parc fermé* afterwards, I couldn't help noticing also that it was the racing drivers' cars which had fewest scars. The first four home were literally unscratched, but some of the others . . . Honourable exceptions would be Will Sparrow and Andrew Cowan, who both put up exceptional performances anyway.

People kept asking what team orders had been given to Roger and me. The answer is

"absolutely none." This was particularly surprising to me, because everyone was very conscious of my limited rallying experience, which consisted of one write-off. Which I refuse to discuss any further. Then, in the rush to get everything ready for the start, I suppose somebody forgot to give us any orders. Roger and I seemed to be well matched at Mallory, and that's how things continued for the rest of the event since it all seemed to keep the crowds on their toes, and we weren't actually intending to drive into each other. Honestly !

My Escort RS 2000 turned a wheel for the first time in the drive up to Birmingham for scrutineering on Thursday morning. The drive was not without incident, because at the last minute we changed from a standard 3.5 axle (which we had used for all our testing) to the optional 4.1. This was mainly my idea, but on the drive up the motorway I got cold feet about it, since the engine was revving round to 7000 rpm in top, which didn't seem to bode well for its chances of survival. I was so worried that Peter Ashcroft checked his calculations, which showed that 7000 was equivalent to exactly 120 mph, which apparently is just what the doctor ordered. So we stayed with it and I crossed my fingers.

Ford Motor Co is contracted to use Dunlop tyres. Finding the right one presented a few problems, which were only partly solved by some testing at Snetterton three days before the event. The SP4s which we eventually chose were by no means the ultimate in performance (Avon will be pleased to hear !), but on durability they were tops. We gave the nearside fronts a pasting at Mallory Park, yet at the dreaded half-hour race round abrasive old Snetterton we took off only one millimetre of tread.

Otherwise, there was very little work for our service crew to do. We changed brake pads as a precautionary measure before Oulton Park and adjusted the rockers after Long Marston. The rocker business was the only real problem, since it had already happened to Roger at Oulton (putting him on to three cylinders), and I noticed mine just in time to get it fixed at Long Marston itself. This was exemplary behaviour from an engine with which Ford had absolutely nil previous Gp 1 experience.

Don't get the idea from this that Ford weren't organised. They had four mechanics in two service Granada "barges" leapfrogging around the route, and everyone buckled to when required. Even Roger got underneath to help change the pads on my car !

I do believe that the Ford hierarchy were surprised at just how competitive the Escort RS 2000 turned out to be. Roger's was showing 138 bhp (mine 136) on the Weslake brake (less than the Vauxhall Magnums), but the handling, braking and traction must have been better.

There's no truth in the story that we "staged" the whole event. But it looked good on Saturday night with Roger and me level-legging in 2nd place behind Lanfranchi's BMW after the circuit events and before the stages. I must admit to being very apprehensive of the last day's stages, particularly those in Wales. I had no experience of this sort of thing, but surprised even myself by keeping up with the dyed-in-the-wool rallymen. On Eppynt 3 and up Loton Park I beat Roger, setting ftd at Loton by two seconds. It was at Loton that Peter Hilliard had a sudden encounter between his "ice-cream" Alfa and a deer.

Congratulations to the Alfa Romeo Club for winning the club team award. I thought that the BRDC had this one sewn up with a team comprising myself, Lanfranchi and "Whizzo" Williams. But "Whizzo" had an incident on the road with a non-member of the UnKloggers movement—not Barrie's fault at all—and ended up walking home. He was lying around 7th overall at the time, with chances of improvement on the Welsh stages. You'll have seen that the Mazdas were not showing the Dolomite-beating

sparkle of the Group 1 rounds. Something to do with the narrow rims they have to use, I believe, and it also seems that a road exhaust system "kills" a lot of the power they develop in track form.

The Chrysler team won the Manufacturers' Team award with the Avengers of Bernard Unett, Colin Malkin and Simon Kirkby. They celebrated so well that Bernie wound up in the pool, twice ! First time in he just happened to be wearing his new never-worn-before suit. Is it true, Bernard, that the chlorine rots the stitching ? King of Donegal Derek McMahon—who's even bigger than me at 22 stone—navigated Alec Poole to the private entrant's award in Derek's Avenger.

Looking back, in fact, it seems that the Tour itself was not very wearing at all. It was the parties afterwards that did the damage ! I just hope I shall have recovered in time for Grand Prix weekend, which I plan to be doubly busy since I plan to race at Ingliston on Sunday in the Ventora V8 as well as in the Castrol race with a new Magnum coupe. Unhappily we shall be without the comforts of DTV's new hospitality caravan.

Above: John Dignan's Magnum kicks up the dust at Dodington

Left: fast man on Eppynt and elsewhere, Russell Brookes

Below: John Dooley's flying Alfetta on Eppynt

Above: very spectacular Capri driver is Roger Platt

Left: John Cooper's spectacular BMW drive ended at Castle Combe; here he is at Oulton

the BRSCC (who looks much better in her Hesketh tee shirt than I do, especially around teddy's ears!) can now catch up on her sleep. I shan't forget Jeremy Walton of Ford, who said how pleased he was to be cheering for me without risking the sack. Ford's Peter Ashcroft and Tony Mason need no thanks from me (the results speak for them) but I am sure that Stuart Turner has granted them benediction.

And last, but most certainly not least, Paul White—my co-driver—who was totally unflappable (except when trying to get me to leave the bar and go to bed on Saturday night) and did more than I could ever have expected from the passenger's seat. I can only say that without him it would have been impossible.

Can you imagine 7000 rpm in top (122 mph) over Eppynt with sheer drops all around and nothing in your hands except a map and a stick of chewing gum . . .

PS: There was a misprint in last week's interview with Roger Clark. Lanfranchi's BMW was doing 140 mph on the straight, not 114 mph as stated.

Thank you . . .

I'd have bought you all a drink, but couldn't get to the bar for Gerry Marshall and Tony Lanfranchi, so this paragraph is a big thank you too:

Peter Browning and all the BRSCC headquarters staff; BRSCC officials and marshals all over the country; marshals from other clubs who backed them up, especially Brecon MC, who ran Eppynt; The Post House, Great Barr, manager Bob Griffin and all his staff; The Esso Motor Hotel, Bristol; Olivetti for calculating machinery; Plessey for remote copying equipment; Rank Xerox for duplicating facilities; Nescafe for keeping us going during the event and Courvoisier for all the expensive rounds afterwards. Next one's yours, Gerry!

Hamish Cardno

Latest word on this is that some Vaux-ite rolled it while trying to "clean" the first stage on Eppynt.

The disappointment of the Tour must have been the early disappearance of the two Grand Prix stars. Fellow-columnist James Hunt tells his story elsewhere in this issue, while Jody Scheckter seemed less than happy with his Capri. I wonder how Adlards and Elf felt with him after he'd put it out of its misery at Oulton Park!

Another Capri driver who I thought would finish higher was Gordon Spice, who didn't seem to be as quick as last year. It would appear that the retention of road tyres handicapped the larger cars, which includes the Capris. Of the few that got through to the finish, my personal accolade for the most damage would be a tie between Gordon, Stuart Rolt and one Roger Platt.

A special GM award, too, goes to Noel and Gill Edmonds, who were going really well until their Eppynt epic. The sponsors should be happy, too, for this incident got the Tour on to the front page of every newspaper in the land.

The balance between racing and rallying was just right. If it had been wet, there's no doubt in my mind that the rallymen would have pulled out a bigger advantage on the stages. To my mind the balance is perfect. Don't believe the Clark propaganda about going into the forests (this would frighten off every racing driver including me): the only improvement would be to lengthen the event to the distance planned before the fuel shortages obliged the organisers to shorten it.

Peter Browning and Hamish Cardno, the Motor staff and Avon all deserve a special word of thanks. And Anne Bradshaw of

Position	Drivers	Car	Penalties*	Tyres
1	Roger Clark/Jim Porter	Escort RS2000	7729	Dunlop SP4
2	Gerry Marshall/Paul White	Escort RS2000	7747	Dunlop SP4
3	Tony Lanfranchi/Antoine Lurst	BMW 3.0 CSi	7758	Michelin XWX
4	John Handley/John Clegg	Dolomite Sprint	7771	Avon Radial
5	Tony Dron/Henry Liddon	Dolomite Sprint	7784	Dunlop SP Sport Super
6	Adrian Boyd/John Davenport	Capri 3-Litre	7935	Michelin XWX
7	Andrew Cowan/Ross Finlay	Magnum Coupe	7964	Michelin XWX
8	Will Sparrow/Richard Hudson-Evans	Magnum Coupe	7974	Michelin XWX
9	Holman Blackburn/Chris Hollinghorn	Capri 3-Litre	8014	Dunlop SP Super Sport
10	Peter Hanson/Robin Turvey	Commodore GSE	8018	Michelin XWX
11	Russell Brookes/Pete Lyons	Escort RS2000	8035	Avon Wide Safety GT
12	Bernard Unett/Geraint Phillips	Avenger GT	8049	Dunlop SP Super Sport
13	Colin Malkin/Brian Coyle	Avenger GT	8977	Dunlop SP Super Sport
14	Nigel Rockey/Don Davidson	Escort RS2000	8092	Goodyear G800
15	John Dooley/Brian Rouse	Alfetta	8136	Goodyear G800
16	Graham Birrell/Andrew Morrison	Hunter GLS	8148	Avon
17	Simon Kirkby/Monty Peters	Avenger GT	8174	Dunlop SP Sport Super
18	Alec Poole/Derek McMahon	Avenger GT	8200	Dunlop Formula 60
19	Gavin Waugh/Peter Handy	Avenger GT	8231	Dunlop SP Super Sport
20	Peter Hilliard/Nicholas Price	Alfa Romeo 2000 GTV	8238	Michelin XWX
21	Roger Platt/John Platt	Capri 3-Litre	8286	Avon Wide Safety GT
22	John Dignan/Pauline Dignan	Magnum Coupe	8359	Avon Radial
23	Clive Baker/Claes Uddgren	Escort RS2000	8374	Avon Wide Safety GT
24	Colin Walker/Ian Walker	Avenger GT	8377	Kleber V10 GT
25	Chris Rathen/John Doyle	Capri 3-Litre	8396	Dunlop Formula 70
26	Mike Smith/Bob Constandouros	Escort RS2000	8422	Avon Wide Safety GT
27	Brian Marshall/Andrew Gardiner	Mazda RX3	8426	Avon Wide Safety GT
28	Leo Bertorelli/Robert Woods	Alfetta	8454	Michelin XWX
29	Christopher Field/Keith Read	Avenger GT	8490	Dunlop SP Super Sport
30	Chris Daisy/Paul Beeson	Avenger GT	8507	Dunlop SP Super Sport
31	Graham Hollis/Eurst Jones	Escort Mexico	8515	Dunlop SP Sport
32	John Collins/John Dandy	Escort RS2000	8518	Avon Wide Safety GT
33	Hugh Oliver-Bellasis/Martin Neal	Avenger GT	8537	Kleber V10 GT
34	Robert James/Brian Tilley	Escort RS2000	8571	Avon Wide Safety GT
35	Tony Fall/Mike Broad	Commodore GSE	8594	Michelin XWX
36	Vin Huxley/Colin Francis	Dolomite Sprint	8597	Kleber V10 GT
37	David Johnson/Robin Mason	Escort RS2000	8624	Avon Wide Safety GT
38	J-P Magalhaes/Daniel Erculisse	Alfa 2000 GTV	8635	Kleber V10 GT
39	Billy Coleman/Jody Carr	Capri 3-Litre	8636	Dunlop SP Sport Super
40	Stuart Brown/Rodger Turnbull	BMW 2002 Tii	8643	Avon Wide Safety GT
41	Stuart Rolt/Adrian Hamilton	Capri 3-Litre	8678	Dunlop SP Super Sport
42	John Ferguson/John Billett	Escort Mexico	8696	Avon Wide Safety GT
43	Ian Bracey/Brian Chick	Avenger 1500 GT	8718	Avon Wide Safety GT
44	Llewelyn Ranson/Brian Rainbow	Mazda RX3	8748	Kleber V10 GT
45	Chris Fitton/Michael Kempley	Commodore	8754	Michelin XWX
46	John Heppenstall/Dick Mullis	Consul	8812	Michelin XWX
47	Geoff Loos/John Kappler	Escort Mexico	8884	Avon Wide Safety GT
48	Rodney Wiltshire/Anne Bertram	Escort Mexico	8982	Avon Wide Safety GT
49	Andy Dawson/Kevin Gormley	Imp Sport	9018	Avon Wide Safety GT
50	Gordon Spice/Stanley Robinson	Capri 3-Litre	9075	Dunlop SP Sport Super
51	Tony Stubbs/John Conder	Moskvich 412	9084	Kleber V10 GT
52	Peter Jopp/Mark Kahn	Moskvich 412	9095	Kleber V10 GT
53	John Parsons/David Knight	Avenger GT	9096	Kleber V10 GT
54	Terry Sanger/Ashley Juniper	Honda Civic 2GM	9137	Avon Wide Safety GT
55	Mike Manning/Philip Gosling	Escort RS2000	9183	Dunlop SP Sport
56	Linda Jackson/Christine Mitchell	Escort RS2000	9255	Uniroyal Rallye
57	John Lyon/Jonathan Mathias	Moskvich 412	9335	Avon Wide Safety GT
58	Brian Peachy/Ted Beaney	Moskvich 412	9347	Avon Wide Safety GT
59	William Oliver/Robert Reed	Mazda RX4	9404	Avon Wide Safety GT
60	Scott Dalgiesh/Roger MacFarlane	Datsun 1200 Coupe	9478	Esso Radial
61	Michael Anderson/Nicholas Shirley	Escort Sport	9628	Avon Wide Safety GT
62	Derek Wileman/Rodney Posner	Imp Sport	9711	Avon Wide Safety GT
63	Chris Clark/Mike Morgan	Opel Ascona	9883	Dunlop Formula 70
64	Gethin Jones/Frank Rutter	Moskvich 412	9916	Avon Wide Safety GT
65	Chris Hiatt-Baker/Bob Mason	Moskvich 412	10627	Avon Wide Safety GT

* in seconds

RACE RESULTS
1961–2004

The following tables are the result of my project to collate the results Dad achieved during his career. Some people didn't believe Dad's claim of 625 wins, but he was very modest about his achievements – away from motor racing he would not discuss them.

I may not have got 625 exactly (at the time of writing), but I have found over 600 race and class wins and while this book had a deadline, I don't, so I will continue to research all of Dad's results.

Any corrections/additions to this data are greatly received!

Gregor Marshall
April 2010

Year	Month	Date	Circuit	Race	Car	Spec	Details	No.	Qualifying	Result
1961	September	15th	Brands Hatch – Club	Chiltern Circle and Harrow Car Club Sprint	Austin	A35	TBC	TBC	1st	DNS
	October	1st	Eelmore Plain	Allard Owners Club – Sprint	Austin	A35	TBC	TBC	N/A	2nd in Class
	TBC	TBC	TBC	Sprint	MG	A	TBC	TBC	N/A	TBC
	November	TBC	Brands Hatch – Club	MG Car Club Sprint	MG	YB – 1466cc	TBC	TBC	2nd in Class	2nd in Class
1963	February	TBC	Brands Hatch – Club	Chiltern Circle and Harrow Car Club Sprint	Austin	Mini	TBC	TBC	N/A	1st in Class
	February	TBC	Brands Hatch – Club	Chiltern Circle and Harrow Car Club Sprint	Austin	Mini	TBC	TBC	N/A	Retired
	June	14th	Firle	MG Car Club (SE Centre) and BARC Firle Hill-Climb	Sunbeam	Rapier	TBC	TBC	N/A	2nd in Class
	August	18th	Snetterton	Astely Trophy for Saloon Cars	Austin	Mini Cooper 997	Newtune	17	TBC	TBC
	August	30th	Brands Hatch – Club	BARC and Circle Car Club Sprint	Austin	Mini Cooper	YCD436	TBC	N/A	1st in Class
	September	1st	Brands Hatch – Club	London Motor Club Sprint	Austin	Mini Cooper	YCD436	TBC	N/A	2nd in Class
	September	15th	Brands Hatch – Sprint	Chiltern Circle and Harrow Car Club Sprint	Austin	Mini Cooper	YCD436	TBC	N/A	2nd in Class
	October	11th	Brands Hatch – Club	BARC and Circle Car Club Sprint	Austin	Mini Cooper	YCD436	TBC	N/A	1st in Class
	October	20th	Brands Hatch – Sprint	MG Car Club (SE Centre)	Austin	Mini Cooper	YCD436	TBC	N/A	4th in Class
	October	27th	Snetterton	Cambridge University Automobile Car Club Sprint	Austin	Mini Cooper	YCD436	TBC	N/A	2nd in Class
1964	February	16th	Brands Hatch – Sprint	Chiltern Circle and Harrow Car Club Sprint	Austin	Mini Cooper	YCD436	TBC	1st in Class	DNS
	February	23rd	Brands Hatch – Sprint	Surrey Sporting Motor Club Sprint	Austin	Mini Cooper S 1071	CMK855A	TBC	N/A	2nd in Class
	March	1st	Snetterton	Cambridge Automobile Club	Austin	Mini Cooper	YCD436	TBC	N/A	1st in Class
	March	14th	Snetterton	BRSCC Saloon Cars up to 1000cc	Austin	Mini Cooper	YCD436	TBC	TBC	5th Overall
	March	22nd	Blackbushe Slalom	London Motor Club	Austin	Mini Cooper	YCD436	TBC	N/A	1st in Class
	March	30th	Snetterton	SMRC Event 5 – Saloons Up to 1000cc	Austin	Mini Cooper	YCD436	TBC	TBC	1st in Class
	April	5th	Snetterton	Romford Enthusiasts Car Club – Saloon cars up to 1200cc	Austin	Mini Cooper	YCD436	TBC	TBC	1st in Class
	April	5th	Snetterton	Romford Enthusiasts Car Club – Unlimited Saloon Cars	Austin	Mini Cooper	YCD436	TBC	TBC	3rd Overall
	April	12th	Snetterton	BRSCC Saloon Cars up to 1000cc	Austin	Mini Cooper	YCD436	133	TBC	5th Overall
	April	19th	Mallory Park	BRSCC Saloon Cars up to 1000cc	Austin	Mini Cooper	Newtune	131	TBC	DNS
	April	26th	Brands Hatch – Club	BRSCC Saloon Car	Austin	Mini Cooper	Newtune	TBC	TBC	1st Overall
	May	25th	Snetterton	Romford Enthusiasts Car Club Sprint	Austin	Mini Cooper	Newtune	TBC	N/A	3rd in Class
	July	5th	Snetterton	BRSCC Saloon Car	Austin	Mini Cooper	Newtune	TBC	1st	1st Overall
	July	5th	Snetterton	BRSCC	Jaguar	E-Type	TBC	112	TBC	TBC
	November	1st	Snetterton	Cambridge Universtiy Automobile Car Club Speed Trial	TBC	TBC	TBC	TBC	TBC	1st in Class
	November	15th	Brands Hatch – Club	Chiltern Circle and Harrow Car Club Sprint	Austin	Mini Cooper S	Borrowed	TBC	N/A	1st in Class
	December	26th	Mallory Park	BRSCC Saloon Car	Austin	Mini	TBC	TBC	TBC	TBC
	TBC	TBC	Duxford Sprint	London Motor Club Spring Slalom	Austin	Mini Cooper	Newtune	TBC	N/A	1st in Class
1965	January	31st	Brands Hatch – Club	Molyslip Trohpy for Saloon Cars	Austin	Mini Cooper	Newtune	TBC	TBC	2nd in Class
	February	14th	Brands Hatch – Club	Chiltern Circle and Harrow Car Club Sprint	Austin	Mini Cooper S	TBC	TBC	N/A	1st in Class
	March	7th	Snetterton	Cambridge University Automobile Car Club Spring Sprint	Austin	Mini Cooper S 1071	Borrowed	TBC	N/A	4th in Class
	March	13th	Brands Hatch – GP	BRSCC British Saloon Car – The Race of Champions	Austin	Mini Cooper S 970	Newtune	85	30th	Retired
	March	20th	Silverstone – International	BARC Saloon Car Race	Austin	Mini Cooper S 999	Newtune	99	TBC	Race Cancelled
	April	4th	Brands Hatch – Club	Ilford Films Trophy Race for Saloon Cars	Austin	Mini Cooper S 999	Newtune	28	TBC	DNS
	April	10th	Snetterton	BRSCC British Saloon Car Championship	Austin	Mini Cooper S 999	Newtune	72	TBC	2nd in Class
	April	19th	Snetterton	BRSCC Saloon Cars 851cc to 1000cc	Austin	Mini Cooper S 999	Newtune	TBC	TBC	1st in Class
	April	25th	Snetterton	Romford & Essex Car Clubs – Saloon cars up to 1300cc	Austin	Mini Cooper S 999	Newtune	TBC	TBC	4th Overall
	April	25th	Snetterton	Romford & Essex Car Clubs – Newhouse & General Trophy	Austin	Mini Cooper S 999	Newtune	TBC	TBC	1st in Class
	May	9th	Snetterton	BRSCC Saloon Cars Class B	Austin	Mini Cooper S 999	Newtune	TBC	1st in Class	2nd in Class
	May	15th	Silverstone – International	BRSCC British Saloon Car Championship – International "Senior Service"	Austin	Mini Cooper S 999	Newtune	4	TBC	4th in Class
	May	29th/30th	Tholt-y-Will	European Mountain Championship	Austin	Mini Cooper S 970	Newtune	4	3rd in Class	TBC
	June	6th	Mallory Park	Saloon Car Race	Austin	Mini Cooper S 970	Newtune	TBC	TBC	1st in Class
	June	7th	Crystal Palace	BRSCC British Saloon Car Championship	Austin	Mini Cooper S 970	Newtune	144	13th	2nd in Class
	June	20th	Brands Hatch – Club	Redex GT Championship	TVR	Mk3 1800	XPG1	TBC	TBC	2nd in class
	July	18th	Snetterton	Saloon Car Race "A" for special saloon cars up to 1000cc	Austin	Mini Cooper S 999	Newtune	154	TBC	TBC
	August	15th	Snetterton	BRSCC 500 Kms – European Touring Car Championship	Austin	Mini Cooper S 1293	Newtune	35	TBC	1st in Class
	September	5th	Eelmore Plain	Allard OC, Herts County A & AAC, North London ECC & Triumph CC	Lotus	Elan 1650	BAR1	TBC	N/A	2nd in Class
	September	5th	Eelmore Plain	Allard OC, Herts County A & AAC, North London ECC & Triumph CC	TVR	Griffith V8	MMT7C	TBC	N/A	1st in Class
	September	12th	Duxford Sprint	BARC North Thames Class H	TBC	TBC	TBC	TBC	N/A	1st in Class
	September	19th	Mallory Park	London Motor Club Lakeside Trophy – GT cars upto 1150 & over 2500	TVR	Griffith V8	MMT7C	20	TBC	6th Overall
	September	26th	Snetterton	Romford Enthusiasts Car Club	TBC	TBC	TBC	TBC	TBC	TBC
	October	3rd	Brands Hatch – GP	Redex Championship for Special Grand Touring Cars	TVR	Griffith V8	MMT7C	152	TBC	1st Overall
	October	3rd	Brands Hatch – GP	Redex Championship for Special Grand Touring Cars	Lotus	Elan 1650	BAR1	180	TBC	6th Overall
	October	17th	Mallory Park	BRSCC GT cars 1601-2500cc	Lotus	Elan 1650	BAR1	TBC	TBC	2nd Overall
	October	17th	Mallory Park	BRSCC GT cars	TVR	Griffith V8	MMT7C	TBC	TBC	6th Overall
	October	24th	Lydden Hill	Austin Healey Club – All-comers Race	Lotus	Elan 1650	BAR1	TBC	2nd	2nd Overall
	November	7th	Brands Hatch – Club	East Surrey Motor Club Sprint	Lotus	Elan 1650	BAR1	72	N/A	1st in Class
	November	14th	Brands Hatch – Club	BARC and Circle Car Club Sprint	Lotus	Elan 1650	BAR1	TBC	N/A	1st in Class
	November	21st	Brands Hatch – Club	Surrey Sporting Motor Club Sprint	Lotus	Elan 1650	BAR1	TBC	N/A	1st in Class
	November	28th	Brands Hatch – Club	London Motor Club	Lotus	Elan 1650	BAR1	TBC	TBC	1st in Class
	November	TBC	TBC	Sprint	TBC	TBC	TBC	TBC	TBC	1st in Class
	December	27th	Brands Hatch – Club	BRSCC Redex Trophy Race for GT Cars	Lotus	Elan 1650	BAR1	83	2nd	1st in Class
	September/October	TBC	Snetterton	Romford Enthusiasts Car Club – Marque & GT Race	Lotus	Elan 1650	BAR1	TBC	TBC	Retired

Year	Month	Date	Circuit	Race	Car	Spec	Details	No.	Qualifying	Result
1965	TBC	TBC	TBC	Shrimpton Challenge Cup Surrey Motor Club	TBC	TBC	TBC	TBC	TBC	1st in Class
	TBC	TBC	Cadwell Park	TBC	Lotus	Elan 1650	BAR1	TBC	TBC	TBC
1966	February	6th	Brands Hatch – Club	Chiltern Circle and Harrow Car Club Sprint	TVR	Griffith V8	MMT7C	96	N/A	1st in Class
	February	25th	Brands Hatch – Club	Sutton and Cheam Motor Club	TVR	Griffith V8	MMT7C	TBC	N/A	1st in Class
	March	6th	Brands Hatch – Club	BRSCC – Autosport Cup	TVR	Griffith V8	MMT7C	92	TBC	TBC
	March	6th	Brands Hatch – Club	Edward Lewis Trophy Race "B" for Special Saloon Cars	Austin	Mini Cooper S 1293	Roy Ensor's Car	187	TBC	4th Overall
	March	13th	Snetterton	BRSCC GT and Marque Race	TVR	Griffith V8	MMT7C	88	1st	Retired
	March	19th	Goodwood	BARC Grand Touring Race	Lotus	Elan	BAR1	52	3rd	Retired
	March	20th	Brands Hatch – Club	Maidstone and Mid-Kent Motor Club GT Race	Lotus	Elan	BAR1	TBC	2nd	Retired
	April	8th	Woburn Hillclimb	Sporting Owner Drivers Club	TVR	Griffith V8	MMT7C	TBC	N/A	1st in Class
	April	11th	Brands Hatch – Club	BRSCC – British Eagle Trophy Race for Special Grand Touring Cars	Lotus	Elan	BAR1	78	TBC	TBC
	April	24th	Snetterton	Romford Enthusiasts Car Club – Marque & GT Race	TVR	Griffith V8	MMT7C	TBC	1st	1st Overall
	May	8th	Brands Hatch – TBC	BOAC 500 Six Hour Race	TVR	1800 S	LHV41D	TBC	TBC	Retired
	May	29th	Brands Hatch – GP	BRSCC Special GT cars	TVR	Griffith V8	MMT7C	TBC	TBC	1st in Class
	May	30th	Snetterton	BRSCC Formule Libre, Formula 3 and Special GT cars	TVR	Griffith V8	MMT7C	TBC	TBC	1st in Class
	May	30th	Snetterton	BRSCC Marque Sportscars 1151cc to 3000cc	TVR	1800 S	LHV41D	173	TBC	1st in Class
	June	5th	Snetterton	Romford Enthusiasts Car Club	TVR	Griffith V8	MMT7C	TBC	N/A	1st in Class
	June	12th	Snetterton	Mini Seven Club Marque and GT Cars	TVR	Griffith V8	MMT7C	TBC	1st	1st Overall
	June	19th	Brands Hatch – Club	London Motor Club (Radio London) GT Cars	TVR	Griffith V8	MMT7C	TBC	2nd	2nd Overall
	July	10th	Brands Hatch – Club	MG Car Club Grand Touring Cars up to 1600	Lotus	Elan	BAR1	TBC	1st	2nd Overall
	July	17th	Brands Hatch – Club	Jaguar Drivers Club & BP Auto Club Sprint	Lotus	Elan	BAR1	TBC	TBC	Retired
	July	24th	Lydden Hill	Romford Enthusiasts Car Club – GT up to 1600	Lotus	Elan 1650	TBC	TBC	TBC	Winner
	July	24th	Lydden Hill	Romford Enthusiasts Car Club – GT over 1600	Lotus	Elan 1650	TBC	TBC	TBC	Winner
	July	31st	Brands Hatch – Club	BARC and Circle Car Club Sprint	Lotus	Elan	BAR1	TBC	N/A	Retired
	August	6th	Silverstone – TBC	750 Motor Club Holland Birkett Six Hour Relay Race	TVR	Griffith V8	TBC	TBC	1st	Retired
	August	6th	Silverstone – TBC	750 Motor Club Holland Birkett Six Hour Relay Race	TVR	1800 S	TBC	TBC	TBC	Retired
	September	5th	Snetterton	BRSCC Marque cars over 3000cc	TVR	Griffith V8	MMT7C	TBC	TBC	1st Overall
	September	11th	Snetterton	BRSCC Marque Sportscars 1151cc to 3000cc	TVR	1800 S	TBC	TBC	TBC	1st in Class
	September	17th	Oulton Park	Daily Express – International Gold Cup	TVR	Griffith V8	MMT7C	55	TBC	7th Overalll
	September	24th/25th	Tholt-y-Will	Guards Cigarettes – European Hillclimb Championship	TVR	Griffith V8	MMT7C	TBC	N/A	1st in Class
	October	1st	Silverstone – International	Eight Clubs Clubmen's Championship GT Car Race over 1600cc	TVR	Griffith V8	MMT7C	224	TBC	TBC
	October	2nd	Brands Hatch – GP	RAC Guards Trophy Race GT Cars (F3)	TVR	Griffith V8	MMT7C	93	TBC	DNS
	October	9th	Woburn Hillclimb	Sporting Owner Drivers Club	TVR	Griffith V8	MMT7C	TBC	N/A	1st in Class
	October	16th	Snetterton	Autosport Championship Final Race – BRSCC Special Saloon Car	Austin	Mini 850	Ken Ayres	TBC	TBC	3rd in Class
	October	16th	Snetterton	Autosport Championship Final Race – BRSCC Special GT & Marque Car	TVR	Griffith V8	MMT7C	TBC	TBC	5th Overall
	October	23rd	Lydden Hill	West Essex Car Club – Event 2 – GT Race	TVR	Griffith V8	MMT7C	TBC	3rd	1st Overall
	November	6th	Snetterton	Cambridge University AC GM Slalom	TVR	Griffith V8	MMT7C	TBC	N/A	Retired
	November	13th	Brands Hatch – Club	Tunbridge Wells & Rochester Motor Clubs GT Race	TVR	Griffith V8	MMT7C	TBC	DNS	Retired
	November	27th	Brands Hatch – TBC	London Motor Club Race 8 GT Cars	TVR	Griffith V8	MMT7C	203	1st	1st in Class
	December	27th	Mallory Park	BRSCC GT Cars	TVR	Grantura Mk3	Tommy Entwhistle	TBC	TBC	1st in Class
	December	27th	Mallory Park	BRSCC Modsports	TVR	Grantura Mk3	Tommy Entwhistle	TBC	1st	Retired
	December	27th	Mallory Park	BRSCC Saloons up to and over 1300cc	Austin	Mini Cooper S 1293	Roy Ensor's Car	TBC	1st	1st in Class
	TBC	TBC	Elstree	Players No.6 Autocross Championship	TVR	Griffith V8	MMT7C	TBC	N/A	1st Overall
1967	February	5th	Brands Hatch – Club	Chiltern Circle and Harrow Car Club Sprint	TVR	Griffith V8	MMT7C	TBC	N/A	1st Overall
	February	12th	Brands Hatch – Club	Saloons up to 850cc	Austin	Mini 850	Ken Ayres	TBC	TBC	1st Overall
	March	1st	Snetterton	Cambridge University Automobile Car Club Spring Sprint	TVR	Griffith V8	MMT7C	TBC	N/A	1st in Class
	March	12th	Brands Hatch – TBC	Race of Champions	TBC	TBC	TBC	TBC	TBC	TBC
	March	19th	Monza	4 Hours – European Touring Car Challenge	Austin	Mini Cooper S 1275	Rex Finnegan	TBC	TBC	Retired
	March	23rd/24th	Snetterton	The Autosport Trophy Race – British Sports Car Championship	Lotus	Elan	Barnet Motor Company	85	TBC	12th
	March	27th	Silverstone – International	The Autosport Trophy Race – British Sports Car Championship	Lotus	Elan	Barnet Motor Company	TBC	TBC	16th Overall
	April	2nd	Woburn Hillclimb	Sporting Owner Drivers Club	Jaguar	E-Type	TBC	TBC	N/A	1st in Class
	May	7th	Elstree	Players No.6 Autocross Championship – Chess Valley Motor Club	TVR	Griffith V8	MMT7C	TBC	N/A	1st in Class
	May	19th	Tholt-y-Will	Lancs AC Hillclimb	TVR	Griffith V8	MMT7C	TBC	N/A	1st in Class
	May	27th	Woburn Hillclimb	Sporting Owner Drivers Club	TBC	TBC	TBC	TBC	N/A	1st in Class
	May	27th	Woburn Hillclimb	Sporting Owner Drivers Club	TBC	TBC	TBC	TBC	N/A	1st in Class
	June	4th	Brands Hatch – Club	Thames Estuary Automobile Club & MSAC – Special GT Cars	TVR	Griffith V8	MMT7C	212	TBC	2nd Overall
	June	11th	Snetterton	BRSCC Special Saloon Car up to 850cc	Austin	Mini 850	Ken Ayres	TBC	TBC	1st Overall
	June	18th	Brands Hatch – TBC	London Motor Club	Austin	Mini 850	Ken Ayres	141	TBC	Retired
	June	29th	TBC	Romford Enthusiasts MiniSprint	TVR	TBC	TBC	TBC	TBC	TBC
	July	2nd	Nürburgring	Grosser Preis der Tourenwagen – European Touring Car Challenge	Austin	Mini Cooper S 1275	Rex Finnegan	TBC	TBC	Retired
	July	9th	Snetterton	BRSCC Festival of Saloon Car Two hour endurance for Special Saloons	Austin	Mini 850	Ken Ayres	35	TBC	TBC
	August	5th/6th	Brands Hatch – TBC	Seven Oaks & District Motor Club – AGK	TBC	TBC	TBC	TBC	TBC	TBC
	September	3rd	Autocross	Players No.6 Autocross Championship – Taunton MC Western Area Final	TBC	TBC	TBC	TBC	N/A	TBC
	September	11th	N/A	Left Barnet Motor Company	N/A	N/A	N/A	N/A	N/A	N/A
	September	14th	Rally	LAP RAC Rally	TBC	TBC	TBC	TBC	TBC	TBC
	September	16th	Oulton Park	Autosport Championship Final Race	TVR	1800 S	Barnet Motor Company	71	TBC	TBC
	September	17th	Snetterton	500Km Archie Scott-Brown Trophy – European Touring Car Challenge	Austin	Mini Cooper S 1293	TBC	TBC	4th	Retired
	September	24th	Tholt-y-Will	European Hillclimb Championship	Jaguar	E-Type	TBC	TBC	N/A	1st in Class
	October	13th	Blackbushe	TBC	TBC	TBC	TBC	TBC	TBC	TBC
	October	22nd	Lydden Hill	West Essex Car Club	Vauxhall	Viva	S&K 1258	TBC	TBC	TBC
	October	28th	Rally	TBC	TBC	TBC	TBC	TBC	TBC	TBC
	October	29th	Snetterton	Cambridge University Automobile Car Club Spring Sprint	Vauxhall	Viva	S&K 1258	TBC	N/A	1st in Class
	November	12th	Brands Hatch – Club	Sevenoaks District Motor Club Sevenoaks Cup	Vauxhall	Viva	S&K 1258	TBC	TBC	TBC
	November	19th	Brands Hatch – TBC	Romford Dictrict Motor Club – Swiftsure Challenge	Vauxhall	Viva	S&K 1258	TBC	TBC	8th Overall
	November	24th	Rally	Sporting Owners Drivers Club	TBC	TBC	TBC	TBC	TBC	TBC
	November	25th	Silverstone – TBC	National Saloon Car Championship	Vauxhall	Viva	S&K 1258	TBC	TBC	TBC
	November	26th	Brands Hatch – Club	Guards Trophy Race	Ginetta	G12 1594	TBC	16	TBC	DNS
	November	26th	Brands Hatch – Club	Redex Gold Cross	Vauxhall	Viva	S&K 1258	217	TBC	TBC
	November	26th	Brands Hatch – Club	November Trophy Race for Formula Libre Cars	Ginetta	G12 1594	TBC	16	TBC	TBC
	December	10th	Brands Hatch – Club	Mini Seven Club	Vauxhall	Viva	S&K 1258	TBC	TBC	TBC
	December	26th	Lydden Hill	Thames Estuary Motor Club	Vauxhall	Viva	S&K 1258	TBC	TBC	Retired
	TBC	TBC	TBC	TBC	Hillman	Imp	Alan Fraser	TBC	TBC	TBC
	TBC	TBC	Snetterton	TBC	Austin	Mini 850	Bill Blydenstein	TBC	TBC	1st in Class
	TBC	TBC	TBC	TBC	Austin	Mini 850	Bill Blydenstein	TBC	TBC	1st in Class

Year	Month	Date	Circuit	Race	Car	Spec	Details	No.	Qualifying	Result
1968	March	3rd	Snetterton	Cambridge University Automobile Car Club Spring Sprint	Vauxhall	Viva	S&K 1258	TBC	N/A	2nd in Class
	March	TBC	Woburn Hillclimb	TBC	Vauxhall	Viva GT	S&K 2 litre	TBC	N/A	TBC
	May	26th	TBC	Sprint	Vauxhall	Viva	TBC	TBC	N/A	4th in Class
	May	26th	Chacil End	Vauxhall Motors Sprint	Vauxhall	Viva GT	S&K 2 litre	TBC	N/A	5th in Class
	June	9th	Brands Hatch – Club	BARC	Vauxhall	Viva GT	S&K 2 litre	TBC	TBC	3rd in Class
	July	14th	Brands Hatch – Mini	TBC	Vauxhall	Viva GT	S&K 2 litre	TBC	TBC	2nd Overall
	July	20th	Lydden Hill	Thames Estuary Automobile Club Saloons over 1300cc	Vauxhall	Viva GT	S&K 2 litre	TBC	1st	1st Overall
	July	21st	Woburn Hillclimb	TBC	Vauxhall	Viva GT	S&K 2 litre	TBC	N/A	3rd Overall
	August	3rd	Silverstone – TBC	750 Motor Club Holland Birkett Six Hour Relay Race	Vauxhall	Viva GT	S&K 2 litre	TBC	TBC	3rd Overall
	August	11th	Lydden Hill	East Sussex Motor Club	Vauxhall	Viva GT	S&K 2 litre	TBC	2nd	Retired
	August	25th	Snetterton	TBC	Vauxhall	Viva GT	S&K 2 litre	TBC	TBC	Retired
	September	2nd	Snetterton	BARC Saloon Car Race	Vauxhall	Viva GT	S&K 2 litre	TBC	TBC	Retired
	September	8th	Beaulieu	Councours	Vauxhall	Viva	HB SL	TBC	N/A	1st
	September	8th	Beaulieu	Gymkhana	Vauxhall	Viva	HB SL	TBC	N/A	3rd Overall
	September	15th	Harewood Hill	Hillclimb	Vauxhall	Viva	TBC	TBC	N/A	7th in Class
	September	22nd	Lydden Hill	750 Motor Club Viva Race	Vauxhall	Viva	1971	TBC	TBC	1st Overall
	September	29th	Santa Pod	London Motor Club Sprint Slalom	Vauxhall	Viva	TBC	TBC	N/A	2nd
	September	29th	Santa Pod	London Motor Club Sprint Slalom	Vauxhall	Viva	TBC	TBC	N/A	Award
	October	6th	Woburn Hillclimb	TBC	Vauxhall	Viva GT	S&K 2 litre	TBC	N/A	3rd in Class
	October	13th	Mallory Park	TBC	Vauxhall	Viva GT	S&K 2 litre	TBC	5th	2nd Overall
	October	20th	Lydden Hill	TBC	Vauxhall	Viva GT	S&K 2 litre	TBC	TBC	4th Overall
	October	27th	Snetterton	Cambridge University Automobile Car Club Grand Saloon	Vauxhall	Viva GT	S&K 2 litre	TBC	TBC	1st in class
	October	27th	Snetterton	Cambridge University Automobile Car Club Grand Saloon	Vauxhall	Viva GT	S&K 2 litre	TBC	TBC	Award
	November	2nd	Silverstone – GP	Sprint	Vauxhall	Viva GT	S&K 2 litre	TBC	N/A	3rd in Class
	November	10th	Brands Hatch – Club	Redex	Vauxhall	Viva GT	S&K 2 litre	TBC	TBC	2nd Overall
	November	16th/20th	Rally	LAP RAC Rally	Vauxhall	Viva	TBC	TBC	TBC	TBC
	November	17th	Rochester, Chatham & District MC Special Saloons		Vauxhall	Viva GT	S&K 2 litre	TBC	1st	Retired
	November	23rd/24th	Brands Hatch – Club	Saloon Car Race	Vauxhall	Viva	Mike Davies	TBC	4th	2nd Overall
	December	1st	Brands Hatch – Club	TBC	Vauxhall	Viva GT	S&K 2 litre	TBC	1st	2nd Overall
	December	8th	Lydden Hill	Chess Valley Motor Club Valvoline Trophy Autocross	Vauxhall	Viva	Coburn Rallycross Car	TBC	N/A	2nd in Class
	December	27th	Brands Hatch – Club	BRSCC	Vauxhall	Viva GT	S&K 2 litre	TBC	3rd	2nd Overall
1969	January	19th	Brands Hatch – Club	BRSCC Special Saloon Car over 1300cc	Vauxhall	Viva GT	S&K 2 litre	134	TBC	2nd in Class
	March	2nd	Snetterton	Cambridge University Automobile Car Club Spring Sprint	Vauxhall	Viva GT	S&K 2 litre	TBC	N/A	1st in Class
	March	9th	Mallory Park	Redex Gold Cross Saloon Car Race	Vauxhall	Viva GT	S&K 2 litre	TBC	1st	1st in Class
	March	15th	Oulton Park	Redex Gold Cross	Vauxhall	Viva GT	S&K 2 litre	TBC	2nd	2nd in Class
	March	23rd	Snetterton	Saloon Race Shaw & Kilburn Vauxhall Viva	Vauxhall	Viva	TBC	TBC	TBC	2nd Overall
	March	30th	Duxford Sprint	Sprint	Vauxhall	Viva	TBC	TBC	N/A	1st in Class
	April	4th	Oulton Park	BRSCC Gold Cup	Vauxhall	Viva GT	S&K 2 litre	104	2nd	1st Overall
	April	7th	Brands Hatch – TBC	BRSCC Redex Gold Cross	Vauxhall	Viva GT	S&K 2 litre	152	TBC	2nd Overall
	April	12th	Snetterton	Guards 500kms for Group 5 Special Touring Cars	Austin	Mini	TBC	TBC	TBC	3rd in Class
	April	27th	Woburn Hillclimb	Sprint	Vauxhall	Viva	TBC	TBC	N/A	1st in Class
	May	3rd	Oulton Park	Lancashire & Cheshire Car Club Redex Gold Cross	Vauxhall	Viva GT	S&K 2 litre	TBC	3rd	2nd Overall
	May	4th	Mallory Park	Redex – BARC East Midlands Centre	Vauxhall	Viva GT	S&K 2 litre	TBC	1st	2nd Overall
	May	11th	Brands Hatch – Club	Maidstone and Mid-Kent Motor Car Club	Vauxhall	Viva	TBC	TBC	TBC	5th in Class
	May	26th	Mallory Park	Redex Gold Cross	Vauxhall	Viva GT	S&K 2 litre	TBC	4th	Retired
	June	7th	Oulton Park	Mid Cheshire MRC Redex Gold Cross	Vauxhall	Viva GT	S&K 2 litre – New car	TBC	4th	Retired
	June	15th	Brands Hatch – Club	Redex Gold Cross	Vauxhall	Viva	TBC	TBC	1st	2nd Overall
	June	22nd	Duxford Sprint	Herts Aero County Club Sprint	Vauxhall	Viva	TBC	TBC	N/A	2nd in Class
	June	29th	Snetterton	Romford Enthusiast Car Club	Vauxhall	Viva	TBC	TBC	1st	Retired
	June	29th	Snetterton	Romford Enthusiast Car Club – Formula Ford	Lotus	61	TBC	TBC	5th	Retired
	July	13th	Mallory Park	Formula Ford	Lotus	61L	TBC	TBC	TBC	10th
	July	13th	Mallory Park	Formula Ford	Lotus	61L	TBC	TBC	TBC	7th Overalll
	July	13th	Mallory Park	Redex Gold Cross	Vauxhall	Viva GT	S&K 2 litre	TBC	1st	Retired
	July	20th	Brands Hatch – Club	Formula Ford	Lotus	61L	TBC	TBC	TBC	5th Overall
	July	27th	Snetterton	Formula Ford	Lotus	61L	TBC	TBC	TBC	Retired
	July	27th	Snetterton	Redex Gold Cross	Vauxhall	Viva GT	2300	TBC	TBC	Retired
	August	3rd	Brands Hatch – Club	Sutton & Cheam Redex Gold Cross	Vauxhall	Viva GT	2300	246	TBC	2nd Overall
	August	9th	Silverstone – Club	750 Motor Club Holland Birkett Six Hour Relay Race	Vauxhall	Viva	TBC	TBC	TBC	1st Overall
	August	10th	Snetterton	Redex Gold Cross	Vauxhall	Viva	TBC	TBC	1st	Retired
	August	10th	Snetterton	Formula Ford	Lotus	61L	TBC	TBC	5th	4th Overall
	August	17th	Brands Hatch – Club	Redex Gold Cross	Vauxhall	Viva	TBC	TBC	TBC	1st Overall
	August	17th	Brands Hatch – Club	Formula Ford – Heat	Lotus	61L	TBC	TBC	TBC	8th Overall
	August	17th	Brands Hatch – Club	Formula Ford – Final	Lotus	61L	TBC	TBC	TBC	17th Overall
	August	24th	Snetterton	Formula Ford – Romford Enthusiasts Car Club	Lotus	61L	TBC	TBC	TBC	2nd Overall
	Aug/Sep	29th/1st	Oulton Park	Redex Gold Cross	Vauxhall	Viva GT	2300	TBC	TBC	1st Overall
	Aug/Sep	29th/1st	Mallory Park	Formula Ford	Lotus	61L	TBC	TBC	TBC	DNS
	Aug/Sep	31st/1st	Mallory Park	TBC	Vauxhall	Viva	TBC	TBC	TBC	Retired
	September	7th	Chaul End	Sprint	Vauxhall	Viva	TBC	TBC	N/A	2nd in Class
	September	13th/14th	Phoenix Park	Irish MRC	Vauxhall	Viva GT	TBC	TBC	1st	Retired
	September	20th	Oulton Park	BARC NW Redex Special Saloon Car Race	Vauxhall	Viva	TBC	TBC	TBC	Winner
	September	21st	Snetterton	BRSCC East Anglia Redex Gold Cross	Vauxhall	Viva	TBC	TBC	TBC	3rd Overall
	September	28th	Brands Hatch – GP	BRSCC Redex Gold Cross	Vauxhall	Viva	TBC	TBC	4th	Retired
	October	4th	Oulton Park	TBC	Austin	Mini 1275S	Hugh Denton	TBC	Back of Grid	Retired
	October	5th	Woburn Hillclimb	TBC	Vauxhall	Viva	TBC	TBC	TBC	1st in Class
	October	17th/18th	Silverstone – GP	Saloon Cars for the Boley Pittard Trophy Clubmans Championship (BRDC)	Vauxhall	Viva GT	2015	131	1st	1st in Class
	October	26th	Brands Hatch – Club	BRSCC	Vauxhall	Viva GT	S&K	TBC	2nd	2nd Overall
	November	9th	Brands Hatch – Club	Redex Gold Cross Saloon Car Race	Vauxhall	Viva GT	2300	42	1st	2nd Overall
	November	9th	Brands Hatch – Club	Redex Gold Cross Saloon Car Race	Vauxhall	Viva GT	2300	42	1st	1st Overall
	November	15th	Thruxton	BARC BBC Televised Race	Vauxhall	Viva GT	2300	TBC	TBC	2nd in Class
	November	16th	Mallory Park	TBC	Vauxhall	Viva GT	TBC	TBC	TBC	3rd Overall
	November	23rd	Brands Hatch – TBC	Romford Enthusiasts Car Club	Austin	Mini 1275S	Hugh Denton	TBC	TBC	DNS
	November	30th	Brands Hatch – TBC	London Motor Club	TBC	TBC	TBC	TBC	TBC	DNS
	December	14th	Brands Hatch – Club	Sprint	Vauxhall	Viva	TBC	TBC	N/A	1st in Class
	December	27th	Brands Hatch – Club	BRSCC Saloons over 1000cc	Vauxhall	Viva GT	2300	TBC	1st	Race Cancelled
	December	28th	Mallory Park	BRSCC (Midland)	Austin	Mini Cooper S 970	Robbie Gordon	TBC	TBC	1st in Class

Year	Month	Date	Circuit	Race	Car	Spec	Details	No.	Qualifying	Result
1970	February	1st	Brands Hatch – Club	Chiltern Circle and Harrow Car Club Sprint	Vauxhall	Viva	TBC	TBC	N/A	1st in Class
	March	1st	Snetterton	Cambridge University Automobile Car Club Spring Sprint	Vauxhall	Viva	TBC	TBC	N/A	1st in Class
	March	8th	Thruxton	Osram GEC	Vauxhall	Viva GT	TBC	TBC	TBC	1st in Class
	March	15th	Snetterton	Osram GEC	Vauxhall	Viva	TBC	TBC	TBC	1st Overall
	March	21st/22nd	Brands Hatch – GP	RAC British Saloon Car Championship – ROC Guards Trophy Heat 1	Vauxhall	Viva GT	S&K 1994	109	16th	10th Overall
	March	21st/22nd	Brands Hatch – GP	RAC British Saloon Car Championship – ROC Guards Trophy Heat 2	Vauxhall	Viva GT	S&K 1994	109	16th	DNF
	March	27th	Snetterton	BRSCC RAC British Saloon Car Championship	Vauxhall	Viva GT	S&K 1994	TBC	32nd	DNQ
	March	28th/30th	Thruxton	BARC RAC British Saloon Car Championship	Vauxhall	Viva GT	S&K 1994	TBC	19th	12th Overall
	April	12th	Duxford Sprint	TBC	Vauxhall	Viva	TBC	TBC	N/A	1st in Class
	April	18th	Castle Combe	Osram GEC	Vauxhall	Viva GT	S&K 2315	TBC	3rd	3rd Overall
	April	24th/25th/26th	Silverstone – GP	GKN Forgings Trophy – BRDC RAC British Saloon Car Championship	Vauxhall	Viva GT	S&K 1994	52	11th	3rd in Class
	May	3rd	Thruxton	Osram GEC	Vauxhall	Viva GT	TBC	TBC	TBC	1st Overall
	May	9th10th	Zolder	Grand Prix de Zolder – National races	Vauxhall	Viva	2 litre	TBC	5th	13th
	May	15th/16th	Spa-Francorchamps	Coupes de Spa	Vauxhall	Viva	1975	10	2nd	4th Overall
	May	17th	Spa-Francorchamps	World Sports Car Championship 1000kms	Brabham	BT8 – Climax	SC-4-64	7	30th	Retired
	May	23rd/25th	Crystal Palace	BARC RAC British Saloon Car Championship	Vauxhall	Viva	S&K 1994	TBC	16th	7th in Class
	May	24th	Brands Hatch – Club	FordSport Day	Ford	Galaxie	TBC	TBC	TBC	Retired
	May	31st	Silverstone – Club	Osram GEC 100kms Trophy Race for Saloon Cars	Vauxhall	Viva	TBC	TBC	4th	18th
	June	6th	Silverstone – International	Wipac Trophy – AMOC RAC British Saloon Car Championship	Vauxhall	Viva GT	S&K 1994	21	14th	5th in Class
	June	21st	Croft	Osram GEC	Vauxhall	Viva	TBC	TBC	TBC	1st Overall
	June	21st	Croft	Invitation Race	Vauxhall	Viva	TBC	TBC	TBC	1st Overall
	June	27th	Silverstone – GP	RAC Tourist Trophy – British Saloon Car Championship – Heat 1	Vauxhall	Viva GT	S&K 1994	57	TBC	16th Overall
	June	27th	Silverstone – GP	RAC Tourist Trophy – British Saloon Car Championship – Heat 2	Vauxhall	Viva GT	S&K 1994	57	16th	11th in Class
	July	5th	Brands Hatch – Club	Osram GEC	Vauxhall	Viva	TBC	TBC	3rd	3rd Overall
	July	10th/11th	Croft	BARC RAC British Saloon Car Championship	Vauxhall	Viva GT	S&K 1994	12	5th	6th in Class
	July	10th/11th	Croft	BARC RAC British Saloon Car Championship	Vauxhall	Viva GT	S&K 1994	12	5th	6th in Class
	July	11th	Castle Combe	Osram GEC	Vauxhall	Viva	TBC	TBC	TBC	3rd Overall
	July	16th/17th/18th	Brands Hatch – GP	RAC British Saloon Car Championship	Vauxhall	Viva GT	S&K 1994	TBC	17th	13th Overall
	July	26th	Mallory Park	Osram GEC BARC Special Saloons	Vauxhall	Viva GT	2300	150	TBC	1st Overall
	August	2nd	Brands Hatch – Club	TBC	Rawlson	Ford 997cc	CR7	TBC	1st	Retired
	August	8th	Silverstone – TBC	750 Motor Club Holland Birkett Six Hour Relay Race	Vauxhall	Viva GT	S&K 1994	TBC	TBC	4th Overall
	August	15th	Silverstone – GP	Grand Touring Cars & Modified Sports Cars	Rawlson	Ford 997cc	CR7	88	2nd	Retired
	August	15th	Silverstone – GP	Special Saloons – Group 2	Austin	Mini Cooper S 970	Ian Blaunt	137	2nd	3rd in Class
	August	16th	Brands Hatch – TBC	Motoring News Grand Touring Cars	Rawlson	Ford 997cc	CR7	TBC	DNS	DNS
	August	16th	Brands Hatch – TBC	TBC	Vauxhall	Viva	TBC	196	TBC	Retired
	August	21st/22nd	Oulton Park	Gold Cup RAC British Saloon Car Championship – Mid Cheshire Motor RC	Vauxhall	Viva GT	S&K 1994	TBC	9th	4th in Class
	August	30th	Thruxton	Osram GEC	Vauxhall	Viva	TBC	TBC	TBC	DNS
	August	31st	TBC	TBC	Austin	Healey 3000	Robbie Gordon	TBC	3rd	2nd in Class
	September	5th/6th	Zolder	Bekers van de Toekomst	Vauxhall	Viva	TBC	TBC	TBC	4th Overall
	September	5th/6th	Zolder	Bekers van de Toekomst	Vauxhall	Viva	TBC	TBC	TBC	8th Overall
	September	12th	Crystal Palace	Osram GEC BARC Championship	Vauxhall	Viva GT	2300	TBC	10th	2nd Overall
	September	18th/19th/20th	Spa-Francorchamps	Trophee des Ardennes	Vauxhall	Viva	TBC	TBC	TBC	Retired
	September	26th/27th	Brands Hatch – GP	TBC	Rawlson	Ford 997cc	CR7	TBC	DNS	Retired
	October	3rd	Castle Combe	Osram GEC	Vauxhall	Viva GT	S&K	TBC	TBC	Retired
	October	4th	Silverstone – National	TBC	Austin	Healey 3000	Robbie Gordon	TBC	TBC	2nd in Class
	October	11th	Thruxton	TBC	Rawlson	Ford 997cc	CR7	TBC	TBC	DNS
	October	11th	Thruxton	Osram GEC	Vauxhall	Viva	TBC	TBC	TBC	DNS
	October	31st	Silverstone – TBC	Herts County & Aero Sprint	Vauxhall	Viva GT	TBC	TBC	N/A	Retired
	November	1st	Brands Hatch – TBC	TBC	Rawlson	Ford 997cc	CR7	TBC	DNS	DNS
	November	8th	High Beech, Loughton	Stone Cross Autotest	TBC	TBC	TBC	TBC	N/A	2nd in Class
	November	8th	High Beech, Loughton	Stone Cross Autotest	TBC	TBC	TBC	TBC	N/A	Award
	November	8th	High Beech, Loughton	Stone Cross Autotest	TBC	TBC	TBC	TBC	N/A	Award
	November	14th	Thruxton	British Saloon Car Championship (Televised Race)	Vauxhall	Viva GT	TBC	TBC	DNS	1st in Class
	November	28th	Silverstone – TBC	Sporting Owner Drivers Club	Austin	Mini Cooper S 998	Barry Boults	TBC	N/A	DNS
	December	26th	Mallory Park	Group 2	Austin	Mini 1000cc	Rob Mason	TBC	TBC	1st
	December	27th	Brands Hatch – TBC	TBC	TBC	TBC	TBC	TBC	TBC	DNS
1971	January	17th	Brands Hatch – Club	Consortium Clubs Race Racing Car Show Meeting	Vauxhall	Viva GT	S&K 2.2	TBC	1st	1st Overall
	February	7th	Brands Hatch – Club	Chiltern Circle and Harrow Car Club Sprint	Vauxhall	Viva	TBC	TBC	N/A	1st in Class
	February	14th	Brands Hatch – Club	Consortium Sprint	Vauxhall	Viva	TBC	TBC	N/A	1st in Class
	February	14th	Brands Hatch – Club	Consortium Sprint	Vauxhall	Viva	XXD388H	TBC	N/A	2nd in Class
	February	28th	Snetterton	Cambridge University Automobile Car Club Spring Sprint	Vauxhall	Viva	TBC	TBC	N/A	1st in Class
	March	14th	Silverstone – Club	National Saloon Car Championship – Triplex > 1000cc	Vauxhall	Viva	2.2	TBC	7th	Retired
	March	20th	Castle Combe	Osram GEC	Vauxhall	Viva GT	S&K 2.2	TBC	2nd	2nd Overall
	March	28th	Duxford Sprint	Cambridge Car Club Sprint	Vauxhall	Viva	TBC	TBC	N/A	1st in Class
	April	4th	Silverstone – TBC	Osram GEC	Vauxhall	Viva GT	TBC	TBC	TBC	5th in Class
	April	9th	Cadwell Park	Osram GEC	Vauxhall	Viva GT	TBC	TBC	TBC	1st in Class
	April	18th	Duxford Sprint	Cambridge University Automobile Car Club Sprint	Vauxhall	Viva	TBC	TBC	N/A	1st in Class
	April	20th	Lydden Hill	Blue Peter Viva Race	Vauxhall	Viva GT	TBC	TBC	3rd	1st Overall
	April	23rd	N/A	Blue Peter visit Shepreth	Vauxhall	Viva GT	TBC	TBC	N/A	N/A
	May	2nd	Snetterton	Castrol Mexico Challenge	Ford	Escort Mexico	TBC	24	TBC	1st Overall
	May	8th	Crystal Palace	Sprint – Mexico	Ford	Escort Mexico	TBC	TBC	N/A	2nd Overall
	May	15th	Oulton Park	Osram GEC	Vauxhall	Viva	TBC	TBC	TBC	1st Overall
	May	23rd	Brands Hatch – Club	Osram GEC	Vauxhall	Viva GT	2.6	TBC	TBC	Retired
	May	30th	Thruxton	Osram GEC 100kms Trophy Race for Saloon Cars	Vauxhall	Viva	TBC	TBC	1st	1st Overall
	May	31st	Llandow	Castrol Mexico Challenge	Ford	Escort Mexico	TBC	24	TBC	3rd Overall
	June	7th	Mondello Park	Saloon Invitation	Vauxhall	Viva GT	John Pope's 2.6	TBC	1st	1st Overall
	June	7th	Mondello Park	Kildare Trophy Saloons over 1000cc	Vauxhall	Viva GT	John Pope's 2.6	TBC	1st	3rd Overall
	June	12th	Oulton Park	Castrol Mexico Challenge	Ford	Escort Mexico	TBC	24	TBC	1st Overall
	June	13th	Thruxton	Osram GEC	Vauxhall	Viva	TBC	TBC	TBC	2nd Overall
	June	18th	Crystal Palace	TBC	Vauxhall	Viva GT	TBC	TBC	TBC	3rd Overall
	June	26th	Silverstone – TBC	TBC	Ford	Mustang	Dave Enstone	TBC	TBC	Retired
	July	11th	Brands Hatch – Club	Castrol Mexico Challenge	Ford	Escort Mexico	TBC	24	TBC	6th Overall
	July	11th	Brands Hatch – Club	BRSCC Production Saloon Handicap	Ford	Capri	GTW132H	91	Fast! (Scratch)	DNF
	July	18th	Cadwell Park	Osram GEC	Vauxhall	Viva GT	TBC	TBC	1st	1st Overall
	July	25th	Mallory Park	Castrol Mexico Challenge	Ford	Escort Mexico	TBC	24	1st	Retired
	August	1st	Snetterton	West Essex Car Club Scott-Brown Memorial Trophy – Saloon Cars	Vauxhall	Viva GT	S&K 2.5	TBC	1st	1st Overall

Year	Month	Date	Circuit	Race	Car	Spec	Details	No.	Qualifying	Result
1971	August	7th	Crystal Palace	Castrol Mexico Challenge	Ford	Escort Mexico	TBC	24	TBC	Retired
	August	8th	Croft	Osram GEC	Vauxhall	Viva GT	2.5	TBC	1st	1st Overall
	August	15th	Thruxton	750 Motor Club Holland Birkett Six Hour Relay Race	Vauxhall	Viva GT	2.2	TBC	N/A	1st in Class
	August	15th	Thruxton	750 Motor Club Holland Birkett Six Hour Relay Race	Vauxhall	Firenza	EXE685J	TBC	N/A	1st in Class
	August	22nd	Thruxton	TBC	Vauxhall	Viva GT	TBC	TBC	TBC	DNS
	August	29th	Thruxton	Chevron Trophy GT Cars up to 1600cc	Costin	Amigo	TBC	41	TBC	1st in Class
	August	29th	Thruxton	Saloon Handicap	Vauxhall	Firenza	EXE685J	TBC	N/A	8th Overall
	August	30th	Castle Combe	Castrol Mexico Challenge	Ford	Escort Mexico	TBC	24	TBC	1st Overall
	September	5th	Brands Hatch – Club	Osram GEC	Vauxhall	Viva GT	2.5	TBC	2nd	1st Overall
	September	9th	N/A	Press Launch for Thames TV	Vauxhall	Firenza	Old Nail	N/A	TBC	Demo
	September	11th	Crystal Palace	Osram GEC	Vauxhall	Viva GT	2.5	71	TBC	1st Overall
	September	12th	Cadwell Park	Castrol Mexico Challenge	Ford	Escort Mexico	TBC	24	TBC	4th Overall
	September	26th	Llandow	Saloons over 1000cc	Vauxhall	Firenza 2.5	Old Nail	TBC	3rd	1st Overall
	September	26th	Llandow	Modsports/Allcomers	Vauxhall	Firenza 2.5	Old Nail	TBC	1st	1st Overall
	September	26th	Llandow	Castrol Mexico Challenge	Ford	Escort Mexico	TBC	24	2nd	4th Overall
	October	3rd	Croft	Castrol Mexico Challenge	Ford	Escort Mexico	TBC	24	TBC	2nd Overall
	October	10th	Ingilston	Race	Vauxhall	Firenza	Old Nail	TBC	1st	1st Overall
	October	10th	Ingilston	Race	Vauxhall	Firenza	Old Nail	TBC	1st	3rd in Class
	October	17th	Thruxton	Osram GEC	Vauxhall	Viva	Roger Bell's 2.2	TBC	1st	1st Overall
	October	31st	Brands Hatch – Club	Castrol Mexico Challenge	Ford	Escort Mexico	TBC	24	1st	1st Overall
	October	31st	Brands Hatch – Club	Race	Vauxhall	Viva GT	TBC	TBC	TBC	3rd Overall
	November	7th	Santa Pod	BDHRA	Vauxhall	Viva	TBC	TBC	N/A	TBC
	November	14th	Brands Hatch – TBC	TBC	Vauxhall	Viva	TBC	TBC	TBC	TBC
	November	20th	Lydden Hill	Thames Estuary Automobile Club	Vauxhall	Firenza	Old Nail	TBC	1st	1st Overall
	November	21st	Brands Hatch – TBC	Sevenoaks District Motor Club	Vauxhall	Firenza	Old Nail	TBC	1st	1st Overall
	November	28th	Brands Hatch – Club	Saloons over 1000cc	Vauxhall	Firenza	Old Nail	TBC	1st	1st Overall
	November	28th	Brands Hatch – Club	Fastest Saloons	Vauxhall	Firenza	Old Nail	TBC	1st	1st Overall
	December	5th	Brands Hatch – Club	Special Saloons	Vauxhall	Firenza	TBC	TBC	2nd	1st Overall
	December	27th	Brands Hatch – Club	Special Saloons – The Arco Trophy Race "B"	Vauxhall	Firenza	Old Nail	145	TBC	1st Overall
1972	February	27th	Snetterton	Cambridge University Automobile Car Club Spring Sprint	Vauxhall	Firenza	Old Nail	TBC	N/A	1st in Class
	February	27th	Snetterton	Cambridge University Automobile Car Club Spring Sprint	Vauxhall	Firenza	2000	TBC	N/A	1st in Class
	March	5th	Brands Hatch – TBC	Britax Production Saloon	Vauxhall	Firenza	TBC	TBC	1st	2nd in Class
	March	12th	Mallory Park	Forward Trust Special Saloon Car Championship	Vauxhall	Firenza	2000 SL (2.5)	58	2nd	2nd Overall
	March	17th	Mondello Park	Saloons over 1300cc County Kildare Motor Club	Vauxhall	Viva GT	John Pope's S&K 2.5	TBC	TBC	1st Overall
	March	18th	Oulton Park	Castrol Production Saloon Car Championship (Group One)	Vauxhall	Firenza	TBC	TBC	TBC	1st in Class
	March	19th	Thruxton	Britax Production Saloon	Vauxhall	Firenza	TJE535K	TBC	1st	1st
	March	20th	Mondello Park	Large Capacity Saloons	Vauxhall	Viva GT	John Pope's S&K 2.5	TBC	1st	1st Overall
	March	26th	Mallory Park	Castrol Production Saloon Car Championship (Group One)	Vauxhall	Firenza	2000	50	3rd in Class	2nd in Class
	April	1st	Rufforth	Escort Mexico Challenge	Ford	Escort Mexico	Jeff Uren	TBC	TBC	Retired
	April	3rd	Brands Hatch – Club	Castrol Production Saloon Car Championship (Group One)	Vauxhall	Firenza	DTV	9	TBC	1st in Class
	April	16th	Silverstone – Club	Forward Trust Special Saloon – 100kms	Vauxhall	Firenza	Old Nail	TBC	TBC	2nd Overall
	April	29th	Oulton Park	Castrol Production Saloon Car Championship (Group One)	Vauxhall	Firenza	TBC	TBC	1st in Class	Retired
	April	30th	Mallory Park	Castrol Production Saloon Car Championship (Group One)	Vauxhall	Firenza	EXE685J	98	3rd	3rd Overall
	May	7th	Croft	Forward Trust Special Saloon Car Championship	Vauxhall	Firenza	Old Nail	TBC	1st	1st Overall
	May	14th	Ingilston	Club Race	Vauxhall	Firenza	Old Nail	TBC	2nd	1st Overall
	May	14th	Ingilston	Castrol Production Saloon Car Championship (Group One)	Vauxhall	Firenza	TBC	TBC	TBC	1st in Class
	May	21st	Brands Hatch – TBC	Castrol Production Saloon Car Championship (Group One)	Vauxhall	Firenza	TBC	TBC	2nd	1st in Class
	May	27th	Rufforth	Castrol Production Saloon Car Championship (Group One)	Vauxhall	Firenza	TBC	TBC	TBC	2nd in Class
	May	29th	Oulton Park	Forward Trust Special Saloon Car Championship	Vauxhall	Firenza	Old Nail	TBC	TBC	Winner
	June	5th	Mondello Park	Forward Trust Special Saloon Car Championship	Vauxhall	TBC	TBC	TBC	TBC	1st Overall
	June	18th	Thruxton	Forward Trust Special Saloon Car Championship	Vauxhall	Firenza	Old Nail	TBC	TBC	1st Overall
	July	2nd	Silverstone – Club	Britax Production Saloon	Vauxhall	Firenza	Silver/Orange	319	TBC	DNS
	July	2nd	Silverstone – Club	Forward Trust Special Saloon Car Championship	Vauxhall	Firenza	Old Nail	166	TBC	3rd Overall
	July	8th	Oulton Park	Castrol Production Saloon Car Championship (Group One)	Vauxhall	Firenza	2.3	TBC	TBC	1st in Class
	July	16th	Cadwell Park	Forward Trust Special Saloon Car Championship	Vauxhall	Firenza	Old Nail	TBC	TBC	1st Overall
	July	22nd/23rd	Spa-Francorchamps	Spa 24-hours	Opel	Commodore 2.8	TBC	7	14th	Retired
	July	23rd	Mallory Park	Castrol Production Saloon Car Championship (Group One)	Vauxhall	Firenza	TBC	TBC	TBC	1st in Class
	July	30th	Snetterton	Castrol Production Saloon Car Championship (Group One)	Vauxhall	Firenza	TBC	TBC	TBC	2nd Overall
	July	30th	Thruxton	Forward Trust Special Saloon Car Championship	Vauxhall	Firenza	Old Nail	TBC	TBC	1st Overall
	August	6th	Silverstone – GP	JCB Historic Championship	Maserati	Birdcage Tipo 61	Hexagon	26	TBC	Retired
	August	6th	Oulton Park	Forward Trust Special Saloon Car Championship	Vauxhall	Firenza	Old Nail	TBC	TBC	1st Overall
	August	13th	Brands Hatch – TBC	Castrol Production Saloon Car Championship (Group One)	Vauxhall	Firenza	TBC	111	1st	Retired
	August	20th	Brands Hatch – Club	Britax Production Saloon	Ford	Escort	Alan Wilkinson	TBC	TBC	Retired
	August	26th	Oulton Park	Castrol Production Saloon Car Championship (Group One)	Vauxhall	Firenza	TBC	TBC	TBC	2nd Overall
	August	27th	Mallory Park	Castrol Production Saloon Car Championship (Group One)	Vauxhall	Firenza	TBC	TBC	TBC	1st Overall
	August	31st	Brands Hatch – TBC	Castrol Production Saloon Car Championship (Group One)	Vauxhall	Firenza	TBC	TBC	TBC	1st in Class
	September	3rd	Brands Hatch – TBC	Forward Trust Special Saloon Car Championship	Vauxhall	Firenza	Old Nail	TBC	TBC	1st Overall
	September	3rd	Brands Hatch – Club	Britax Production Saloon	Ford	Escort	GT	TBC	2nd	2nd
	September	4th	Croft	Forward Trust Special Saloon Car Championship	Vauxhall	Firenza	TBC	TBC	TBC	1st Overall
	September	4th	TBC	N/A	Ford	GT40	N/A	N/A	N/A	N/A
	September	4th	TBC	N/A	Jaguar	Lister	WTM446	N/A	N/A	N/A
	September	9th	Crystal Palace	Motoring News/Castrol Sports GT for Hexagon Trophy	Jaguar	Lister	WTM446	102	4th	2nd in Class
	September	9th	Crystal Palace	Forward Trust Special Saloon – Hexagon Trophy Meeting	Vauxhall	Firenza	Old Nail	151	TBC	1st Overall
	September	10th	Brands Hatch – Club	Castrol Production Saloon Car Championship (Group One)	Vauxhall	Firenza	TBC	TBC	TBC	Retired
	September	23rd	Crystal Palace	AMOC Daily Mirror Historic Car Race Meeting	Jaguar	Lister	WTM446	175	2nd	1st Overall
	September	24th	Silverstone – International	RAC Tourist Trophy – Castrol Group One – UNIFLO	Vauxhall	Firenza	TBC	TBC	TBC	1st in Class
	October	1st	Brands Hatch – TBC	Mini Seven	Austin	Mini	TBC	TBC	TBC	2nd in Class
	October	8th	Mallory Park	Forward Trust Special Saloon Car Championship	Vauxhall	Firenza	Old Nail	TBC	TBC	1st Overall
	October	8th	Mallory Park	Castrol Production Saloon Car Championship (Group One)	Vauxhall	Firenza	TBC	TBC	TBC	2nd in Class
	October	14th	Oulton Park	Castrol Production Saloon Car Championship (Group One)	Vauxhall	Firenza	TBC	TBC	TBC	1st in Class
	October	29th	Snetterton	Castrol Production Saloon Car Championship (Group One)	Vauxhall	Firenza	TBC	61	TBC	Retired
	October	29th	Thruxton	Forward Trust Special Saloon Car Championship	Vauxhall	Firenza	Stan Burge	TBC	DNS	1st in Class
	November	11th/12th	Estoril	Group One Race	Vauxhall	Firenza 2.3	DTV	TBC	TBC	3rd in Class
	November	19th	Brands Hatch – Club	Forward Trust Special Saloon – Sevenoaks District Motor Club	Vauxhall	Firenza	Old Nail	TBC	TBC	1st Overall
	November	26th	Brands Hatch – Club	Forward Trust Special Saloon – Romford Enthusiasts Car Club	Vauxhall	Firenza	Old Nail	TBC	TBC	1st Overall

Year	Month	Date	Circuit	Race	Car	Spec	Details	No.	Qualifying	Result
1972	December	3rd	Brands Hatch – Club	Forward Trust Special Saloon – Rochester and Tunbridge Wells Motor Club	Vauxhall	Firenza	Old Nail	TBC	1st	1st Overall
	December	3rd	Brands Hatch – Club	Group One – Rochester and Tunbridge Wells Motor Club	Vauxhall	Firenza	TJE535K	TBC	1st	1st Overall
	December	10th	Brands Hatch – TBC	Forward Trust Special Saloon – Banbury Trophy M7C	Vauxhall	Firenza	Old Nail	TBC	TBC	1st Overall
	December	10th	Brands Hatch – TBC	Group One Race	Vauxhall	Firenza	TBC	TBC	TBC	2nd Overall
	December	26th	Brands Hatch – Club	Forward Trust Special Saloon – Racing Car Show Trophy	Vauxhall	Firenza	Old Nail	53	1st	1st Overall
	December	26th	Brands Hatch – Club	MOTOR Group One	Vauxhall	Firenza	2.3	11	1st	1st in Class
	March/ April/May	TBC	Chobham	Thames Television	Vauxhall	Firenza	Old Nail	TBC	TBC	TBC
	TBC	TBC	TBC	TBC	Honda	600cc	Bill Sydenham	TBC	TBC	TBC
1973	January	28th	Brands Hatch – Club	Group One Race	Vauxhall	Firenza	TJE535K	TBC	TBC	1st Overall
	January	28th	Brands Hatch – Club	Special Saloons	Vauxhall	Firenza	Old Nail	TBC	TBC	1st Overall
	March	3rd	Brands Hatch – TBC	Castrol Production Saloon Car Championship (Group One)	BMW	3.0 Si	Tony Lanfranchi	158	1st	3rd Overall
	March	11th	Mallory Park	Forward Trust Special Saloon Car Championship	Vauxhall	Firenza	Old Nail	1	1st	1st Overall
	March	11th	Mallory Park	Castrol Production Saloon Car Championship (Group One)	BMW	3.0 Si	Tony Lanfranchi	TBC	TBC	TBC
	March	24th	Silverstone – TBC	TBC	Lotus	Elan	VRM	TBC	1st	Retired
	March	25th	Thruxton	TBC	Lotus	Elan	VRM	TBC	1st	3rd in Class
	March	25th	Thruxton	Forward Trust Special Saloon Car Championship	Vauxhall	Firenza	Old Nail	1	1st	3rd Overall
	April	1st	Snetterton	Forward Trust Special Saloon Car Championship	Vauxhall	Firenza	Old Nail	TBC	TBC	1st Overall
	April	8th	Cadwell Park	Forward Trust Special Saloon Car Championship	Vauxhall	Firenza	Old Nail	TBC	TBC	1st Overall
	April	15th	Ingilston	Castrol Production Saloon Car Championship (Group One)	Vauxhall	Viva	1800	TBC	TBC	3rd in Class
	April	15th	Ingilston	Special Saloons – Heat	Vauxhall	Viva	1800	TBC	TBC	6th Overall
	April	15th	Ingilston	Special Saloons – Final	Vauxhall	Viva	1800	TBC	TBC	DNS
	April	23rd	Thruxton	Vauxhall Selling Plate	Vauxhall	Firenza SL	TBC	TBC	TBC	4th Overall
	May	6th	Mallory Park	Forward Trust Special Saloon Car Championship	Vauxhall	Firenza	Old Nail	1	1st	1st Overall
	May	13th	Silverstone – Club	Britax Production Saloon	Austin	Marina	MYX775L	TBC	DNS	2nd in Class
	May	13th	Silverstone – Club	Blue Circle Modsports	Lotus	Elan	VRM	29	1st	Retired
	May	20th	TBC	Britax Production Saloon	Austin	Marina	MYX775L	TBC	TBC	TBC
	May	19th or 25th	Rally	Chesterfield & District Motor Club Gearbox Rally	Vauxhall	Magnum	TJE535K	31	Rally	Retired
	May	27th	Brands Hatch – Club	FordSport Day Celebrity Race	Ford	Consul GT	TBC	TBC	1st	DNS
	June	1st	Thruxton	Modified Sports Car	Lotus	Elan	VRM	64	1st	Retired
	June	1st	Thruxton	SuperSaloon Race	Vauxhall	Firenza	Old Nail	TBC	1st	1st Overall
	June	10th	Silverstone – Club	Blue Circle Modsports	Lotus	Elan	VRM	TBC	1st	2nd in Class
	June	10th	Silverstone – Club	Forward Trust Special Saloon Car Championship	Vauxhall	Firenza	Old Nail	TBC	1st	DNS
	June	16th	Castle Combe	FordSport Celebrity Race	Ford	Consul GT	TBC	TBC	TBC	TBC
	June	16th/17th	Mondello Park	SuperSaloon Race	Vauxhall	Firenza	Old Nail	1	TBC	DNS
	June	24th	Silverstone	NDRC Drag Race	Vauxhall	Firenza	Old Nail	DM12	N/A	2nd in Class
	July	7th	Oulton Park	Vauxhall Trophy Chase	Vauxhall	Firenza	Old Nail	TBC	N/A	1st Overall
	July	8th	Thruxton	Forward Trust Special Saloon Car Championship	Vauxhall	Firenza	Old Nail	TBC	1st	1st Overall
	July	15th	Cadwell Park	Britax Production Saloon	Austin	Marina	MYX775L	TBC	TBC	TBC
	July	21st	Oulton Park	Forward Trust Special Saloon Car Championship	Vauxhall	Firenza	Old Nail	123	1st	Winner
	July	29th	Llandow	Forward Trust Special Saloon Car Championship	Vauxhall	Firenza	Old Nail	71	1st	1st Overall
	August	5th	Thruxton	Alcoa Special Saloons – Non Championship	Vauxhall	Firenza	Old Nail	TBC	1st	3rd in Class
	August	12th	Knebworth Park	Car and Car Conversions	Ford	Consul GT	TBC	TBC	N/A	N/A
	August	19th	Brands Hatch – Club	Castrol Production Saloon Car Championship (Group One)	Ford	Capri	TBC	TBC	TBC	DNS
	August	19th	Brands Hatch – Club	Forward Trust Special Saloon Car Championship	Vauxhall	Firenza	Old Nail	TBC	1st	2nd Overall
	August	19th	Brands Hatch – Club	BMW Celebrity Race	BMW	2002	TBC	TBC	1st	6th Overall
	August	26th	Mallory Park	FordSport Day Celebrity Race	Ford	Escort	TBC	TBC	4th	1st Overall
	August	27th	Castle Combe	Britax Production Saloon	Vauxhall	Magnum	GN	TBC	10th	3rd in Class
	September	2nd	Rufforth	Britax Production Saloon	Vauxhall	Firenza	GN	TBC	DNS	3rd Overall
	September	9th	Silverstone – Club	Forward Trust Special Saloon Car Championship	Vauxhall	Firenza	Old Nail	114	3rd	2nd Overall
	September	16th	Thruxton	Forward Trust Special Saloon Car Championship	Vauxhall	Firenza	Old Nail	14	2nd	1st Overall
	September	22nd	Oulton Park	FordSport Day	TBC	TBC	TBC	TBC	TBC	TBC
	September	23rd	Croft	Forward Trust Special Saloon Car Championship	Vauxhall	Firenza	Old Nail	TBC	1st	Retired
	September	23rd	Brands Hatch – TBC	Romford Enthusiasts Car Club	TBC	TBC	TBC	TBC	TBC	1st in two events
	September	23rd	Silverstone – GP	RAC Tourist Trophy	Vauxhall	Firenza	TBC	41	TBC	DNS
	September	29th	Silverstone – TBC	750 Motor Club Holland Birkett Six Hour Relay Race	Clan	Crusader	TBC	60	TBC	21st/25th
	October	6th	Silverstone – GP	Forward Trust Special Saloon – Westwood Trophy	Vauxhall	Firenza	Old Nail	TBC	3rd	2nd Overall
	October	7th	Brands Hatch – TBC	Forward Trust Special Saloon – TV Times Race of ths Stars Meeting	Vauxhall	Firenza	Old Nail	36	TBC	1st Overall
	October	14th	Lydden Hill	Forward Trust Special Saloon – West Essex Car Club Thames Television	Vauxhall	Firenza	Old Nail	TBC	TBC	1st Overall
	October	14th	Lydden Hill	Formule Libre – West Essex Car Club – Event 10	Vauxhall	Firenza	Old Nail	TBC	TBC	1st Overall
	October	28th	Thruxton	Britax Production Saloon	Hillman	Hunter	1.7	TBC	TBC	2nd in Class
	October	28th	Thruxton	Forward Trust Special Saloon Car Championship	Vauxhall	Firenza	Old Nail	5	3rd	1st Overall
	November	18th	Brands Hatch – TBC	Sevenoaks District Motor Club	TBC	TBC	TBC	TBC	TBC	1st
	December	TBC	Brands Hatch – Club	ShellSport Celebrity Race	Ford	Escort Mexico	TBC	TBC	TBC	1st Overall
	TBC	TBC	Brands Hatch – TBC	MSAC Thames Estuary Automobile Club Special Saloons over 1,000cc	Vauxhall	Firenza	TBC	TBC	TBC	Winner
	TBC	TBC	TBC	Forward Trust Special Saloon Car Championship	Vauxhall	Firenza	TBC	TBC	TBC	1st in Class
	TBC	TBC	Thruxton	Thruxton Circuit Supporters Club	TBC	TBC	TBC	TBC	TBC	Winner
	TBC	TBC	Brands Hatch – TBC	R&T WMC – Over 1301cc Class	TBC	TBC	TBC	TBC	TBC	1st in Class
1974	March	3rd	Brands Hatch – TBC	Simoniz Special Saloons	Vauxhall	Firenza DS	Old Nail	TBC	2nd	1st Overall
	March	9th	Oulton Park	Simoniz Special Saloons	Vauxhall	Firenza DS	Old Nail	TBC	2nd	1st Overall
	March	10th	Mallory Park	Castrol Anniversary British Touring Car – Group One	Chevrolet	Camaro 5600	London Sports Car Centre	TBC	3rd	Retired
	March	11th	Brands Hatch – TBC	Simoniz Special Saloons	Vauxhall	Firenza DS	Old Nail	55	TBC	DNS
	March	17th	Brands Hatch – GP	Castrol Anniversary British Touring Car – Race of Champions	Chevrolet	Camaro 5600	London Sports Car Centre	TBC	24th	DNS
	March	24th	Snetterton	Simoniz Special Saloons	Vauxhall	Firenza DS	Old Nail	TBC	1st	2nd Overall
	March	31st	Silverstone – Club	Simoniz Special Saloons	Vauxhall	Ventora	Big Bertha	TBC	1st	1st Overall
	April	5th/6th/7th	Silverstone – International	Castrol Anniversary British Touring Car – Group One	Vauxhall	Firenza	Tim Stock	56	TBC	Retired
	April	12th	Oulton Park	Saloons	Vauxhall	Firenza	TBC	TBC	TBC	TBC
	April	14th	Snetterton	Simoniz Special Saloons	Vauxhall	Ventora	Big Bertha	TBC	TBC	Retired
	April	14th	Snetterton	Triplex – Production Saloon	Vauxhall	Magnum	Jock Robertson	TBC	TBC	Retired
	April	15th	Thruxton	Castrol Anniversary British Touring Car – Group One	Vauxhall	Magnum	TBC	TBC	TBC	6th in Class
	April	21st	Brands Hatch – TBC	ShellSport Celebrity Race	TBC	TBC	TBC	TBC	TBC	4th Overall
	April	21st	Brands Hatch – TBC	TBC	Vauxhall	Firenza	TBC	TBC	TBC	2nd Overall
	April	27th	Oulton Park	Britax Production Saloon	Austin	Marina	MYX775L	134	TBC	TBC
	April	28th	Mallory Park	Special Saloons	Vauxhall	Firenza DS	Old Nail	7	1st	1st Overall

Year	Month	Date	Circuit	Race	Car	Spec	Details	No.	Qualifying	Result
1974	May	5th	Brands Hatch – TBC	Special Saloons	Vauxhall	Firenza DS	Old Nail	TBC	2nd	1st Overall
	May	12th	Silverstone – GP	Castrol Anniversary British Touring Car – Martini International Meeting	Vauxhall	Magnum	DTV	56	14th	Retired
	May	19th	Brands Hatch – TBC	Simoniz Special Saloons	Vauxhall	Firenza DS	Old Nail	TBC	TBC	3rd Overall
	May	27th	Thruxton	Forward Trust Special Saloon Car Championship	Vauxhall	Ventora	Big Bertha	1	2nd	Retired
	May	27th	Thruxton	Castrol Anniversary British Touring Car – Group One	Vauxhall	Firenza	Tim Stock	56	TBC	7th in Class
	May	27th	Thruxton	Vauxhall Spring Cup	Vauxhall	Firenza DS	OTP554M	17	TBC	2nd Overall
	June	3rd	Mondello Park	Special Saloons – Heat	Vauxhall	Firenza DS	Old Nail	TBC	TBC	Retired
	June	3rd	Mondello Park	Special Saloons – Final	Vauxhall	Firenza DS	Old Nail	TBC	TBC	Retired
	June	9th	Silverstone – National	Simoniz Special Saloons	Vauxhall	Ventora	Big Bertha	45	1st	1st Overall
	June	15th/16th	Mondello Park	Simoniz Special Saloons	Vauxhall	Firenza DS	Old Nail	TBC	TBC	1st Overall
	June	23rd	Mallory Park	Simoniz Special Saloons	Vauxhall	Ventora	Big Bertha	55	TBC	1st Overall
	June	30th	Brands Hatch – Club	Simoniz Special Saloons	Vauxhall	Firenza DS	Old Nail	TBC	2nd	1st Overall
	July	12th/13th/14th	Rally	Avon Tour of Britain	Ford	Escort RS 2000	PVX446M	40	Rally	2nd Overall
	July	19th/20th	Brands Hatch – GP	Castrol Anniversary British Touring Car – Group 1	Vauxhall	Magnum	DTV	TBC	20th	6th in Class
	July	21st	Ingilston	Simoniz Special Saloons	Vauxhall	Firenza DS	Old Nail	TBC	TBC	2nd Overall
	July	27th	Oulton Park	Simoniz Special Saloons	Vauxhall	Firenza DS	Old Nail	221	1st	2nd Overall
	July	28th	Mallory Park	Simoniz Special Saloons	Vauxhall	Firenza DS	Old Nail	TBC	TBC	1st Overall
	August	4th	Silverstone – Club	Simoniz Special Saloons	Vauxhall	Ventora	Big Bertha	1	3rd	Retired
	August	11th	Mallory Park	Simoniz Special Saloons	Vauxhall	Firenza DS	Old Nail	TBC	TBC	2nd Overall
	August	17th	Ingilston	Castrol Anniversary British Touring Car – Group One	Vauxhall	Firenza	TBC	TBC	9th	Retired
	August	24th	Kirkistown	Special Saloons	Vauxhall	Firenza	Jackie Peterson	TBC	TBC	1st Overall
	August	24th	Kirkistown	Production Saloons	Honda	Civic	Patsie McGarity	TBC	TBC	3rd in Class
	August	26th	Snetterton	Simoniz Special Saloons	Vauxhall	Firenza DS	Old Nail	TBC	TBC	2nd in Class
	September	9th	Silverstone – Club	Simoniz Special Saloons	Vauxhall	Firenza DS	Old Nail	TBC	TBC	6th Overall
	September	12th	Rally	Castrol Manx Trophy Rally	Vauxhall	Magnum	RBU83XM	TBC	Rally	2nd in Class
	September	21st/22nd	Silverstone – GP	ACCESS RAC Tourist Trophy	Vauxhall	Magnum	2.3	34	TBC	6th in Class
	September	29th	Mallory Park	Simoniz Special Saloons	Vauxhall	Firenza DS	Old Nail	TBC	3rd	2nd Overall
	October	6th	Snetterton	Castrol Anniversary British Touring Car – Group One	Vauxhall	Firenza	TBC	TBC	5th	5th Overall
	October	13th	Brands Hatch – Club	Simoniz Special Saloons	Vauxhall	Firenza DS	Old Nail	TBC	TBC	2nd Overall
	October	26th	Oulton Park	Simoniz Special Saloons	Vauxhall	Firenza DS	Old Nail	TBC	1st	1st Overall
	October	27th	Thruxton	Castrol Production Saloon Car Championship (Group One)	Hillman	Avenger	TBC	TBC	TBC	1st in Class
	October	27th	Thruxton	Forward Trust Special Saloons	Vauxhall	Firenza DS	Old Nail	TBC	2nd	Retired
	November	3rd	Brands Hatch – Club	Castrol Production Saloon Car Championship (Group One)	Hillman	Avenger	TBC	TBC	TBC	Retired
	November	16th	Thruxton	Simoniz Special Saloons	Vauxhall	Firenza DS	Old Nail	TBC	TBC	DNS
	November	17th	Brands Hatch – TBC	Special Saloons – Sevenoaks District Motor Club	Vauxhall	Firenza DS	Old Nail	TBC	TBC	1st Overall
	November	24th	Brands Hatch – TBC	Special Saloons – Romford Enthusiasts Car Club	Vauxhall	Firenza DS	Old Nail	TBC	TBC	1st
	December	1st	Brands Hatch – TBC	Special Saloons – RMC Brands	Vauxhall	Firenza DS	Old Nail	TBC	TBC	1st in Class
	December	8th	Brands Hatch – TBC	Special Saloons – RMC Brompton Motors Saloon over 1000cc	Vauxhall	Firenza DS	Old Nail	TBC	TBC	Winner
	December	26th	Brands Hatch – Club	Special Saloons – Freebie Bean Trophy	Vauxhall	Firenza DS	Old Nail	1	1st	1st Overall
	TBC	TBC	Snetterton	Cambridge University Automobile Car Club Spring Sprint	TBC	TBC	TBC	TBC	TBC	1st in Class
	TBC	TBC	Croft	Special Saloons	Vauxhall	Firenza DS	Old Nail	TBC	TBC	1st Overall
1975	March	2nd	Brands Hatch – TBC	Special Saloon Non Championship Race	Vauxhall	Firenza DS	Old Nail	TBC	1st	1st Overall
	March	2nd	Brands Hatch – TBC	Radio 1 Production Saloon	Vauxhall	Firenza	Hamilton Motors	TBC	TBC	1st in Class
	March	8th	Oulton Park	Simoniz Special Saloons	Vauxhall	Firenza DS	TBC	TBC	TBC	TBC
	March	8th	Oulton Park	Radio 1 Production Saloon	Vauxhall	Firenza	Hamilton Motors	TBC	TBC	2nd in Class
	March	16th	Silverstone – Club	Castrol Production Saloon Car Championship (Group One)	Vauxhall	Magnum	TBC	TBC	TBC	Retired
	March	16th	Silverstone – Club	Radio 1 Production Saloon	Vauxhall	Magnum	Hamilton Motors	127	TBC	5th in Class
	March	16th	Silverstone – Club	Simoniz Special Saloons	Vauxhall	Firenza DS	Old Nail	6	1st	3rd Overall
	March	30th	Snetterton	Simoniz Special Saloons	Vauxhall	Firenza DS	Old Nail	1	1st	1st Overall
	March	31st	Brands Hatch – TBC	Radio 1 Production Saloon	Vauxhall	Firenza	Hamilton Motors	TBC	TBC	2nd in Class
	April	12th/13th	Ingilston	Tricentrol Special Saloon Car Championship – Rossleigh Trophy	Vauxhall	Firenza DS	Old Nail	94	2nd	2nd Overall
	April	12th/13th	Ingilston	The Radio Forth Race	Vauxhall	Magnum	SMT	175	1st	1st Overall
	April	12th/13th	Ingilston	Tricentrol Special Saloon Car Championship – Rossleigh Trophy	Vauxhall	Firenza DS	Old Nail	94	2nd	1st Overall
	April	20th	Thruxton	Radio 1 Production Saloon	Vauxhall	Firenza	Hamilton Motors	TBC	1st	1st in Class
	April	20th	Thruxton	Forward Trust Special Saloon Car Championship	Vauxhall	Firenza DS	TBC	TBC	TBC	TBC
	April	26th	Oulton Park	ShellSport 4000 (Special Saloons & Group One)	Vauxhall	Firenza DS	Old Nail	TBC	3rd	2nd Overall
	April	27th	Silverstone – Club	Radio 1 Production Saloon	Vauxhall	Firenza	Hamilton Motors	261	TBC	4th in Class
	April	27th	Silverstone – Club	Forward Trust Special Saloon Car Championship	Vauxhall	Firenza	TBC	TBC	TBC	TBC
	May	4th	Silverstone – Club	Tricentrol Special Saloon Car Championship	Vauxhall	Firenza DS	Old Nail	18	Back of Grid	4th Overall
	May	18th	Mallory Park	Radio 1 Production Saloon	Vauxhall	Firenza	Hamilton Motors	261	TBC	5th in Class
	May	22nd	Snetterton	Test Day	Vauxhall	Firenza DS	Baby Bertha	N/A	N/A	N/A
	May	25th	Brands Hatch – Club	FordSport Super Saloon Day – BRSCC Super Saloon Championship	Vauxhall	Firenza DS	Baby Bertha	6	4th	Retired
	May	26th	Snetterton	Radio 1 Production Saloon	Vauxhall	Firenza	Hamilton Motors	TBC	TBC	1st in Class
	June	1st	Cadwell Park	Britax Production Saloon	Vauxhall	Firenza	Hamilton Motors	TBC	TBC	2nd in Class
	June	2nd	Mondello Park	Tricentrol Special Saloon Car Championship – CKMC Motorcraft Races	Vauxhall	Firenza DS	Baby Bertha	1	1st	1st Overall
	June	2nd	Mondello Park	Tricentrol Special Saloon Car Championship – CKMC Motorcraft Races	Vauxhall	Firenza DS	Baby Bertha	1	1st	1st Overall
	June	8th	Silverstone – TBC	Simoniz Special Saloons	Vauxhall	Firenza DS	Baby Bertha	TBC	TBC	1st Overall
	June	8th	Silverstone – TBC	Simoniz Special Saloons	Vauxhall	Firenza DS	Baby Bertha	TBC	TBC	1st Overall
	June	8th	Silverstone – TBC	Britax Production Saloon	Vauxhall	Firenza	Hamilton Motors	TBC	TBC	1st in Class
	June	15th	Snetterton	Britax Production Saloon	Vauxhall	Firenza	Hamilton Motors	TBC	TBC	2nd in Class
	June	15th	Snetterton	Simoniz Special Saloons	Vauxhall	Firenza DS	Baby Bertha	TBC	TBC	1st Overall
	June	22nd	Croft	Britax Production Saloon	TBC	TBC	TBC	TBC	TBC	Retired
	June	28th	Oulton Park	Tricentrol Special Saloon Car Championship	Vauxhall	Firenza DS	Baby Bertha	TBC	2nd	2nd Overall
	June	28th	Oulton Park	Britax Production Saloon	Vauxhall	Firenza	Hamilton Motors	TBC	TBC	4th
	June	29th	Mallory Park	Radio 1 Production Saloon	TBC	TBC	TBC	TBC	TBC	Retired
	July	6th	Silverstone – Club	Tricentrol Special Saloon Car Championship	Vauxhall	Firenza DS	Baby Bertha	1	1st	1st Overall
	July	13th	Cadwell Park	Britax Production Saloon	Vauxhall	Firenza	Hamilton Motors	TBC	TBC	4th in Class
	July	19th	Silverstone – GP	Tricentrol Special Saloon Car Championship	Vauxhall	Firenza DS	Baby Bertha	27	3rd	1st Overall
	July	26th	Oulton Park	Britax Production Saloon	Vauxhall	Firenza	Hamilton Motors	261	TBC	3rd in Class
	July	27th	Snetterton	Radio 1 Production Saloon	Vauxhall	Firenza	Hamilton Motors	261	TBC	3rd in Class
	August	1st/2nd/3rd	Rally	Avon Tour of Britain	Vauxhall	Magnum	WXE944M	12	Rally	2nd Overall
	August	9th	Oulton Park	Radio 1 Production Saloon	Vauxhall	Magnum	TBC	TBC	TBC	3rd in Class
	August	10th	Mallory Park	Radio 1 Production Saloon	Vauxhall	Magnum	TBC	TBC	TBC	4th in Class
	August	17th	Thruxton	Tricentrol Special Saloon Car Championship	Vauxhall	Firenza DS	Baby Bertha	1	1st	1st Overall
	August	24th	Mallory Park	SuperSaloon Race	Vauxhall	Firenza DS	Baby Bertha	TBC	TBC	1st Overall

Year	Month	Date	Circuit	Race	Car	Spec	Details	No.	Qualifying	Result
1975	August	25th	Brands Hatch – Club	Radio 1 Production Saloon	Vauxhall	Magnum	TBC	TBC	TBC	Retired
	August	25th	Silverstone – National	Esso Uniflo Special Saloon Car Race	Vauxhall	Firenza DS	Baby Bertha	TBC	TBC	1st Overall
	August	31st	Silverstone – GP	Britax Production Saloon	Vauxhall	Firenza	Hamilton Motors	261	TBC	3rd Overall
	September	7th	Brands Hatch – Club	Radio 1 Production Saloon	Vauxhall	Firenza	Hamilton Motors	TBC	TBC	1st in Class
	September	7th	Brands Hatch – Club	Simoniz Special Saloons	Vauxhall	Firenza DS	Baby Bertha	TBC	TBC	1st Overall
	September	14th	Thruxton	Britax Production Saloon	Vauxhall	Magnum	Allam Motor Services	TBC	TBC	1st in Class
	September	15th	Rally	Manx Trophy Rally	Vauxhall	Magnum	WXE944M	TBC	Rally	Retired
	September	20th	Oulton Park	Tricentrol Special Saloon Car Championship	Vauxhall	Firenza DS	Baby Bertha	TBC	TBC	1st Overall
	September	21st	Mallory Park	Radio 1 Production Saloon	Vauxhall	Firenza	Hamilton Motors	261	DNS	TBC
	September	27th/28th	Silverstone – GP	Esso Uniflo Special Saloons – Clubmans Championship	Vauxhall	Firenza DS	Baby Bertha	7	1st	1st Overall
	October	4th/5th	Silverstone – GP	ACCESS RAC Tourist Trophy	Vauxhall	Magnum	DTV	21	19th	Retired
	October	19th	Snetterton	Special Saloon Non Championship Race – Thames Estuary Automobile Club	Vauxhall	Firenza DS	Baby Bertha	TBC	TBC	1st Overall
	October	19th	Snetterton	Radio 1 Production Saloon – Thames Estuary Automobile Club	Triumph	Dolomite Sprint	Bob Saunders	TBC	TBC	1st in Class
	October	26th	Thruxton	Britax Production Saloon	Triumph	Dolomite Sprint	Bob Saunders	TBC	TBC	2nd Overall
	October	26th	Thruxton	Forward Trust Special Saloon Car Championship	Vauxhall	Firenza DS	Baby Bertha	1	1st	1st Overall
	November	2nd	Brands Hatch – Club	ShellSports Escorts, Victoria vs Windsor Castle	Ford	Escort	TBC	TBC	TBC	2nd Overall
	November	2nd	Brands Hatch – Club	Radio 1 Production Saloon	Vauxhall	Magnum	TBC	TBC	TBC	3rd in Class
	November	9th	Brands Hatch – TBC	RMC Promotasport Trophy	Vauxhall	Firenza DS	Baby Bertha	TBC	TBC	1st Overall
	November	15th	Thruxton	SuperSaloon Race	Vauxhall	Firenza DS	Baby Bertha	TBC	TBC	1st Overall
	November	23rd	Brands Hatch – TBC	Forward Trust Special Saloon Car Championship	Vauxhall	Firenza DS	Baby Bertha	TBC	TBC	1st Overall
	December	7th	Brands Hatch – TBC	SuperSaloon Race	Vauxhall	Firenza DS	Baby Bertha	TBC	TBC	1st Overall
	December	7th	Brands Hatch – TBC	Formule Libre	Vauxhall	Firenza DS	Baby Bertha	TBC	TBC	1st Overall
	December	13th	Brands Hatch – Club	Promotorsport Trophy Race for Classic Saloon Cars	Ford	Zephyr 2.5	Bill Wykeham	20	7th	1st Overall
	December	27th	Brands Hatch – Club	The Melaware Challenge Production Saloon Race	Vauxhall	Firenza	Hamilton Motors	261	TBC	5th in Class
	December	27th	Brands Hatch – Club	The Kent Special Saloon Car Race	Vauxhall	Firenza DS	Baby Bertha	1	1st	1st Overall
	December	27th	Brands Hatch – Club	Jack Brabham Libre Race	Vauxhall	Firenza DS	Baby Bertha	1	8th	4th Overall
1976	March	7th	Brands Hatch – TBC	Radio 1 Production Saloon	Vauxhall	Firenza	Hamilton Motors	TBC	TBC	4th
	March	13th/14th	Brands Hatch – GP	Keith Prowse Group One – Race of Champions	Vauxhall	Magnum	Tim Stock	TBC	9th	1st in Class
	March	14th	Silverstone – Club	BBC Radio 1 Production Saloon	Vauxhall	Firenza	Hamilton Motors	35	TBC	TBC
	March	20th/21st	Mallory Park	Radio 1 Production Saloon	Vauxhall	Firenza	Hamilton Motors	35	TBC	2nd Overall
	April	4th	Thruxton	Radio 1 Production Saloon	Vauxhall	Firenza	Hamilton Motors	35	3rd	Retired
	April	10th/11th	Silverstone – GP	Keith Prowse Group One	Vauxhall	Magnum	DTV	29	8th	4th in Class
	April	16th	Oulton Park	Keith Prowse Group One	Vauxhall	Magnum	DTV	TBC	TBC	2nd in Class
	April	17th/19th	Thruxton	Keith Prowse Group One – Joanna Carlin Touring Car race sponsored DJM Records	Vauxhall	Magnum	DTV	29	7th	1st in Class
	April	18th	Snetterton	Radio 1 Production Saloon	Vauxhall	Firenza	Hamilton Motors	TBC	TBC	1st in Class
	April	TBC	Silverstone – TBC	Graham Hill Tribute Demonstration	Lotus	XI	168	TBC	N/A	Demo
	May	2nd	Mallory Park	Radio 1 Production Saloon	Vauxhall	Firenza	TBC	TBC	TBC	1st in Class
	May	8th/9th	Silverstone – GP	Tricentrol Special Saloon Car Championship	Vauxhall	Firenza DS	Baby Bertha	10	1st	2nd Overall
	May	8th/9th	Silverstone – GP	World Championship of Makes	Porsche	Carrera RSR	Raymond Touroul	34	DNS	DNS
	May	9th	Thruxton	Keith Prowse Group One	Vauxhall	Magnum	DTV	29	10th	2nd in Class
	May	15th	Oulton Park	BBC Radio 1 Production Saloon	Vauxhall	Firenza	Hamilton Motors	TBC	TBC	1st in Class
	May	22nd	Rally	Red Dragon Rally	Vauxhall	Chevette	1200	TBC	N/A	1st in Class
	May	22nd	Rally	Dragon Valley WMC	Vauxhall	Chevette	1200	TBC	TBC	2nd
	May	30th	Brands Hatch – Club	BBC Radio 1 Production Saloon	Vauxhall	Firenza	Hamilton Motors	TBC	TBC	1st in Class
	May	31st	Silverstone – Club	Keith Prowse Group One	Vauxhall	Magnum	DTV	29	8th	3rd in Class
	June	6th	Silverstone – Club	Tricentrol Special Saloon Car Championship	Vauxhall	Firenza DS	Baby Bertha	1	2nd	1st Overall
	June	6th	Silverstone – Club	Britax Production Saloon	TBC	TBC	TBC	TBC	TBC	TBC
	June	20th	Silverstone – Club	BBC Radio 1 Production Saloon	Vauxhall	Firenza	Hamilton Motors	35	TBC	1st in Class
	June	27th	Croft	Britax Production Saloon	TBC	TBC	TBC	TBC	TBC	TBC
	July	4th	Silverstone – Club	Tricentrol Special Saloon Car Championship	Vauxhall	Firenza DS	Baby Bertha	1	3rd	Retired
	July	9th/10/11th	Rally	Texaco Tour of Britain	Vauxhall	Magnum	4DTV	TBC	Rally	4th Overall
	July	10th	Silverstone – GP	St John H – 27th – Goddard & Smith Trophy for GT & Sports Cars	Sunbeam	Tiger Le Mans	Green ADU 180B/179B	29	TBC	1st in Class
	July	10th	Silverstone – GP	St John H – 27th – The Philips Electrical Trophy Race	Sunbeam	Tiger Le Mans	Green ADU 180B/179B	29	TBC	TBC
	July	16th/17th/18th	Brands Hatch – GP	Grand Prix Celebrity Race	Ford	Escort	MTW157P	TBC	TBC	Retired
	July	16th/17th/18th	Brands Hatch – GP	Keith Prowse Group One	Vauxhall	Magnum	DTV	TBC	TBC	2nd in Class
	July	24th/25th	Spa-Francorchamps	Spa 24-hours	Vauxhall	Magnum	TBC	27	26th	27th Overall
	July	31st	Snetterton	Keith Prowse Group One	Vauxhall	Magnum	DTV	TBC	TBC	2nd in Class
	August	1st	Snetterton	Radio 1 Production Saloon	Vauxhall	Magnum	TBC	TBC	1st	1st
	August	8th	Thruxton	Britax Production Saloon	Ford	Capri	TBC	TBC	TBC	1st Overall
TBC	TBC	Thruxton	Alcoa of Great Britain	Ford	Capri	ICS	TBC	4th	1st Overall
	August	14th	Oulton Park	Britax Production Saloon	TBC	TBC	TBC	TBC	TBC	TBC
	August	15th	Brands Hatch – Club	Tricentrol Special Saloon Car Championship	Vauxhall	Firenza DS	Baby Bertha	TBC	1st	Retired
	August	29th	Mallory Park	Keith Prowse Group One	Vauxhall	Magnum	DTV	29	7th	1st Overall
	August	29th	Mallory Park	Radio 1 Production Saloon	Vauxhall	Firenza	Hamilton Motors	35	10th	1st
	August	30th	Snetterton	Radio 1 Production Saloon	TBC	TBC	TBC	TBC	TBC	1st
	September	5th	Silverstone – TBC	Britax Production Saloon	TBC	TBC	TBC	TBC	TBC	TBC
	September	11th	Castle Combe	Tricentrol Special Saloon Car Championship	Vauxhall	Firenza DS	Baby Bertha	1	1st	1st Overall
	September	12th	Brands Hatch – Club	Radio 1 Production Saloon	Vauxhall	Firenza	Hamilton Motors	TBC	TBC	1st
	September	17th/18th	Oulton Park	Radio 1 Production Saloon	Vauxhall	Magnum	TBC	TBC	TBC	1st
	September	17th/18th/19th	Silverstone – GP	ACCESS RAC Tourist Trophy	Vauxhall	Magnum	DTV	48	21st	6th in Class
	September	26th	Mallory Park	Britax Production Saloon	Vauxhall	Magnum	TBC	TBC	TBC	1st
	October	2nd	Silverstone – GP	Marshall Wingfield Production Saloon Car Race	Vauxhall	Firenza	Hamilton Motors	35	TBC	1st Overall
	October	2nd	Silverstone – GP	Esso Uniflo Special Saloon Car Race	Vauxhall	Firenza DS	Baby Bertha	7	1st	1st Overall
	October	3rd	Snetterton	BBC Radio 1 Production Saloon	Vauxhall	Firenza	Hamilton Motors	35	TBC	1st in Class
	October	3rd	Snetterton	Keith Prowse Group One	Vauxhall	Magnum	DTV	29	TBC	2nd in Class
	October	10th	Mallory Park	Tricentrol Special Saloon Car Championship	Vauxhall	Firenza DS	Baby Bertha	1	1st	1st Overall
	October	10th	Mallory Park	Radio 1 Production Saloon	Vauxhall	Firenza	Hamilton Motors	35	6th	1st
	October	17th	Brands Hatch – Club	SuperSaloon Race	Vauxhall	Firenza DS	Baby Bertha	TBC	TBC	1st Overall
	October	23rd/24th	Brands Hatch – GP	BBC Radio 1 Production Saloon	Vauxhall	Firenza	Hamilton Motors	35	TBC	1st
	October	23rd/24th	Brands Hatch – GP	Keith Prowse Group One – Motor Show 200	Vauxhall	Magnum	DTV	29	1st	1st in Class
	October	31st	Thruxton	SuperSaloon Race	Vauxhall	Firenza DS	Baby Bertha	TBC	TBC	1st Overall
	October	31st	Thruxton	Production Saloon	BMW	3.0 Si	TBC	TBC	TBC	1st Overall
	November	21st	Thruxton	November Cup Special Saloon Car Challenge	Vauxhall	Firenza DS	Baby Bertha	1	1st	1st Overall
	November	28th	Brands Hatch – TBC	RMC Drake & Fletcher – Unlimited Saloons	Vauxhall	Firenza DS	Baby Bertha	TBC	TBC	1st Overall
	December	27th	Brands Hatch – Club	Christmas Cup Special Saloon Car Race	Vauxhall	Firenza DS	Baby Bertha	1	1st	1st Overall

Year	Month	Date	Circuit	Race	Car	Spec	Details	No.	Qualifying	Result
1977	February	13th	Brands Hatch – Club	Chiltern Circle and Harrow Car Club Sprint	Vauxhall	Firenza DS	666DTV	57	TBC	1st in Class
	March	6th	Silverstone – International	Tricentrol British Touring Car Championship	Vauxhall	Magnum	DTV	35	5th Overall	3rd in Class
	March	12th	Silverstone – TBC	Classic Saloon Car Championship	Jaguar	Mk2 2.4	TVC254	33	TBC	1st Overall
	March	18th/19th/20th	Brands Hatch – TBC	Race of Champions	Vauxhall	Firenza	Hamilton Motors	TBC	TBC	2nd in Class
	March	18th/19th/20th	Brands Hatch – TBC	Tricentrol British Touring Car Championship	Vauxhall	Magnum	DTV	TBC	6th Overall	2nd in Class
	March	27th	Thruxton	Britax Production Saloon	Vauxhall	Firenza	Hamilton Motors	TBC	TBC	1st in Class
	March	27th	Thruxton	Classic Saloon Car Championship	Jaguar	Mk2 2.4	TVC254	33	TBC	1st Overall
	April	3rd	Silverstone – Club	Britax Production Saloon	Vauxhall	Firenza	Hamilton Motors	TBC	3rd in Class	2nd in Class
	April	8th	Oulton Park	Tricentrol British Touring Car Championship	Vauxhall	Magnum	DTV	TBC	1st	4th in Class
	April	11th	Thruxton	Tricentrol British Touring Car Championship	Vauxhall	Magnum	DTV	35	7th	1st in Class
	April	16th/17th	Dijon	French bs British Group 1 Race	Vauxhall	Magnum	DTV	TBC	1st in Class	Retired
	April	24th	Silverstone – Club	BRMB British Radio Production Saloon Car	Vauxhall	Firenza	Hamilton Motors	20	TBC	TBC
	May	1st	Snetterton	Britax Production Saloon	Vauxhall	Firenza	Hamilton Motors	TBC	TBC	1st in Class
	May	8th	Spa-Francorchamps	Spa 600kms	Vauxhall	Firenza	TBC	TBC	TBC	Retired
	May	15th	Silverstone – GP	Kosset World Manufacturers 6 hours	BMW	3.0 Si	TBC	49	TBC	21st
	May	21st/22nd	Mallory Park	Radio Trent Production Saloon Car	Vauxhall	Firenza	Hamilton Motors	20	TBC	1st in Class
	May	28th	Donington Park	Else Motor Group Super Saloons	Vauxhall	Firenza DS	Baby Bertha	1	TBC	TBC
	May	29th	Brands Hatch – Club	Britax Production Saloon	Vauxhall	Firenza	Hamilton Motors	20	TBC	1st in Class
	June	6th	Silverstone – Club	Tricentrol British Touring Car Championship	Vauxhall	Magnum	DTV	35	10th	2nd in Class
	June	7th	Donington Park	Britax Production Saloon	Vauxhall	Firenza	Hamilton Motors	TBC	TBC	1st in Class
	June	12th	Brands Hatch – TBC	Debenhams Escort Celebrity Race	Ford	Escort	TBC	TBC	TBC	TBC
	June	19th	Thruxton	Tricentrol British Touring Car Championship	Vauxhall	Magnum	DTV	35	6th	3rd in Class
	June	26th	Brands Hatch – Club	Britax Production Saloon	Vauxhall	Firenza	Hamilton Motors	TBC	TBC	Retired
	July	3rd	Brands Hatch – Club	Debenhams Escort Celebrity Race	Ford	Escort	Celebrity Car	TBC	TBC	TBC
	July	8th/9th	Donington Park	Tricentrol British Touring Car Championship	Vauxhall	Magnum	DTV	TBC	4th	Retired
	July	10th	Snetterton	Britax Production Saloon	TBC	TBC	TBC	TBC	TBC	Retired
	July	16th	Silverstone – GP	Tricentrol British Touring Car Championship	Vauxhall	Magnum	DTV	TBC	10th	2nd in Class
	July	22nd/23rd	Spa-Francorchamps	Spa 24-hours	Vauxhall	Magnum	DTV	56	25th	2nd Overall
	July	22nd/23rd	Spa-Francorchamps	Spa 24-hours	Vauxhall	Magnum	DTV	56	25th	Teams Cup
	July	22nd/23rd	Spa-Francorchamps	Spa 24-hours	Vauxhall	Magnum	DTV	56	25th	1st in Class
	July	22nd/23rd	Spa-Francorchamps	Spa 24-hours	Vauxhall	Magnum	DTV	56	25th	N/A
	July	23rd/24th	Spa-Francorchamps	Spa 24-hours	Vauxhall	Magnum	DTV	56	25th	N/A
	July	31st	Donington Park	Britax Production Saloon	Vauxhall	Magnum	TBC	TBC	TBC	1st in Class
	August	11th	Donington Park	Tricentrol British Touring Car Championship	Vauxhall	Magnum	DTV	TBC	TBC	3rd in Class
	August	12th/13th/14th	Jyllands-Ringen	Group One – Grand Prix Danmark	Vauxhall	Magnum	TBC	TBC	TBC	Retired
	August	12th/13th/14th	Jyllands-Ringen	Group One – Grand Prix Danmark	Vauxhall	Magnum	TBC	TBC	TBC	3rd Overall
	August	12th/13th/14th	Jyllands-Ringen	Group One – Grand Prix Danmark	Vauxhall	Magnum	TBC	TBC	TBC	DNS
	August	12th/13th/14th	Jyllands-Ringen	Special Saloons – Group 2 & Group 5 – Grand Prix Danmark	Vauxhall	Firenza DS	Baby Bertha	TBC	TBC	4th Overall
	August	12th/13th/14th	Jyllands-Ringen	Special Saloons – Group 2 & Group 5 – Grand Prix Danmark	Vauxhall	Firenza DS	Baby Bertha	TBC	TBC	5th Overall
	August	12th/13th/14th	Jyllands-Ringen	Special Saloons – Group 2 & Group 5 – Grand Prix Danmark	Vauxhall	Firenza DS	Baby Bertha	TBC	TBC	4th Overall
	August	28th/29th	Brands Hatch – GP	Tricentrol British Touring Car Championship	Vauxhall	Magnum	DTV	35	4th	2nd in Class
	August	28th/29th	Brands Hatch – GP	Capital Radio Production Saloon	Vauxhall	Firenza	Hamilton Motors	20	TBC	2nd in Class
	September	4th	Silverstone – National	Britax Production Saloon	Vauxhall	Firenza	Hamilton Motors	20	TBC	2nd in Class
	September	11th	Thruxton	Tricentrol British Touring Car Championship	Vauxhall	Magnum	DTV	TBC	TBC	2nd in Class
	September	18th	Silverstone – GP	RAC Tourist Trophy – Access	Vauxhall	Magnum	DTV	29	15th	Retired
	September	18th	Silverstone – GP	Classic Saloon Car Club	Jaguar	Mk2 2.4	TVC254	33	TBC	TBC
	October	2nd	Mount Panorama Bathurst	Hardie Ferodo 1000	Holden	Torana A9X	TBC	24	18th	30th Overall
	October	16th	Brands Hatch – Club	Tricentrol British Touring Car Championship	Vauxhall	Magnum	DTV	35	4th	Retired
	October	16th	Brands Hatch – Club	Capital Radio Production Saloon	Vauxhall	Firenza	Hamilton Motors	20	TBC	3rd in Class
	October	23rd	Mallory Park	BARC Special Saloon Race	Vauxhall	Firenza DS	Baby Bertha	TBC	1st	1st Overall
	October	23rd	Mallory Park	Britax Production Saloon	Vauxhall	Firenza	Hamilton Motors	TBC	TBC	1st in Class
	October	30th	Thruxton	SuperSaloon Race	Vauxhall	Firenza DS	Baby Bertha	TBC	2nd	1st Overall
	October	30th	Thruxton	Britax Production Saloon	Vauxhall	Firenza	Hamilton Motors	TBC	TBC	Retired
	November	4th	N/A	N/A	Vauxhall	Firenza DS	Baby Bertha	N/A	TBC	N/A
	November	12th	Thruxton	Eleanor's Chase for Production Saloons	BMW	3.0 Si	TBC	20	4th	Retired
	November	13th	Brands Hatch – Club	Classic Saloon Car Race	Austin	A35	Andy McLennan	TBC	TBC	Retired
	TBC	TBC	TBC	Classic Saloon Car Club	TBC	TBC	TBC	TBC	TBC	TBC
	TBC	TBC	Donington Park	SuperSaloon Race	Vauxhall	Firenza DS	Baby Bertha	TBC	TBC	1st Overall
1978	February	5th	Brands Hatch – Club	Chiltern Circle and Harrow Car Club Sprint	Vauxhall	Chevette HS2300	4DTV	TBC	N/A	1st in Class
	February	5th	Brands Hatch – Club	Chiltern Circle and Harrow Car Club Sprint	Vauxhall	Firenza DS	Old Nail	84	N/A	1st in Class
	March	5th	Brands Hatch – Club	ShellSport Derwent Production Saloon	Triumph	Dolomite Sprint	TBC	1	1st in Class	1st in Class
	March	11h	Oulton Park	ShellSport Derwent Production Saloon	Triumph	Dolomite Sprint	TBC	1	1st in Class	2nd in Class
	March	12th	Thruxton	Britax Production Saloon	Triumph	Dolomite Sprint	TBC	1	1st	1st in Class
	March	19th	Silverstone – GP	Tricentrol British Touring Car Championship	Ford	Capri 3.0	CC Engineering	14	7th	1st in Class
	March	23rd	Oulton Park	Tricentrol British Touring Car Championship	Ford	Capri 3.0	CC Engineering	14	7th	Retired
	March	27th	Thruxton	Tricentrol British Touring Car Championship	Ford	Capri 3.0	CC Engineering	14	DNS	DNS
	March	26th/27th	Brands Hatch – GP	ShellSport Derwent Production Saloon	Triumph	Dolomite Sprint	TBC	1	1st in Class	1st in Class
	April	1st	Brands Hatch – Club	Tricentrol British Touring Car Championship	Ford	Capri 3.0	CC Engineering	14	8th	4th in Class
	April	2nd	Silverstone – National	Britax Production Saloon	Triumph	Dolomite Sprint	TBC	1	1st in Class	1st in Class
	April	9th	Thruxton	ShellSport Derwent Production Saloon	Triumph	Dolomite Sprint	TBC	1	2nd in Class	1st in Class
	April	15th/16th	Snetterton	ShellSport Derwent Production Saloon	Triumph	Dolomite Sprint	TBC	1	1st in Class	1st in Class
	April	22nd	Oulton Park	Britax Production Saloon	Triumph	Dolomite Sprint	Marshall Wingfield	1	2nd in Class	1st in Class
	April	29th	Silverstone – TBC	Tricentrol British Touring Car Championship	Ford	Capri 3.0	CC Engineering	14	TBC	4th Overall
	April	30th	Donington Park	Britax Production Saloon	Triumph	Dolomite Sprint	Marshall Wingfield	1	1st	1st Overall
	May	1st	Brands Hatch – Club	Tricentrol British Touring Car Championship	Ford	Capri 3.0	CC Engineering	14	TBC	4th in Class
	May	7th	Brands Hatch – Club	ShellSUPERLIFE Celebrity Escort Race	Ford	Escort	Celebrity Car	6	3rd	5th Overall
	May	7th	Brands Hatch – Club	Britax Production Saloon	Triumph	Dolomite Sprint	Marshall Wingfield	1	1st in Class	1st in Class
	May	14th	Mallory Park	Britax Production Saloon	Triumph	Dolomite Sprint	Triplex	1	1st in Class	1st in Class
	May	21st	Donington Park	Porsche 924 Championship	Porsche	924	Gordon Lamb	11	TBC	TBC
	May	21st	Donington Park	Britax Production Saloon	Triumph	Dolomite Sprint	TBC	TBC	TBC	1st in Class
	May	28th	Brands Hatch – Club	ShellSport Derwent Production Saloon	Triumph	Dolomite Sprint	Triplex	1	1st in Class	1st in Class
	May	29th	Silverstone – Club	Tricentrol British Touring Car Championship	Ford	Capri 3.0	CC Engineering	14	8th	4th Overall
	June	4th	Silverstone – Club	Britax Production Saloon	Triumph	Dolomite Sprint	Triplex	1	1st in Class	1st in Class
	June	4th	Silverstone – Club	Porsche 924 Championship	Porsche	924	Gordon Lamb	11	TBC	TBC
	June	11th	Brands Hatch – Club	Britax Production Saloon	Triumph	Dolomite Sprint	Triplex	1	1st in Class	1st in Class
	June	11th	Brands Hatch – Club	Porsche 924 Championship	Porsche	924	Gordon Lamb	11	TBC	TBC

Year	Month	Date	Circuit	Race	Car	Spec	Details	No.	Qualifying	Result
1978	June	18th	Snetterton	ShellSport Derwent Production Saloon	Triumph	Dolomite Sprint	Triplex	TBC	1st	1st Overall
	June	24th	Oulton Park	Porsche 924 Championship	Porsche	924	Gordon Lamb	11	3rd	3rd Overall
	June	24th/25th	Donington Park	Tricentrol British Touring Car Championship	Ford	Capri 3.0	CC Engineering	14	3rd	Retired
	July	2nd	Mallory Park	Tricentrol British Touring Car Championship	Ford	Capri 3.0	CC Engineering	14	5th	Retired
	July	2nd	Mallory Park	Britax Production Saloon	Triumph	Dolomite Sprint	Triplex	1	3rd	1st in Class
	July	8th	Oulton Park	ShellSport Derwent Production Saloon	Triumph	Dolomite Sprint	Triplex	1	1st in Class	1st in Class
	July	9th	Snetterton	Porsche 924 Championship	Porsche	924	Gordon Lamb	11	1st	Retired
	July	14th/15th/16th	Brands Hatch – GP	Tricentrol British Touring Car Championship	Ford	Capri 3.0	CC Engineering	14	12th	18th
	July	22nd/23rd	Spa-Francorchamps	Spa 24-hours	Ford	Capri 3.0	CC3	33	8th	Retired
	July	30th	Brands Hatch – Club	ShellSport Derwent Production Saloon	Triumph	Dolomite Sprint	Triplex	1	3rd in Class	1st in Class
	August	6th	Donington Park	International Historic Single Seater Sports Car	Jaguar	Lister	Barry Simpson	32	5th	3rd Overall
	August	6th	Donington Park	Tricentrol British Touring Car Championship	Ford	Capri 3.0	CC Engineering	14	8th	6th Overall
	August	6th	Donington Park	ShellSport Derwent Production Saloon	Triumph	Dolomite Sprint	Triplex	1	1st in Class	2nd in Class
	August	27th	Snetterton	ShellSport Derwent Production Saloon	Triumph	Dolomite Sprint	Triplex	1	1st in Class	1st in Class
	August	28th	Brands Hatch – GP	Tricentrol British Touring Car Championship	Ford	Capri 3.0	CC Engineering	14	DNE	DNE
	August	28th	Thruxton	Britax Production Saloon	Triumph	Dolomite Sprint	Triplex	1	1st in Class	1st in Class
	September	3rd	Silverstone – Club	ShellSport Derwent Production Saloon	Triumph	Dolomite Sprint	Triplex	1	1st in Class	1st in class
	September	10th	Thruxton	Porsche 924 Championship	Porsche	924	Gordon Lamb	11	1st	Retired
	September	10th	Thruxton	Tricentrol British Touring Car Championship	Ford	Capri 3.0	CC Engineering	14	12th	Retired
	September	16th	Oulton Park	Britax Production Saloon	Triumph	Dolomite Sprint	Triplex	1	Last	Retired
	September	17th	Silverstone – GP	Diners Club Trans-Europe Trophy Race	Ford	Capri 3.0	CC Engineering	20	13th	4th Overall
	September	17th	Silverstone – GP	RAC Tourist Trophy – Diner's Club	Ford	Capri 3.0	CC Engineering	20	6th in Class	3rd in Class
	September	24th	Snetterton	Britax Production Saloon	Triumph	Dolomite Sprint	Triplex	1	TBC	1st in Class
	October	7th	Oulton Park	Tricentrol British Touring Car Championship	Ford	Capri 3.0	CC Engineering	14	8th	Retired
	October	14th	Croft	Britax Production Saloon	Triumph	Dolomite Sprint	Triplex	1	1st	1st in Class
	October	15th	Brands Hatch – Club	ShellSport Derwent Production Saloon	Triumph	Dolomite Sprint	Triplex	1	1st in Class	1st in Class
	October	21st	Snetterton	Tricentrol Production Car Night Races	Alfa Romeo	Alfetta GTAm	Jon Dooley	27	3rd	Retired
	October	29th	Thruxton	Britax Production Saloon	Triumph	Dolomite Sprint	Triplex	1	1st in Class	1st in Class
	November	4th	Brands Hatch – Club	Shell Super Escort Instructors Race	Ford	Escort	Sports	TBC	TBC	2nd Overall
1979	February	4th	Brands Hatch – Club	Chiltern Circle and Harrow Car Club Sprint	Triumph	Dolomite Sprint	Triplex	TBC	N/A	1st in Class
	February	9th/10th/11th	Rally	Henley Forklift Galway Rally	Ford	Escort	TBC	TBC	N/A	TBC
	March	4th	Brands Hatch – Club	Demon Tweeks 4 Shocks Production Saloon	Triumph	Dolomite Sprint	Triplex	22	TBC	1st in Class
	March	11th	Thruxton	Demon Tweeks 4 Shocks Production Saloon	Triumph	Dolomite Sprint	Triplex	22	6th	1st in Class
	March	18th	Donington Park	Tricentrol British Touring Car Championship – Race of Champions	Triumph	Dolomite Sprint	TBC	22	N/A	Race Cancelled
	March	18th	Donington Park	Demon Tweeks 4 Shocks Production Saloon	Triumph	Dolomite Sprint	TBC	22	N/A	Race Cancelled
	March	24th/25th	Silverstone – International	Tricentrol British Saloon Car Championship	Triumph	Dolomite Sprint	Triplex	22	3rd in Class	Retired
	April	1st	Snetterton	Demon Tweeks 4 Shocks Production Saloon	Triumph	Dolomite Sprint	Triplex	22	1st in Class	1st in Class
	April	8th	Silverstone – Club	ShellSport Derwent Production Saloon	Triumph	Dolomite Sprint	Triplex	22	1st in Class	1st in Class
	April	12th/13th	Oulton Park	Tricentrol British Saloon Car Championship	Triumph	Dolomite Sprint	Triplex	22	3rd in Class	2nd in Class
	April	14th/16th	Thruxton	Tricentrol British Saloon Car Championship	Triumph	Dolomite Sprint	Triplex	22	2nd in Class	6th in Class
	April	29th	Lydden Hill	Demon Tweeks 4 Shocks Production Saloon	Triumph	Dolomite Sprint	Triplex	22	TBC	1st in Class
	April	29th	Brands Hatch – TBC	European Touring Car Championship Race	Chevrolet	Camaro	Scottish Owned	TBC	DNE	DNE
	May	6th	Cadwell Park	Demon Tweeks 4 Shocks Production Saloon	Triumph	Dolomite Sprint	Triplex	22	1st in Class	Retired
	May	7th	Brands Hatch – Club	ShellSport Derwent Production Saloon	Triumph	Dolomite Sprint	Triplex	22	9th	Retired
	May	12th	Oulton Park	Demon Tweeks 4 Shocks Production Saloon	Triumph	Dolomite Sprint	Triplex	22	5th	1st in Class
	May	19th/20th	Snetterton	Demon Tweeks 4 Shocks Production Saloon	Triumph	Dolomite Sprint	Triplex	22	11th	2nd in Class
	May	28th	Silverstone – Club	Tricentrol British Saloon Car Championship	Triumph	Dolomite Sprint	Triplex	22	3rd in Class	3rd in Class
	June	3rd	Mallory Park	Demon Tweeks 4 Shocks Production Saloon	Triumph	Dolomite Sprint	Triplex	22	1st in Class	1st in Class
	June	16th/17th	Snetterton	ShellSport Derwent Production Saloon	Triumph	Dolomite Sprint	Triplex	22	2nd in Class	1st in Class
	June	23rd	Silverstone – Club	St John Horsfall – 30th – Lloyds & Scottish Historic Sports Car Championship	Jaguar	Lister	BHL130/YCD422	TBC	TBC	Retired
	June	24th	Brands Hatch – Club	ShellSport Derwent Production Saloon	Triumph	Dolomite Sprint	Triplex	22	DNE	DNE
	June	24th	Donington Park	Tricentrol British Saloon Car Championship	Triumph	Dolomite Sprint	Triplex	22	3rd in Class	3rd in Class
	July	1st	Brands Hatch – Club	Demon Tweeks 4 Shocks Production Saloon	Triumph	Dolomite Sprint	Triplex	22	TBC	1st in Class
	July	7th	Oulton Park	ShellSport Derwent Production Saloon	Triumph	Dolomite Sprint	Triplex	22	1st in Class	1st in Class
	July	7th	Oulton Park	Debenhams Escort Challenge Race	Ford	Escort	TBC	1	4th	5th Overall
	July	12th/13th/14th	Silverstone – GP	Tricentrol British Saloon Car Championship	Triumph	Dolomite Sprint	Triplex	22	3rd in Class	Retired
	July	12th/13th/14th	Silverstone – GP	Lloyds & Scottish Historic Sports Car Championship	Jaguar	Lister	BHL130/YCD422	38	TBC	DNS
	July	21st	Spa-Francorchamps	Spa 24-hours	Triumph	Dolomite Sprint	Triplex	57	34th	Retired
	August	26th/27th	Brands Hatch – GP	Lloyds & Scottish Historic Sports Car Championship	Jaguar	Lister	BHL130/YCD422	47	TBC	DNS
	August	26th/27th	Brands Hatch – GP	Tricentrol British Saloon Car Championship	Triumph	Dolomite Sprint	Triplex	22	3rd in Class	2nd in Class
	September	2nd	Silverstone – Club	Demon Tweeks 4 Shocks Production Saloon	Triumph	Dolomite Sprint	Triplex	22	1st in Class	1st in Class
	September	9th	Thruxton	Tricentrol British Saloon Car Championship	Triumph	Dolomite Sprint	Triplex	22	2nd in Class	5th in Class
	September	15th	Oulton Park	Demon Tweeks 4 Shocks Production Saloon	Triumph	Dolomite Sprint	Triplex	22	8th	1st in Class
	September	15th/16th	Silverstone – International	RAC Tourist Trophy – Pentax	Triumph	Dolomite Sprint	Triplex	65	2nd in Class	4th in Class
	September	15th/16th	Silverstone – International	RAC Tourist Trophy – Pentax	Triumph	Dolomite Sprint	Triplex	66	1st in Class	5th in Class
	September	15th/16th	Silverstone – International	Lloyds & Scottish Historic Sports Car Championship	Jaguar	Lister	BHL130/YCD422	38	DNQ	Retired
	September	23rd	Croft	Demon Tweeks 4 Shocks Production Saloon	Triumph	Dolomite Sprint	Triplex	22	3rd	1st in Class
	September	29th	Oulton Park	ShellSport Derwent Production Saloon	Triumph	Dolomite Sprint	Triplex	22	1st in Class	1st in Class
	September	29th	Oulton Park	Tricentrol British Saloon Car Championship	Triumph	Dolomite Sprint	Triplex	22	4th in Class	Retired
	September	30th	Thruxton	Demon Tweeks 4 Shocks Production Saloon	Triumph	Dolomite Sprint	Triplex	22	1st in Class	1st in Class
	October	7th	Brands Hatch – Indy	ShellSport Derwent Production Saloon	Triumph	Dolomite Sprint	Triplex	22	2nd in Class	1st in Class
	October	14th	Mallory Park	Demon Tweeks 4 Shocks Production Saloon	Triumph	Dolomite Sprint	Triplex	22	2nd in Class	2nd in Class
	October	21st	Snetterton	ShellSport Derwent Production Saloon	Triumph	Dolomite Sprint	Triplex	22	TBC	1st in Class
	October	28th	Thruxton	Demon Tweeks 4 Shocks Production Saloon	Triumph	Dolomite Sprint	Triplex	22	1st in Class	1st in Class
	December	26th	Brands Hatch – Indy	Prodsports	Triumph	TR7 V8	Tony Hill – Dodge City	TBC	TBC	TBC
1980	March	2nd	Brands Hatch – Indy	Monroe Shock Absorbers Production Saloon Car Championship	Triumph	Dolomite Sprint	TBC	24	TBC	1st in Class
	March	16th	Silverstone – Club	Monroe Shock Absorbers Production Saloon Car Championship	Ford	Capri 3.0	TBC	24	2nd	2nd Overall
	March	23rd	Brands Hatch – Indy	Monroe Shock Absorbers Production Saloon Car Championship	Triumph	Dolomite Sprint	TBC	24	9th	2nd in Class
	March	30th	Brands Hatch – Indy	Wilcomatic 3000 Production Saloon	Ford	Capri 3.0	TBC	15	9th	9th in Class
	April	5th	Mallory Park	Wilcomatic 3000 Production Saloon	Ford	Capri 3.0	TBC	15	2nd	4th Overall
	April	7th	Silverstone – Club	Lloyds & Scottish Historic Sports Car Championship	Jaguar	Lister	BHL130/YCD422	55	1st	Retired
	April	13th	Mallory Park	Monroe Shock Absorbers Production Saloon Car Championship	Ford	Capri 3.0	TBC	15	2nd	4th in Class
	April	26th/27th	Donington Park	Donington Trophy for Production Saloon – Non Championship	Ford	Capri 3.0	TBC	15	2nd	2nd Overall
	April	27th	Thruxton	Monroe Shock Absorbers Production Saloon Car Championship	Ford	Capri 3.0	TBC	15	4th	1st Overall
	May	5th	Brands Hatch – Indy	Debenhams RS Fiesta Challenge – Harpers & Queen Trophy Stirling Moss	Ford	Fiesta	TBC	14	3rd	3rd Overall

Year	Month	Date	Circuit	Race	Car	Spec	Details	No.	Qualifying	Result
1980	May	10th	Oulton Park	Monroe Shock Absorbers Production Saloon Car Championship	BMW	3.0 Si	TBC	15	1st in Class	1st Overall
	May	11th	Brands Hatch – Club	Lloyds & Scottish Historic Sports Car Championship	Jaguar	Lister	BHL130/YCD422	55	1st	1st Overall
	May	11th/12th	Silverstone – TBC	World Championship of Makes 6-Hours	Porsche	Carrera 2.8	Tony Wingrove	TBC	TBC	DNS
	May	25th	Oulton Park	Wilcomatic 3000 Production Saloon	Triumph	Dolomite Sprint	TBC	24	1st in Class	1st in Class
	May	26th	Snetterton	Production Saloon – Non-Championship	Triumph	Dolomite Sprint	TBC	24	1st	1st Overall
	June	1st	Cadwell Park	Monroe Shock Absorbers Production Saloon Car Championship	Opel	Commodore 2.8	Paul Everett	15	3rd	4th Overall
	June	1st	Cadwell Park	Monroe Shock Absorbers Production Saloon Car Championship	Triumph	Dolomite Sprint	TBC	24	1st	1st Overall
	June	8th	Brands Hatch – Indy	Wilcomatic 3000 Production Saloon	Triumph	Dolomite Sprint	TBC	24	1st in Class	1st in Class
	June	14th	Oulton Park	Lloyds & Scottish Historic Sports Car Championship	Jaguar	Lister	BHL130/YCD422	55	1st	1st Overall
	June	14th/15th	Donington Park	Production Saloon & ASCARS – Non Championship	BMW	3.0 Si	TBC	15	2nd in Class	2nd in Class
	June	21st/22nd	Snetterton	Willhire 24-hour race	Ford	Capri 3.0	TBC	10	TBC	2nd Overall
	June	28th	Silverstone – Club	St John H – 31st – Lloyds & Scottish Historic Sports Car wChampionship	Jaguar	Lister	BHL130/YCD422	55	2nd	2nd Overall
	June	29th	Brands Hatch – Indy	Monroe Shock Absorbers Production Saloon Car Championship	Ford	Capri 3.0	TBC	15	7th	5th in Class
	July	5th	Castle Combe	Wilcomatic 3000 Production Saloon	Triumph	Dolomite Sprint	TBC	24	1st in Class	1st in Class
	July	6th	Silverstone – Club	Monroe Shock Absorbers Production Saloon Car Championship	Ford	Capri 3.0	TBC	15	12th	2nd Overall
	July	11th/12th/13th	Brands Hatch – GP	Lloyds & Scottish Historic Sports Car Championship	Jaguar	Lister	BHL130/YCD422	55	4th	2nd in Class
	July	26th	Aintree	Wilcomatic 3000 Production Saloon	Triumph	Dolomite Sprint	TBC	24	TBC	1st in Class
	August	9th	Oulton Park	Wilcomatic 3000 Production Saloon	Triumph	Dolomite Sprint	TBC	24	1st	2nd in Class
	August	10th	Brands Hatch – Indy	Monroe Shock Absorbers Production Saloon Car Championship	Ford	Capri 3.0	TBC	15	5th	3rd in Class
	August	24th	Snetterton	Monroe Shock Absorbers Production Saloon Car Championship	Ford	Capri 3.0	TBC	15	4th	1st Overall
	August	24th/25th	Brands Hatch – GP	Lloyds & Scottish Historic Sports Car Championship	Jaguar	Lister	BHL130/YCD422	55	1st in Class	1st Overall
	August	31st	Silverstone – Club	Monroe Shock Absorbers Production Saloon Car Championship	Ford	Capri 3.0	TBC	15	5th	4th Overall
	September	7th	Mallory Park	Debenhams RS Fiesta Challenge	Ford	Fiesta	Celebrity Car	TBC	TBC	9th Overall
	September	14th	Silverstone – GP	Lloyds & Scottish Historic Sports Car Championship	Jaguar	Lister	WTM446 (Barry Simpson)	57	1st in Class	1st in Class
	September	14th	Snetterton	Wilcomatic 3000 Production Saloon	Triumph	Dolomite Sprint	TBC	24	DNS	1st in Class
	September	19th/20th	Oulton Park	Monroe Shock Absorbers Production Saloon Car Championship	Ford	Capri 3.0	TBC	15	2nd	1st Overall
	September	28th	Mallory Park	Wilcomatic 3000 Production Saloon	Triumph	Dolomite Sprint	TBC	24	2nd in Class	1st in Class
	October	12th	Snetterton	Monroe Shock Absorbers Production Saloon Car Championship	Ford	Capri 3.0	TBC	15	7th	2nd Overall
	October	18th	Oulton Park	Monroe Shock Absorbers Production Saloon Car Championship	Ford	Capri 3.0	TBC	15	3rd	2nd Overall
	October	19th	Brands Hatch – Indy	Wilcomatic 3000 Production Saloon	Triumph	Dolomite Sprint	TBC	24	1st in Class	Retired
	October	26th	Thruxton	Monroe Shock Absorbers Production Saloon Car Championship	Ford	Capri 3.0	TBC	15	1st	1st Overall
	November	8th	Thruxton	Wendy Wools Production Saloon Race	Ford	Capri 3.0	TBC	15	2nd	1st Overall
	November	9th	Brands Hatch – Indy	BARC London and Home Counties Production Saloon	Ford	Capri 3.0	TBC	15	3rd	1st Overall
1981	March	1st	Brands Hatch – Indy	Monroe Shock Absorbers Production Saloon Car Championship	Ford	Capri 3.0	Autoplan	6	1st	1st Overall
	March	8th	Thruxton	Monroe Shock Absorbers Production Saloon Car Championship	Ford	Capri 3.0	Autoplan	6	1st	1st Overall
	March	15th	Silverstone – National	Monroe Shock Absorbers Production Saloon Car Championship	Ford	Capri 3.0	Autoplan	6	1st	1st Overall
	March	22nd	Thruxton	Monroe Shock Absorbers Production Saloon Car Championship	Ford	Capri 3.0	Autoplan	6	1st	1st Overall
	March	29th	Snetterton	Wilcomatic 3000 Production Saloon	Ford	Capri 3.0	Autoplan	6	1st	1st Overall
	April	5th	Brands Hatch – Indy	Wilcomatic 3000 Production Saloon	Ford	Capri 3.0	Autoplan	6	1st	2nd Overall
	April	12th	Cadwell Park	Monroe Shock Absorbers Production Saloon Car Championship	Ford	Capri 3.0	Autoplan	6	1st	1st Overall
	April	17th	Snetterton	Monroe Shock Absorbers Production Saloon Car Championship	Ford	Capri 3.0	Autoplan	6	2nd	1st Overall
	April	20th	Silverstone – National	Lloyds & Scottish Historic Sports Car Championship	Aston	DBR4	RB/250/1 & RB6/300/1	69	TBC	2nd Overall
	May	3rd/4th	Brands Hatch – GP	Wilcomatic 3000 Production Saloon	Ford	Capri 3.0	Autoplan	6	1st	1st Overall
	May	3rd/4th	Brands Hatch – GP	Wilcomatic 3000 Production Saloon	Ford	Capri 3.0	Autoplan	6	1st	1st Overall
	May	9th	Oulton Park	Monroe Shock Absorbers Production Saloon Car Championship	Ford	Capri 3.0	Autoplan	6	3rd	1st Overall
	May	10th	Snetterton	Monroe Shock Absorbers Production Saloon Car Championship	Ford	Capri 3.0	Autoplan	6	1st	1st Overall
	May	17th	Brands Hatch – Indy	Pace Petroleum FIA Championship Race	Aston	DBR4	RB/250/1 & RB6/300/1	5	1st	1st Overall
	May	25th	Snetterton	Monroe Shock Absorbers Production Saloon Car Championship	Ford	Capri 3.0	Autoplan	6	1st	1st Overall
	May	31st	Silverstone – Club	Wilcomatic 3000 Production Saloon	Ford	Capri 3.0	Autoplan	6	1st	1st Overall
	June	6th	Oulton Park	Monroe Shock Absorbers Production Saloon Car Championship	Ford	Capri 3.0	Autoplan	6	1st	1st Overall
	June	6th/7th	Donington Park	Historic Grand Prix Association Race of the Year	Aston	DBR4	RB/250/1 & RB6/300/1	9	2nd	1st Overall
	June	14th	Thruxton	Shell Super Sunbeam Celebrity Race	Talbot	Sunbeam	Celebrity Car	1	2nd	2nd Overall
	June	14th	Thruxton	Wilcomatic 3000 Production Saloon	Ford	Capri 3.0	Autoplan	6	1st	1st Overall
	June	21st	Mallory Park	Monroe Shock Absorbers Production Saloon Car Championship	Ford	Capri 3.0	Autoplan	6	TBC	1st Overall
	June	27th	Silverstone – Club	St John H – 32nd – Lloyds & Scottish Historic Sports Car Championship	Aston	DBR4	RB/250/1 & RB6/300/1	69	TBC	1st Overall
	June	27th/28th/29th	Snetterton	Willhire 24-hour race	Ford	Capri 3.0	Autoplan	TBC	TBC	2nd Overall
	July	12th	Mallory Park	Monroe Shock Absorbers Production Saloon Car Championship	Ford	Capri 3.0	Autoplan	6	1st	1st Overall
	July	16th/17th/18th	Silverstone – GP	Minolta Trophy for Super Sports Cars	Lola	T70 3b	SL76/148	6	5th	Retired
	July	16th/17th/18th	Silverstone – GP	Lloyds & Scottish Historic Sports Car Championship	Aston	DBR4	RB/250/1 & RB6/300/1	69	TBC	1st Overall
	July	26th	Snetterton	Wilcomatic 3000 Production Saloon	Ford	Capri 3.0	Autoplan	6	1st	1st Overall
	August	2nd	Brands Hatch – Indy	Paul Linard Group Three Hour Race Meeting	Volkswagen	Scirocco	TBC	50	1st in Class	Retired
	August	30th	Mallory Park	Wilcomatic 3000 Production Saloon	Ford	Capri 3.0	Autoplan	6	TBC	1st Overall
	August	30th/31st	Brands Hatch – GP	Lloyds & Scottish Historic Sports Car Championship	Aston	DBR4	RB/250/1 & RB6/300/1	69	2nd	1st Overall
	September	6th	Silverstone – Club	Letchworth Roofing Trophy Race	Ford	Capri 3.0	Autoplan	6	1st	1st Overall
	September	12th/13th	Silverstone – GP	Lloyds & Scottish Historic Sports Car Championship	Aston	DBR4	RB/250/1 & RB6/300/1	69	1st	1st Overall
	September	12th/13th	Silverstone – GP	Lloyds & Scottish Historic Sports Car Championship	Aston	DBR4	RB/250/1 & RB6/300/1	69	1st	1st Overall
	September	12th/13th	Silverstone – GP	RAC Tourist Trophy – Canon	AMC	AMX Spirit	John Markey	5	DNS	DNS
	September	27th	Oulton Park	Monroe Shock Absorbers Production Saloon Car Championship	Ford	Capri 3.0	Autoplan	6	1st	1st Overall
	October	4th	Silverstone – GP	Minolta Trophy for Super Sports Cars	Lola	T70 3b	SL76/148	69	TBC	1st Overall
	October	10th	Oulton Park	Wilcomatic 3000 Production Saloon	Ford	Capri 3.0	Autoplan	6	1st	1st Overall
	October	18th	Brands Hatch – Indy	Wilcomatic 3000 Production Saloon	Ford	Capri 3.0	Autoplan	6	1st	1st Overall
	October	23rd	Thruxton	Monroe Shock Absorbers Production Saloon Car Championship	Ford	Capri 3.0	Autoplan	6	1st	1st Overall
	December	3rd/4th	Dubai	High Speed Parade	Aston	DBR4	RB/250/1 & RB6/300/1	TBC	N/A	N/A
	December	3rd/4th	Dubai	The Marlboro Cup Super Sports Race	Lola	T70 3b	SL76/148	TBC	1st	1st Overall
	TBC	TBC	TBC	Monroe Shock Absorbers Production Saloon Car Championship	Ford	Capri 3.0	TBC	TBC	TBC	1st Overall
	TBC	TBC	TBC	Monroe Shock Absorbers Production Saloon Car Championship	Ford	Capri 3.0	TBC	TBC	TBC	1st Overall
	TBC	TBC	TBC	Monroe Shock Absorbers Production Saloon Car Championship	Ford	Capri 3.0	TBC	TBC	TBC	1st Overall
1982	February	7th	Brands Hatch – Indy	Chiltern Circle and Harrow Car Club Sprint	TBC	TBC	TBC	28	TBC	1st in Class
	March	7th	Brands Hatch – Indy	Monroe Shock Absorbers Production Saloon Car Championship	Ford	Capri	Offord Packaging	1	TBC	2nd Overall
	March	14th	Thruxton	Monroe Shock Absorbers Production Saloon Car Championship	Ford	Capri	Offord Packaging	1	2nd	2nd Overall
	March	27th	Oulton Park	BRSCC Production Saloon Championship	Ford	Capri 2.8	TBC	1	TBC	2nd Overall
	March	28th	Silverstone – National	Monroe Shock Absorbers Production Saloon Car Championship	Ford	Capri 2.8	TBC	1	2nd	1st Overall
	April	9th	Snetterton	BRSCC Production Saloon Championship	Ford	Capri	TBC	1	1st in Class	1st in Class
	April	11th/12th	Brands Hatch – GP	BRSCC Production Saloon Championship	Ford	Capri	TBC	1	1st in Class	2nd in Class
	April	25th	Cadwell Park	Monroe Shock Absorbers Production Saloon Car Championship	Ford	Capri	TBC	1	2nd	2nd Overall
	April	TBC	Mondello Park	TBC	Ford	Capri	TBC	TBC	TBC	TBC

Year	Month	Date	Circuit	Race	Car	Spec	Details	No.	Qualifying	Result
1982	May	2nd	Snetterton	Monroe Shock Absorbers Production Saloon Car Championship	Ford	Capri	TBC	1	2nd	2nd Overall
	May	3rd	Castle Combe	BRSCC Production Saloon Championship	Ford	Capri 3.0	TBC	1	2nd	2nd Overall
	May	8th	Oulton Park	Monroe Shock Absorbers Production Saloon Car Championship	Ford	Capri	TBC	1	1st	1st Overall
	May	16th	Snetterton	BRSCC Production Saloon Championship	Ford	Capri 2.8	TBC	1	1st	1st Overall
	May	31st	Snetterton	Monroe Shock Absorbers Production Saloon Car Championship	Ford	Capri	TBC	1	1st	1st Overall
	June	5th	Oulton Park	Monroe Shock Absorbers Production Saloon Car Championship	Ford	Capri	TBC	1	4th	1st Overall
	June	13th	Brands Hatch – Indy	BRSCC Production Saloon Championship	Ford	Capri	TBC	1	4th	2nd Overall
	June	20th	Mallory Park	Monroe Shock Absorbers Production Saloon Car Championship	Ford	Capri	TBC	1	2nd	1st Overall
	June	26th	Oulton Park	BRSCC Production Saloon Championship	Ford	Capri	TBC	1	3rd	Retired
	June	27th	Silverstone – National	Monroe Shock Absorbers Production Saloon Car Championship	Ford	Capri 2.8	TBC	1	4th	3rd Overall
	July	3rd	Silverstone – Club	St John H – 33rd – PAS Mobile All Comers Historic Sports Car	Vauxhall	Viva	John Pope Special	16	4th	1st in Class
	July	11th	Mallory Park	Monroe Shock Absorbers Production Saloon Car Championship	Ford	Capri 2.8	TBC	1	3rd in Class	2nd Overall
	July	16th/17th/18th	Brands Hatch – GP	HSCC Atlantic Computers Historic GT	Lola	T222	HU7	70	TBC	2nd in Class
	August	7th/8th	Snetterton	Willhire 24-hour race	BMW	323i	TBC	TBC	TBC	2nd Overall
	September	5th	Silverstone – Club	Monroe Shock Absorbers Production Saloon Car Championship	Ford	Capri 2.8	TBC	1	TBC	2nd Overall
	September	12th	Silverstone – GP	RAC Tourist Trophy – Canon	Ford	Capri 2.8	Autoplan	62	2nd in Class	1st in Class
	September	18th	Oulton Park	Atlantic Computers Historic GT Race	Lola	T222	HU7	70	1st	1st Overall
	September	19th	Brands Hatch – Indy	Monroe Shock Absorbers Production Saloon Car Championship	Ford	Capri 2.8	TBC	TBC	1st	2nd Overall
	September	26th	Brands Hatch – Indy	HSCC Atlantic Computers Historic GT	Lola	T222	HU7	70	1st	1st Overall
	October	16th/17th/18th	Brands Hatch – GP	Lucas CAV Productionuction Sports Cars	Lotus	Esprit Turbo	OPW679W	8	1st	2nd Overall
	October	24th	Thruxton	Monroe Shock Absorbers Production Saloon Car Championship	Ford	Capri	TBC	1	2nd	1st Overall
	November	21st	Brands Hatch – Indy	Production Car Race	Lotus	Esprit Turbo	OPW679W	8	1st	1st Overall
1983	February	6th	Brands Hatch – Indy	Chiltern Circle and Harrow Car Club Sprint	Volkswagen	Scirocco	Gli	TBC	N/A	1st in Class
	March	6th	Silverstone – Club	Uniroyal Tyres Production Sports & Saloons	Lotus	Esprit Turbo	OPW679W	11	2nd	3rd Overall
	March	13th	Thruxton	Monroe Shock Absorbers Production Saloon Car Championship	Ford	Capri 3.0	TBC	1	1st	1st Overall
	March	20th	Brands Hatch – Indy	Uniroyal Tyres Production Sports & Saloons	Ford	Capri 3.0	TBC	1	1st	2nd in Class
	March	27th	Donington Park	Monroe Shock Absorbers Production Saloon Car Championship	Ford	Capri 3.0	Eric Cook	1	1st	1st Overall
	April	1st	Snetterton	Uniroyal Tyres Production Sports & Saloons	Ford	Capri 3.0	Lyndon Martin Construction	1	1st in Class	1st in Class
	April	4th	Silverstone – Club	Uniroyal Tyres Production Sports & Saloons	Ford	Capri 3.0	Eric Cook	1	1st	1st in Class
	April	4th	Silverstone – Club	Hewgate Construction Group Trophy for Histoics	Jaguar	Lister	BHL130/YCD422	4	2nd	2nd in Class
	April	17th	Snetterton	Monroe Shock Absorbers Production Saloon Car Championship	Ford	Capri 3.0	Eric Cook	1	1st	1st Overall
	April	24th	Cadwell Park	Monroe Shock Absorbers Production Saloon Car Championship	Ford	Capri 3.0	TBC	1	1st	1st Overall
	May	14th	Oulton Park	Monroe Shock Absorbers Production Saloon Car Championship	Ford	Capri 3.0	TBC	1	2nd	2nd Overall
	May	22nd	Snetterton	Uniroyal Tyres Production Saloon	Ford	Capri 3.0	Lyndon Martin Construction	1	1st	2nd in Class
	May	22nd	Snetterton	Uniroyal Tyres Production Sports	Lotus	Esprit Turbo	OPW679W	11	1st	3rd Overall
	May	29th	Snetterton	Monroe Shock Absorbers Production Saloon Car Championship	Ford	Capri	Martin Mulchrone	1	2nd	2nd Overall
	May	30th	Silverstone – Club	Uniroyal Tyres Production Sports & Saloons	Lotus	Esprit Turbo	OPW679W	111	1st	Retired
	June	4th/5th	Snetterton	Willhire 24-hour race	Ford	Capri 2.8	Chelmsford Car Auctions	21	1st in Class	3rd in Class
	June	12th	Silverstone – International	Uniroyal Tyres Production Sports & Saloons	Lotus	Esprit Turbo	OPW679W	11	1st	Retired
	June	19th	Snetterton	Monroe Shock Absorbers Production Saloon Car Championship	Ford	Capri	TBC	1	3rd	3rd Overall
	June	25th	Silverstone – Club	St John H – 34th – Pace Petroleum Trophy Race	Jaguar	Lister	BHL130/YCD422	4	DNS	Retired
	June	26th	Brands Hatch – Indy	Uniroyal Tyres Production Sports & Saloons	Lotus	Esprit Turbo	OPW679W	11	1st	1st Overall
	July	10th	Brands Hatch – Indy	Uniroyal Tyres Production Saloon	Ford	Capri	TBC	1	5th in Class	5th in Class
	July	10th	Brands Hatch – Indy	Uniroyal Tyres Production Sports	Lotus	Esprit Turbo	OPW679W	11	1st	1st Overall
	July	14th/15th/16th	Silverstone – GP	Vandervell Trophy Car Race	Jaguar	Lister	BHL130/YCD422	4	9th	2nd in Class
	July	14th/15th/16th	Silverstone – GP	Atlantic Computers Historic GT Race	Lola	T222	HU7	41	4th in Class	Retired
	July	24th	Donington Park	Uniroyal Tyres Production Saloon	Ford	Capri 3.0	TBC	1	2nd	2nd Overall
	July	24th	Donington Park	Uniroyal Tyres Production Sports	Lotus	Esprit Turbo	OPW679W	11	1st	3rd Overall
	August	6th	Oulton Park	Uniroyal Tyres Production Sports	Lotus	Esprit Turbo	OPW679W	11	1st	1st Overall
	August	7th	Lydden Hill	Monroe Shock Absorbers Production Saloon Car Championship	Ford	Capri 3.0	TBC	1	TBC	3rd Overall
	August	20th	Oulton Park	Monroe Shock Absorbers Production Saloon Car Championship	Ford	Capri	TBC	1	2nd	3rd Overall
	August	28th	Snetterton	Monroe Shock Absorbers Production Saloon Car Championship	Ford	Capri 3.0	TBC	1	1st	1st Overall
	August	29th	Silverstone – Club	Uniroyal Tyres Production Saloon	Ford	Capri 3.0	TBC	1	5th in Class	3rd in Class
	September	4th	Silverstone – National	Monroe Shock Absorbers Production Saloon Car Championship	BMW	323i	Chelmsford Car Auctions	1	6th	6th Overall
	September	11th	Oulton Park	Monroe Shock Absorbers Production Saloon Car Championship	Ford	Capri 3.0	TBC	TBC	TBC	3rd Overall
	October	1st/2nd	Silverstone – International	Uniroyal Tyres Production Sports & Saloons	Ford	Capri 3.0	Chelmsford Car Auctions	1	1st in Class	4th in Class
	October	1st/2nd	Silverstone – International	Atlantic Computers Historic GP	Lola	T222	HU7	41	1st in Class	2nd Overall
	October	8th	Castle Combe	Uniroyal Tyres Production Sports & Saloons	Ford	Capri 3.0	Chelmsford Car Auctions	1	3rd in Class (6th)	Retired
	October	9th	Brands Hatch – Indy	Monroe Shock Absorbers Production Saloon Car Championship	Ford	Capri 3.0	TBC	1	2nd	1st Overall
	October	16th	Snetterton	Monroe Shock Absorbers Production Saloon Car Championship	Ford	Capri 3.0	TBC	1	1st	1st Overall
	October	23rd	Thruxton	Monroe Shock Absorbers Production Saloon Car Championship	Ford	Capri 3.0	TBC	1	1st	1st Overall
	October	30th	Snetterton	Atlantic Computers Trophy Race	Lola	T222	HU7	41	5th	Retired
	October	30th	Snetterton	Historic Sports Car Endurance Race	Jaguar	Lister	BHL130/YCD422	2	2nd	2nd Overall
	November	12th	Thruxton	City Desk BBC Grandstand Special Saloon Race	Vauxhall	Firenza DS	Baby Bertha	1	7th	2nd in Class
	November	13th	Brands Hatch – Indy	BARC BBC Grandstand Special Saloons	Vauxhall	Firenza DS	Baby Bertha	1	DNS	Demo
	November	13th	Brands Hatch – Indy	BARC BBC Grandstand Production Saloon	Ford	Capri 3.0	TBC	1	1st	1st Overall
	November	22nd	Thruxton	Monroe Shock Absorbers Production Saloon Car Championship	Ford	Capri	Chelmsford Car Auctions	TBC	1st	1st Overall
1984	February	5th	Brands Hatch – Indy	Chiltern Circle and Harrow Car Club Sprint	Ford	Capri 2.8	TBC	41	N/A	1st in Class
	March	4th	Silverstone – Club	Uniroyal Tyres Production Saloon	Opel	Monza	Yellow	1	2nd	3rd Overall
	March	10th	Silverstone – Club	Inter-Marque Race	MG	B GT	Colin Pearcy's Car	100	2nd	1st Overall
	March	11th	Thruxton	Monroe Shock Absorbers Production Saloon Car Championship	Opel	Monza	Yellow	1	1st	2nd Overall
	March	18th	Silverstone – Club	Monroe Shock Absorbers Production Saloon Car Championship	Opel	Monza	Yellow	1	2nd	2nd Overall
	March	31st	Oulton Park	Monroe Shock Absorbers Production Saloon Car Championship	Opel	Monza	Yellow	1	TBC	4th Overall
	April	7th/8th	Mondello Park	Production Saloon	Opel	Monza	Yellow	1	TBC	DNS
	April	7th/8th	Mondello Park	Production Saloon Handicap	Opel	Monza	Yellow	1	N/A	9th Overall
	April	15th	Snetterton	Monroe Shock Absorbers Production Saloon Car Championship	Opel	Monza	Yellow	1	2nd	1st Overall
	April	20th	Snetterton	Uniroyal Tyres Production Saloon	Opel	Monza	Yellow	1	4th	10th
	April	22nd/23rd	Brands Hatch – Indy	Racing for Britain Celebrity Escort Race	Ford	Escort XR3i	Celebrity Car	10	1st	1st Overall
	April	22nd/23rd	Brands Hatch – GP	Uniroyal Tyres Production Saloon	Opel	Monza	Yellow	1	5th	6th Overall
	April	29th	Cadwell Park	Monroe Shock Absorbers Production Saloon Car Championship	Opel	Monza	Yellow	1	1st	1st Overall
	May	6th	Brands Hatch – Indy	Uniroyal Tyres Production Saloon	Opel	Monza	Yellow	1	6th	6th Overall
	May	20th	Donington Park	Monroe Shock Absorbers Production Saloon Car Championship	Opel	Monza	Yellow	1	2nd	2nd Overall
	May	27th	Snetterton	Monroe Shock Absorbers Production Saloon Car Championship	Opel	Monza	Yellow	1	TBC	2nd Overall
	May	28th	Silverstone – Club	Uniroyal Tyres Production Saloon	Opel	Monza	Yellow	1	2nd	3rd Overall
	June	2nd/3rd	Snetterton	Willhire 24-hour race	Opel	Monza	Yellow	1	8th	Retired
	June	17th	Snetterton	Wendy Wools Special Saloon Championship	Opel	Monza	Yellow	1	6th	3rd in Class
	June/July	30th/1st	Snetterton	Trimoco British Saloon Car Championship	TBC	TBC	TBC	TBC	TBC	DNS

Year	Month	Date	Circuit	Race	Car	Spec	Details	No.	Qualifying	Result
1984	July	1st	Brands Hatch – Indy	Uniroyal Tyres Production Saloon	Opel	Monza	Yellow	1	7th	6th Overall
	July	1st	Brands Hatch – Indy	Metro Breaker Modified Saloon Car	TBC	TBC	TBC	29	11th	TBC
	July	8th	Donington Park	Uniroyal Tyres Production Saloon	Opel	Monza	Yellow	TBC	TBC	TBC
	August	15th	Braefield	Acorn Computer Hot Rod Supreme Championship	Ford	Escort	Norman Abbott Rentarod	TBC	TBC	TBC
1986	February	9th	Brands Hatch – Indy	Chiltern Circle and Harrow Car Club Sprint	Fiat	Strada Arbarth 2.0	130T C29FBH	TBC	N/A	1st in Class
	March	9th	Thruxton	Monroe Shock Absorbers Production Saloon Car Championship	Opel	Monza	Teroson	21	1st	1st in Class
	March	16th	Silverstone – Club	Monroe Shock Absorbers Production Saloon Car Championship	Opel	Monza	Teroson	21	3rd in Class	2nd in Class
	March	23rd	Cadwell Park	Monroe Shock Absorbers Production Saloon Car Championship	Opel	Monza	Teroson	21	1st in Class	2nd in Class
	March	30th/31st	Brands Hatch – GP	Celebrity Race	Ford	Escort XR3i	TBC	10	TBC	1st Overall
	March	30th/31st	Brands Hatch – GP	Uniroyal Tyres Production Saloon	Opel	Monza	Teroson	21	5th in Class	2nd in Class
	April	5th/6th	Donington Park	The Donington 500: FIA European Touring Car Championship	Toyota	Corolla GT16	Geoff Kimber-Smith	105	31st	30th Overall
	April	20th	Thruxton	Monroe Shock Absorbers Production Saloon Car Championship	Opel	Monza	Teroson	21	1st in Class	DNS
	May	5th	Castle Combe	Uniroyal Tyres Production Saloon	Opel	Monza	Teroson	21	5th	4th in Class
	May	11th	Mallory Park	Uniroyal Tyres Production Saloon	Opel	Monza	Teroson	21	7th	3rd Overall
	May	18th	Donington Park	Monroe Shock Absorbers Production Saloon Car Championship	Opel	Monza	Teroson	21	4th in Class	3rd in Class
	May	25th	Snetterton	Monroe Shock Absorbers Production Saloon Car Championship	Opel	Monza	Teroson	21	4th in Class	2nd in Class
	May	26th	Silverstone – National	GM Dealers Trophy Meeting	Opel	Monza	Teroson	21	3rd in Class	4th in Class
	June	1st	Mallory Park	Monroe Shock Absorbers Production Saloon Car Championship	Opel	Monza	Teroson	21	1st	3rd in Class
	June	8th	Silverstone – International	Uniroyal Tyres Production Saloon	Opel	Monza	Teroson	21	3rd in Class	2nd in Class
	June	14th/15th	Snetterton	Willhire 24-hour race	Opel	Monza	Teroson	21	13th	33rd (Retired)
	June	21st	Silverstone – Club	SKF Components Systems race for HSCC Historic Car Championship	Aston	DB4	RB/250/1 & RB6/300/1	TBC	TBC	4th Overall
	June	28th	Oulton Park	Monroe Shock Absorbers Production Saloon Car Championship	Opel	Monza	Teroson	21	TBC	Retired
	July	6th	Brands Hatch – Indy	Uniroyal Tyres Production Saloon	Ford	Escort RS Turbo	B276XVX	21	2nd in Class	5th in Class
	July	20th	Silverstone or Donington – GP	Uniroyal Tyres Production Saloon	Ford	Escort RS Turbo	B276XVX	21	13th in Class	3rd in Class
	August	3rd	Cadwell Park	Uniroyal Tyres Production Saloon	Ford	Escort RS Turbo	B276XVX	21	2nd in Class	3rd in Class
	August	9th	Oulton Park	Classic Saloon Car Club Pre '65 Saloon Championship	Ford	Lotus Cortina	TBC	200	2nd	1st Overall
	August	9th	Oulton Park	Monroe Shock Absorbers Production Saloon Car Championship	Ford	Escort RS Turbo	B276XVX	21	4th	2nd in Class
	August	16th	Donington Park or Oulton Park	Uniroyal Tyres Production Saloon	Ford	Escort RS Turbo	B276XVX	21	1st in Class	Retired
	August	24th	Snetterton	Monroe Shock Absorbers Production Saloon Car Championship	Ford	Escort RS Turbo	B276XVX	21	1st in Class	13th in Class
	August	25th	Castle Combe	Thundersaloon Championship – Shell Oils	Vauxhall	Chevette	Mike Smith	52	2nd in Class	6th in Class
	August	31st	Brands Hatch – Indy	Monroe Shock Absorbers Production Saloon Car Championship	Ford	Escort RS Turbo	B276XVX	21	4th in Class	3rd in Class
	September	6th/7th	Silverstone – International	Uniroyal Tyres Production Saloon	Ford	Escort RS Turbo	B276XVX	21	2nd in Class	2nd in Class
	September	6th/7th	Silverstone – International	RAC Tourist Trophy – The Istel	Toyota	Corolla GT16	Geoff Kimber-Smith	105	3rd in Class	Retired
	September	13th/14th	Brands Hatch – GP	Uniroyal Tyres Production Saloon	Ford	Escort RS Turbo	B276XVX	21	6th in Class	4th in Class
	September	21st	Oulton Park	Monroe Shock Absorbers Production Saloon Car Championship	Ford	Escort RS Turbo	B276XVX	21	1st in Class	1st in Class
	September	28th	Snetterton	HSCC John Scott Insurance Endurance Race	Sunbeam	Tiger	NME883E	14	9th	DNS
	September	28th	Snetterton	HSCC John Scott Insurance Endurance Race	MG	B	Colin Pearcy's Car	TBC	TBC	TBC
	October	11th/12th	Donington Park	Motor Show 4-hour Production Saloon Car	Mitsubishi	Colt Starion	Graham Scarborough	1	1st	Retired
	October	19th	Snetterton	Monroe Shock Absorbers Production Saloon Car Championship	Ford	Escort RS Turbo	B276XVX	21	1st in Class	Retired
1987	February	15th	Brands Hatch – Club	Brands Hatch Racing Club Kentagon Sprint	MG	B	189DMO	TBC	N/A	1st in Class
	February	15th	Brands Hatch – Club	Brands Hatch Racing Club Kentagon Sprint	Ford	Escort RS Turbo	B276XVX	TBC	N/A	1st in Class
	March	22nd	Silverstone – TBC	BRDC	MG	B	189DMO	TBC	N/A	5th Overall
	March	22nd	Silverstone – Club	Saab Turbo Mobil Challenge	Saab	900 Turbo	TBC	TBC	N/A	5th Overall
	March	29th	Brands Hatch – Club	Thundersaloon Championship – Shell Oils	Ford	Escort Cosworth	Joe Ward	7	TBC	TBC
	April	5th	Snetterton	Dutton Forshaw MG Car Club BCV8 Championship	MG	B	TBC	55	2nd	Retired
	April	20th	Thruxton	Saab Turbo Mobil Challenge	Saab	900 Turbo	TBC	TBC	DNS	Disqualified
	May	3rd	Brands Hatch – Indy	Thoroughbred Sports Car Championship	Aston	DB4	455YYC (919R)	74	1st	Retired
	May	17th	Brands Hatch – Indy	Saab Turbo Challenge	Saab	900 Turbo	TBC	3	9th	6th Overall
	May	25th	Silverstone – Club	Thoroughbred Sports Car Championship	Aston	DB4	455YYC (919R)	74	1st in Class	1st Overall
	May	31st	Mallory Park	Thoroughbred Sports Car Championship – Jaguar Owners Club	Aston	DB4	455YYC (919R)	74	TBC	1st Overall
	June	6th/7th	Brands Hatch – GP	Classic Sportscar and Thoroughbred Sports Car Championship	Aston	DB4	455YYC (919R)	74	1st in Class	Retired
	June	6th/7th	Brands Hatch – GP	The International FISA Cup	MG	B 1840/1963	TBC	40	9th in Class	Retired
	June	12th/13th/14th	Rally	25th Anniversary Cavalino International	Ferrari	250 GTO	TBC	TBC	TBC	N/A
	June	20th	Silverstone – Club	HSCC Guildford Estates Classic Sports Car	MG	B 1840/1963	TBC	70	TBC	TBC
	June	20th	Silverstone – Club	St John H – 38th – SKF Materials Race for the Thoroughbred Sports	Aston	DB4	455YYC (919R)	74	TBC	1st Overall
	June	28th	Snetterton	Thundersaloon Championship – Shell Oils	Ford	Sierra Cosworth	Tony Strawson	TBC	TBC	TBC
	July	26th	Silverstone – TBC	Thundersaloon Championship – Shell Oils	Ford	Sierra Cosworth	Tony Strawson	18	TBC	TBC
	August	9th	Brands Hatch – TBC	Thundersaloon Championship – Shell Oils	Ford	Sierra Cosworth	Tony Strawson	TBC	TBC	Retired
	August	22nd	Oulton Park	Dunlop British Touring Car Championship	Toyota	Corolla GT16	Geoff Kimber-Smith	77	12th	3rd in Class
	August	31st	Silverstone – Club	Dutton Forshaw MG Car Club BCV8 Championship	MG	B 1840	TBC	55	4th in Class	3rd in Class
	September	20th	Mallory Park	Dutton Forshaw MG Car Club BCV8 Championship	MG	B	TBC	55	3rd in Class	1st in Class
	September	27th	Snetterton	HSCC Guildford Estates Classic Sports Car	MG	B	TBC	40	3rd in Class	4th in Class
	September	27th	Snetterton	HSCC Endurance Race	MG	B	TBC	40	11th	5th in Class
	October	17th	Donington Park	Arquati Production Saloon 4 hour Race	Ford	Sierra Cosworth	Jerry Mahoney	18	4th	Retired
	October	25th	Snetterton	Dutton Forshaw MG Car Club BCV8 Championship	MG	B 1840	TBC	55	TBC	2nd Overall
	TBC	TBC	Snetterton	TBC	TBC	TBC	TBC	TBC	TBC	TBC
	TBC	TBC	Donington Park	TBC	TVR	420 SEAC	TBC	TBC	TBC	TBC
	TBC	TBC	Donington Park	TBC	TVR	420 SEAC	TBC	TBC	TBC	TBC
1988	March	27th	Brands Hatch – Indy	Thundersaloon Championship – Norcross	Rover	Vitesse	TBC	10	6th in Class	7th in Class
	March	27th	Brands Hatch – Indy	Thundersaloon Championship – Norcross	Vauxhall	Firenza DS	Transpeed	100	2nd in Class	2nd in Class
	April	1st	Snetterton	Thundersaloon Championship – Norcross	Rover	Vitesse	TBC	10	5th in Class	3rd in Class
	April	1st	Snetterton	Thundersaloon Championship – Norcross	Vauxhall	Firenza DS	Transpeed	100	2nd in Class	2nd in Class
	May	1st	Brands Hatch – Indy	MIBA FIA European Championship	Aston	DB4	RB/250/1 & RB6/300/1	55	1st in Class	1st in Class
	May	21st	Oulton Park	Uniroyal Tyres Production Saloon	Suzuki	Swift Gti	TBC	117	4th in Class	Retired
	May	22nd	Brands Hatch – Indy	Saab Turbo Challenge	Saab	900 Turbo	Jonathan Collett-Jobey	16	14th	4th in Class
	May	28th	Silverstone – National	Wilky MG Car Club BCV8 Championship	MG	B	TBC	54	TBC	2nd Overall
	May	30th	Thruxton	Saab Turbo Challenge	Saab	900 Turbo	Jonathan Collett-Jobey	16	5th	Retired
	June	4th/5th	Brands Hatch – GP	AMOC/HSCC pre-60 Historic Car Championship	Aston	DBR4	RB/250/1 & RB6/300/1	55	1st	1st Overall
	June	4th/5th	Brands Hatch – GP	HSCC Classic Championship	MG	B	TBC	52	TBC	1st in Class
	June	4th/5th	Brands Hatch – GP	The Rolfe Judd Tophy Race – FISA Cup for Historic GT Cars	MG	B	Colin Pearcy's Car	44	DNQ	1st in Class
	June	4th/5th	Brands Hatch – TBC	HSCC International Historic Superprix	TBC	TBC	TBC	TBC	TBC	1st in Class
	June	4th/5th	Brands Hatch – TBC	HSCC International Historic SuperPrix	TBC	TBC	TBC	TBC	TBC	Winner
	June	4th/5th	Brands Hatch – TBC	HSCC International Historic SuperPrix	TBC	TBC	TBC	TBC	TBC	1st in Class
	June	18th	Silverstone – Club	St John H – 39th – HSCC Classic Championship	MG	B 1950	189DMO	52	TBC	1st in class
	June	18th	Silverstone – Club	St John H – 39th – SKF Tollo for the AMOC/HSCC Pre-60 Historics	Aston	DBR4	RB/250/1 & RB6/300/1	55	TBC	3rd Overall

Year	Month	Date	Circuit	Race	Car	Spec	Details	No.	Qualifying	Result
1988	June	25th	Brands Hatch – Indy	Uniroyal P100 Challenge	Ford	P100	TBC	10	2nd	TBC
	June	26th	Brands Hatch – Indy	British Truck Grand Prix	TBC	TBC	TBC	TBC	TBC	TBC
	June	26th	Brands Hatch – Indy	British Truck Grand Prix	TBC	TBC	TBC	TBC	TBC	TBC
	July	3rd	Snetterton	BRSCC Dunlop Historic Racing Saloons	Ford	Anglia	TBC	47	8th	1st Overall
	July	17th	Donington Park	HSCC Classic Championship	MG	C	TBC	52	TBC	1st in Class
	July	30th/31st	Snetterton	Saab Turbo Challenge	Saab	900 Turbo	Jonathan Collett-Jobey	16	TBC	3rd in Class
	September	18th	Snetterton	Saab Turbo Challenge	Saab	900 Turbo	Jonathan Collett-Jobey	16	3rd	1st Overall
	September	24th	Silverstone – Club	HSCC Classic Championship	MG	C GTS	TBC	65	TBC	Race Cancelled
	October	8th	Thruxton	Saab Turbo Challenge	Saab	900 Turbo	Jonathan Collett-Jobey	16	1st	2nd Overall
	October	9th	Cadwell Park	Uniroyal P100 Challenge	Ford	P100	TBC	6	7th	2nd Overall
	October	16th	Snetterton	HSCC Endurance Race	MG	B	TBC	TBC	TBC	1st in Class
1989	April	30th	Brands Hatch – Indy	AMOC Intermarque Championship – Gordon Russell	Aston	V8 5340	Silver Dream 10330	96	1st	1st Overall
	April	30th	Brands Hatch – Indy	Autoglym Post-War Aston Martin Race	Aston	V8 5340	Silver Dream 10330	96	1st	DNS
	May	1st	Oulton Park	Thundersaloon Championship – Johnson Tiles	Opel	Manta Pontiac	Stars & Stripes	11	3rd	2nd Overall
	May	6th/7th	Donington Park	Esso British Touring Car Championship – One Hour Race	BMW	M3	John Llewellyn	44	5th in Class	2nd in Class
	May	6th/7th	Donington Park	TVR Tuscan Challenge	TVR	Tuscan 4500	David Gerald	55	21st	Retired
	May	14th	Mallory Park	AMOC Intermarque Championship – Gordon Russell	Aston	V8 5340	Silver Dream 10330	46	1st	1st Overall
	May	19th/20th/21st	Zandvort	Thundersaloon Championship – Johnson Tiles	Opel	Manta Pontiac	Stars & Stripes	11	3rd	15th Overall
	May	19th/20th/21st	Zandvort	Thundersaloon Championship – Johnson Tiles	Opel	Manta Pontiac	Stars & Stripes	11	5th	16th Overall
	May	29th	Silverstone – National	AMOC Intermarque Championship – Gordon Russell	Aston	V8 5340	Silver Dream 10330	96	1st	1st Overall
	May	29th	Castle Combe	TVR Tuscan Challenge	TVR	Tuscan 4500	David Gerald	TBC	DNQ	DNQ
	June	3rd/4th	Brands Hatch – GP	FIA Cup for Historical Grand Touring Cars – Rolfe Judd Trophy	MG	B	665FXF	49	8th in Class	5th in Class
	June	11th	Brands Hatch – Indy	TVR Tuscan Challenge	TVR	Tuscan 4500	David Gerald	55	3rd	2nd Overall
	June	16th/17th/18th	Snetterton	Willhire 24-hour race	Ford	Sierra Cosworth	Jess Yates	10	8th in Class	Retired
	June	25th	Mallory Park	TVR Tuscan Challenge	TVR	Tuscan 4500	David Gerald	55	5th	2nd Overall
	July	1st	Castle Combe	AMOC Intermarque Championship – Gordon Russell	Aston	V8	Silver Dream 10330	96	1st	1st Overall
	July	9th	Donington Park	TVR Tuscan Challenge	TVR	Tuscan 4500	David Gerald	55	3rd	3rd Overall
	July	9th	Donington Park	Thundersaloon Championship – Johnson Tiles	Opel	Manta Pontiac	Stars & Stripes	TBC	TBC	TBC
	July	15th	Pembrey	AMOC Intermarque Championship – Gordon Russell	Aston	V8	Silver Dream 10330	96	1st	1st Overall
	July	15th	Pembrey	Jaguar Car Club – Aston Martin vs Jaguars	Aston	V8	Silver Dream 10330	96	1st	1st Overall
	July	TBC	Cadwell Park	AMOC Intermarque Championship – Gordon Russell	Aston	TBC	TBC	TBC	TBC	1st in Class
	July	30th	Silverstone – National	TVR Tuscan Challenge	TVR	Tuscan 4500	David Gerald	55	1st	4th Overall
	August	19th	Oulton Park	TVR Tuscan Challenge	TVR	Tuscan 4500	David Gerald	55	3rd	2nd Overall
	August	28th	Castle Combe	TVR Tuscan Challenge	TVR	Tuscan 4500	David Gerald	55	8th	6th Overall
	September	10th	Brands Hatch – GP	TVR Tuscan Challenge	TVR	Tuscan 4500	David Gerald	55	8th	1st Overall
	September	13th	Pembrey	AMOC Intermarque Championship – Gordon Russell	Aston	V8	Silver Dream 10330	96	1st	1st Overall
	September	13th	Pembrey	Jaguar Car Club – Aston Martin vs Jaguars	Aston	V8	Silver Dream 10330	96	1st	1st Overall
	September	30th	Snetterton	TVR Tuscan Challenge	TVR	Tuscan 4500	David Gerald	55	1st	1st Overall
	October	1st	Mallory Park	Dunlop Historic Racing Saloon Cars	Ford	Anglia	TBC	38	1st	2nd in Class
	October	8th	Cadwell Park	TVR Tuscan Challenge	TVR	Tuscan 4500	David Gerald	55	TBC	2nd Overall
	October	15th	Snetterton	Dunlop Historic Racing Saloon Cars	Ford	Anglia	TBC	38	1st	2nd Overall
	October	21st	Oulton Park	TVR Tuscan Challenge	TVR	Tuscan 4500	David Gerald	55	3rd	3rd Overall
	October	22nd	Snetterton	HSCC Cressy Endurance Race	MG	B	TBC	88	3rd in Class	3rd in Class
1990	April	12th/13th	Oulton Park	TVR Tuscan Challenge	TVR	Tuscan 4500	David Gerald	55	TBC	Retired
	April	21st	Silverstone – TBC	Vintage Sports Car Club	BRM	F1 H16	TBC	N/A	N/A	Demo
	April	28th/29th	Donington Park	TVR Tuscan Challenge	TVR	Tuscan 4500	David Gerald	55	2nd	2nd Overall
	May	6th	Brands Hatch – Indy	AMOC Intermarque Championship – Proteus Petroleum	Aston	V8	Silver Dream 10330	55	18th	2nd Overall
	May	6th	Brands Hatch – Indy	SKF Engineering Production Historic Car Championship	Aston	DBR4	RB/250/1 & RB6/300/1	55	1st	1st Overall
	May	28th	Castle Combe	TVR Tuscan Challenge	TVR	Tuscan 4500	David Gerald	55	4th	4th Overall
	June	2nd/3rd	Brands Hatch – Indy	40th Anniversary Celebrity Race	Ford	Fiesta	Celebrity Car	5	1st	1st Overall
	June	10th	Brands Hatch – TBC	TVR Tuscan Challenge	TVR	Tuscan 4500	David Gerald	55	TBC	Retired
	June	23rd	Silverstone – National	St John H – 41st – Proteus Petroleum AMOC Intermarque	Aston	V8	Silver Dream 10330	55	3rd	DNS
	June	23rd	Silverstone – National	St John H – 41st – SKF Engineering Historic Car Championship	Aston	DBR4	RB/250/1 & RB6/300/1	55	2nd	Winner
	June	22nd/23rd/24th	Snetterton	Esso Willhire 24-Hours	Ford	Sierra Cosworth	TBC	10	TBC	5th in Class
	June	22nd/23rd/24th	Snetterton	TVR Tuscan Challenge	TVR	Tuscan 4500	David Gerald	55	TBC	Retired
	July	8th	Donington Park	TVR Tuscan Challenge	TVR	Tuscan 4500	David Gerald	55	TBC	Retired
	July	8th	Pembrey	Classic Cars Magazine Trophy Race	TVR	Griffith 4727	Ronnie Farmer	43	1st	Retired
	July	21st/22nd	Donington Park	HSCC Donington "100" Endurance Race	TVR	Griffith 4727	Ronnie Farmer	11	TBC	10th in Class
	July	28th/29th	Silverstone – International	AMOC Intermarque Championship – Proteus Petroleum	Aston	V8	Silver Dream 10330	55	1st	5th Overall
	August	4th	Castle Combe	AMOC Intermarque Championship – Proteus Petroleum	Aston	V8 5340	Silver Dream 10330	55	1st	1st Overall
	August	12th	Cadwell Park	TVR Tuscan Challenge	TVR	Tuscan 4500	David Gerald	55	TBC	Retired
	August	18th/19th	Brands Hatch – GP	AMOC Intermarque Championship – Proteus Petroleum	Aston	V8 5340	Silver Dream 10330	55	TBC	1st in Class
	September	9th	Brands Hatch – TBC	TVR Tuscan Challenge	TVR	Tuscan 4500	David Gerald	55	TBC	Retired
	September	15th	Oulton Park	AMOC Intermarque Championship – Proteus Petroleum	Aston	V8	Silver Dream 10330	55	1st	2nd Overall
	September	15th	Oulton Park	Coys of Kensington Historic Car	Aston	DBR4	RB/250/1 & RB6/300/1	55	2nd	1st Overall
	September	29th/30th	Silverstone – Club	TVR Tuscan Challenge	TVR	Tuscan 4500	David Gerald	55	TBC	Retired
	October	6th/7th	Silverstone – National	AMOC Intermarque Championship – Proteus Petroleum	Aston	V8	Silver Dream 10330	55	1st	1st Overall
	October	13th/14th	Donington Park	TVR Tuscan Challenge	TVR	Tuscan 4500	Celebrity Car	1	4th	1st Overall
	October	20th	Oulton Park	TVR Tuscan Challenge	TVR	Tuscan 4500	TBC	TBC	TBC	Retired
	October	28th	Snetterton	HSCC 50 Lap Edurance Race	TVR	Griffith 4727	Ronnie Farmer	2	1st	1st Overall
1991	February	TBC	Brands Hatch – Indy	Chiltern Circle and Harrow Car Club Sprint	TBC	TBC	TBC	TBC	TBC	TBC
	March/April	31st /1st	Brands Hatch – Indy	TVR Tuscan Challenge	TVR	Tuscan 4500	Celebrity Car	1	4th	2nd Overall
	April	28th	Donington Park	TVR Tuscan Challenge	TVR	Tuscan 4500	Celebrity Car	1	1st	Retired
	May	5th	Brands Hatch – Indy	AMOC Intermarque Championship	Aston	V8 5340	Silver Dream 10330	55	1st	1st Overall
	May	6th	Snetterton	TVR Tuscan Challenge	TVR	Tuscan 4500	Martin Crass	21	1st	1st Overall
	May	19th	Mallory Park	Sakura Multisports Championship	Van Diemen	Multisport	TBC	8	4th	4th Overall
	May	27th	Mallory Park	TVR Tuscan Challenge	TVR	Tuscan 4500	Martin Crass	21	3rd	1st Overall
	May	27th	Mallory Park	TVR Tuscan Challenge	TVR	Tuscan 4500	Martin Crass	21	3rd	1st Overall
	June	1st/2nd	Magny Cours	Super GTS	Aston	DB5	358DLW	1	1st	1st Overall
	June	9th	Brands Hatch – GP	BRSCC/Fast Car Thundersaloon Championship	Vauxhall	Firenza DS	Transpeed	54	10th in Class	7th in Class
	June	14th/15th/16th	Snetterton	TVR Tuscan Challenge	TVR	Tuscan 4500	Martin Crass	21	4th	Retired
	June	22nd	Silverstone – Club	St John H – 42nd – SKF Limited Intermarque	Aston	V8 5340	Silver Dream 10330	55	1st	2nd Overall
	June	23rd	Donington Park	TVR Tuscan Challenge	TVR	Tuscan 4500	Martin Crass	21	1st	Retired
	June	27th/28th	Brands Hatch – TBC	TVR Tuscan Challenge	TVR	Tuscan 4500	Martin Crass	21	TBC	1st Overall
	June	27th/28th	Brands Hatch – TBC	TVR Tuscan Challenge	TVR	Tuscan 4500	Martin Crass	21	TBC	1st Overall
	July	6th/7th	Donington Park	TVR Tuscan Challenge	TVR	Tuscan 4500	Martin Crass	21	1st	1st Overall
	July	27th/28th	Brands Hatch – Indy	TVR Tuscan Challenge	TVR	Tuscan 4500	Martin Crass	21	1st	1st Overall
	July	27th/28th	Brands Hatch – Indy	Caterham Vauxhall Challenge	Caterham	Vauxhall	Celebrity Car	15	11th	TBC

Year	Month	Date	Circuit	Race	Car	Spec	Details	No.	Qualifying	Result
1991	August	3rd	Castle Combe	Caterham Vauxhall Challenge	Caterham	Vauxhall	Celebrity Car	27	8th	3rd Overall
	August	11th	Snetterton	Firestone Productionuction Car	Vauxhall	Astra GTE	Tony Lanfranchi	70	3rd in Class	5th in Class
	August	16th/17th/18th	Brands Hatch — GP	AMOC Intermarque Championship	Aston	V8 5340	Silver Dream 10330	55	2nd	DNS
	August	26th	Castle Combe	TVR Tuscan Challenge	TVR	Tuscan 4500	Martin Crass	21	1st	1st Overall
	September	1st	Cadwell Park	Classic Cars Magazine Trophy Race — Jaguar Car Club	Caterham	Vauxhall	TBC	3	1st	1st Overall
	September	7th	Mondello Park	TVR Tuscan Challenge	TVR	Tuscan 4500	Martin Crass	21	1st	1st Overall
	September	8th	Mondello Park	TVR Tuscan Challenge	TVR	Tuscan 4500	Martin Crass	21	1st	1st Overall
	September	14th	Oulton Park	AMOC Intermarque Championship	Aston	V8	TBC	TBC	TBC	TBC
	September	22nd	Silverstone — Club	TVR Tuscan Challenge	TVR	Tuscan 4500	Martin Crass	21	1st	1st Overall
	October	6th	Cadwell Park	TVR Tuscan Challenge	TVR	Tuscan 4500	Martin Crass	21	4th	2nd Overall
	October	12th	Donington Park	Porsche 1 Hour Race	Porsche	Carrera	Richard Cabburn	94	10th in Class	7th in Class
	October	19th	Oulton Park	TVR Tuscan Challenge	TVR	Tuscan 4500	Martin Crass	21	2nd	Retired
	October	27th	Snetterton	The Cressy Sports Car Endurance Race	TVR	Griffith 4727	Yellow	69	3rd in Class	1st in Class
1992	May	3rd	Brands Hatch — Indy	Frank Short Sportswear Modified Porsche	Porsche	RSR	Richard Cabburn	34	DNS	DNS
	May	4th	Thruxton	TVR Tuscan Challenge — Mobil	TVR	Tuscan 4500	Martin Crass	21	1st	1st Overall
	June	7th	Brands Hatch — TBC	TVR Tuscan Challenge — Mobil	TVR	Tuscan 4500	TBC	TBC	TBC	3rd Overall
	June	14th	Silverstone — Club	St John H — 43rd — AMOC Intermarque Championship	Aston	V8 5340	TBC	55	TBC	TBC
	June	14th	Silverstone — Club	St John H — 43rd — PAS Post War Aston Martin Race	Aston	DBSV8	DRY840K	55	TBC	1st in Class
	July	25th/26th	Silverstone — GP	BRDC 60s GT Race	Aston	Zagato	TBC	3	TBC	TBC
	July	25th/26th	Silverstone — GP	BRDC 60s GT Race	Jaguar	E-Type	TBC	9	TBC	4th Overall
	August	31st	Castle Combe	BRDC/BRSCC Saloon Car Championship	Ford	Sapphire Cosworth	Mike McGoun	12	4th	4th Overall
	August	31st	Castle Combe	TVR Tuscan Challenge — Mobil	TVR	Tuscan 4500	Graham Nash	29	DNS	5th Overall
	September	12th/13th	Silverstone — National	BRDC/BRSCC Saloon Car Championship Part 1	Ford	Sapphire Cosworth	Mike McGoun	11	5th	TBC
	September	12th/13th	Silverstone — National	BRDC/BRSCC Saloon Car Championship Part 2	Ford	Sapphire Cosworth	Mike McGoun	11	TBC	TBC
	September	12th/13th	Silverstone — National	TVR Tuscan Challenge — Mobil	TVR	Tuscan 4500	TBC	TBC	TBC	TBC
	September	19th	Oulton Park	AMOC Intermarque Championship	Aston	V8	V8R02 10526	TBC	TBC	Retired
	November	14th	Snetterton	750 Motor Club Holland Birkett Six-Hour Relay Race	Caterham	Vauxhall	TBC	32	TBC	3rd Overall
	December	9th	Silverstone — National	BRDC/BRSCC Saloon Car Championship	Ford	Sapphire Cosworth	Mike McGoun	11	1st	TBC
	TBC	TBC	Oulton Park	TVR Tuscan Challenge — Mobil	TVR	Tuscan 4500	TBC	21	DNS	6th Overall
	TBC	TBC	Cadwell Park	TVR Tuscan Challenge — Mobil	TVR	Tuscan 4500	TBC	TBC	3rd	2nd Overall
	TBC	TBC	Mallory Park	BRDC/BRSCC Saloon Car Championship	Ford	Sapphire Cosworth	Mike McGoun	12	1st	Retired
1993	April	24th/25th	Donington Park	National Saloon Car Cup One-Hour Race	Vauxhall	Astra GTE	Tony Lanfranchi	22	2nd in Class	1st in Class
	May	2nd	Brands Hatch — Indy	AMOC Intermarque Championship — MBIA	Aston	V8 5340	V8R02 10526	55	1st	1st Overall
	May	8th/9th	Silverstone — GP	BRDC National Sports GT Challenge	Aston	V8 5340	V8R02 10526	69	TBC	2nd in Class
	June	5th/6th	Brands Hatch — TBC	The Seaboard Donald Healey Memorial Trophy	Austin	Healey 3000	DD300	69	2nd	Winner
	June	5th/6th	Brands Hatch — TBC	HSCC Donald Healy	TBC	TBC	TBC	69	TBC	1st in Class
	June	13th	Silverstone — National	St John H — 44th — AMOC Intermarque Championship	Aston	V8 5340	V8R02 10526	55	TBC	1st Overall
	July	18th	Brands Hatch — Indy	AMOC Intermarque Championship	Aston	V8	V8R02 10526	55	1st	1st Overall
	July	24th/25th	Silverstone — GP	Coys of Kensington	Austin	Healey 3000	DD300	21	TBC	TBC
	July	24th/25th	Silverstone — GP	Coys of Kensington	Austin	Healey 3000	DD300	21	TBC	TBC
	August	22nd	Silverstone — Club	BRDC National Sports GT Challenge	Aston	V8 5340	V8R02 10526	69	TBC	3rd Overall
	September	11th/12th	Brands Hatch — GP	BRDC National Sports GT Challenge	Aston	V8 5340	V8R02 10526	69	TBC	1st Overall
	September	18th	Oulton Park	AMOC Intermarque Championship	Aston	V8	V8R02 10526	TBC	TBC	1st Overall
	October	9th	Oulton Park	Classic Saloon Car Club Pre '83 Group One	Rover	Vitesse	TWR005	7	TBC	TBC
1994	May	1st	Brands Hatch — Indy	AMOC Intermarque Championship	Aston	V8	V8R02 10526	55	1st	1st Overall
	May	1st	Brands Hatch — Indy	AMOC Crandchester Post War Aston Martin Race	Aston	V8	V8R02 10526	55	1st	1st Overall
	May	1st	Brands Hatch — Indy	AMOC Thoroughbred Sportscars	Aston	DB4	991YBF	53	2nd	TBC
	May	6th	Brands Hatch — GP	HARA Trans AM Challenge Race	Chevrolet	Corvette	TBC	3	3rd	2nd Overall
	May	21st	Silverstone — National	Goldsmith & Young Thoroughbred Sports Car	Aston	DB4	TBC	93	1st	1st Overall
	May	30th	Thruxton	TVR Tuscan Challenge	TVR	Tuscan 4500	Giles Cooper	69	8th	9th Overall
	June	4th/5th	Brands Hatch — GP	HARA Trans AM Challenge Race	Chevrolet	Corvette	7.2 Hank Danby	3	TBC	2nd Overall
	June	12th	Silverstone — Club	St John H — 45th — AMOC Intermarque Race	Aston	V8 5340	V8R02 10526	55	1st	1st Overall
	June	12th	Silverstone — Club	St John H — 45th — Grantchester Post War	Aston	DB4 Vantage 3670	CJB949B	55	1st in Class	1st in Class
	June	12th	Silverstone — Club	St John H — 45th — Feltham Aston Martin & Pre-War Sports	Aston	DB3S	OKE472	20	1st	1st Overall
	June	26th	Thruxton	AMOC Intermarque Championship	Aston	V8 5340	V8R02 10526	55	1st	1st Overall
	July	3rd	Donington Park — Short	AMOC Intermarque Championship	Aston	V8 5340	V8R02 10526	55	1st	1st Overall
	July	3rd	Donington Park — Short	Goldsmith & Young Thoroughbred Sports Car	Aston	DB4	DB4/675/R 788CUV 197	93	TBC	TBC
	July	17th	Cadwell Park	TVR Tuscan Challenge	TVR	Tuscan 4500	Giles Cooper	69	4th	Retired
	July	30th	Oulton Park	TVR Tuscan Challenge	TVR	Tuscan 4500	Giles Cooper	69	5th	Retired
	August	6th/7th	Snetterton	TVR Tuscan Challenge	TVR	Tuscan 4500	Giles Cooper	69	4th	Retired
	August	7th	Mallory Park	Goldsmith & Young Thoroughbred Sports Car	Aston	DB4	TBC	93	TBC	7th in Class
	August	29th	Silverstone — Club	TVR Tuscan Challenge	TVR	Tuscan 4500	Giles Cooper	69	8th	Retired
	September	10th/11th	Snetterton	TVR Tuscan Challenge	TVR	Tuscan 4500	Giles Cooper	69	TBC	Retired
	September	10th/11th	Snetterton	TVR Tuscan Challenge	TVR	Tuscan 4500	Giles Cooper	69	18th	Retired
	September	17th	Oulton Park	AMOC Intermarque Championship	Aston	DB4	DB4/675/R 788CUV 197	93	5th in Class	4th in Class
	September	17th	Oulton Park	Goldsmith & Young Thoroughbred Sports Car	Aston	DB4	DB4/675/R 788CUV 197	93	1st	1st Overall
	September	24th	Snetterton	Goldsmith & Young Thoroughbred Sports Car	Aston	DB4	TBC	93	DNS	DNS
	October	1st/2nd	Silverstone — International	BRDC National Sports GT Challenge	Aston	V8	V8R02 10526	25	3rd	DNS
	October	1st/2nd	Silverstone — International	TVR Tuscan Challenge	TVR	Tuscan 4500	Giles Cooper	69	4th	Retired
	October	15th	Brands Hatch — Indy	TVR Tuscan Challenge	TVR	Tuscan 4500	Giles Cooper	69	5th	10th
	October	15th	Silverstone — Club	Goldsmith & Young Thoroughbred Sports Car	Aston	DB4	DB4/675/R 788CUV 197	93	TBC	1st Overall
1995	May	20th/21st	Silverstone — National	Goldsmith & Young Thoroughbred Sports Car	Aston	DB4	DB4/675/R 788CUV 197	96	1st in Class	1st in Class
	May	29th	Thruxton	Goldsmith & Young Thoroughbred Sports Car	Aston	DB4	DB4/675/R 788CUV 197	96	1st	1st Overall
	June	11th	Silverstone — Club	St John H — 46th — ERF Intermarque Championship	Aston	V8 5340	TBC	55	3rd	1st Overall
	June	11th	Silverstone — Club	St John H — 46th — Patrick Hackett Memorial Trophy — Goldsmith & Young	Aston	DB4	DB4/675/R 788CUV 197	96	1st	Winner
	July	1st2nd	Brands Hatch — GP	AMOC Intermarque Championship — ERF	Aston	V8	V8R02 10526	55	1st	Retired
	July	29th/30th	Silverstone — GP	Coys of Kensington GT Race	MG	B 1860	Colin Pearcy's Car	31	TBC	TBC
	July	29th/30th	Silverstone — GP	Donald Healey Memorial Race	Austin	Healey 100S	RWD323	3	4th in Class	2nd in Class
	July	29th/30th	Silverstone — GP	Coys of Kensington GT Race	MG	B 1860	Colin Pearcy's Car	31	TBC	TBC
	August	13th	Mallory Park	AMOC Intermarque Championship — ERF	Aston	V8	V8R02 10526	55	1st	1st Overall
	August	27th/28th	Thruxton	AMOC Intermarque Championship — ERF	Aston	V8	V8R02 10526	55	1st	1st Overall
	August	27th/28th	Thruxton	Goldsmith & Young Thoroughbred Sports Car	Aston	DB4	DB4/675/R 788CUV 197	96	1st	1st Overall
	August	27th/28th	Thruxton	AMOC One-Hour Endurance Race	Aston	V8	David Heynes	55	1st	1st Overall
	September	24th	Brands Hatch — GP	750 Motor Club Goldsmith & Young Thoroughbred	Aston	DB4	DB4/675/R 788CUV 197	96	TBC	1st Overall
1996	April	20th	Silverstone — National	AMOC Intermarque Championship	Aston	V8	V8R02 10526	55	2nd	2nd Overall
	May	6th	Brands Hatch — Indy	AMOC Intermarque Championship — ERF	Aston	V8 5340	V8R02 10526	55	DNS	1st Overall
	June	30th	Thruxton	AMOC Intermarque Championship — ERF	Aston	V8	V8R02 10526	55	1st	Retired

Year	Month	Date	Circuit	Race	Car	Spec	Details	No.	Qualifying	Result
1996	July	6th/7th	Brands Hatch — Indy	AMOC Intermarque Championship — ERF	Aston	V8	V8R02 10526	55	TBC	TBC
	August	18th	Mallory Park	AMOC Intermarque Championship — ERF	Aston	DB4	DB4/675/R 788CUV 197	55	4th in Class	4th in Class
	August	18th	Mallory Park	AMOC Post War Aston Martin Race	Aston	DB4	DB4/675/R 788CUV 197	55	1st in Class	2nd Overall
1997	October	5th	Donington Park	AMOC Intermarque Championship	Aston	V8	TBC	55	8th	3rd Overall
1998	May	2nd/3rd	Silverstone — National	Richardson Hosken Classic Sports Car Championship 1-hour race	Jaguar	E-Type	PFO416	41	9th	1st in Class
	May	3rd/4th	Brands Hatch — Indy	AMOC Post War Aston Martin Race	Aston	V8 6145	TBC	55	1st	1st Overall
	May	3rd/4th	Brands Hatch — Indy	Classic Sports Car 1-Hour Endurance	Aston	DB4	David Heynes	69	1st	1st in Class
	May	3rd/4th	Brands Hatch — Indy	AMOC Intermarque Championship	Aston	V8	V8R02 10526	55	1st	DNS
	June	14th	Silverstone — TBC	AMOC Intermarque Championship	Aston	V8	V8R02 10526	55	TBC	3rd Overall
	June	27th/28th	Donington Park	AMOC Intermarque Championship	Aston	V8 6145	V8R02 10526	55	4th	2nd Overall
	July	5th	Mallory Park	AMOC Intermarque Championship	Aston	V8 6145	V8R02 10526	55	1st	2nd Overall
	July	24th/25th/26th	Silverstone — GP	Coys of Kensington pre 1964 GT Car	Jaguar	E-Type	CUT7/8600004	39	1st	3rd Overall
	July	TBC	Brands Hatch — Indy	AMOC Intermarque Championship	Aston	V8	TBC	TBC	TBC	2nd Overall
	August	1st/2nd	Zolder	FIA European Championship for Historical Cars	Ford	Lotus Cortina	TBC	24	5th in Class	Retired
	August	23rd	Brands Hatch — Indy	AMOC Intermarque Championship	Aston	V8 6145	TBC	55	1st	3rd in Class
	September	4th/5th/6th	Donington Park	Historic Touring Cars	Ford	Lotus Cortina	Max Rostron	24	5th in Class	TBC
	September	27th	Brands Hatch — Indy	BARC/CSCC Group One Touring Car	Ford	Capri 3.0	TBC	99	5th in Class	Retired
1999	April	3rd/4th	Paul Ricard	FIA European Challenge for Historic Touring Cars	Ford	Lotus Cortina	Max Rostron	24	3rd in Class	2nd in Class
	April	18th	Donington Park	HSCC/HSRS Historic Racing Saloon Cars	Ford	Mustang	Bob Sherring	15	1st in Class	DNS
	May	2nd/3rd	Brands Hatch — Indy	Classic Sports Car 1-Hour Endurance	Aston	DB4	991YBF	83	1st	1st Overall
	May	2nd/3rd	Brands Hatch — Indy	Classic Sports Car 1-Hour Endurance	Aston	DB4	991YBF	83	1st	1st Overall
	May	2nd/3rd	Brands Hatch — Indy	AMOC Aston Martin Race Meeting	Aston	DB4	991YBF	83	1st	1st Overall
	May	2nd/3rd	Brands Hatch — Indy	AMOC Intermarque Championship	Aston	V8 6145	V8EVO4 10330	55	2nd	2nd Overall
	May	8th/9th	Zandvort	FIA European Challenge for Historic Touring Cars	Ford	Lotus Cortina	Max Rostron	24	3rd	Retired
	May	22nd/23rd	Monza	FIA European Challenge for Historic Touring Cars	Ford	Lotus Cortina	Max Rostron	24	6th	5th Overall
	May	31st	Crystal Palace	Sevenoaks District Motor Club Sprint	Ford	Escort RS 1800	Les Lyons	124	1st	1st in Class
	June	5th/6th	Donington Park	AMOC Intermarque Championship	Aston	V8 6145	V8EVO4 10330	55	3rd	Retired
	June	5th/6th	Donington Park	AMOC FPD Savills	Aston	DB4	991YBF	83	1st	1st Overall
	June	20th	Snetterton	AMOC FPD Savills	Aston	DB4	991YBF	83	1st	1st Overall
	July	4th	Mallory Park	AMOC Intermarque Championship	Aston	V8 6145	V8EVO4 10330	55	2nd	Race Cancelled
	July	18th	Brands Hatch — Indy	AMOC Intermarque Championship	Aston	V8 6145	V8EVO4 10330	55	4th	3rd Overall
	July/August	30th/31st/1st	Silverstone — GP	Coys of Kensington pre 1964 GT Car	Jaguar	E-Type	CUT7/8600004	19	6th	Retired
	August	8th	Silverstone — Club	St John H — 50th — AMOC Intermarque Championship	Aston	V8 6145	V8EVO4 10330	55	2nd	Race Cancelled
	August	8th	Silverstone — Club	St John H — 50th — FPD Savills Aston Martin Championship	Aston	DB4	991YBF	83	1st	Race Cancelled
	August	21st/22nd	Zolder	FIA European Challenge for Historic Touring Cars	Ford	Lotus Cortina	Max Rostron	24	4th	3rd Overall
	September	3rd/4th/5th	Donington Park	FIA European Challenge for Historic Touring Cars	Ford	Lotus Cortina	Max Rostron	24	2nd in Class	4th in Class
	September	3rd/4th/5th	Donington Park	FIA Cup for Historic Grand Touring Cars	Jaguar	E-Type	André Bailly	24	TBC	4th
	September	17th/18th/19th	Goodwood	St Mary's Trophy	Ford	Lotus Cortina	Max Rostron	18	2nd	1st Overall
	October	10th	Donington Park	AMOC Intermarque Championship	Aston	V8 6145	V8EVO4 10330	55	4th	3rd Overall
	October	10th	Donington Park	AMOC FPD Savills	Aston	DB4	991YBF	83	1st	1st Overall
	October	10th	Donington Park	Flemings Thoroughbred Sports Car Championship	Aston	DB4	991YBF	83	1st	1st Overall
	October	16th	Silverstone — Club	Richardson Hosken Classic Sports — Historic Sports Car Club	Marcos	1800 GT	Dave Methley	7	2nd	1st Overall
2000	May	27th/28th	Silverstone — National	Pre '65 Touring Cars 1-Hour Race	Ford	Mustang	Miles Townshend	4	3rd	Retired
	May	TBC	Silverstone — National	Top Hat Endurance Series Historic Cars	TBC	TBC	TBC	TBC	TBC	TBC
	June	3rd/4th	Donington Park	Clifford Chance Aston Martin Championship	Aston	DB4	DB4/675/R 788CUV 197	96	1st	1st Overall
	June	18th	Lydden Hill	Millers Oils Post Historic Touring Car	Vauxhall	Firenza DS	Peter Blincow	39	4th in Class	DNS
	June	24th	Silverstone — National	St John H — 50th — Clifford Chance Aston Martin Championship	Aston	DB4	DB4/675/R 788CUV 197	96	1st	1st Overall
	June	24th	Silverstone — National	St John H — 50th — Feltham Aston Martin Race	Aston	DB3S	SR34	23	2nd in Class	3rd in Class
	July	8th/9th	Brands Hatch — Indy	Feltham Aston Martin Race	Aston	DB3S	SR34	23	1st in Class	1st in Class
	July	8th/9th	Brands Hatch — Indy	Clifford Chance Aston Martin Championship	Aston	DB4	DB4/675/R 788CUV 197	96	1st	1st Overall
	July	23rd	Thruxton	Clifford Chance Aston Martin Championship	Aston	DB4	DB4/675/R 788CUV 197	96	1st	1st Overall
	August	6th	Snetterton	Clifford Chance Aston Martin Championship	Aston	DB4	DB4/675/R 788CUV 197	96	2nd in Class	Winner
	September	8th/9th/10th	Spa Francorchamps	HSCC Top Hat Touring	Ford	Mustang	TBC	55	TBC	4th in Class
	September	15th/16th/17th	Goodwood	St Mary's Trophy	Ford	Mustang	Max Rostron	19	4th	2nd Overall
	September	15th/16th/17th	Goodwood	Fordwater Trophy	Austin	Healey 100S	RWD323	8	3rd	2nd Overall
	September	15th/16th/17th	Goodwood	RAC Tourist Trophy Celebration	Chevrolet	Corvette Stingray	TBC	9	25th	DNS
	September	24th	Dijon	FIA European Challenge for Historic Touring Cars	Ford	TBC	TBC	55	2nd in Class	Retired
	October	1st	Donington Park	Clifford Chance Aston Martin Championship	Aston	DB4	DB4/675/R 788CUV 197	96	2nd in Class	Winner
	October	1st	Donington Park	Half-Hour Classic Invitation Race	Triumph	TR6	TBC	99	TBC	1st in Class
	October	28th	Snetterton	750 Motor Club Holland Birkett Six-Hour Relay Race	Ford	Escort RS 2000	Steve Cripps	19	TBC	TBC
2001	April	28th/29th	Brands Hatch — Indy	Clifford Chance Aston Martin Championship	Aston	DB4	DB4/675/R 788CUV 197	96	1st	1st in Class
	May	5th/6th	Donington Park	Top Hat Cloth Cap 1-Hour Sports Car	AC	Cobra	CSX2153	4	TBC	2nd Overall
	May	5th/6th	Donington Park	Top Hat Endurance Series Historic Cars	Ford	Mustang	Max Rostron	1	10th in Class	17th Overall
	May	19th/20th	Monza	FIA European Challenge for Historic Touring Cars	Ford	Mustang	Max Rostron	84	3rd	3rd in Class
	May	26th/27th	Zandvort	25th Historic FIA European Challenge	Ford	Mustang	Max Rostron	TBC	TBC	1st in Class
	June	9th/10th	Anderstorp	FIA European Challenge for Historic Touring Cars	Ford	Mustang	Max Rostron	55	TBC	3rd in Class
	June	22nd/23rd/24th	Zolder	FIA European Challenge for Historic Touring Cars	Ford	Mustang	Max Rostron	TBC	3rd in Class	2nd in Class
	July	7th/8th	Goodwood Hillclimb	Festival of Speed	Vauxhall	Firenza DS	Baby Bertha	171	N/A	2nd in Class
	August	10th/11th/12th	Nürburgring	29th Alfa Romeo Oldtimer Grand Prix	Ford	Mustang	Max Rostron	TBC	3rd in Class	1st in Class
	August	25th/26th/27th	Silverstone — GP	The Jack Sears Trophy for pre '65 Touring Cars	Ford	Galaxie	7.2	30	TBC	TBC
	September	14th/15th/16th	Goodwood	St Mary's Trophy	Ford	Lotus Cortina	828CDL	9	2nd	1st Overall
	September	14th/15th/16th	Goodwood	RAC Tourist Trophy Celebration	Chevrolet	Corvette Stingray	John Young	15	16th	Retired
	September	22nd/23rd	Dijon	FIA European Challenge for Historic Touring Cars	Ford	Mustang	Max Rostron	55	1st in Class	Retired
	September	30th	Donington Park	Clifford Chance Aston Martin Championship	Aston	DB4	DB4/675/R 788CUV 197	96	TBC	1st in Class
	October	1st	Donington Park	3rd Team Half-Hour Invitation Race	TBC	TBC	TBC	TBC	4th	TBC
	October	14th	Rockingham	Classic Saloon and Historic Touring Car Race	Ford	Lotus Cortina	Chris Sanders	1	6th	2nd in Class
	October	14th	Rockingham	Classic Touring and Race Car Club Post Historic Touring Car Championship	Ford	Lotus Cortina	Chris Sanders	1	3rd in Class	2nd in Class
	October	20th/21st	Snetterton	Cloth Cap Sports Cars	AC	Cobra	CSX2153	18	5th in Class	5th in Class
	October	20th/21st	Snetterton	Top Hat Jack Sears Tribute Trophy Race for pre '65 Touring Cars	Ford	Mustang	Max Rostron	55	6th in Class	Retired
2002	April	20th/21st	Oulton Park	Heritage Grand Touring Car Challenge	Aston	V8	Boysie Thurtle	70	1st in Class	Retired
	May	5th/6th	Donington Park	Cloth Cap Sports Cars	AC	Cobra	COB6008	18	3rd in Class	1st in Class
	May	5th/6th	Brands Hatch — Indy	AMOC Aston Martin Championship Race	Aston	DB4	DB4/675/R 788CUV 197	96	1st	1st Overall
	May	5th/6th	Brands Hatch — Indy	AMOC Intermarque Championship	Aston	V8	Baysie Thurtle	70	1st in Class	1st in Class
	July	14th	Goodwood Hillclimb	Festival of Speed	Vauxhall	Firenza DS	Baby Bertha	152	N/A	1st in Class
	July	27th	Snetterton	Heritage Grand Touring Car Challenge	Aston	V8	Boysie Thurtle	70	1st in Class	Retired
	August	3rd	Thruxton	AMOC Aston Martin Championship Race	Aston	DB4	DB4/675/R 788CUV 197	96	1st	1st in Class
	August	25th/26th	Brands Hatch — Indy	Heritage Grand Touring Car Challenge	Aston	DB4	DB4/675/R 788CUV 197	96	4th in Class	4th in Class

Year	Month	Date	Circuit	Race	Car	Spec	Details	No.	Qualifying	Result
2002	August	25th/26th	Brands Hatch — Indy	Heritage Grand Touring Car Challenge	Aston	DB4	DB4/675/R 788CUV 197	96	TBC	DNS
	September	6th/7th/8th	Goodwood	Fordwater Trophy	Austin	Healey 100S	RWD323	10	3rd	2nd Overall
	September	6th/7th/8th	Goodwood	St Mary's Trophy	Jaguar	Mk 1	TBC	15	3rd	2nd Overall
	September	6th/7th/8th	Goodwood	RAC Tourist Trophy Celebration	Chevrolet	Corvette Stingray	TBC	15	15th	11th Overall
	September	28th	Silverstone — National	AMOC Aston Martin Championship Race	Aston	DB4	DB4/675/R 788CUV 197	96	1st	1st in Class
2003	April	27th	Thruxton	Colonade Sporstcar Residental Championship	Aston	DB4	DB4/675/R 788CUV 197	96	1st	1st Overall
	May	4th	Mallory Park	AMOC Aston Martin Championship Race	Aston	DB4	DB4/675/R 788CUV 197	96	2nd in Class	Winner
	May	4th	Mallory Park	Colonade Sporstcar Residental Championship	Aston	DB4	DB4/675/R 788CUV 197	96	1st	1st Overall
	June	7th/8th	Silverstone — International	Heritage Grand Touring Car Challenge	Aston	DB4	DB4/675/R 788CUV 197	96	1st	3rd in Class
	June	7th/8th	Silverstone — International	Heritage Grand Touring Car Challenge	Aston	DB4	DB4/675/R 788CUV 197	96	4th	3rd in Class
	June	28th	Silverstone — National	St John H — AMOC Aston Martin Race Meeting	Aston	DB4	DB4/675/R 788CUV 197	96	1st in Class	2nd in Class
	July	5th/6th	Shelsley Walsh	The Vauxhall Centenary Weekend	Vauxhall	Firenza DS	Baby Bertha	TBC	N/A	Demo
	July	11th/12th	Goodwood Hillclimb	Festival of Speed	Vauxhall	Firenza DS	Baby Bertha	128	N/A	4th in Class
	August	8th/9th	Snetterton	Heritage Grand Touring Car Challenge	Aston	V8	Boysie Thurtle	70	1st in Class	Retired
	August	8th/9th	Snetterton	Heritage Grand Touring Car Challenge	Aston	V8	Boysie Thurtle	70	N/A	Demo
	August	24th/25th	Brands Hatch — Indy	Heritage Grand Touring Car Challenge	Aston	DB4	DB4/675/R 788CUV 197	96	3rd in Class	3rd in Class
	August	24th/25th	Brands Hatch — Indy	Heritage Grand Touring Car Challenge	Aston	DB4	DB4/675/R 788CUV 197	96	9th	Retired
	August	31st	Brands Hatch — TBC	Demo	Vauxhall	Firenza DS	Baby Bertha	128	N/A	Demo
	September	5th/6th/7th	Goodwood	St Mary's Trophy	Ford	Lotus Cortina	828CDL	19	5th	Retired
	September	5th/6th/7th	Goodwood	RAC Tourist Trophy Celebration	Chevrolet	Corvette Stingray	TBC	9	DNQ	10th
	September	13th	Brighton Speed Trial	Sports Libre Cars over 1600cc	Vauxhall	Firenza DS	Baby Bertha	192	N/A	12th in Class
	September	27th	Oulton Park	Classic Group One Touring Cars	Mazda	RX7	Stacy Vickers	1	1st	1st Overall
	October	4th/5th	Brands Hatch — Indy	AMOC Aston Martin Championship Race	Aston	DB4	DB4/675/R 788CUV 197	96	2nd in Class	1st in Class
	October	4th/5th	Brands Hatch — Indy	Colonade Sporstcar Residental Championship	Aston	DB4	DB4/675/R 788CUV 197	96	2nd	1st Overall
	October	11th	Silverstone — National	HSCC/HSRS Historic Racing Saloon Cars	Ford	Mustang	Max Rostron	18	1st	2nd Overall
	October	12th	Donington Park	AMOC Aston Martin Race Meeting	Aston	DB4	DB4/675/R 788CUV 197	96	3rd in Class	3rd in Class
	October	12th	Donington Park	Colonade Sporstcar Residental Championship	Aston	DB4	DB4/675/R 788CUV 197	96	2nd	1st Overall
2004	April	12th	Castle Combe	Cloth Cap/Octane European Historic Sports Car	AC	Cobra	COB6008	98	6th in Class	4th in Class
	July	4th	Thruxton	AMOC UBS Championship	Aston	DB4	DB4/675/R 788CUV 197	96	1st in Class	Retired
	July	4th	Thruxton	Colonade Sporstcar Residental Championship	Aston	DB4	DB4/675/R 788CUV 197	TBC	1st	3rd Overall
	July	17th	Goodwood	AMOC Sprint	Aston	DB4	DB4/675/R 788CUV 197	TBC	N/A	Retired
	August	22nd	Pembrey	AMOC UBS Championship	Aston	DB4	DB4/675/R 788CUV 197	96	3rd	1st Overall
	September	3rd/4th/5th	Goodwood	St Mary's Trophy	Alvis	Grey Lady	PUE769	4	5th	2nd Overall
	September	3rd/4th/5th	Goodwood	Freddie March Memorial Trophy	Austin	Healey 100S	RWD323	8	6th	3rd Overall
	September	3rd/4th/5th	Goodwood	RAC Tourist Trophy Celebration	Ferrari	330 LMB	TBC	17	4th	8th Overall
	September	11th	Silverstone — National	St John H — AMOC Aston Martin Jim Broadey Memorial Trophy	Aston	DB4	DB4/675/R 788CUV 197	96	3rd	2nd Overall
	September	11th	Silverstone — National	St John H — AMOC UBS Aston Martin Race Meeting	Aston	DB4	DB4/675/R 788CUV 197	96	TBC	1st Overall
	September	11th	Silverstone — National	St John H — Heritage Grand Touring Car Challenge	Aston	DB4	DB4/675/R 788CUV 197	96	2nd in Class	1st in Class
	September	25th/26th	Brands Hatch — TBC	AMOC UBS Championship	Aston	DB4	DB4/675/R 788CUV 197	TBC	TBC	TBC
	September	25th/26th	Brands Hatch — TBC	Colonade Sporstcar Residental Championship	Aston	DB4	DB4/675/R 788CUV 197	TBC	TBC	TBC
	October	10th	Donington Park	AMOC UBS Championship	Aston	DB4 4.2	DB4/675/R 788CUV 197	96	2nd in Class	Retired
	October	10th	Donington Park	Colonade Sporstcar Residental Championship	Aston	DB4 4.2	DB4/675/R 788CUV 197	TBC	2nd in Class	2nd Overall
	November	6th/7th	Silverstone — National	BRDC Members Race	Ford	Lotus Cortina	Michael Steele	25	16th	15th Overall
2005	April	21st	Silverstone — National	Testing	Chevrolet	Camaro	IROC	TBC	N/A	N/A

KEY

TBC - To be confirmed

DNF - Did not finish

DNQ - Did not qualify

N/A - Not applicable

CHAMPIONSHIPS & AWARDS BY SEASON: 1965–2004

Year	Status	Date	Circuit	Title	Result
1965	SEASON	N/A	N/A	British Saloon Car Championship	2nd in Class
1967	SEASON	N/A	N/A	Redex Championship	2nd in Class
1968	SEASON	N/A	N/A		N/A
1969	March	2nd	Snetterton	Cambridge University Automobile Car Club Spring Sprint	Award
	SEASON	N/A	N/A	Redex Saloon Car Championship	2nd
	SEASON	N/A	N/A		34th
1970	SEASON	N/A	N/A		N/A
	CHAMPIONSHIP	N/A	N/A	Osram GEC	1st in Class
1971	CHAMPIONSHIP	N/A	N/A	Ford Escort Mexico Champion	Championship Winner
	CHAMPIONSHIP	N/A	N/A	Osram GEC	1st in Class
	SEASON	N/A	N/A		N/A
1972	August	27th	Mallory Park	Man of the Meeting	Award
	October	14th	Oulton Park	BP Man of the Meeting	1st in Class
	CHAMPIONSHIP	N/A	N/A	BARC Forward Trust Special Saloon Car Championship	Championship Winner
	CHAMPIONSHIP	N/A	N/A	Castrol Production Saloon Car Championship (Group One)	1st in Class
	AWARD	N/A	N/A	BARC President's Cup	Championship Winner
	October	N/A	N/A	BARC President's Cup	Award
1973	CHAMPIONSHIP	N/A	N/A	BARC Forward Trust Class Champion	1st in Class
	SEASON	N/A	N/A		N/A
1974	March	31st	Silverstone – Club	Allied Polymer Group	Award
	September	12th	Rally	Castrol Manx Trophy Rally	Award
	September	12th	Rally	Castrol Manx Trophy Rally	Award
	September	12th	Rally	Castrol Manx Trophy Rally	3rd Navigator
	CHAMPIONSHIP	N/A	N/A	Simoniz Saloon Car Championship	Championship Winner
1975	July	6th	Silverstone – TBC	Allied Polymer Group	Award
	CHAMPIONSHIP	N/A	N/A	Tricentrol Special Saloon Car Championship	Championship Winner
	CHAMPIONSHIP	N/A	N/A	Forward Trust Champion	Championship Winner
	SEASON	N/A	N/A	RESULTS	N/A
	CHAMPIONSHIP	N/A	N/A	Scottish Saloon Car Championship	Championship Winner
1976	CHAMPIONSHIP	N/A	N/A	Tricentrol Special Saloon Car Championship	Championship Winner
	CHAMPIONSHIP	N/A	N/A	RAC British Saloon Car Championship	1st in Class
	CHAMPIONSHIP	N/A	N/A	Radio 1 Production Saloon	1st in Class
	AWARD	TBC	Thruxton	Aloca Driver of the Meeting	Award
	AWARD	TBC	TBC	Post 2 Trophy	Award
1977	October	30th	Thruxton	Phil Winter Memorial Trophy	Award
	CHAMPIONSHIP	N/A	N/A	Tricentrol Special Saloon Car Championship	Championship Winner
	AWARD	N/A	N/A	BRDC – ERA Trophy	Award
1978	September	6th	Snetterton	Commanders Cup 24-hour record	N/A
	CHAMPIONSHIP	N/A	N/A	Tricentrol British Touring Car Championship	8th in Class
	CHAMPIONSHIP	N/A	N/A	Britax Production Saloon	Championship Winner
	CHAMPIONSHIP	N/A	N/A	ShellSport Derwent Television Champion – Production Saloon	Championship Winner
1979	July	19th/20th	Snetterton	British National 2000km Class E Record	Record
	CHAMPIONSHIP	N/A	N/A	Demon Tweeks 4 Shocks Production Saloon	Championship Winner
	CHAMPIONSHIP	N/A	N/A	Demon Tweeks 4 Shocks Production Saloon	1st in Class
1980	CHAMPIONSHIP	N/A	N/A	Wilcomatic 3000 Production Saloon	Championship Winner
	CHAMPIONSHIP	N/A	N/A	Lloyds & Scottish Sports Car Champion	1st in Class
	CHAMPIONSHIP	N/A	N/A	Monroe Shock Absorbers Production Saloon Car Championship	1st in Class
1981	CHAMPIONSHIP	N/A	N/A	Monroe Shock Absorbers Production Saloon Car Championship	Championship Winner
	CHAMPIONSHIP	N/A	N/A	Lloyds & Scottish Sports Car Champion	1st in Class
	CHAMPIONSHIP	N/A	N/A	Wilcomatic 3000 Production Saloon	Championship Winner
	October	6th	Snetterton	Class D 2000kms 24-hour record – ICS Trophy	Award
	AWARD	N/A	N/A	BARC President's Cup	Award
1982	February	7th	Brands Hatch – Indy	Chiltern Circle and Harrow Car Club Sprint	Award
	CHAMPIONSHIP	N/A	N/A	Monroe Shock Absorbers Production Saloon Car Championship	Championship Winner
	AWARD	N/A	N/A	Stapleton Trophy	Award
	AWARD	TBC	Newport Pagnell	AMOC Summer concourse	Award
1983	CHAMPIONSHIP	N/A	N/A	Monroe Shock Absorbers Production Saloon Car Championship	Championship Winner
	CHAMPIONSHIP	N/A	N/A	BRDC/BRSCC Production Car Challenge	3rd Overall
	CHAMPIONSHIP	N/A	N/A	Uniroyal Tyres Production Saloon Car Championship	6th Overall
	CHAMPIONSHIP	N/A	N/A	Uniroyal Tyres Production Sports Car Championship	5th Overall
	AWARD	N/A	N/A	Stapleton Trophy	Award
	AWARD	N/A	N/A	BARC President's Cup	Award
1984	AWARD	N/A	N/A	Stapleton Trophy	Award
1986	SEASON	N/A	N/A	Monroe Shock Absorbers Production Saloon Car Championship	2nd in Class
1987	AWARD	N/A	N/A	Stapleton Trophy	Award
1988	AWARD	N/A	N/A	Stapleton Trophy	Award
1989	CHAMPIONSHIP	N/A	N/A	TVR Tuscan Challenge	4th Overall
	AWARD	N/A	N/A	Stapleton Trophy	Award
	AWARD	N/A	N/A	Stapleton Trophy	Award
1990	CHAMPIONSHIP	N/A	N/A	SKF Engineering Productionucts Historic Car Championship	Championship Winner
1991	August	3rd	Castle Combe	The Hyperion Cup Caterham	Award
	AWARD	N/A	N/A	Stapleton Trophy	Award
	AWARD	TBC	N/A	Roger St John Hart Challenge Trophy	Award
1992	August	31st	Castle Combe	Abraham's Jewellers	Award
1993	AWARD	N/A	N/A	Roger St John Hart Challenge Trophy	Award
1994	AWARD	N/A	N/A	Roger St John Hart Challenge Trophy	Award
1996	AWARD	N/A	N/A	Roger St John Hart Challenge Trophy	Award
1999	TBC	TBC	TBC	Jaybrand Most Resilient Driver	Award
	AWARD	N/A	N/A	Roger St John Hart Challenge Trophy	Award
2000	AWARD	N/A	N/A	Roger St John Hart Challenge Trophy	Award
	AWARD	N/A	N/A	Martini Trophy	1st in Class
2001	September	14th/15th/16th	Goodwood	Driver of the Day	Award
2002	AWARD	N/A	N/A	BARC	Award

INDEX